D0065336

The Social Misconstruction of Reality

The Social Misconstruction of Reality
Validity and Verification in the Scholarly Community

Richard F. Hamilton

Yale University Press   New Haven and London

Published with assistance from the Mary Cady Tew Memorial Fund.

Designed by Rebecca Gibb.
Set in Fournier type by Alexander Graphics, Ltd., Indianapolis, Indiana.
Printed in the United States of America by
BookCrafters, Inc., Chelsea, Michigan.

Library of Congress Cataloging-in-Publication Data

Hamilton, Richard F.
    The social misconstruction of reality : validity and verification
in the scholarly community / Richard F. Hamilton.
        p.   cm.
    Includes bibliographical references and index.
    ISBN 0-300-06345-8 (cloth : alk. paper)
    1. Historiography—Case studies.   2. Knowledge, Sociology of—Case
studies.   I. Title.
D13.H282   1996
907.2--dc20

                                                        95-30970
                                                        CIP

A catalogue record for this book is available from the
British Library.

The paper in this book meets the guidelines for
permanence and durability of the Committee on
Production Guidelines for Book Longevity of the
Council on Library Resources.

10 9 8 7 6 5 4 3 2 1

For Bill Form, a good friend and generous colleague

Contents

Tables

Preface

The evidence of personal biography and the evidence of social and historical scholarship seldom overlap. At best, personal experience may provide insights or hunches that might not occur to someone else. Once expressed, however, such insights face the same basic scientific problems as would any other statement. Are the insights accurate? Can the hunches be supported? Is the personal experience typical? Or does it hold only for a small minority? Or is it perhaps unique?

The autobiographical information presented here does not address substantive issues. It is intended, rather, to address a methodological question raised by a reader of the manuscript: Why, in the face of a consensus among scholars, have I seen things differently?

Somewhere along the line, early in my school years, I reviewed my intellectual experience and drew a couple of conclusions. We had considered American history maybe three times by then. Each new version was more complex, and more critical and, in effect, undid some of the earlier conclusions. It occurred to me that we were learning, in textbooks and in class, a "preliminary version" of what had actually happened. One teacher, I think it was Mr. Marlak, confirmed my suspicion. We would get the "real story" later, he said; it would be taught at university.

Recognizing that the information we had been given was imperfect or false, I developed a skeptical attitude that sought the reality behind those appearances. Since I read widely, I was able on many occasions to discover errors, to detect implausible arguments, and to raise pertinent questions about other possibilities.

Several years later, at university, we read Descartes and there I was gratified to find support for this procedure. His call for skepticism, for doubt, provided welcome justification for a tendency which, I had discovered, was not always viewed with favor. Shortly thereafter, I learned that Max Weber also had this dual attitude, the sense that another reality was hidden behind the initial appearances.

This critical attitude led me to look favorably on the work of Karl Marx. At that point, in the late 1940s and early 1950s, he was not widely read and certainly was not approved. His ideas were new and different; they were also provocative and challenging. The Marx-Engels dramaturgy helped. The two men were endlessly "unveiling" things, letting their readers know that the manifest fact X was in reality the hidden fact Y. Or, to borrow another of their favorite metaphors, we were watching a drama as it unfolded on the stage. And they, the master dramatists (and stage managers), disabused us of our illusions, telling us what was really happening "behind the scenes" (*hinter den Kulissen*).

It is easy to say "I developed a skeptical attitude," but between the attitude and a genuinely critical practice, there can often be a large (and embarrassing) gap. Many of the positions I have since argued against were ones I originally accepted and defended. Until some time in the early sixties, I taught and defended the familiar lower-middle-class thesis, that the threatened petty bourgeoisie was reactionary and somehow dangerous. At about that time, while doing research to support one version of the claim (the conservatism of independent businessmen), I discovered evidence from surveys in the United States that led me to reject the thesis. Skepticism, when practiced consistently, has cumulative impacts. That initial rejection led me to review the claim in other contexts, the most important of which was Germany. This research will be reviewed here in Chapter 4.

Similarly, for many years I taught Max Weber's Protestant ethic thesis, giving it credence through the early 1970s before gradually recognizing and discovering many serious difficulties. My findings on this subject are reported here in Chapter 3. In the late 1960s and early 1970s, when marxism experienced a new flowering, I again turned to the Marx-Engels originals and, over time, discovered much that was problematic. Some of these findings appear in my previous book, *The Bourgeois Epoch: Marx and Engels on Britain, France, and Germany.* Through an accident of fate, in the late 1970s I read Michel Foucault's *Discipline and Punish.* At that time I knew next to nothing about the historical experience he described and analyzed. Again I approached the subject with considerable skepticism and, by then, had a fair amount of practical experience in scholarly detective work. The results of my research on Foucault's study appear here in Chapter 6.

On the whole, the skeptical attitude has served me well. It has allowed me to get behind texts that other readers have taken at face value; it opened up possibilities for research and discovery that had been missed. Armed with that predisposition, I have been skeptical in many instances where, after review, my suspicions proved unjustified. No great loss was involved. Time and effort were required, but, in recompense, useful knowledge was gained. The approach is akin to tapping the foundations of a house prior to purchase: one is better off for it, no matter what the outcome.

This work reviews six examples of social misconstruction, that is, of collective misreadings of evidence. Those involving Columbus, Mozart, and the duke of Wellington are reviewed in the opening chapters. They are intended to introduce and illustrate the problem, the misreadings having persisted now for more than a century. In all three, both the "facts" and the "larger implications" involve misleads. The subsequent chapters will then detail the three principal examples, those just reviewed.

No special plan or principle of selection governed the choice of these case studies. They are, rather, an ad hoc lot, a minuscule and obviously nonrandom sample drawn from the vast universe of scholarly productions. They are examples that came to my attention in the course of teaching, research, and leisure reading. This diversity of cases allows the exploration of misconstructions that differ in origins, in the methods and evidence used, and in theoretical implications.

The effort is basically inductive. It begins with the review of cases and ends with a discussion of factors likely to contribute to and sustain such misconstructions. Most of those factors are social psychological. They are not binding (as with necessary and sufficient conditions), nor are they likely to have the weight social scientists often assign to "structures." My sense is that they should be seen, as in most normal science, as involving probabilities. They are factors having some impact on intellectual outcomes. This study, however, cannot provide answers with regard to the extent of influence. Some evidence will be presented showing conformity. But it is not possible here to establish the quantities: How much was there? How strong was it? How persistent was (or is) the tendency?

There is, I realize, another methodological preference. One could begin with a well-defined theory, formulate testable hypotheses, select appropriate "cases" for study, and then proceed to investigation. That would be my ordinary preference. But much of the crucial evidence needed for such a study is inaccessible. One must know the minds of the researchers, teachers, or commentators in the course of their work. That kind of project is not feasible in this case and, accordingly, I have chosen this largely inductive alternative, one that is primarily behavioral in orientation.

A persistent question arises in this connection: How much of scholarly work is misconstruction? Is it half, or 30 percent, or only 3 percent? While an understandable concern, this study cannot provide an answer. An adequate answer would require a prodigious research effort, involving a representative sample of studies, possibly one hundred from a defined universe of say twenty thousand, that followed by an independent investigation and assessment of those selected. For complex multifaceted researches, the problems involved would be enormous. Given the costs and difficulties of such an assessment, that kind of project will probably never be realized.

From another perspective, the incidence question is aside from the point. If the rate of error were close to 100 percent, we might consider closing the universities. If, however, the rate were low, say 7 percent (viewing matters more optimistically), the question of the precise incidence would lose importance. The key concern should be with the flawed cases. For researchers, teachers, and citizens, any misconstruction is (or should be) too much.

Everyday scholarly activity involves specific claims, arguments, and theories. The key question in any given case is whether those specifics are accurate, valid, or proven. If one is skeptical about theory Q, and if those doubts prove justified, that discovery should lead to a reconstruction, to a more appropriate analysis of the case. If theory Q is faulty, because based on mistaken assumptions, or because the key predictions are not sustained, one should either repair it or abandon it. The key task is to provide a better theory. In each of the examples reviewed here, some consideration of likely alternatives will be provided.

William Form, a friend, colleague, and co-worker, to whom this book is dedicated, has performed heroic service in helping with the writing of this volume. He read and commented extensively on all of the chapters. Four other friends, colleagues, and co-workers, Richard Ogmundson, Michael Smith, Henry A. Turner, and Axel van den Berg, also read the entire work and were exceptionally generous in provision of comment and suggestion. If academics gave out medals, I would award all five a *pour le mérite*.

For expert assistance on the subject of prisons, I wish to thank Simon Dinitz. For expert assistance on the subject of Protestantism, I wish to thank Wayne Baker, George Becker, and James Kittelson. And for their expert assistance on the subject of the military, I thank John F. Guilmartin, Williamson Murray, and David Shewchuk. A seminar paper by Shewchuk provided the basis and impulse for the discussion of the military in Chapter 6.

Others who in one way or another assisted with this project are: Robert Bremner, Steven Brint, Edward Crenshaw, G. William Domhoff, Jürgen Falter, Richard Gunther, Lowell Hargens, Jeffrey Herf, Gisela J. Hinkle, Peter C. Hoffmann, Charles Krauskopf, Gerhard Lenski, Allan Megill, Anthony Masi, Neil McLaughlin, Donald H. Naftulin, James Phelan, Maurice Pinard, Guenther Roth, Lars Sandberg, Suzanne Schmeidl, James Wright, Ekkart Zimmermann, and several anonymous reviewers. I am very grateful for all of their efforts.

A special note of appreciation is due to Frank Turner for two exceptional contributions. For his outstanding editorial and diplomatic services, I wish to thank Charles Grench.

I wish also to thank the many people in the Ohio State University's Inter-Library Loan Department. Their diligence in locating and retrieving fugitive source material is gratefully acknowledged.

An early version of Chapter 4, "Hitler's Electoral Support: Recent Findings and Theoretical Implications," appeared in the *Canadian Journal of Sociology* 11 (1986): 1–34.

Last, and certainly not least, I would like to thank Irene Hamilton for her contributions, both direct and indirect, that helped in this effort.

1

On Social Misconstructions

The expression "social misconstruction," as used here, refers to a collective error, to a widespread agreement about facts or interpretation that is mistaken. A range of examples will be reviewed in this work, all of which have three distinct features: they involve errors, mistakes, or misreading of evidence; the errors have been widely accepted; and they have persisted over many years.

The examples vary considerably in importance. Some might best be described as curiosities in that nothing remarkable follows from recognition of the error. The duke of Wellington, it is reported, assigned unusual importance to "the playing fields of Eton." As will be seen, this claim appears to be mistaken. Our understanding of Wellington, of the Napoleonic Wars, or of British institutions is not significantly altered by recognition of this fact. An opposite example, one of considerable importance, involves Max Weber's famous Protestant ethic thesis. Weber claimed there was a strong linkage between Protestantism and worldly success. The driving energies generated by a new religious doctrine, he argued, provided an explanation for "the rise of the West." If the initial fact, the linkage of religion and success, were mistaken, then the larger argument would also fall.

The principal task of this book is to describe and document some examples of such misconstruction. Although stated as a conclusion, the judgment of error or misrepresentation, at this point, is perhaps best viewed as a hypothesis: it is my hypothesis that these events have been misrepresented. The chapters will review both logic and evidence. With "the case" spelled out, the reader may then agree with, reject, or amend the offered solution.

The second aim of this work is to consider positive alternatives. If the Protestant ethic hypothesis is rejected, what alternative explanations might better explain the rise of the West? Was it maritime superiority—better ships and sailors? Was it military superiority—better cannons? Or was it technological breakthroughs—innovations in spinning, weaving, the steam engine, or the use of coke in smelting? Only limited attention is given here to this second aim; exploration and assessment of the alternative hypotheses would take us far afield. The best that may be done in this brief space is the provision of hypotheses, of alternative logic or argument, and/or references to appropriate literature.

Some scholarly errors prove to be remarkably persistent. Some baseless information has persisted for more than 150 years despite the attention of ever-growing numbers of self-declared critical scholars. The basic claims of one such history, the Mozart story (discussed in Chapter 2), have been thoroughly rejected in recent decades. Nevertheless, the elements of that position are still accepted and recounted by persons who should know better. As opposed to the assumption that new findings will be easily accepted and assimilated is the frequent problem of "stickiness." Some people appear to be attached to traditional or handed-down views, hanging onto them even in the face of new and compelling evidence. The third aim of this work is to account for the persistence of these errors.

The chapters in this volume are all, in one way or another, concerned with the sociology of knowledge. That phrase refers to the social constraints or influences affecting knowledge and understanding. This view stands in opposition to the simple "reflection" theory, which claims that knowledge stems from a direct apprehension of "the facts." The sociology of knowledge argument holds that knowledge is somehow mediated by various social factors. Perceptions and understandings are, in part at least, social products. Children ordinarily learn things—language, usages, norms, and so forth—from their parents and later from friends, teachers, co-workers, and through various media of communication. The insight that knowledge has social roots is merely a special application of the basic sociological assumption that people influence each other.

Many epistemological discussions, regrettably, have focused on the extreme cases as if these were the only options: either knowledge, all of it, is directly learned *or* it is a social construction. There is no reason, a priori, why that should be the case. One may easily think of intermediate options, all of which involve some notion of the partitive. Most of our knowledge is mediated, somehow or other socially transmitted. This is clearly the case with events distant in time and space. Some person (or persons) edited, transmitted, and perhaps provided a judgment of the credibility of that information. Some knowledge, a small part of the total, is unmediated, gained through direct experience, and potentially subject to unique personal interpretation. In any given instance, some combination of social influence and individual judgment is likely, the key question being one of weight or preponderance.

Science: The Polar Views

Many scientists in the nineteenth century saw their effort as one of accumulation and refinement. They observed, tested, and experimented, bringing data to bear on a range of propositions which, after comprehensive testing, would be declared laws. Scientific truth was to be found through ever-closer approximation, through a process of correction and adjustment. That truth resulted from an asymtotic progress toward an ultimate or definitive knowledge. Various philosophers of science, Auguste Comte among others, presented and argued the case, and this position was termed positivism. Theories and hypotheses would be put forward, so it was assumed, and evidence would be generated to support, reject, or modify those claims. With methods involving built-in corrective procedures, the result would be a uniquely high quality of knowledge. That knowledge, called scientific, was explicitly contrasted with other, less adequate varieties, with mystical or theological knowledge based on feeling, revelation, or logical deduction. There was also, of course, a wide range of traditional knowledge, of handed-down understandings lacking any clear indication as to source or validity.[1]

A countering position, the opposite extreme, has had some following at all times in the modern era. Somewhat surprisingly, it has gained considerable currency in the second half of the twentieth century, in an era said to be permeated by the scientific ethos. The extreme view holds that all knowledge is social construction; there is no objective reality. Even the productions of science, it is said, are no more than "agreements" imposed by the positivists who control the major academic institutions and the leading scholarly publications. If that were an adequate reading, an important lesson would follow, one of profound relativism. Where scientific (or "positive") knowledge has a binding character, one that obliges attention, this opposite argument suggests that all readings are arbitrary and have equal claims to validity.

All knowledge, it is argued, is transmitted through the use of concepts, that is, through the use of agreed-upon symbols. All such symbols are learned in the course of social experience or training. Our knowledge is bound by the available symbols (or discourse); they provide a cage from which no escape is possible. The "choice" of symbols (terms of analysis) from among the available conceptual options predetermines the result, that is, how we will perceive, know, and understand "reality."

One reading of the human situation might be termed the pluralist variant of the argument. A diversity of social constructions is assumed. Groups throughout the society work out a multiplicity of competing meanings or understandings. Families, men and women, ethnic groups, religious bodies, racial communities, and regional communities provide various readings of "the world." Schoolteachers, in different levels and types of schools, develop and communicate other readings. University professors, scientists, artists, journalists, and members of the intelligentsia develop and pass on still other conceptions. For some advocates, again the extreme case, these social constructions all have equal claims to validity. The productions of "science" are no more than an elaborate pretense. Those claims are held to be no more credible than the understandings produced by backyard gossips.[2]

Another reading of the argument invokes some notion of power, dominance, or hegemony. This will be referred to as the elitist version of the social construction position. Powerful persons or groups (business leaders or politicians, for example, those dominating the mass media, or the leading figures in academia) impose the terms that determine the readings or understandings of others. The latter are portrayed as victims, as prisoners of those "controls." The Italian marxist Antonio Gramsci was an early proponent of this view. Louis Althusser, Nicos Poulantzas, and various members of the Frankfurt school of sociology, most notably Herbert Marcuse, have also provided formulations of this position.[3]

Although the arguments of elite dominance and control are richly embellished with "therefores," the connecting tissue of logic and evidence is ordinarily lacking. Some support for such claims is needed, that being at least a formal possibility. Although perhaps a difficult task, one might provide evidence showing "the powerful" plotting the terms of public discourse. One could perhaps more easily, through examination of media contents, demonstrate the successful control of the messages provided for mass consumption. Still another option is that one could show how "the masses" have accepted elite viewpoints or, the obvious alternative, show them unable to develop their own countering terms of analysis. Without that supporting evidence, the claim is, at best, an untested hypothesis. At worst, it is a paranoid fantasy—"they" are controlling our thoughts and behavior. A wide range of studies in the United States has shown a deterioration of trust in many established institutions and in most groups of leaders, beginning in the early 1960s. Those findings point to a serious loss of control over public "discourse" by those much-interested elites. The elite constructionists, however, typically do not concern themselves with such evidence.[4]

Another critique of science, one having greater merit than the positions just reviewed, offers an argument of failed controls. Here the focus is on scientific malfeasance, instances in which the supposedly disinterested scientists either distorted or faked the evidence needed to support some preferred conclusion. This might be termed the feet-of-clay approach, the point being that even the great luminaries did it. One can readily grant the specific point, because it is well documented. The extension of the argument, its application as a claim about "all knowledge," however, is unjustified, a clear non sequitur. The discovery of instances of malfeasance in the work of Galileo or Mendel does not prove such behavior to be universal or even typical in their work or in the sciences generally. That Newton at some point did something unacceptable says nothing about his contributions on other occasions, those for which he is remembered. Nor does the supposed a fortiori case say anything about science (or intellectual effort generally) at any other time or place. The discovery of instances says nothing about incidence or frequency within the larger universe of experience. The major contributions of those three men remain valid to this day. The sweeping conclusion, justifying the bold relativist claim, goes far beyond what the evidence warrants.

An important correlated line of criticism appears in this connection. The basic concept of science assumes some repeated testing of the findings. Replication, to use the relevant term, is assumed to be the standard practice. Scholarly error will be "found out" in those subsequent tests. The critics, quite rightly, point to the failure of the corrective mechanism. Fraudulent research has appeared in the literature and stayed there, in some cases for decades, before the "obvious" problems were recognized.[5] It is a serious concern, but again, the subsequent step, the move from instances to a general case (or to general condemnation) also poses an obvious problem—it is a non sequitur.

It is easy to concede the principal claims of both arguments reviewed here. Yes, all knowledge is conceptual. But far from being prisoners of received language, people can develop new concepts; they can and do generate new terms to frame new insights. Galileo, Newton, and Mendel did that. Our contemporaries, scientists and nonscientists alike, do the same on a regular basis. If there were any lingering doubt, one could point to the work of the critics being discussed here. They announce regularly that they, in their "critical" texts, have broken out of the received frameworks to discover the higher truths.[6]

As for the second line of critique, scientist fallibility, that too is easily conceded. Yes, people, even the most capable, make mistakes and, much more seriously, some of them have engaged in questionable or outright dishonest practice. As already implied, this criticism is obviously flawed, moving as it does from instances to the general case. One can recognize also that "the marketplace of ideas" does not work as it is supposed to, that is, yielding automatic, ineluctable correction. But the problems are those of frequency (how often does the supposed correction fail?) and timing (how long do discovery and correction take?). As opposed to the sweeping denial of the scientific enterprise, another line of endeavor seems appropriate—exploration of the conditions facilitating (or hindering) discovery and correction.

This line of criticism, relativism based on instances of malfeasance, is rather ingenuous. The standard for judgment is a fictive pure case, the researcher who never cheats, who never distorts, who never makes a self-serving decision. The underlying standard, demand, or expectation, saintly virtue, seems an unrealistic one for assessment of this-worldly behavior. An easy and more appropriate alternative standard is that one will, without question, find instances of malfeasance. The basic concerns then are those of incidence, seriousness, persistence, discovery, and correction. Partitive usage is also appropriate.[7]

The Transmission of Knowledge

The extreme readings of the scientific enterprise—direct empirical appreciation of "the facts" versus social construction—are unrealistic options, neither of them accepted by serious commentators. Most knowledge, in one way or another, is mediated. Most knowledge is transmitted through social networks and subject to various interpersonal influences. Only a small part of any individual's knowledge stems from original, direct perception of events.

Knowledge is perhaps best seen as something produced and transmitted in a series (or chain) of episodes. Abel sees something, formulates it, and passes that knowledge on to Baker. He (or she) then passes the knowledge on, possibly with some reformulation, to Charley. Each of the participants is involved in four basic processes: perception, formulation, assessment, and transmission. Abel senses something (makes the original observation). He formulates it, that is, puts it into words. Some assessment is made, some judgments of validity, of importance, and/or of usefulness. Finally, some decisions with respect to transmission are made: Should the information be passed on? If so, what to pass on? To whom should it be passed? How shall it be communicated? Abel, in the course of conversation, tells Baker, "It is warm today." For Baker, who has not yet been outside, this information is indirect, that is, mediated. The next steps, decisions actually, are identical in form to those undertaken by Abel. Baker may accept the statement as given or may alter it. Different judgments of validity or of importance may be made. And some judgments about transmission will be made. One possibility is that Baker passes the exact same message on to Charley.

The "knowledge" transmitted in this illustration is clearly of trivial importance, but the same processes would be involved if we substituted Max Weber for Abel. Weber's conclusion, based on his sweeping review of historical experience, held that Protestantism, inadvertently, played a major role in the development of modern capitalism. Baker subsequently read Weber's famous monograph and recommended it to students, one of whom was Charley, who accepted the claim and, never hearing any objections or critical comment, passed it on to many generations of students.

Given the volume of information available, some selection is required. People continuously make editorial judgments. They can vouch for and accredit the information received, approving it for retransmission, or they can make decisions to discard. If judged to be important, however, that information could be passed along through, say, seven steps and arrive unchanged. Each subsequent "processor" would have accepted the formulation as valid and important and relayed it without alteration. Another possibility would involve a significant change at, say, step two. It might then be relayed without change in all subsequent reports. Still another possibility would be a series of minor modifications at each step, the cumulative effect being a markedly altered formulation by step seven.

One of the assumptions underlying scientific knowledge is that a systematic effort will be made to assess information and to correct errors. In historical study, for example, a basic requirement is recourse to original sources. The aim is to review the primary evidence and the judgments drawn at the earliest steps in a sequence. But variation may occur in those assessments, ranging from none to considerable. As opposed to the assumption of an automatic (and ineluctable) correction process, a more "relaxed" reading seems appropriate. If that review is not regular and insistent, the tendencies or distortions that have crept into our understandings would continue. These might be termed inertial errors.

In the following chapter, two examples of such misconstruction, of failed controls, and of long-term inertial tendencies will be considered. Chapters 3 through 6 will review and assess three important historical and sociological formulations that involve misconstruction. Those chapters will also deal with processes of transmission and of subsequent reception. Such processes involve interpersonal or small group influences, matters usually discussed and researched in social psychology; one aim of the present effort is to apply the findings of that discipline to the scholarly enterprise. The assumption is that the social processes discovered in the experimental studies appear generally throughout the society and, more precisely, are present and have influence within academia, in the field of journalism, and, more broadly, in the ranks of the intelligentsia. To give some sense of the themes to be discussed, a brief review along with some illustrations follows. This subject, the "social psychology of scholarly wisdom," will be considered again at greater length in Chapter 7.

The Role of Interpersonal Influences

The portrait of Abel, Baker, and Charley is unrealistic in that it has them making rational and individual decisions. Each of the participants has been portrayed as making purely internal judgments. But most people's calculations involve some consideration of others' reactions, those of friends, associates, colleagues, and so forth. A basic concern, for most people, would be the question of impacts or effects. Would the message be well received? Or would it, in one way or another, be rejected? If the latter, would there be unpleasant consequences?

The conformity studies undertaken by Solomon Asch, involving perception and formulation, are relevant here. These small group experiments showed that some people misreported simple empirical realities— the length of lines. They followed the erroneous cues provided by other individuals in the group rather than depending on their own judgments. Later experiments by Stanley Milgram indicated that some people would inflict considerable pain on others, in response to the instructions provided by the experimenter. They accepted the experimenter's confident judgment that it was all right to proceed, even though the "victims" appeared to be suffering enormously. In both the Asch and Milgram experiments, many subjects conformed to the cues given them even though they had only passing acquaintance with the "peer group" or with the experimenter providing the instructions.[8] No serious sanctions, no threats or punishments followed nonconforming behavior, that is, provision of an accurate reading or a responsible moral judgment.

These experiments suggest a psychological tendency, a need to "go along" or to accept direction, an effect that transcends mere practical expediency. It is easy to assume that results of this sort apply to someone else. The subjects are typically drawn from student populations. It might, therefore, reflect only the naïvete of beginning students. Or, in a broader reading, such results might appropriately be applied to a wider population, to those lost within "the mass society."

Other experience, however, does not accord with such restricted readings. David Halberstam, the noted journalist, reported the following case. In September 1961, the United Nations' secretary-general, Dag Hammarskjöld, was in the Congo (later Zaire) attempting to bring an end to the civil war there. A group of reporters were at Ndola Airport (in what was then Northern Rhodesia) awaiting his arrival. For security reasons they were kept off the field behind a wire fence several hundred feet from

the landing area. It was dark when, at the appropriate time, a plane arrived. Some men walked out and greeted the man who got off. The figure
was "about the size of Hammarskjöld." A reporter with field glasses said,
"It's Hammarskjöld." A guard confirmed that conclusion and an official
from the Rhodesian ministry of information concurred. A large black car
drove off. There was no press conference. One reporter filed a story reporting a conversation between the secretary-general and a political lead-
er. Two reporters who were not convinced by what they had seen and
heard did not file stories. The others, the majority of the group, sent out
the news of his safe arrival. But that was not the case: the plane had
crashed and Hammarskjöld was dead. What does this experience show? In
the face of a "diffuse stimulus," experienced journalists had interpreted
the event and agreed on "the facts" of the case. There was, it is important
to note, some variation in the responses. Most of the participants had
gone along with the group reading, but some, here a minority of two, had
not.[9]

Another example is provided by Timothy Crouse, who described the
efforts of journalists reporting the 1972 presidential campaign. His major
theme was "pack journalism," the tendency for reporters to adopt a common line. The pack, Crouse wrote, "followed the wire-service men when-
ever possible. Nobody made a secret of running with the wires; it was an
accepted practice." Editors reinforced this conformity by calling reporters
to query them about variant readings of the day's news. As opposed to
the image of publishers and editors giving direct orders with regard to
news coverage, the more frequent experience, some have argued (with
evidence), is the provision of cues. The journalist is then expected to
"sense policy" and to react accordingly.[10]

Irving Janis applied some of the lessons from the conformity studies in
an important work concerned with major policy decisions that proved disastrous. On the evening of 6 December 1941, a group of top-level naval
commanders and their wives met at a dinner party in Pearl Harbor. In the
course of discussion, one participant, who was recognized as "brilliant,"
argued the likelihood of a Japanese attack. A unanimous response is reported: "everybody" present thought the person to be "crazy." There
were good grounds for concern: accurate intelligence reports had been received in the previous weeks, reports gained through the breaking of
codes. They revealed that Japan was preparing for massive military opera-

tions. The Japanese fleet, including eight aircraft carriers, had disappeared, its whereabouts unknown.

In another case, Janis reviews the actions of British leaders in 1938, men who systematically rejected "dissonant" information, evidence that cast doubt on the good intentions of their negotiating partner, one Adolf Hitler. In still another case, early in 1961, a group of men (described in one later account as "the best and the brightest") listened to and accepted as a plausible scenario, a plan for an invasion of Cuba, for a landing on a beach that was almost entirely surrounded by swamp. Not a single voice was raised to challenge the judgment of the planners.[11]

These cases were far removed from both the "naive" sophomores and "the great unwashed." All of these episodes involved matters of perception and formulation. Small groups of decision makers were, in one way or another, assessing information and drawing conclusions. In the process, they were rejecting plausible alternative readings or hypotheses.

Another social psychological study dealt directly with members of academia and discovered similar social psychological processes. The researchers hypothesized that academics responded to the "form" of a communication as much as to the content.[12] To test this possibility, they concocted a meaningless lecture entitled "Mathematical Game Theory as Applied to Physical Education." They hired a professional actor who "looked distinguished and sounded authoritative." He became Dr. Myron L. Fox. One of the experimenters coached the actor on presentation and on the handling of the question and answer period. Dr. Fox was trained in the use of double-talk, neologisms, non sequiturs, and contradictory statements, all of this to be interspersed with "parenthetical humor and meaningless references to unrelated topics." Outfitted with an impressive but fictitious curriculum vitae, he spoke before a group of highly trained educators. The presentation was videotaped for subsequent viewing by other groups of educators. On each of three occasions, questionnaires were distributed asking for evaluation and assessment. Here are some of the reactions: "Excellent presentation, enjoyed listening. Has warm manner. Good flow, seems enthusiastic. What about the two types of games, zero-sum and non-zero sum? Too intellectual a presentation. My orientation is more pragmatic."

The first videotape presentation was to a group of psychiatrists, psychologists, psychiatric social workers, all working as mental health educators. One of them reported having read some of Dr. Fox's publications. A third audience consisted of thirty-three educators and administrators in a graduate-level course on university educational philosophy. Their comments: "Lively examples. His relaxed manner of presentation was a large factor in holding my interest. Extremely articulate. Interesting, wish he dwelled more on background. Good analysis of subject that has been personally studied before. Very dramatic presentation. He was certainly captivating." Not all comments were positive. Dr. Fox was found to be "somewhat disorganized" by one viewer, "frustratingly boring" by another, and "unorganized and ineffective" by a third. But others in the audience found him to be "articulate" and "knowledgeable."

The principal lesson to be gained from this study is simple: prior training plays an important role in determining perceptions and judgments. In this instance, the training involved an appreciation of appearances, clues, style, and mannerisms often associated with professorial researchers (as opposed to logic, research procedures, weight of evidence, and so forth). In this case, the educators involved proved to be unexpectedly conformist. The investigators drew the following conclusions: "The three groups of learners in this study, all of whom had grown up in the academic community and were experienced educators, obviously failed as 'competent crap detectors' and were seduced by the style of Dr. Fox's presentation. Considering the educational sophistication of the subjects, it is striking that none of them detected the lecture for what it was."[13]

Discussions of conformity are often categorical in character. People, it is said, "are conformists." That statement overlooks some significant details, however, those of frequency and circumstance. The Asch study cited here indicates that conformity was the minority experience: "One-third of all the estimates in the critical group were errors identical with or in the direction of the distorted estimates of the majority. . . .The preponderance of estimates in the critical group (68 per cent) was correct despite the pressure of the majority." Asch reported "extreme individual differences"; some subjects "remained independent without exception" while others "went nearly all the time with the majority." Two replications of the Asch studies report nonconfirming results, that is, groups wherein little or no conformity was found. The authors of one of these studies, Marie-France Lalancette and Lionel Standing, argue against both the categorical readings and the notion of conformity as a fixed character trait. They conclude that "conformity is not universal, but appears momentarily in certain groups, at particular times. Rather than postulate a fixed conformity tendency, we must view it as a dependent variable, whose magnitude provides a measure of personality, group characteristics, or cultural influences."[14]

The incidence of conformity in the "real-life" cases reviewed here was much greater than the one-third reported by Asch. Only two of the reporters at Ndola Airport dissented. There was no dissent among the Bay of Pigs decision makers and none was reported among Dr. Fox's listeners. One facile but mistaken reaction to experimental studies of conformity— condescension toward the naive subjects and a discounting because of the artificial conditions—overlooks a much more serious problem: high levels of conformity among journalistic, political, military, and academic elites in real-life situations.[15]

The social psychological studies reviewed here all involve direct, face-to-face relationships. That experience, therefore, is not precisely analogous to the scholarly enterprise since one central activity, writing up results, is typically an individual effort, undertaken (so far as possible) in isolation. That circumstance, however, does not eliminate the social influence factor, which is instead indirect, one or more steps away from the immediate activity. The researcher (or commentator) would have internalized attitudes, values, outlooks, and normative cues in earlier training. The text must be approved by editors and referees, factors the author might take into account. The responses of later reviewers are also likely to be considered. Commentators, most of them, would have in mind the reactions of their peers, friends, co-workers, and acquaintances.

The anticipation of peer group reactions is the analogue of the directly experienced influences described in the face-to-face examples. It is a reasonable hypothesis that the anticipated reactions would have greater impact than the cues experienced in the Asch and Milgram experiments. Researchers know those peers personally; they wish to have the approval of those "significant others," of those reference groups. The subjects in the experiments had only casual contacts with their "peers," however, and, knowing the time limits involved, had no long-term psychological investment in those relationships. The much higher incidence of conformity in the real-life circumstances of Kennedy's cabinet discussions and Dr. Fox's lecture supports this hypothesis.

Three social psychological considerations have been delineated in this discussion. There is the matter of prior training, or what might be termed the learning of preferences. There are technical or instrumental judgments

involving "economic" calculations or cost/benefit analyses (what information to retain, pass on, discard) and, in another context, those made with a
view to the demands of publishers or referees. Finally, there are the judgments based on personal feelings, those made with regard to likely impacts on social relationships.

Questions of honesty and dishonesty are unavoidably present in discussion of these themes. Was the researcher aware of the bias? Was there
intent? Or was it a result of systematic, unchallenged training? Did the researcher who was committed to a given theoretical orientation simply see
the result as patently obvious, as an unquestioned fact of life? Did an innocent dismissal of "inessential information" yield support for a given
position? Or was dissonant information knowingly discarded (or discounted) so as to "save" a preferred position? Did the researcher select
and present evidence, unwittingly, in accordance with the constraints of
an accepted theory? Or was selection made so as to maintain harmonious
relationships with a given reference group?

Some of the dynamics, and some of the difficulties, may be seen in an
episode involving two leading intellectuals. Max Eastman was once a
prominent figure on the American Left. He was intelligent, charismatic,
and also a humane person. He had published much and his writings were
well received. In the early 1920s, following a trip to the Soviet Union, he
wrote a critical account reporting his observations, a book entitled *Since
Lenin Died.* Eastman knew that "he was exposing himself, but he underes-
timated the danger." Virtually everyone in his reference group turned
against him; the once-idolized intellectual became an object of contempt.
Lincoln Steffens, in an unusual and frank declaration of intent, provided
the guideline: whatever happened, he wrote, nothing "must jar our perfect
loyalty to the party and its leaders."[16] Since few intellectuals have been
quite so open as Steffens, questions of intent can rarely be as satisfactorily
answered. Accordingly, such questions will, for the most part, be neglected in the following chapters. With infrequent exception, the accounts
will be strictly "behavioral," reviewing and commenting on intellectual
productions but without comment on underlying "phenomenological"
processes.

Because of the complex interrelationships of the intended and unintended, interested and disinterested procedure, one further observation on
the social psychology of intellectual life may prove useful. The second
volume of Alexis de Tocqueville's *Democracy in America* opens with a dis-

cussion of what later scholars would call the sociology of knowledge. The volume carries the subtitle "The Social Influence of Democracy." The first section deals with the "Influence of Democracy on the Action of Intellect in the United States." Chapter 1 addresses the "Philosophical Method of the Americans" and chapter 2 "The Principal Source of Belief among Democratic Nations." In the latter chapter, Tocqueville points to an important and unavoidable *social* component present in human knowledge and understanding. He notes: "If man were forced to demonstrate for himself all the truths of which he makes daily use, his task would never end. . . . As, from the shortness of his life, he has not the time, nor, from the limits of his intelligence, the capacity, to act in this way, he is reduced to take on trust a host of facts and opinions which he has not had either the time or the power to verify for himself. . . . There is no philosopher in the world so great but that he believes a million things on the faith of other people and accepts a great many more truths than he demonstrates." Tocqueville carries the argument a step further, shifting from an empirical to a normative judgment: "This is not only necessary but desirable." Since no one can research "a million things," we must all accept many things "on faith." The question, Tocqueville declares, is "not to know whether any intellectual authority exists . . . but simply where it resides and by what standard it is to be measured."[17]

Tocqueville was pointing to a technical reason for reliance on a "collective heritage," that is, the compelling need for economy. That technical requirement could, in a well-ordered arrangement, yield a reasonably accurate reading of contemporary or historical realities. A problem would arise, however, with misinformation, with items that, somehow or other, became part of that heritage. The routine transmission and acceptance of such information—"on the faith of other people"—means it would not be subject to any systematic review or check. Rather than drawing an extreme relativist conclusion, however, one can again draw on the Tocqueville observations. He does not see *all* knowledge as the product of "social construction." Each "philosopher," as he sees things, would investigate a small range of problems and, presumably, an exchange of information would follow. Thus, the sum total of scholarly knowledge would be the product of two factors, original research and what might be called a social heritage.

A problem arises, however, from the failure to make systematic review of the knowledge contained in that heritage. First is the ever-present issue of personal preference, of bias. Additional problems are involved in the transmission of that heritage. People make choices about what information is to be transmitted and about what they are willing to receive. The social psychological studies, moreover, indicate that another range of extraintellectual factors is operating: tendencies toward conformity and deference to "authority," or to persons or texts having the appearance of authority.

Nowhere is this more evident than in the scholarly habit of citing previous work to establish intellectual credibility. In a continuation of our hypothetical chain, Daedelus, a researcher, depended on the work of Charley, who cited Baker, who in turn was citing Abel, who, it turned out, gave no source. Each of the subsequent commentators had judged the representation of the predecessor as accurate and had vouched for its adequacy. The regular appearance of such citation chains in the scholarly literature provides striking proof of Tocqueville's claim that "philosophers" take many statements "on the faith of other people." This should not be a serious problem in scholarly work that adheres to the requirement that, wherever possible, one must go to the original sources. Given the constraints of time and given a fallible human nature, however, there will always be a temptation to take shortcuts. Citation chains are a constant problem; two examples allow consideration of the implications.

The first comes from the work of Philip D. Curtin. It is one of the longest citation chains in modern scholarly literature. The question addressed is a simple factual one: How many persons were transported from Africa to the New World as slaves? The "consensus answer" to the question is: about fifteen million persons from beginning to end over the centuries. That number is generally indicated as a low estimate. Curtin provides several examples: Basil Davidson, in *Black Mother* (1961), gives the fifteen million figure, labelling it conservative. Davidson in turn cites R. R. Kuczynski, *Population Movements* (1936), as his source. Roland Oliver and J. D. Fage, in *A Short History of Africa* (1962), give the fifteen million figure together with a table showing the result broken down by century, and they too cite Kuczynski. Robert Rotberg's *Political History of Tropical Africa* (1965) gives a twenty-five million estimate, this on the assumption that the more frequent fifteen million figure is conservative. He cites Kuczynski plus a second source. The second source in this case is pointless since it too depends on Kuczynski.

All roads lead to Kuczynski. The reference in Davidson's text comes embellished with a brief description of Kuczynski, who is described, quite accurately, as "an eminent student of population statistics." The "eminent student" had not made an independent review and estimate, however; he had borrowed from an earlier source, in this case, a paper written by W. E. B. Du Bois in 1911. Du Bois provided two rather casual sentences which gave estimates by century. His conclusion was that there may have been perhaps "15,000,000 in all." Kuczynski's contribution was to put those sentences into tabular form. Du Bois, for his part, had borrowed from an article by Edward E. Dunbar, an American publicist who, in 1861, had first provided the set of estimates by century. He gave them as his estimates and indicated that they were probably low. Du Bois rounded the figures upward, thus adding roughly 5 percent to Dunbar's original. Curtin refers to the confident references made in the 1960s as providing an "impressive tower of authority." But, he adds, the ultimate source should have been indicated as the writing of "an obscure American publicist" rather than as "an eminent student." The argument, in either case, he notes, would be ad hominem.[18]

A basic rule of scholarly practice, that wherever possible one should go to original sources, was regularly neglected in this long history. If one does not check those sources, the following assumptions are being accepted on faith: first, that original evidence actually exists; second, that the evidence is credible, without problem or difficulty; and, third, that it has been accurately reproduced in all subsequent tellings. The probability of all three assumptions being valid would, on any occasion, be rather low.

The second example comes from a remarkable brief monograph by Jeffrey Burton Russell. He reviewed the history of what might be called the flat-earth question. The citation chains in this case are more extensive and have lasted even longer than in the case reviewed by Curtin. It is reported in the familiar histories that Christopher Columbus challenged the ignorant scholars of his age, those who believed the earth to be flat. His 1492 voyage, so it is said, proved the world to be round. Russell reviewed the scholarship on the subject from the ancients through the Middle Ages up to the time of Columbus. At all times, he reports, global conceptions (also termed sphericity) were dominant among scholars and the educated. Some writers, recognizing the accurate understandings of ancient scholars, argued a reversion hypothesis, that a flat-earth view had appeared in the "dark ages," but even that claim was mistaken. Russell indicates that in the first fifteen centuries of the Christian Era, only five rather atypical writers "seem to have denied the globe, and a few others were ambiguous and uninterested in the question." At all times "nearly unanimous scholarly opinion pronounced the earth spherical, and by the fifteenth century all doubt had disappeared." It was, Russell continues, several "nineteenth- and twentieth-century writers [who] flattened the medieval globe.[19]

In 1828, Washington Irving, an early propagator of the flat-earth mythology, published a biography, *History of the Life and Voyages of Christopher Columbus*. This account, Russell writes, "mingled fiction with what he announced as a historical reconstruction." In one "dramatic" scene, Irving has Columbus challenging a "council of Salamanca." His Columbus is "a simple mariner, standing forth in the midst of an imposing array of professors, friars and dignitaries of the church; maintaining his theory with natural eloquence, and, as it were, pleading the cause of the new world." A later Columbus biographer, Samuel Eliot Morison, describes Irving's account as "pure moonshine." Morison writes that Irving, "scenting his opportunity for a picturesque and moving scene, took a fictitious account of this nonexistent university council published 130 years after the event, elaborated on it, and let his imagination go completely. . . .The whole story is misleading and mischievous nonsense. . . .The sphericity of the globe was not in question. The issue was the width of the ocean; and therein the opposition was right.[20]

The transformation of medieval scholarship is traced by Russell to, among others, the work of a popular writer, John W. Draper, in particular to his *History of the Conflict between Religion and Science* (1874). Another contributor, Andrew Dickson White, an academic, published works on the same theme, among them *The Warfare of Science* (1876) and a "fully documented" two-volume study, *History of the Warfare of Science with Theology in Christendom* (1896). White misrepresented his sources and "constructed" the medieval flat earth. This allowed him a further contribution, a portrait of Columbus, as "the brave navigator 'at war' with ignorant theologians." The rhetoric, it is said, "captured the imagination of generations of readers, and [White's] copious references, still impressive, have given his work the appearance of sound scholarship, bedazzling even twentieth-century historians who should know better." Russell points out that "many authors great and small have followed the Draper-White line down to the present. The educated public, seeing so many eminent scientists, philosophers, and scholars in agreement, concluded that they must be right. In fact, the reason they were in agreement is that they imitated one another.[21] Again, conformity and citation chains are evident problems.

Russell reiterates his basic point later in a pair of conclusions: "Educated medieval opinion was virtually unanimous that the earth was round," and, "the idea that 'Columbus showed that the world was round' is an invention." The nineteenth-century writers, Russell argues, were apostles of enlightenment and, to make their case, assigned backward ideas to their opponents. It made a good story. One aspect of their method involves what would be called, in other contexts, sampling error. To make their case, the "few actual medieval flat-earthers were belabored to confirm the prejudice, and the bulk of the evidence on the other side was ignored." Although long-since exposed, "the Error continues to be almost as persistent . . . as it was nearly a century ago."[22]

It would be easy to think of—or to define—the flat-earth fiction as an isolated example. It "must be" a peculiar exception, one instance in which the normal scholarly checks somehow failed. A review of several major public affairs issues discussed over the last several decades shows, however, that round-to-flat transformations are remarkably frequent. In the late 1950s, some academics generated considerable alarm about the "threat of automation." The wholesale elimination of jobs would bring mass unemployment; these changes, they claimed, were imminent realities. In the late sixties, the student uprisings signaled a massive change in contemporary values. This was "documented" in several popular works, the most notable of which was Charles Reich's *The Greening of America*. In the early seventies, recognizing that those students, the bearers of the new values, were entering the labor force, arguments about a "rebellion in the workplace" became commonplace. At the same time, although the attitudes of whites toward blacks had shown steady improvement, the notion of an imminent "white backlash" was widely propagated. When the predictions offered in these confident scenarios did not come to pass, they were quietly abandoned. Few of the academic experts who had sounded the alarm subsequently addressed the problem, for example, indicating the error or attempting to explain its sources. The media followed the same tack; the issues were simply dropped.[23]

The chapters in this volume all deal with some kind of social misconstruction. Max Weber's *Protestant Ethic and the Spirit of Capitalism* (first published in 1905) is widely cited within sociology (and to some extent in works of cultural or intellectual history). In those contexts it is, for the most part, cited with approval. In two scholarly fields, Reformation history and economic history, the work receives little attention and when considered it is seldom approved. Sociologists, on the whole, seem to be neither aware nor interested in the findings produced in those other fields. Weber's essay provides an extensive explanation for differences in "worldly success" associated with religion. Nowhere in that text, with its rich array of sources, does he successfully document that initial claim. Weber was explaining a difference he had not established.

For a half-century, academic specialists had a ready explanation for the "rise of Nazism": Germany's threatened lower middle class provided the mass support that made Hitler and his party an important political force. The argument and evidence for that claim are reviewed in Chapter 4, which summarizes and extends the findings of my book *Who Voted for Hitler?* (1982). The basic conclusion, in brief, is that the hypothesis was never supported. The lower-middle-class claim survived for some five decades without benefit of serious supporting evidence. Substantially different lines of analysis are required to account for the National Socialist electoral victories.

Chapter 5 gives further consideration to the lower-middle-class thesis. It reviews the history of citation, of mutual support, pointing to the social dynamics that sustained the view in absence of evidence. Now, more than six decades after the last elections of the Weimar Republic, some academics still treat the claim as if it were well-documented fact. Several of the strategies used to maintain this "construction" will be reviewed.

Michel Foucault's *Discipline and Punish* (1977 [original 1975]) argues a pervasive sinister tendency within modern society. An unidentified "power," with extraordinary cunning and subtlety, has been extending its control into all areas of existence. The documentation for this case is most questionable, one central claim being based on an outright fiction. Foucault is, nevertheless, among the most cited of all twentieth-century authors, and most of that citation is with evident approval.

The next chapter will consider two modest instances of the social misconstruction problem, these involving Mozart and Wellington.

2

Mozart's Poverty, Wellington's Epigram

The Neglected Genius

A persistent social misconstruction appears in most accounts of the life of Wolfgang Amadeus Mozart. The well-known history involves a range of factual elements that are organized in terms of an underlying theory. The basic portrait has been summed up by a recent biographer, Volkmar Braunbehrens: "Mozart, the wunderkind celebrated throughout Europe, a child showered with gifts by the empress, the pope, kings, and princes, was a forgotten man when he died at thirty-five and was buried in an unmarked pauper's grave. Thus, with many variations, has Wolfgang Mozart's life always been presented to us: as a brilliant rise to success followed by a single, uninterrupted period of decline. This version is found in novels, children's books, biographical films, and even works that claim to be scholarly.... All this may have a certain fascination, but it does not stand up to historical scrutiny."[1]

On leaving Salzburg for Vienna in 1781, the twenty-five-year-old Mozart gave up a position that assured him of 450 florins per year. A primary-school teacher in Austria at that time earned between 120 and 250 florins, a secondary-school teacher 300. In Vienna, a permanent position for most musicians, according to Braunbehrens, "normally meant around 400 florins per year," an amount exceeded by only a handful of conductors and virtuoso soloists. In 1782 Mozart wrote that with 1,200 florins per year "a man and his wife can manage in Vienna if they live quietly and in the retired way we desire." Beginning in 1783, "he earned almost twice that amount and managed to spend all of it." The last Mozart apartment, that of the final and supposedly desolate year, 1791, had five rooms. Two of them, a study and living room, were of fair size, approximately fifteen by eighteen feet. The apartment itself had more than fifteen hundred square feet of floor space. Mozart's fortepiano was located in the study, a room with three windows facing the street. Another room contained a billiard table. The furnishings of this last dwelling make clear that Mozart was not living in extreme want. The problem "lay in his style of living and was not the result of actual poverty." A careful review of the composer's known income puts his 1791 earnings at 3,725 florins, the best showing for his decade in Vienna. After 1787, he was assured of an annual salary of 800 florins from the Austrian court. Braunbehrens's conclusion: "Mozart was far from poor."[2]

Two later biographical accounts, by H. C. Robbins Landon and William Stafford, covered much of the same ground and reached similar conclusions. In Stafford's judgment Braunbehrens and Landon exaggerated Mozart's income. Stafford's conclusion, however, accords with the recent revisionism rather than with the portrait of poverty: "Without doubt," he writes, "Mozart's income, and wealth as represented by his possessions, put him firmly in the middle classes—perhaps in the top 10 per cent of the Viennese population." Stafford seems troubled by this conclusion. In his next sentence, he claims "this does not mean that [Mozart] was comfortably off." Andrew Steptoe, one of Stafford's sources, offers the following summary: "Mozart did in fact earn a healthy but variable income. . . . Even in his last years, Mozart was not poor; rather he suffered occasional periods of want."[3]

In 1790, the composer received an invitation to visit London. He was assured the equivalent of 2,400 florins for a six-month tour. He would, in addition, have received earnings from his own concerts given there. But for several reasons, he postponed the opportunity (it was agreed that Haydn, the older composer, would go first). At that time Mozart's "works were on sale in all the leading Viennese music shops. . . . His operas were being performed everywhere." Mozart gained nothing directly from the many opera performances since the going arrangement provided for a one-time payment, that is, a fixed commission. His evident fame had major implications for subsequent earnings, however: his commissions for operas doubled twice between 1786 and 1791. And there was no shortage of opportunities—he "had been inundated with commissions at least since March" of 1791. The most famous of these was for the *Requiem*. After 1787, he began composing (among many other things) dances for *Fasching* balls, "minuets, German dances, *Ländler*, and contredanses." Many of these works "were advertised in the *Wiener Zeitung* during Mozart's last years, bringing him substantial fees from publishers."[4]

The most striking evidence of the composer's fame, because the most visible, came with the death of Emperor Joseph II early in 1790 and the installation of his successor, Leopold II. Mozart made an expensive trip to Frankfurt for the crowning of the new emperor. That does not appear to have produced any significant financial return for the composer. Some months later, Leopold was crowned as king of Bohemia during a week-long celebration in Prague in September 1791. Mozart was commissioned to write an opera, *La Clemenza di Tito*, for the occasion, and two other Mozart operas, *Così fan tutte* and *Don Giovanni*, were also performed. Mozart was the most-performed composer during the week. *Die Zauberflöte* received its first performance later in the month and was an immediate success. It received "almost daily" performances in Vienna and was performed eighteen times in Frankfurt before packed houses.[5]

The composer's illness, death, and burial were reviewed in the early 1970s in a book-length account by Carl Bär. The attending doctor during Mozart's last weeks, he reports, was Dr. Thomas Closset, one of the most famous and sought-after physicians in Vienna. In the composer's last days Closset was joined by Dr. Mathias Sallaba, also one of the best and most renowned physicians in the city.[6]

Mozart died on 5 December 1791. That day, according to Sophie Haibel (sister of Constanze Mozart, Wolfgang's wife), "many people stood in front of the house and showed their sympathy in various ways." The following day Mozart's body was displayed at St. Stephen's Cathedral. Haibel, considered by Braunbehrens to be the "most authentic source" on the composer's last days, reported that "crowds of people walked past his corpse, weeping and wailing for him." Four thousand mourners appeared at a service in Prague. The contemporary sources say nothing about a "pauper's grave"—that all came later. Mozart was buried in an unmarked common grave but that was the general practice of the age, a circumstance that "applied to 85 percent of the bourgeois population." Braunbehrens writes that "in the Josephine period, a communal grave was an expression neither of shabbiness nor of thoughtlessness, but rather a reflection of the sober rationalism that promoted—not without reason—what were then the most advanced ideas about hygiene."[7]

On the day of the burial, the *Wiener Zeitung* reported the composer's death. It declared that "from childhood on he was known throughout Europe for his most exceptional musical talent. Through the successful development and diligent application of his extraordinary natural gifts, he scaled the heights of the greatest masters. His works, which are loved and admired everywhere, are proof of his greatness."[8] One further proof of the composer's continuing fame is indicated by an event that occurred three days before his death. The emperor named him to be music director of St. Stephen's Cathedral.

Evidence attesting to the family's financial well-being, curiously, appears with frequency in the Mozart biographies. Constanze, in continuous ill health, spent weeks in a nearby spa, Baden-bei-Wien. Mozart arranged for two rooms there in May 1791, and his wife was accompanied by two maids. Their son Karl was enrolled in an expensive boarding school. "There are no letters from this period," Braunbehrens reports, "in which Mozart bewails his money problems." It is an extraordinary history. Mozart was extremely popular and very well-off and, had he lived, was clearly destined to achieve even greater fame and material rewards. Yet despite readily available evidence, this odd history of poverty and neglect was generated, and sustained, and in some quarters—even in the face of documented corrections—has been maintained and repeated to the present.[9]

By way of explanation, Braunbehrens signals the importance of the first major scholarly biography, Otto Jahn's two-volume work, *W. A. Mozart*, published in 1856 and 1859. All of "the key points," Braunbehrens declares, "have remained basically the same" since its publication. That conclusion, which appears in the opening paragraph of the preface, is plainly hyperbolic: for stylistic effect, Braunbehrens dramatically simplified a complex history. Stafford's work provides the detail, tracing the strands of the "basic revised history" through many decades of biographical production. Many of the elements of the basic history were in print within decades of the composer's death. Then, through diligent copy-work and active embellishment, doubtful material came to be viewed as well-established fact.

The uncritical acceptance of prior work could be either innocent (as with random error) or in some way "motivated," that is to say, the product of some predisposition. Conclusions may be accepted "on faith" because of their surface plausibility, there being no immediate grounds for doubt. Alternatively, they may be accepted because they agree with prior training or preference. Many writers, it seems, took the romantic paradigm of the neglected and suffering artist and turned "the evidence" to fit that scheme. It seems likely that the romantic paradigm (or romantic prejudice) was a decisive factor for many biographers and "guided" their interpretations throughout the more than 160 years of the Mozart mythology.[10]

The comments in the preceding paragraph touch on some unanswerable questions—hence the qualifications and indications of likelihood. We cannot know the workings of the minds of those many commentators when they wrote their versions of the basic tale. Were they producing mindless copy-work, or did they actually see the contrary evidence but overlook it because it did not accord with their understanding? The citation-chain problem, noted in the previous chapter, was present throughout this history of misconstruction. On the simple question of the composer's appearance, for example, Stafford reports, biographers are "heavily indebted" to three early accounts by Schlichtegroll, Niemetschek, and Nissen. But, he continues, "Nissen plagiarized Niemetschek who in turn plagiarized Schlichtegroll. Where then did Schlichtegroll, who never saw Mozart as far as we know, get his information?" Nissen reviewed a mass of relevant material for his biography, published in 1828. He covered some twenty earlier biographies but, according to Stafford, found that "seventeen or eighteen simply repeated each other."[11]

Some authors no doubt did review original sources but still offered the portrait of neglect and privation (despite the evidence of the coronation week, the spa, the private school, and so on). For them, the problem is an uncritical (or naive) acceptance of the romantic paradigm. In many cases, both processes may have been involved: a simple reworking of the old tale and an easy acceptance of the plausible (because so often heard) framework even in the face of contrary evidence.

One difficulty facilitating that easy acceptance was the failure to consider alternative hypotheses. Steptoe, for example, refers to a "catastrophic decline in Mozart's popularity in the second half of the decade." He points to the decline of Mozart's public performances, which fell off dramatically after 1785, but he gives no direct evidence to support his specific claim that public tastes had changed. One possibility is that Mozart had turned his attention elsewhere. *Figaro* was composed in 1786, *Don Giovanni* in 1787, and both were enthusiastically received. Some major political events occurred at that point and these had far-reaching consequences for Austrian cultural life. The Habsburg monarchy was at war with Turkey from midyear 1787 to September 1790, with more than 280,000 men mobilized for the effort. Simultaneously, there were uprisings in the Netherlands and Hungary. Concert-going declined as young aristocrats were called to the front and as economies at home became necessary. Braunbehrens reviews the linkage between war and concert opportunities at length. At the same time, however, he indicates the continued affection of the composer's leading patrons. Mozart's fortunes recovered in 1791, which, he notes, was "also a year of recovery for Austria."[12]

The elitist version of the social construction argument claims that knowledge is somehow "interested" or purposeful: the dominant discourse is an imposition devised and disseminated by the powerful. The Mozart myth allows a test of the claim or, at least, an occasion for speculation about its validity. It is difficult, a priori, to see the Mozart myth as interested knowledge, as something serving "the needs" of the powerful. One would have to imagine Jahn and subsequent biographers (Marcia Davenport, for example) following the directives of some manipulative planners. It is not immediately clear that "the powerful" (Emperor Franz Joseph, Louis Napoleon Bonaparte, Otto von Bismarck, and perhaps William Gladstone) would wish to have "the masses" trained in romantic imagery. It is unlikely, moreover, that they would have had time to manage such fine details of cultural life. The "powerful" bourgeoisie, one might assume, would have preferred the more realistic portrait of Mozart the entrepreneur, the man who wrote music on commission, who closely followed market preferences, and, in accordance with the liberal view, the successful composer who rose to the top of his profession.

One should always consider alternative hypotheses. One might put that insinuating question: Who benefits? Who stands to gain through propagation of the romantic fiction? One possible answer is easy—"the artist" would gain. The underlying theme (or subtext) is that artists, the talented, the creative minds, or intellectuals are not paid enough.

Two lessons follow from this case study. First, this example shows that intellectuals can produce and maintain discourse (or hegemonic ideas) independently of political or economic elites. The record of intellectual activity over much of the modern era provides a serious challenge to the assumption that the powerful have exclusive dominance or control. Second, this narrative points again to "uncritical critics." With remarkable persistence, generations of intellectuals (and their immediate audience, the well educated) have proved curiously accepting. They have taken conclusions as coin of the realm even when there were serious grounds for doubt or skepticism. The merchants of culture, moreover, have provided themselves with a convenient double standard. If haberdashers, grocers, or hardware dealers had put forward such flagrantly self-serving claims, critical intellectuals would have subjected them to merciless ridicule.[13]

Eton's Playing Fields

A second social misconstruction involves the duke of Wellington's famous epigram: "The Battle of Waterloo was won on the playing fields of Eton." Elizabeth Longford, author of the outstanding biography of Wellington, concludes that "probably he never said or thought anything of the kind." Longford reports that the duke, then Arthur Wesley, did not finish his studies at Eton. He left "after his three inglorious years, having been neither happy nor successful." The boy was small, an odd-man-out, and appears to have spent his spare time in the Manor House garden. In the decades following the most famous of his victories, he "never returned . . . except when he had to." In 1841, when asked for a contribution for new buildings at Eton, he declined with, as Longford puts it, a "cold reference to Eton as just another foundation."[14]

The first version of the famous statement, Longford reports, came in 1855, three years after Wellington's death. The count de Montalembert, an eminent author, visited the school and was inspired to comment on its significance. He wrote that the duke, in his declining years, revisited "the beauteous scenes where he had been educated," and there, "remembering the games of his youth, and finding the same precocious vigour in the descendants of his comrades, [he] said aloud: '*C'est ici qu'a été gagnée la bataille de Waterloo.*'" A later commentator, Sir Edward Creasy, added a minor refinement to that original. He reported that the aged duke, when passing the playing fields, commented on the "manly character" nurtured there. In this version, the duke is reported to have said: "There grows the stuff that won Waterloo." In 1889, Sir William Fraser, the "excellent club raconteur," repeated Montalembert's statement, put it into English for the first time, joined it with Creasy's comment about the playing fields, and gave us the version that has come down to the present.

The famous epigram, in short, appears to be a posthumous social construction generated over several decades, the product of several creators. That is one aspect of the tale; the rest is a history of repetition, of transmission by scores of later commentators. The uncritical transmission of a saying over many decades points to a failing, albeit a modest one, in the scholarly enterprise. Those many commentators had accepted the statement on faith, vouched for its validity, and passed it on to subsequent audiences. The scholarly admonition, the need for doubt, for skepticism, or for critical thinking, appears to have gone unheeded in this now century-old history.

Apart from the question of a source, one might argue that there was no immediate reason for questioning the credibility of the claim as given. But was that the case? One might begin with a simple line of questioning: What does the statement mean? What did the playing-field activities have to do with the later battle? What games were played there? What was the relationship between those schoolboy romps and the ordered squares and the disciplined firing that were decisive on the field of battle? The faint indications of meaning attributed to the statement typically focus on character—either the manly variety stressed by Creasy or some other, usually unspecified, leadership abilities. Another possibility is that the statement applies to Wellington himself. But, Longford notes, there "were no compulsory, organized games at Eton and even the most casual cricket or boating did not attract Arthur," who is described as "lonely and withdrawn."[15] One other fact: he attended Eton from his twelfth to his fourteenth year. It seems unlikely, under those circumstances, that he had acquired leadership skills there.

One should at least speculate about alternatives. The easiest hypothesis of all would be a simple rejection of the claim—the skills required of British officers at Waterloo were *not* developed on Eton's playing fields. One might put the matter even more forcefully: the required skills had nothing whatsoever to do with the famous playing fields. The absence of evident meaning should have stimulated doubts and led to research by someone among those many commentators. The manifest absence of such skepticism points to a different lesson, mentioned earlier: a remarkable degree of uncritical acceptance (or quiet conformity) is present within the ranks of the intelligentsia.[16]

The second variant of the relativist position, elite constructionism, argues that knowledge is generated and sustained by the holders of power; it somehow serves their interests. Is the Eton-Waterloo statement interested knowledge? Does it serve the purposes of the powerful? To support such a claim and to move beyond mere allegation would require a considerable effort. One would ordinarily begin with a hypothesis, with some guess as to the instrumental purpose. The aim, presumably, was to generate respect or deference among the masses; the populace was to be taught the importance of established institutions and the capability of the leaders trained there. The purpose, put simply, would be legitimation. One must then demonstrate that this was the intention of the creators and propagators of this "knowledge." In the last link of the serve-the-purposes argument, one would have to prove success, that the masses learned the lesson and responded with appropriate obeisance.

It is by no means obvious that gullible acceptance of the claim served the interests of "power," since an alternative reading is readily available, namely, that the traditional schools did a poor job in the training of leaders. George Orwell offered a stunning challenge to the received wisdom of the Eton-Wellington apothegm. Writing in 1941, he referred to "the immobility of the public schools, which have barely altered since the 'eighties of the last century." He pointed to "the military incompetence which has again and again startled the world. Since the 'fifties every war in which England has engaged has started off with a series of disasters, after which the situation has been saved by people comparatively low in the social scale. The higher commanders, drawn from the aristocracy, could never prepare for modern war, because in order to do so they would have had to admit to themselves that the world was changing. They have always clung to obsolete methods and weapons, because they inevitably saw each war as a repetition of the last."[17] Maybe those disasters were produced, somehow, on the playing fields of Eton and the other great public schools. If so, the interested apologist (or the critical thinker) might be moved to rethink the cliché.

One of Britain's nineteenth-century prime ministers, Robert Cecil, better known as Lord Salisbury, came from an ancient and influential aristocratic family. His father was a cousin to the duke of Wellington; the duke stood as the boy's godfather. From an early age, the boy showed exceptional intellectual and political capacities. He was, as a matter of course, sent off to Eton but the experience proved "a nightmare." A biographer reports that his "lack of animal spirits and superior mental development did not commend him to his fellows." His "only Eton friend," Lord Dufferin, wrote later that he "was badly knocked about for his precocity." His father eventually consented to his withdrawal. The years between Eton and Oxford were spent at Hatfield, the family estate, with private tutoring. While only a single case, this experience does suggest some alternative hypotheses: such schools might teach (or require) a pointless conformity; they might discourage independent thinking, doing little good for weak egos; and they might harm strong egos. The achievements of Wellington and Salisbury, conceivably, were possible only because they left Eton at an early point, before the damage was done.[18]

Another bit of evidence providing a striking challenge to the received claims about the merits of such schools (and a confirmation of Orwell's reading) is found in a little-noted lesson from the first of the great disasters of the twentieth century. In the midst of World War I, it became clear that the British establishment and the famous schools had failed entirely. The leadership of the wartime coalition government was turned over to David Lloyd George, a man whose early experience was far removed from "the great schools." His father, a schoolteacher, died when the boy was in his nineteenth month. An uncle, a shoemaker, appears to have been the most important influence in his formative years. The boy was educated in a village school in Llanystumdwy (Wales) where one of his teachers undertook unusual efforts of tutelage. The family—father, mother, and uncle—were devoted Baptists, this too being far removed from the normal "establishment" experience. The school was Anglican and the students, although overwhelmingly nonconformist, were required to learn the catechism. At age thirteen, the boy organized a revolt, "a unanimous refusal by the students . . . to recite the creed."[19]

Some intellectuals have argued that "we" are prisoners of our conceptions or of those provided by "the powerful," but another reading is possible and likely. The genuine skeptic would have noted, first, the absence of citation accompanying the Wellington epigram; second, the implausible character of the statement as given, and third, the ready existence of evidence challenging the general point of the claim. Maybe, somehow, power was serving "its" purposes with this hegemonic idea. Maybe the establishment self-interestedly overlooked the problems just reviewed. Perhaps it was "in their interest" to overlook those problems. But there was no obstacle preventing any intellectual from engaging in a routine analytic effort. One alternative to the prisoner image is personal failing or incapacity. The invocation of the prisoner image might be an excuse to cover up that inadequacy.

The Columbus, Mozart, and Wellington examples are intended as first illustrations of the social misconstruction problem. All three involve persistent collective errors that have lasted for a century or more. The analysis has reviewed the factual errors and has provided some explanation of how they originated and were sustained. Some larger issues are involved, beyond the basic questions of fact. Two of the erroneous readings provided "evidence" that, supposedly at least, sustained the romantic "theory" of the world. The Wellington epigram, the alleged fact, also fits within a larger framework that provides legitimacy to an established institution and its graduates.

A general recognition of these errors would probably have no major consequences for intellectual life. That Mozart's genius, for example, was appreciated to the end of his days and that he was well rewarded for his efforts will not change our enjoyment of his music. That he showed unusual commercial sense, producing goods for an ever-changing market, that he and Constanze lived well, that they were spendthrifts, should force an abandonment of the romantic tale of neglect and resulting poverty.

The chapters that follow deal with larger issues. They address theories or interpretative schemes that purport to explain major social changes in modern world. Should those theories prove faulty, another explanation of those changes is in order. One should develop a better explanation.

3

Max Weber and
the Protestant Ethic

This chapter will consider Max Weber's most famous work, *The Protestant Ethic and the Spirit of Capitalism*. In the opening pages, Weber presents evidence to show the connection between Protestantism and various measures of economic achievement in the late nineteenth century. He also provides some judgments about the weight that should be assigned to this causal factor. His conclusions, in brief, are that a religious impact was present in the late nineteenth century, readily observable and easily documented, and that it was of primary importance in explaining individual outlooks and behavior. His subsequent larger argument reaches back to cover several centuries. It holds that "the Protestant ethic" was a key factor in the rise of modern capitalism.

The first task in this chapter is to review Weber's argument and evidence on the initial question, that of the association between religion and achievement in the late nineteenth century. Later, consideration will be given to Weber's explanation of the religion-capitalism association. The conclusions, to anticipate, are: that the initial association is not satisfactorily demonstrated, and that the historical claims are poorly supported. Finally, some consideration will again be given to the sociology of knowledge, specifically, to the treatment given the Protestant ethic thesis in scholarly accounts.

A brief comment on the characteristics of causal arguments is appropriate. The beginning point for research on any such argument is a demonstration of association. The assumed cause must be linked, in the manner predicted, with the effect. If it is argued that metropolitan cities are detrimental to social life, one should, as a first step, show that to be the case. One should present or cite evidence indicating fewer friends or contacts in the large cities as opposed to the towns, villages, and rural areas. If the point is not established, any subsequent comment would have begged the initial question. Put differently, one might be "explaining" a nonexistent difference.

Causal arguments typically come with some indication of weights or importance. A given factor might be associated with some end-result but the impact might be small or even trivial. If one were arguing importance (for example, that community size has a major impact on social life), then one ought to see sizable differences in the anticipated direction. If, however, the claim were supported, but only by a few percentage points, the assumption of importance would be immediately challenged. If this point were not researched, if it too were bypassed, one might again be addressing the wrong question. In this case, begging the question would lead to the neglect of more important, weightier causes.

Weber's Opening Argument

The Protestant Ethic and the Spirit of Capitalism begins with the following sentences (to facilitate later discussion, the letter *n* has been inserted before Weber's footnotes):[1]

A glance at the occupational statistics of any country of mixed religious composition brings to light with remarkable frequency[n2] a situation which has several times provoked discussion in the Catholic press and literature,[n3] and in Catholic congresses in Germany, namely, the fact that business leaders and owners of capital, as well as the higher grades of skilled labour, and even more the higher technically and commercially trained personnel of modern enterprises, are overwhelmingly Protestant.[n4] This is true not only in cases where the difference in religion coincides with one of nationality, and thus of cultural development, as in Eastern Germany between Germans and Poles. The same thing is shown in the figures of religious affiliation almost wherever capitalism, at the time of its great expansion, has had a free hand to alter the social distribution of the population in accordance with its needs, and to determine its occupational structure. The more freedom it has had, the more clearly is the effect shown. It is true that the greater relative participation of Protestants in the ownership of capital,[n5] in management, and the upper ranks of labour in great modern industrial and commercial enterprises,[n6] may in part be explained in terms of historical circumstances[n7] which extend far back into the past, and in which religious affiliation is not a cause of the economic conditions, but to a certain extent appears to be a result of them.

The first phrase of the opening sentence suggests that occupational statistics broken down by religion are readily available for several countries of mixed religious composition. Those comparisons, moreover, show consistently that "the higher grades" are "overwhelmingly" Protestant. One fact about "the Weber thesis" has gone largely unnoticed: Weber presented no statistics supporting his claim. This failure is all the more remarkable given Weber's penchant for thorough documentation. In Talcott Parsons's translation, *The Protestant Ethic* has 148 pages of text (with large type); they are accompanied by 98 pages of small-type notes. To avoid an excess of notes, references to this source will be given in parentheses in the text.

A detailed examination of Weber's documentation of these initial claims is instructive. The chapter title, "Religious Affiliation and Social Stratification," is footnoted. The opening paragraph is embellished with six notes (numbers two through seven). The note appended to the chapter title reviews several later discussions of Weber's original publication; it is by far the longest of the seven. One statement stands out: writing some fifteen years later, Weber announced that in the revised version he had not "left out, changed the meaning of, weakened, or added materially different statements to, a single sentence of my essay which contained any essential point. There was no occasion to do so, and the development of my exposition will convince anyone who still doubts" (187). The phrase "nicht einen einzigen Satz" (not a single sentence) was emphasized.

The second footnote comes after "remarkable frequency." It discusses exceptions to the not-yet-expressed rule and considers the kind of statistics needed. The note itself provides no statistics. The passage about discussion in the Catholic press and literature is followed by his footnote 3.

Two works are cited that discuss the presumed fact; they do not, however, contain any evidence on the point.

The key passage, which declares that the high-level occupations are "overwhelmingly Protestant," is also footnoted. The reference here is to a work by Martin Offenbacher, a student of Weber.[2] That work is said to contain "the most complete statistical material we possess on this subject: the religious statistics of Baden" (188). But the note does not report anything about the relationship between *occupation* and religion. In contrast to the generous promise of the opening text passage—"statistics of any country"—the content of this note proves unexpectedly modest. Baden, a small state within Germany, would provide information on a minuscule segment of the European population.

The fifth footnote, which appears after "ownership of capital," is the first to provide evidence. It contains data from Offenbacher in support of Weber's claim about the "relative participation of Protestants in the ownership of capital." He provides figures for Baden on the taxable capital of Protestants and Catholics. A substantial difference is indicated, which is clearly consonant with Weber's main argument. Again, however, no statistics on occupation are provided. The last two lines of this note report that "the Jews . . . were far ahead of the rest," their taxable capital being more than four times that of the Protestants. Although of possible relevance to "the spirit of capitalism," Weber does not return to this point.[3] The sixth note, appended to the subsequent clause after "commercial enterprises," refers again to Offenbacher. The one-sentence statement reads: "On this point compare the whole discussion in Offenbacher's study." The seventh note, after "historical circumstances," is another one-sentence reference to Offenbacher.

Weber's opening discussion continues with a consideration of a causal possibility, suggesting that the association may in part result from some distant historical fact. Occupancy of leading economic positions "usually involves some previous ownership of capital, and generally an expensive education; often both." These, he notes, "are to-day largely dependent on the possession of inherited wealth." A "majority of the wealthy towns," Weber writes, "went over to Protestantism in the sixteenth century," and this yielded handed-down advantages that were still present at the time of his writing.

The connection between cities and Protestantism was evident and much discussed in the sixteenth century. It has also been the subject of much scholarly attention in recent decades. While it is apparent that the majority of towns "went over" to Protestantism, Weber's specification, his focus on the *wealthy* towns, does not appear justified. Weber provides no supporting evidence or references on that point.

To guard against an all-too-easy inference, two quotations from the work of Lewis W. Spitz, a leading Reformation historian, may be helpful: "It was in the cities that the movement made sensational progress during the first two decades. The initiative and dynamic of the urban populace that carried it forward were propelled by the gospel preaching of evangelists and pamphleteers and by negative feelings such as anticlericalism, resentment against church dues, and anger at what were now perceived to be fraudulent indulgences. It remained a popular movement into the 1530s and longer." On the social base of the movement, Spitz writes: "The process by which the Reformation became established in the cities was nearly everywhere the same. In no case did the patricians initiate the reform. . . . The pressure for reform came from the populace down below."[4]

Weber repeats the "inheritance" argument again a couple of pages later where, "in part at least," that factor is assigned some causal significance. "But," he adds, "there are certain other phenomena which cannot be explained in the same way." Reintroducing the religious factor, he reports "a great difference discoverable in Baden, in Bavaria, in Hungary, in the type of higher education which Catholic parents, as opposed to Protestant, give their children." Catholics "prefer the sort of training which the humanistic Gymnasium affords" and, in contrast to the Protestants, they avoid "the institutions preparing . . . for technical studies and industrial and commercial occupations" (37–38).

This point is supported by two footnote references to Offenbacher. The data are again for Baden (notes 8 and 9, 188–189). Weber's figures are reproduced here in Table 3.1. Protestants made up 37 percent of the state's population and thus, as may be seen, were overrepresented in all five varieties of secondary schools, constituting nearly half (48 percent) of those enrolled. For three of those schools, the Protestant percentages are not very different from the overall 48 percent figure. The most striking difference appears between attendance in the *Gymnasium* and the *Realgymnasium*. Talcott Parsons, translator and editor of the work, writes that the "main emphasis" in the former school "is on the classics." In the latter, "Greek is dropped and Latin reduced in favour of modern languages, mathematics and science" (189). The Protestant percentages in

Table 3.1　Religion and Schooling: Baden, Bavaria, and Württemberg (circa 1895)

State and School Type	Protestant (%)	Religion Catholic (%)	Jewish (%)
BADEN			
Gymnasien	43	46	9.5
Realgymnasien	69 (59)[a]	31	9
Oberrealschulen	52	41	7
Realschulen	49	40	11
Höhere bürgerschulen	51	37	12
Secondary schools	48	42	10
Baden population	37.0	61.3	1.5
BAVARIA			
Gymnasien	27.3	68.1	4.2
Progymnasien and Lateinschulen	44.4	49.4	6.0
Realgymnasien	54.4	34.8	10.5
Realschulen	41.8	49.5	8.1
Handelsschulen	31.9	48.1	19.8
Bavaria population	28.2	70.7	0.9
WÜRTTEMBERG			
Gymnasien	68.2	28.2	3.4
Lateinschulen	73.2	22.3	3.9
Realschulen	79.7	14.8	4.2
Württemberg population	69.1	30.0	0.7

[a]See discussion in text.
Sources: Weber, *Protestant Ethic*, p. 189 (Baden only); Offenbacher, *Konfession*, pp. 16–18.

those schools, Weber reports, were 43 and 69 percent, respectively. The difference is indeed remarkable. Apart from the historical residues, apart from the fact of inherited fortunes, another factor late in the nineteenth century influenced educational choices and thus affected subsequent occupational choices and life chances. A distinctive outlook was present among "Protestants," more than three hundred years after the Reformation. Here Weber has provided perhaps the most convincing *evidence* in the entire monograph in support of his thesis.

That contemporary evidence is decisive for Weber's argument. It is possible a priori that *all* of the alleged differences between Protestants and Catholics, in wealth, occupation, and education, stemmed from that distant historical fact and from subsequent inheritance of advantages or disadvantages. Were that the case, the task for Germany would be to explain events in the second quarter of the sixteenth century. One might also, perhaps, wish to explain the persistence of the Protestant advantage over 350 years, a span that saw the Thirty Years' War, the many wars of Louis XIV, the Seven Years' War, the Napoleonic Wars, and an assortment of minor tumultuous events. In these pages, with this review of the contemporary evidence, Weber argues the case for his specific contribution: in addition to the early advantage, a unique mentality (*geistige Eigenart*) was still present within the Protestant ranks. That ethic, he argues, made a significant independent contribution, apart from the historical facts, to generate the reported differences.

Almost four decades ago, in a 1957 publication, Kurt Samuelsson reviewed Weber's figures and pointed to an obvious error—the row of percentages for the realgymnasien students adds up to 109 percent. The incorrect figures appeared initially in Offenbacher's work. Weber copied them and passed them on, the unrecognized difficulty appearing in both the 1905 and 1920 editions of *The Protestant Ethic*. Talcott Parsons took over the problematic figures for his English translation. They have appeared there, without comment or correction, in the many subsequent printings and editions, now for more than sixty years.

That row of figures is of decisive importance for Weber's initial discussion. More precisely, it is the Protestant overrepresentation, the 69 percent in the realgymnasien that carries his case. Samuelsson declared the correct figure to be 59 percent. That would still leave a difference in the anticipated direction, but instead of a 21-point overrepresentation of Protestants (relative to the overall secondary school "average" of 48), the difference is only 11 points. A recent reanalysis of the original data for Baden has found Samuelsson's figure to be mistaken. George Becker's study shows the correct figure to be 51 percent, a difference of only 3 points. Samuelsson, it seems, had not recalculated Offenbacher's original figures (which combined the results for a ten-year span) but had simply inferred that the problem was a copying error and that the 69 should have been 59.[5] The 3-point difference, or the 14-point difference vis-à-vis the entire population, is in the right direction for Weber's argument. Even that modest support, however, is misleading.

In Weber's key footnote, the one containing *the* evidence of distinct religious differences, he reported that the "same thing" (*Genau die gleichen*) may be observed in Prussia, Bavaria, Württemberg, Alsace Lorraine, and Hungary. Weber refers again to Offenbacher, who began his key footnote, the one reviewing that other experience, with a conclusion—the comparisons show "very similar results" (*ganz ähnliche Resulte*). Offenbacher ends on the same note—"Everywhere, therefore, the same appearance!" (*Allenthalben also dieselbe Erscheinung!*). His data, however, do not justify that conclusion.[6]

Offenbacher's principal findings for Baden may be summarized as follows:

1. Protestant overrepresentation (versus the general population) in all five kinds of secondary schools.
2. Protestant overrepresentation (versus the secondary school population) in the four school types with more practical orientations.
3. Protestant underrepresentation (again versus the school population) in the classical gymnasium.

The second conclusion gains only weak support in three of the Baden comparisons shown; the decisive case, therefore, involves the choices with respect to the realgymnasium. In that case, one finds:

4. A fair-sized (21-point) overrepresentation of Protestants (versus the school population). This result, it should be remembered, depends on the erroneous 69 percent figure.

On the first finding: Offenbacher provides data allowing comparison of the general population and students in the different kinds of secondary schools in only two instances, Bavaria and Württemberg (shown also in Table 3.1). Those results, incidentally, do not appear in Weber's footnote. In both of those states, the percentages of Protestants in the classical gymnasium are virtually identical to the overall Protestant percentages. In this respect, then, the results do not show "the same thing" as in Baden, where modest overrepresentation was found. For other kinds of schools, the Offenbacher and Weber conclusions are confirmed—some degree of Protestant overrepresentation appears in all other cases.

Offenbacher presented no summary figures for secondary school attenders in any of the five other instances mentioned by Weber. That means the other conclusions (that is, 2, 3, and 4) drawn from the Baden experience cannot be exactly replicated. The best comparison possible is between the general population and attendance in the specific schools. Protestants, as just indicated, are overrepresented in all other kinds of school (that is, apart from the gymnasien). The differences range from minuscule (e.g., in the *Handelsschulen*—commercial schools—of Bavaria and the Latin schools of Württemberg) to sizable.[7] Exact replication is not possible for another reason: the types of schools for which data are given differ in all five cases. Only in the case of Bavaria are figures given for the realgymnasien. In this instance, the difference is sizable—54.4 percent of the students were Protestant as compared to 28.2 percent overall. The respective figures for Catholics were sharply opposite, 34.8 and 70.7.

Although Weber's "same thing" conclusion is not justified, his basic point does gain some limited support. But as opposed to his claim of sweeping confirmation, a differentiated set of conclusions is in order. Compared with the general population: 1) Protestants were overrepresented (by a small margin) in the gymnasien of Baden and were represented proportionally in Bavaria and Württemberg; 2) Protestants were overrepresented in all other school types; 3) the greatest overrepresentation discovered was in the realgymnasien of Bavaria and Baden; and 4) the data reported by Offenbacher for other settings do not allow a judgment on these questions. As will be seen, that key Baden finding proves to be spurious.

Offenbacher provides a potpourri of figures for the other political units. For Prussia, he provides the religious distribution for 1885 together with the distribution of students in "the higher teaching institutions" for 1859 and 1885. He notes the changes (Protestants and Jews increase their representation, Catholics decline), but indicates that this could result from the 1866 annexations. He then digresses, presenting figures on the numbers of Protestant and Catholic gymnasium graduates who chose to study theology. For Hungary, he contrasts the overall religious composition (for 1876) with the representation among gymnasium students. In contrast to Weber's declaration ("great difference . . . in Hungary"), Offenbacher reported the disparities there to be *nicht so prägnant* (not so meaningful). The listing of five religious groups in the population there adds to 85.6 percent, that of the gymnasium students to 93.6 percent. One should not be drawing any conclusions from obviously incomplete data. Weber, nevertheless, saw something for his purposes in those results—"It may further be noted as characteristic that in Hungary those affiliated with the Reformed Church exceed even the average Protestant record of attendance at secondary schools" (189 n9). The "characteristic" findings there, based on an incomplete report, are: a trivial *under*representation of the "average" Protestants, and a 2.2-point edge for the Reformed.

Weber's judgments about the orientations of those religious communities are based on very small "samples." Offenbacher indicates that Baden, in 1895, had a total population of "1,725,464 souls."[8] The relevant student population in the school year 1895–1896 (one learns from Samuelsson) was 12,138, or 0.7 percent of the total. Neither Offenbacher nor Weber indicates the distribution of the 12,138 among the five school types. One clear possibility, however, is that some of the reported differences depend on very small numbers of students. In the 1895–1896 school year, Samuelsson reports, 1,504 students were enrolled in Baden's realgymnasien, 52 percent being Protestant.[9] The 15 percent overrepresentation (versus the total population) depends on an "excess" of 226 Protestant students. The percentages, accordingly, could fluctuate markedly from year to year and also, a possibility noted by Samuelsson, they could be changed through the opening of a new school.

Weber's discussion of educational preferences is followed by a paragraph on contemporary occupational choices. Skilled workers in modern industry, he indicates, are drawn out of the traditional crafts. Again, the shift is "much more true" of Protestant than of Catholic journeymen. The Catholics, Weber writes, "more often become master craftsmen, whereas the Protestants are attracted to a larger extent into the factories in order to fill the upper ranks of skilled labour and administrative positions" (38–39). A brief note is added: "For the proofs see Offenbacher, p. 54, and the tables at the end of his study."

Offenbacher's text contains statements that appear to provide the basis for Weber's claims.[10] But in Offenbacher they are presented as speculative suggestions—a given finding, for example, "allows the supposition" (*lässt ... jedoch vermuten*) that Protestants do not remain in the crafts. No "proofs" appear. Weber paraphrased Offenbacher's observations and, in the process, changed their character, transforming tentative or speculative judgments into confirmed conclusions.

Roughly two-thirds of Offenbacher's hundred-page monograph is given to the religion-occupation linkage. Numbers and percentages are given for many occupations—wheelwright, potter, locksmith, bookbinder, dyer, saddlemaker, and so on. These categories are divided by religion and also by city, region, size of community. If Weber's first paragraph conclusion—"business leaders and owners of capital . . . are overwhelmingly Protestant"—were valid, Protestants would be consistently overrepresented, by large margins, in the key category of "independents." That category contained a wide range of higher positions, such as owners, partners, renters, master craftsmen, entrepreneurs, directors, administrators, also leading civil servants and other managers.

Unfortunately, Offenbacher provided no summary table, only this extraordinary range of detail. There are findings pointing in the direction indicated, for example, in the tobacco industry in the Karlsruhe area, where the Protestant independents formed 33.6 percent of the total versus 15.1 of the local population. That is a fair-sized overrepresentation; the segment is not, however, as Weber expressed it, "overwhelmingly Protestant." In the adjacent columns, one finds an opposite tendency with Protestants underrepresented (39.2 percent versus 55.9 overall) in the much larger tobacco industry of the Mannheim region. In three branches of Baden's textile industry, the Protestant percentages among the independents were: spinning, 32.2; weaving, 24.1; and dyeing, 39.0. The Protestant percentage for all of Baden, it will be remembered, was 37.0. None of the complexity, the inconsistency, and the small differences is captured in Weber's text. His brief footnote—"For the proofs see Offenbacher"—is seriously misleading.[11]

One of Weber's first paragraph footnotes gives data on "taxable capital available for the tax on returns from capital" (188). The figures show an impressive difference in the indicated direction: per 1,000 Protestants, 954,000 marks; per 1,000 Catholics, 589,000 marks. Again, for Weber's source, one is referred to Offenbacher. This subject was also reviewed by Samuelsson in his 1957 publication: "In 1897, taxable wealth in Baden amounted to 4.7 milliard marks. Of this 1.6 milliard belonged to Protestants, 0.3 milliard to Jews and 2.8 milliard to Catholics. Thus Catholics held about 60% of the total wealth known to the tax inspectorate; in other words, their share of statistically recorded wealth corresponded almost exactly with their representation in the total population." Data for three categories of taxes were reported by Offenbacher, the "Land, House, and

Business" category forming well over half of the total. There was also a "Special Income Tax," yielding a small part of the total, and a Capital Dividend Tax" (*Kapitalrentensteuer*). With Protestants forming 37 percent of the Baden population, the respective percentage shares of Protestants in those three forms of capital were 28.1, 37.2, and 45.5. Weber has taken only the part of Offenbacher's report that supports his argument, thus neglecting the opposite pattern in the much larger landed capital category and the "no difference" result with respect to the special income tax. Offenbacher reviewed some explanatory hypotheses, which Weber also overlooked.[12]

Weber links the occupational differences to the home and community environments of Protestants and Catholics. The explanation, he writes, "is undoubtedly that the mental and spiritual peculiarities acquired from the environment, here the type of education favoured by the religious atmosphere of the home community and the parental home, have determined the choice of occupation, and through it the professional career" (39). No evidence or references are provided to support the latter claim, which turns out to be merely an inference.

In this exposition, Weber is pointing to a continuing impact of religious traditions on economic behavior. It is a plausible and testable hypothesis, the one chosen as the beginning point for his monograph. Weber's interpretation of this evidence differs significantly from that suggested by his student and source. Offenbacher's explanation centers on choices of a specific occupation, the clergy. Catholics, more than Protestants, he showed, were oriented to clerical careers.[13] For a student entering the clergy, the humanistic gymnasium, with its many years of Greek and Latin, was the obvious choice. Weber's focus, in contrast, is open-ended with respect to occupation, his discussion covering the entire range of possibilities. Weber was again overlooking an alternative hypothesis. His "atmospheric" reference sets the stage for his "broader" reading, for his consideration of a Protestant ethic which, presumably, had implications for all careers.

The issue is not one of narrow versus wide readings but rather one of accuracy. The approved scholarly procedure reviews and considers all plausible hypotheses, but in this case, Weber has pocketed a serious alternative. There is an appropriate method for investigation of such cases. One should exclude those students aiming for clerical careers and then examine the educational choices among those remaining. The basic question is whether the differences between religions in the choices of secular fields are "great," modest, minuscule, or nonexistent.

Before we proceed to a consideration of another interpretative possibility, five summary observations are in order. First, Weber was describing the then contemporary experience, that is, developments in the late nineteenth century. The impact of Protestantism, he was arguing, was still present and easily established with data from routine statistical sources. Second, the formulation deals with Protestantism, the entire category, not with the Calvinist subcategory. The impact of "Protestantism," at this point in the monograph, is taken to be general. Third, we have an indication of the magnitude of the presumed impact. Weber has suggested that he knows the weight to be assigned this factor—that the higher occupational categories are "overwhelmingly" Protestant suggests we are dealing with a powerful factor. It is the size and importance of the "finding" that justifies the extended effort of explanation. Fourth, the evidence described has the advantage that it links individual traits, unlike the ecological analyses in many discussions that compare the economic development of predominantly Protestant and Catholic nations, for example, "Protestant" Netherlands and "Catholic" Belgium. And fifth, having established to his satisfaction the fact of sizable differences, Weber proceeds to explanation. He thereby overlooks another interpretative option—that the differences might have been due to some other factor. One possibility, suggested by Weber himself, is that of a historical inheritance.

An Alternative Hypothesis

Offenbacher introduced and emphasized the historical factor from the beginning of his monograph. Nineteenth-century Baden was formed through a unification of several smaller states (or "statelets") having diverse religious and economic histories. Offenbacher's work opens, appropriately, with a review of the "natural and political-historical influences." He discusses the complicated history at some length, ending with a three-page summary table showing the religious patterns of thirteen component segments, these resulting from decisions made in the middle of the sixteenth century, from the Treaty of Augsburg of 1555.

Nineteenth-century Baden was located on the right (eastern) side of the Rhine River, extending from the Swiss border north to the city of Mannheim at the confluence of the Neckar River. Basically, it was a thin strip of land on a north-south axis with two arms extending over to the east. In the south, one arm extended eastward along the Swiss border, reaching over to the city of Constance. The second arm, at the northern end of the state, extended to the north and east of Heidelberg (Weber's home city for much of his adult life). The southern counties were overwhelmingly Catholic. They were also agricultural, although the land was of very poor quality. The national border, which reduced the size of the local market, was also an obstacle to development.

In general, variations on the two key variables, religion and economic development, occurred along the state's principal north-south axis. The percentages of Protestants and levels of development both declined as one moved from north to south. That ecological correlation could be offered as "proof" for both the historical and the contemporary influence hypotheses. It is clear that a control for geography (and, in effect, history) was needed before one could demonstrate a contemporary religious influence—a point Offenbacher noted in all discussions.

For some purposes, Offenbacher presented data for the state's four major subdivisions (*Landeskommissariatsbezirke*). From north to south were the following districts, named after their largest cities: Mannheim (containing Baden's largest city, a manufacturing, commercial, and cultural center, and also the city of Heidelberg); Karlsruhe (containing Baden's capital city, in population almost as large as Mannheim); Freiburg (the city was a local commercial center, also a university town); and Constance (a commercial center which, located on Lake Constance, was also a resort area). The respective Protestant percentages were 50.7, 41.7, 33.5, and 9.6.

Samuelsson took up the question of historical inheritance and presented evidence showing an indirect effect. His focus was on the question of access, on the availability of those various schools. Weber had noted the historical fact: cities, in the sixteenth century, generally became Protestant. That circumstance yielded a nineteenth-century fact: Protestants tended to be located in cities, Catholics tended to be located in towns, villages, and in the countryside. When education was extended and schools built, they were generally located in the larger communities. Late in the nineteenth century, the realgymnasien, with their emphasis on "modern languages, mathematics and science," were especially likely to be located in larger communities. That would mean, on the whole, that attendance in such schools was easier for Protestants than for Catholics. Again, a simple control for distance or ease of access is in order.

Following through the implications of his analysis, Samuelsson pointed out that "neither Offenbacher nor Weber tried to ascertain in what proportions the various denominations were represented among the inhabitants of those school districts where Protestants predominated in the schools" (141). For the realgymnasien that determination proved unexpectedly easy, since only six of those schools existed in all of Baden. Three were located in that heavily Protestant northernmost district, one in the city of Mannheim, one in nearby Weinheim, and one in Mosbach, all three, according to Offenbacher's figures, communities with Protestant majorities. A fourth was located in Karlsruhe, the capital city, which also had a Protestant majority. The remaining two were in smaller communities to the south of the capital, both of which had sizable Catholic majorities. Considering only the two Christian denominations, Samuelsson found that, overall, in 1895 "almost exactly 55% of the inhabitants of these districts were Protestants." Since 52 percent of the students attending those schools in 1895–1896 were Protestants, the differences were, at best, very small. Samuelsson made several similar comparisons and concluded:

> Thus, school by school and district by district it appears that the proportions of school children classified by religious faith are almost exactly the same as the corresponding proportion of the total populations of the appropriate district. That the Protestants in Baden as a whole display a "school frequency" higher than their share in the aggregate population is thus due entirely to the fact that more Protestants than Catholics lived in districts where *Realgymnasien, Höhere Bürgerschulen* and *Realschulen* were available. If one reckons not in terms of total population but of inhabitants of districts containing the respective categories of schools, there remain no differences worth mentioning. (141–142)

Samuelsson's findings, based on his review of the Offenbacher-Weber evidence, allow an easy conclusion: the evidence from late nineteenth-century Baden does not reveal any distinctive linkage between "Protestantism" and any behavior or value orientation that one could call a "spirit of capitalism." It might be that some differences existed, that some *geistige Eigenart* was present among Protestants at that time, but Weber did not successfully demonstrate that fact. The geography (or access) factor may also have given rise to the confirmation reported by Offenbacher and

Weber in Bavaria. It is, in any event, a hypothesis that needs to be tested. Samuelsson's findings and conclusions should not be taken as definitive or the last word on the subject. There might easily be some aggregation error (the six *realgymnasien* would have differed in size). Careless typographical errors appear frequently, although they may exist only in the English edition.[14]

The question of religion and school choice in Germany has been reviewed recently by George Becker. His analysis of the Baden evidence shows that when access was controlled, the original Protestant-Catholic differences were markedly reduced but, as against Samuelsson, did not disappear entirely. The remaining differences, Becker shows, were linked to job opportunities. A growing shortage of Catholic clergy led many Catholic students to choose the *gymnasium;* a surplus of Protestant clergy led Protestant students to make other choices. The shortage, on the Catholic side, was due to celibacy (among Protestants, sons frequently, followed fathers in the profession) and to the lingering effects of a recent historical event, the *Kulturkampf.* That anti-Catholic campaign of the 1870s and early 1880s drove many clergy out of Germany and simultaneously discouraged the entry of new aspirants.[15]

Most methods texts list three requirements for a demonstration of causality. The first and foremost of those requirements is "that the two variables be associated." Borrowing from Offenbacher, Weber presented evidence that, to his satisfaction, established a clear association between religion and "worldly success." One would have no difficulty with the second condition, that the causal variable must chronologically precede the presumed effect. The religion (of parents and of students) was acquired prior to schooling and subsequent careers. The third condition is that no other prior third variable can, when held constant, cause the original association to disappear.[16] Weber paid little attention to this last requirement. His treatment of alternative hypotheses is extremely casual. He recognized the importance of the historical factor (he could hardly avoid it), but, making an ad hoc determination of weights, simply argued, without testing, the existence of a strong independent contemporary "cultural" effect, that is, independently of the historical (and geographic) heritage. Casual ad hoc weightings, as has been seen, appear regularly in his text and notes, for example, the initial phrases "overwhelmingly Protestant" (35) and "a great difference" (38). Still another example, possibly the most important in these confident judgments, reads: "Thus the principal explanation of this difference must be sought in the permanent intrinsic character of their religious beliefs, and not only in their temporary external historico-political situations" (40).

To this point the concern has been with Weber's use of statistical evidence. He also makes generous use of qualitative information, referring to many observers who, presumably, have seen the same connections between Protestantism and business success: "For Scotland, Buckle, and among English poets, Keats, have emphasized these same relationships" (44). The accompanying footnote does not document those claims. Instead, more undocumented testimonial statements are provided: "Lavelye [*sic*], Matthew Arnold, and others already perceived it" (191 n23). Later, Weber provides another list of persons who had recognized "these relationships"—"poets like Heine and Keats, as well as historians like Macaulay, Cunningham, Rogers, or an essayist such as Matthew Arnold, have assumed them as obvious" (280 n96). Again no specific citations are given; consensus on a given point is not the same as evidence on the question.

Jacob Viner, the eminent economic historian, wrote a comprehensive critique of the Weber thesis in which he provided some information on several of these fugitive sources. Some of them, Laveleye and Shell, for example, agreed with Weber about the economic backwardness of Catholic countries but provided other explanations for the differences. Weber cited Henry Thomas Buckle as one of the many who recognized the Calvinism-capitalism linkage, but Viner argued, with a supporting quotation, that Buckle saw Calvinism in an opposite light, as a hindrance to capitalist development. Weber also reported some support from John Keats. That proved to be a mere trace of evidence (a letter to the poet's brother). Viner cites several other observers, all of whom wrote before the publication of Weber's monograph, who commented on "the economic backwardness of Scotland during the period of dominance of orthodox Calvinism." W. L. Mathieson saw the Calvinist religious spirit as "the most serious of all obstacles to industrial progress" in Scotland. From another source we learn that Thomas Babington Macaulay, the British historian, was not a dispassionate commentator. David Thompson describes him as a historian of "shrewd, forceful, and pugnacious qualities," a man who "never hid his strong prejudices" and who "detested Roman Catholicism as much as Jacobinism."[17]

Weber's casual citation procedures appear elsewhere in this opening chapter. The text comments on the tendency "observed at all times" for minorities to be "driven with peculiar force into economic activity" but notes that Catholics prove an exception to this rule (39). In the accompanying note, Weber reports that the tendency is "especially well illustrated by passages in the works of Sir William Petty, to be referred to later." Petty is referred to in the following note (which deals with Protestant absentee landlords in Ireland); no source is given. The next reference to Petty comes ninety pages later in the notes but deals with a different point, and again no specific pages are cited. A single brief quotation from Petty, concerning the basic Protestant ethic theme, appears on page 179 of his text and there a specific reference is provided.

Weber's note 12 also contains a confident declaration: "The typical relationship between Protestantism and capitalism existed in Ireland as well as elsewhere." The next sentence reads: "On the Scotch-Irish see C. A. Hanna, *The Scotch-Irish*, two vols., Putnam, New York." No date is given and, of more importance for a large two-volume work, no page references are provided. Hanna's text contains an extraordinary potpourri of information. A brief chapter titled "The Scotch-Irish in American Politics" argues their prominence in public affairs. It contains page-long listings of names and ends with a question: "In view of these facts can it not with propriety be contended that the Scottish race, in proportion to its relative strength in the New World, has contributed to America a vastly greater number of her leaders in thought and action than has any other?"[18]

Again as a precaution, to guard against easy acceptance, a reference to a subsequent account may prove useful. James G. Leyburn, in a scholarly work on the Scotch-Irish, provided conclusions that are contrary to Weber's confident judgment. The Scotch-Irish and the Germans arrived "simultaneously" in Pennsylvania, settling in "an alternative and parallel movement" in adjacent neighborhoods. These Germans were "chiefly Lutherans and Reformed in religion." The Scotch-Irish were "almost all Presbyterians." Many colonial commentators, Leyburn reports, commented on the differences in temperament between the two peoples. It was usual, he writes, "to expect Germans to be orderly, industrious, carefully frugal." The Scotch-Irish, by contrast, "were regarded as quick-tempered, impetuous, inclined to work by fits and starts, reckless, too much given to drinking. No contemporary observer praised them as model farmers." In politics, they became "active, even tempestuous ... their fame as Indian fighters was to become almost as notable as their reputation for causing trouble with the Indians." James Logan, the provincial secretary, reportedly described them as "troublesome settlers to the government and hard neighbors to the Indians"; he also noted their "audacious and disorderly" habits.[19]

The discussion to this point has dealt only with the brief (eleven-page) opening chapter of *The Protestant Ethic*. That chapter, entitled "Religious Affiliation and Social Stratification," contains Weber's effort to establish the crucial association and to assert its independence. The rest of the work, 136 pages of text, contains Weber's explanation of the initial "finding." Those remaining pages, the heart of the enterprise, are devoted to the explanation of a "cause" that had not been satisfactorily established.

The Larger Argument

Although Weber's initial exposition involved a false step, one might argue that the circumstances in late nineteenth-century Baden and those connected with the larger issues—that is, the relationship of religion and economic life in Europe existing earlier, from the sixteenth century—are separable concerns. If so, the first chapter misstep would not impair the arguments central to "the Weber thesis" offered in the later chapters.

For this purpose, the work of Gordon Marshall proves useful. He published a comprehensive review of claims and evidence on the subject entitled *In Search of the Spirit of Capitalism*. Although Marshall's book is in some ways parallel to Samuelsson's, the two works differ in emphasis. Both are sweeping in their coverage, but where Samuelsson gives much attention to the "nuts and bolts" of Weber's argument, Marshall focuses on the "architectural plans," its basic framework, and points out that many critics, Samuelsson among them, have addressed aspects of some other "plan." The Weber thesis, Marshall writes, is not complicated: it is, "quite simply, that certain Protestant doctrines *caused* the rise of the modern capitalist mentality."[20] The argument is that one set of beliefs gave rise to another set. This thesis includes an important correlated argument, which Marshall reviews at length, namely that the beliefs (or mentality) were closely linked to behavior: the new religious views gave rise to a distinctive work effort.

The framework, Marshall indicates, is easily seen in the progression of the chapters. In the second chapter, Weber explains what he means by "The Spirit of Capitalism." The third chapter is entitled "Luther's Con-

ception of the Calling." Focusing on what he takes to be a key innovation, Weber argues that Luther gave a new meaning to work. No longer a
morally neutral routine, a series of tasks done to make ends meet (or an
activity driven by avarice), work now became a divinely sanctioned effort.
The fourth chapter, "The Religious Foundations of Worldly Asceticism,"
deals with Calvinism, Pietism, Methodism, and the Baptist sects. The notion of a calling is taken over by these movements and, in diverse ways,
the "sanction" involved is said to be even more forceful, more effective
than in the Lutheran original.

The heart of the argument is found in this discussion of Calvinism and
the doctrine of predestination. The fearful Calvinist, desperately yearning
for a sign of salvation, was driven to a highly disciplined work effort that
generated large profits. Those profits, in turn, were reinvested, in adher-
ence to a doctrinal prohibition of self-indulgence. Weber's final chapter,
"Asceticism and the Spirit of Capitalism," elaborates on the mechanisms
involved. The focus once again is on religious doctrines and their unfore-
seen economic consequences.

Before commenting on the principal arguments, it is important to
stress what Weber does *not* say. He does not contend that Protestantism
(in any of its manifestations) gave rise to the institutions of modern capitalism. His "specific" argument is that the new religious orientations gave
rise to a new work ethic, to this new set of attitudes, to this "spirit of capitalism." Weber does not link the religious orientations to the structures or
technologies of modern capitalism, that is, to free markets, factory production, modern banking, insurance, mechanization, and so on. The argument is focused on the "capitalist spirit," on the driving work ethic that
operates within given contexts. Each context involves a different set of elements, institutions, and raw materials; those contextual features require
other, entirely separate lines of analysis. Weber was not indifferent to the
role of such "conditions." Some settings, those with coal and iron ore, for
example, would be more favorable to economic development than a region offering nothing but sandy soil. The argument does not say that
"Protestantism" was a (or the) sufficient condition for the development of
modern capitalism. Those institutions and conditions provide a context
within which the ethic, or the later spirit, operates.

Weber's central argument may be summarized as follows: with other
things equal, "Protestantism" would give rise to considerably greater
work efforts and hence to greater economic growth than would "Catholi-

cism." Although he does not use these terms, he clearly sees the Protestant ethic as a necessary (but not sufficient) condition for the development of modern capitalism in the period from the seventeenth to the nineteenth centuries. Without that contribution, the development would not have occurred.

Kurt Samuelsson has provided a "false copy" of the Weber argument. Weber took some pains to distinguish "the specifically modern capitalist spirit"—his subject matter—from other types of economic activity (see especially 47–59). He also indicated that he was explaining the appearance of this unique "spirit" and not, for example, "the growth of capital mobilisation and credit provision on a large scale," one of Samuelsson's concerns. The shift of definition allowed the critic to discover "capitalism" long before any Protestantism appeared and to find capitalist efforts that are unrelated to any "Protestant" origins. That said, it should also be noted that differentiated judgment is appropriate. Samuelsson's comments on Weber's opening chapter, his analysis of the Baden data, contain important and valid observations. Those comments do not depend on his extended definition of capitalism. Samuelsson's observations on Weber's use of sources with respect to Benjamin Franklin and Jacob Fugger (to be considered immediately in the text) also remain valid. The work is filled with useful and provocative comment, observation, evidence, and documentation. At each point, however, given the indicated difficulty, it is important to establish whether or not the specific claim is on target."[21]

The Spirit of Capitalism

In his discussion of the spirit of capitalism, Weber argues that modern capitalism is characterized by a distinct outlook different from all previous economic orientations. Some form of capitalism had existed in many places previously but, he writes, "this particular ethos was lacking." Two kinds of orientation are found in those other settings. One is simple greed or avarice, which, Weber indicates, is found everywhere; it is the activity of the speculator or the dishonest trader. The "specific characteristic" of that outlook, he explains, is the "universal reign of absolute unscrupulousness in the pursuit of selfish interests by the making of money" (57). The second orientation is traditionalism, working only to achieve a fixed sum, enough to cover a handed-down conception of basic needs. Increased income, Weber argues in a paragraph-long discussion of a hypothetical farm laborer, actually decreases productivity. This "immensely

stubborn resistance," he reports, is the "leading trait of pre-capitalistic labour."

The modern capitalist operates with a different "spirit." It is "above all
the idea of a duty of the individual toward the increase of his capital,
which is assumed as an end in itself" (51). That money-making activity is
carefully distinguished from the efforts of the avaricious speculator, who
wishes money for personal enjoyment, for the satisfaction of selfish
wants. But for the modern capitalist, "the *summum bonum* of this ethic, the
earning of more and more money, [is] combined with the strict avoidance
of all spontaneous enjoyment of life, [and] is above all completely devoid
of any eudaemonistic, not to say hedonistic, admixture." The separation
of acquisition from any obvious goals, Weber points out, makes it appear
"entirely transcendental and absolutely irrational" (53). Although rather
cautiously formulated, another distinctive trait of the modern capitalist is
honesty, a commitment to that virtue as a duty, an orientation going beyond mere utilitarianism. This attitude is repeatedly set in opposition to
the "ruthless acquisition" of other entrepreneurs, those "bound by no ethical norms whatever" (57).

The provision of evidence to support this argument would require an
enormous effort. One would have to draw samples of entrepreneurs from
appropriate settings and demonstrate the predicted differences in their
outlooks. Weber's case, however, rests on an odd-lot assortment of examples, and he offers as the key illustration, he offers an array of quotations,
two and a half pages of maxims from the writings of Benjamin Franklin
(for example, "Remember, that *time* is money . . . *credit* is money"). Weber's conclusion: "That it is the spirit of capitalism which here speaks in
characteristic fashion, no one will doubt" (48–51). Those maxims, he declares, show that the increase of capital was held to be a "duty" for the individual.

In the late 1950s, Samuelsson pointed out that Weber had misrepresented Franklin's position. Franklin, wrote Samuelsson, "was no champion of unremitting labour" but instead had indicated "at an early age" that
"he had planned to make, as quickly as possible, a fortune large enough
to enable him to retire and occupy himself with public duties and intellectual and scientific interests." His moneymaking was clearly directed toward another goal; capital accumulation was not at all "an end in itself." It
is difficult to see how Weber could have missed this aspect of Franklin's
career. He discusses Franklin's activities and orientations for two pages,

correcting possible misreadings that might challenge his position. Weber's conclusion on the point, however, is forceful and without qualification; he tells his readers that his knowledge of the subject is comprehensive: "The earning of money within the modern economic order is, so long as it is done legally, the result and expression of virtue and proficiency in a calling; and this virtue and proficiency are, as it is now not difficult to see, the real Alpha and Omega of Franklin's ethic, as expressed in the passages we have quoted, as well as in all his works without exception" (53–54).[22]

In his *Autobiography,* Franklin clearly indicates the instrumental character of his moneymaking activity: "When I disengaged myself . . . from private business, I flattered myself that, by the sufficient tho' moderate fortune I had acquired, I had secured leisure during the rest of my life for philosophical studies and amusements." Franklin reports on those amusements. During his first stay in London, he writes, "I was pretty diligent, but [spent] a good deal of my earnings in going to plays and other places of amusement," and "that hard-to-be-governed passion of youth had hurried me frequently into intrigues with low women that fell in my way, which were attended with some expense and great inconvenience." Later, in his mature years, he tells of his adjustment to the presence of silver and china in his household which "augmented gradually to several hundred pounds in value." Franklin's life was certainly not devoid of eudaemonistic or hedonistic elements.[23]

Weber, it appears, had reached into the Franklin works and selected some elements that supported his position and neglected those that would challenge his claims. Franklin's "strict Calvinistic father," Weber reports, had "drummed into him again and again in his youth" a quotation from the Bible: " 'Seest thou a man diligent in his business? He shall stand before kings' Prov. xxii. 29" (53). Weber does not give a specific citation on this point. The *Autobiography* does contain the obvious original, but Franklin's statement is not as forceful nor is the proverb as central as in Weber's version. Franklin writes simply of "my father having among his instructions to me when a boy frequently repeated a proverb of Solomon." Franklin's text reports the proverb as saying "a man diligent in his calling." Weber presented the passage, appropriately, as *in seinem Beruf* and emphasized that phrase. He then appended a footnote (which Parsons omitted) indicating that Luther's translation reads *in seinem Geschäfte* and that the older English versions used *business.* Something has been lost here in the retranslation of Franklin.[24]

Franklin does not indicate that his father, Josiah, was a strict Calvinist. The *Autobiography* is not entirely clear on this point but suggests less strenuous demands. The family connection, in any event, was broken at an early point and the principal religious lessons rejected. The family had been Church of England until, late in the reign of Charles II, Franklin's father and an uncle joined Nonconformist conventicles. His mother, Abiah Folger, was a daughter of Peter Folger, who, according to Franklin, had written occasional pieces, one of which asserted liberty of conscience "in behalf of the Anabaptists, Quakers, and other sectaries that had been persecuted." Franklin recalled that his parents "had early given me religious impressions, and brought me through my childhood piously in the dissenting way." Then, at age twelve, Benjamin was apprenticed and boarded out with an older brother. When "scarce fifteen" he began to doubt much that he had learned, a skepticism encouraged by "some books" that fell into his hands. Although "religiously educated as a Presbyterian," some of the dogmas of that persuasion, "such as the eternal decrees of God, election, reprobation, etc., appeared to me unintelligible, others doubtful, and I early absented myself from the public assemblies of the sect, Sunday being my studying-day." He ran away from his native city at age seventeen.[25] Weber has misrepresented his source, at every point claiming a religious influence that is not clearly indicated.

Weber next contrasts Franklin's outlook with that of a traditional capitalist, Jacob Fugger. According to Weber, a business associate who had retired sought to persuade Fugger to do the same, "since he had made enough money and should let others have a chance." But Fugger "thought otherwise, he wanted to make money as long as he could." The spirit of that statement, Weber concludes, "is evidently quite different from that of Franklin" (51). Here too Samuelsson reviewed the original source and found that "it was not a question of Fugger's departure from the management of business affairs but simply of a withdrawal from hazardous enterprises in Hungary." At issue was the question of risk, not retirement. The story, Samuelsson adds, has thus been "improved." Weber had taken a secondhand account, which told nothing of the context (let alone the man's motivation), and boldly announced its meaning.[26]

Gordon Marshall undertook a detailed review of the "spirit of capitalism" question. His conclusion, which is entirely appropriate, reads: "All of this is, of course, empirically dubious. Weber documents his argument with an unconvincing mixture of fictitious illustrations, composite instances drawn from diverse times and places, and anecdotal empirical examples." In another summary, Marshall writes that "Weber offers little or no independent evidence concerning the motives and world-view of either modern or medieval businessmen and labourers. His evidence [on the moderns] apart from the 'provisional description' offered by Franklin's advice, is drawn exclusively from Protestant teaching."[27]

Marshall also considered the question discussed earlier in this chapter, that of the initial association. He noted Weber's exasperated reaction to some unnamed critics who, supposedly, denied any religion-stratification linkage. Marshall argues that the accuracy of Offenbacher's statistics is "beside the point." Weber's purpose was "to illustrate a relationship whose existence had become a platitude in his time." The difference between a relationship and a platitude, however, cannot be dismissed. If Weber's argument is based on a commonplace notion, he might, as is argued here, have been "explaining" a non-thing. The agreement of a wide range of "authorities" does not establish the point at issue.[28]

Two separate lines of argument are interwoven in Weber's text: there are claims about Protestant and Catholic nations and claims about Protestant and Catholic individuals. One might reasonably affirm the claims about nations (for example, the Netherlands and Britain versus Spain and Portugal) without at the same time affirming a parallel claim about individuals (for example, Protestants and Catholics in Baden). Viner reports that he found "no writer, Catholic or non-Catholic, who seriously disputed the claim that Protestant countries were generally more prosperous than Catholic ones."[29] In the opening pages of the essay, however, Weber had affirmed the existence of important differences between Protestant and Catholic individuals in central Europe late in the nineteenth century. His difficulty with respect to those initial claims points to an important conclusion. Some fifteen years intervened between Weber's work for the original and revised editions of *The Protestant Ethic*. If occupational statistics showing the alleged differences were readily available, as he claimed, the appropriate data or sources could have been provided in the revision. It is clear, however, that he had not found the requisite statistical evidence.

Luther and the Calling

Weber's discussion of the Protestant ethic begins with a chapter entitled "Luther's Conception of the Calling." It opens with a confident formulation: "Now it is unmistakable that even in the German word *Beruf*, and perhaps still more clearly in the English *calling*, a religious conception, that of a task set by God, is at least suggested." Tracing "the history of the word through the civilized languages," Weber reports that "neither the predominantly Catholic peoples nor those of classical antiquity have possessed any expression of similar connotation for what we know as a calling." This unique notion, which "has existed for all predominantly Protestant peoples," had its origin in Luther's translation of the Bible. It is through "the spirit of the translator," Weber writes, not of the original text, that the word was used "precisely in our modern sense." From that unexpected beginning, the term "speedily took on its present meaning in the everyday speech of all Protestant peoples, while earlier not even a suggestion of such a meaning could be found in the secular literature of any of them" (79). The twenty-five lines of text are accompanied by seven pages of small-type notes reviewing terms and usages in many settings (204–210).

Following that opening declaration of uniqueness is a discussion of the importance of the concept of a calling. Again, the formulations are bold and confident—"At least one thing was unquestionably new: the valuation of the fulfilment of duty in worldly affairs as the highest form which the moral activity of the individual could assume. This it was which inevitably gave every-day worldly activity a religious significance." And, a few lines later: "The only way of living acceptably to God was not to surpass worldly morality in monastic asceticism, but solely through the fulfilment of the obligations imposed upon the individual by his position in the world" (80). As opposed to the strictly religious calling, as for the clergy or those in monastic life, in this new faith one finds "more and more strongly emphasized, the statement that the fulfilment of worldly duties is under all circumstances the only way to live acceptably to God. It and it alone is the will of God, and hence every legitimate calling has exactly the same worth in the sight of God." Eschewing any concern with documentation, Weber offers another forceful statement: "That this moral justification of worldly activity was one of the most important results of the Reformation, especially of Luther's part in it, is beyond doubt, and may even be considered a platitude" (81).

Luther's attitude toward economic life, Weber indicates, was traditional; it "cannot be claimed for the spirit of capitalism" in the sense he had specified earlier. Luther, "without doubt," would have "sharply repudiated any connection with a point of view like that of Franklin." His statements on usury "from a capitalistic view-point," Weber notes, are "definitely backward." Having carefully laid aside the specific economic positions of the reformer, Weber turns again to the implications of the distinctive religious innovation, the notion of the calling. "The effect of the Reformation as such was only that, as compared with the Catholic attitude, the moral emphasis on and the religious sanction of, organized worldly labour in a calling was mightily increased" (82–83). Weber's ad hoc weighting—mightily—should be noted. The calling has an extremely important impact, but again, no supporting evidence is provided.

The notion of the calling was incorporated in the teachings of other later Protestant movements, most notably, for Weber's argument, in Calvinism. In those later movements, the calling was associated with a drive, a commitment, a level of activity that went far beyond anything seen in Lutheranism. For this reason some authors have focused on Calvinism (and the later sects) as decisive, as if "the Protestant ethic" begins there. Marshall, for example, discounts the importance of Luther and his conception of the calling. It is "of little significance for Weber's argument and serves merely as an introduction to the concept itself." Calvin is the "really decisive figure."[30] Weber's text contains a sentence which, unambiguously, supports that reading: "Thus the mere idea of the calling in the Lutheran sense is at best of questionable importance for the problems in which we are interested" (86). Several pages earlier, however, Weber had provided a diametrically opposite assessment of the calling—it was "one of the most important results of the Reformation" (81). Weber's text clearly indicates a two-stage development: Lutheranism "mightily increased" worldly labor; Calvinism and, to a lesser degree, the sects stimulated a further and more important increase.

In the later pages, Weber stressed that Luther's concept of the calling "remained traditionalistic" (85–86). His translation of the key Bible passage reads: "Bleibe in deinem Beruf" (from Sirach 11:20 and 21), that is, "remain in your calling" (notes 1 and 3, 204, 207). Sirach, a book of the Old Testament, is now widely judged by Protestants to be apocryphal. Translations before Luther's time had used the word *Werk* (work, or job). Weber reports that in "its later and present sense the word *Beruf* did not exist in the German language" (207–208). The implication, Weber indicates, is to work within one's "established station in life." It is a command to adjust or to adapt oneself. In the later Calvinist framework, however, the concept is given a different content.

Calvinism and Predestination

Weber's next chapter, entitled "The Religious Foundations of Worldly Asceticism," provides the key exposition of Calvinism and the predestination doctrine. Weber immediately narrows the focus, rejecting any concern with official teachings and the transmission of the doctrine. His concern is with "something entirely different: the influence of those psychological sanctions which . . . gave a direction to practical conduct and held the individual to it" (97). Weber reviews the predestination doctrine over six pages and then concludes: "This doctrine must above all have had one consequence. . . . That was a feeling of unprecedented inner loneliness of the single individual" (104). Some implications are reviewed for another half dozen-pages. The isolated individual, Weber argues, desperately wishes knowledge of salvation, of election, but that possibility is denied. "On the other hand, in order to attain that self-confidence intense worldly activity is recommended as the most suitable means. It and it alone disperses religious doubts and gives the certainty of grace" (112). Comparison is made with Lutheranism and the power of the Calvinist "sanction" is reaffirmed: "Thus, however useless good works might be as a means of attaining salvation . . . they are indispensable as a sign of election. They are the technical means, not of purchasing salvation, but of getting rid of the fear of damnation" (115). The end result, Weber claims, was a "methodical control over the whole man" (119).

The discussion of Calvinism, of predestination, of the inner loneliness, and of the recommended means for alleviation of doubts is the central argument of the monograph. Weber's argument, it will be noted, is social psychological. The psychological strains have a specific social origin in the Calvinist teachings. The resolution of those strains also depends on a social influence, on the "recommendation" that appears in those teachings. The end result, according to Weber, was an exceptional work effort.

The argument is repeated with many variations. The "central characteristic of this type of religion," he writes, was that "every Christian had to be a monk all his life." Those "passionately spiritual natures" were "now forced to pursue their ascetic ideals within mundane occupations" (121). Comparisons are again made with Lutheranism and other religious developments. Because of "its doctrine of grace, [Lutheranism] lacked a psychological sanction of systematic conduct to compel the methodical rationalization of life." The Calvinist doctrine of predestination was only "one of several possibilities," but, nevertheless, "we have become convinced," Weber declares, "that in its way it had not only a quite unique consistency, but that its psychological effect was extraordinarily powerful" (128).

These claims are no more than statements of possibility. It would be extremely difficult to establish the validity of social psychological claims that deal with the "inner states" of populations living centuries earlier. Weber's sovereign declaration that "we have become convinced" reports his personal judgment. The support for his claims, one assumes, would be found in the footnotes and in the references cited there. The importance Weber assigned to Calvinism and predestination may be seen in the quantity of documentation he supplied: the thirty pages of text are accompanied by twenty-three pages of small-print notes.

Weber reviews various formulations of the doctrine, of "the original body of ideas," but says nothing about the transmission processes, about how it was communicated, or about the conditions of its acceptance. These key questions are addressed, and dismissed, in a brief declaration: "We are naturally not concerned with the question of what was theoretically and officially taught in the ethical compendia of the time, however much practical significance this may have had through the influence of Church discipline, pastoral work, and preaching" (97). Two key steps in the causal sequence are thus excluded. The question of transmission processes, basically that of pastoral efforts, cannot be avoided and, as will be seen, this subject does appear in an important subsequent discussion. The conditions-of-acceptance question—why did people become Calvinists?—is nowhere addressed. Weber does not explore whether one is dealing with individual conversions, an act of faith, or reacting to a ruler's decree, making a prudent tactical response. Begging the question, Weber regularly assumes the former.

After reviewing the predestinarian doctrine, Weber offers that pivotal conclusion with regard to its impact, that the doctrine "must above all" have produced a "feeling of unprecedented inner loneliness" (104). Since it is such an important point, extensive documentation would be appropriate. But the accompanying note is both brief and unexpectedly limited. It reads, in its entirety: " 'The deepest community (with God) is found not in institutions or corporations or churches, but in the secrets of a solitary heart', as Dowden puts the essential point in his fine book *Puritan and Anglican* (p. 234). This deep spiritual loneliness of the individual applied as well to the Jansenists of Port Royal, who were also predestinationists" (221 n16). Dowden's sentence obviously provides no compelling evidence. Weber's undocumented assurance about the inner state of Jansenists merely compounds the problem. This central point in Weber's argument is supported by, at best, a wisp of evidence.[31]

The inner-loneliness theme is reviewed again in Weber's text three pages later, in a discussion beginning with a conclusion: "But for the general religious situation of a man the consequences are evident . . . the Calvinist's intercourse with his God was carried on in deep spiritual isolation" (106–107). A page-long review of literary evidence follows. "To see the specific results of this peculiar atmosphere, it is only necessary to read Bunyan's *Pilgrim's Progress,* by far the most widely read book of the whole Puritan literature" (107). The sentence carries two notes; the first, something of a digression, reports that the predestination doctrine was proscribed repeatedly in the Netherlands. The second note comments on two biographical accounts of Bunyan, and also reports that the writer was "a strict Calvinistic Baptist." Continuing with the text, one learns that Bunyan's account "is somewhat reminiscent" of Gottfried Keller's *Gerechte Kammacher* and of "Alfonso of Liguori, as Döllinger has described him to us." These three are "worlds removed" from Machiavelli's portrait of Florentine citizens. And "of course" it is "even farther from the feelings which Richard Wagner puts into the mouth of Siegmund before his fatal combat." All in all, it is hardly a compelling proof.

The distressed Calvinist cannot know whether he or she is among the elect. In another key step of the argument, Weber reports *the* solution— "intense worldly activity" (112). A key claim requires compelling support. The accompanying footnote, however, provides no specific documentation with regard to this all-important recommendation. The first sentence reads: "Thus, as we shall see later, in countless passages, especially the conclusion, of Baxter's *Christian Directory*" (229 n47). The next sentences digress to a discussion of Pascal and of his entirely different recommendation, "renunciation of the world" and contemplation. The note proceeds then to even more remote topics, to "the orthodox Catholic" and Jansenist versions of "the idea of calling," with a reference to an unpublished study on that subject. The note contains no specific citation of sources to support the central point.

The "inner loneliness" led to (or was directed into) action, the key point being "the necessity of proving one's faith in worldly activity" (121). Calvinism substituted "for the spiritual aristocracy of monks ... the spiritual aristocracy of the predestined saints of God within the world." The accompanying note (n89) provides no supporting evidence or references. It reads, in full: " 'Bless God that we are not of the many' (Thomas Adams, *Works of the Puritan Divines,* p. 138)." The next sentence of Weber's text tells of the "terrifying gulf" between the elect and the damned. The next note (n90) digresses: "The idea of the birthright, so important in history, thus received an important confirmation in England." A quotation on the firstborn and his inheritance follows, this again from Thomas Adams.

This central discussion ends with a statement of the contrast between ascetic Protestantism with its "systematic rational ordering of the moral life as a whole" and the Lutheran faith which "left the spontaneous vitality of impulsive action and naive emotion more nearly unchanged." By way of evidence, Weber tells of the "great difference which was very striking to contemporaries between the moral standards of the courts of Reformed and of Lutheran princes, the latter often being degraded by drunkenness and vulgarity" (126–127). The discrepancy between textual boldness and insufficiency in the "supporting" note is remarkable: one is referred there (n105) to "the gossipy book of Tholuck, *Vorgeschichte des Rationalismus*" (no pages given). In the next sentence of text, Weber reports that "the helplessness of the Lutheran clergy, with their emphasis on faith alone, against the ascetic Baptist movement, is well known." The "typical German quality often called good nature (*Gemütlichkeit*) ... contrasts strongly, even in the facial expressions of people, with ... that thorough destruction of spontaneity ... in the Anglo-American atmosphere." Those "very striking" differences in conduct, according to Weber "clearly originated in the lesser degree of ascetic penetration of life in Lutheranism as distinguished from Calvinism." No support is provided for these claims.

These few paragraphs can provide little more than a brief sketch of Weber's problems with evidence and documentation. The points just discussed are the crucial central themes of his entire argument.

In subsequent discussion, Weber provides various weightings of influence, comparing the power of different religious "sanctions." He also outlines some flows of influence, pointing to developments that maintained or weakened the original religious impulses. Lutheranism and the calling produced a greater work commitment than did the previous religious systems. Calvinism, with its sanction, had the most powerful impact. The other systems, those considered later in his chapter, had weaker effects because of the weaker sanctions. Effectively, there was a falling away from the predestination doctrine "in its magnificent consistency." Whitefield, Methodism's "most consistent thinker," was an adherent of the doctrine. He and some others "prevented a premature collapse into a purely utilitarian doctrine of good works." The latter, Weber argues, "would never have been capable of motivating such tremendous sacrifices for non-rational ideal ends" (125–126).

The claims about the respective weights of psychological sanctions are ad hoc declarations. Those conclusions follow from the logic of Weber's argument but no serious supporting evidence is provided. Such conclusions—which are simultaneously comparative, historical, and social psychological—are, for all practical purposes, beyond the reach of historical and social science methods. Such conclusions, therefore, ought to be signaled as hypothetical options rather than confirmed findings.

Much of Weber's argument depends on the illustrative case, on exemplary persons who are said to be representative of the larger development. Weber's argument also delineates a causal sequence that moves from the religious ethic to the capitalist spirit. Whitefield, for example, argued the key doctrine with its powerful sanction, thus preventing the "premature collapse." Benjamin Franklin was the exemplar of the later capitalist spirit, his quotations stressing diligence, reinvestment, and so forth. The religious basis of that worldly asceticism, Weber declares, "by Franklin's time had died away" (180). Any assumption of sequence, however, would be inappropriate in this case since Franklin and Whitefield were contemporaries.

George Whitefield lived from 1714 to 1770; Franklin lived from 1706 to 1790. Whitefield was Franklin's guest in Philadelphia. Franklin describes the clergyman over several pages in the *Autobiography*. He tells of Whitefield's sermons, of his "extraordinary influence" on his hearers, and of his efforts to build an orphanage (to which Franklin, moved by the oratory, contributed). Franklin was impressed by the strength of Whitefield's voice and carefully measured its carrying power, estimating the numbers who might have heard him at more than thirty thousand. He discusses the quality of his sermons, recognizing how frequent repetitions allowed a degree of improvement that was not possible for the ordinary clergyman. Franklin printed Whitefield's sermons and journals and was thus "intimately acquainted" with him. Countering some detractors, Franklin judged the clergyman to be "a perfectly *honest man*." His comments, in short, are analytical and respectful. Franklin reports that Whitefield's prayers for his conversion were without effect. Franklin's account says nothing about predestination or psychological sanction.[32]

Both men had considerable influence. Whitefield spoke to sizable crowds in Britain and in the colonies. Franklin's audience was also enormous. *Poor Richard's Almanack* was a best-seller; in the colonies, it was second only to the Bible. In the activities of these two men, a "Protestant ethic" and a "spirit of capitalism" would have appeared as parallel contemporary developments, not as steps in a causal sequence. Whitefield might have prevented a "premature collapse" of the predestination doctrine within some segments of the population. Simultaneously, however, some other segments were already imbued with the secular capitalist spirit, that development aided, presumably, by Franklin's writings. The questions of their respective audiences and of their influence would, of course, require independent investigation.[33]

The Argument Reviewed

Weber's argument may be treated as involving twelve steps, each of which requires independent analysis, investigation, and assessment.

1. The expounding of a new and distinctive religious doctrine: Luther's concept of the calling.
2. The expounding of a doctrine: Calvinism and predestination.
3. Transmission to followers: the calling.
4. Transmission to followers: predestination.
5. Among Calvinists, the predestination doctrine produced extreme salvation anxieties, which were experienced in profound inner isolation.
6. Calvinists were told that intense worldly activity may be taken as a sign of salvation.
7. To gain that assurance, Calvinists engaged in exceptionally disciplined economic activity.
8. Calvinists accumulated large amounts of capital which, following religious strictures, were reinvested.

9. The ethic and the later spirit caused substantial economic growth in Protestant nations, specifically in those influenced by Calvinism and its derivatives.
10. The original attitudes were subsequently transformed; the religious ethic disappeared and was replaced by the secular capitalist spirit.
11. The argument of extension or of diffusion (to be discussed later). The spirit of capitalism spreads out from the early centers and, later, has sweeping, general effects.
12. Late in the nineteenth century, one finds substantial differences in the economic and occupational standing of Protestants and Catholics.

The first of these steps, the argument about the concept of the calling, is an unusual one for sociology. This claim, the cornerstone of the entire thesis, begins with an accident of translation. Martin Luther invested the key term with unique meaning. That meaning was then rapidly disseminated within the Protestant communities where, ultimately, in conjunction with other developments, it had world-historical impact.

The argument is curious: first, it centers on an accident of individual behavior, the idiosyncratic translation of a single word, and second, it is an argument of "etymological determinism." While always possible, the argument goes very much against the general theoretical orientations of most social scientists and historians. It ought, therefore, to be given more attention by critics and defenders alike. The questions of surface plausibility and validity—whether the meaning was unique to Protestantism—have not been prominent in discussions of the Weber thesis. For the most part, Weber's conclusion has been treated as a given. To research this question one would have to review the meanings assigned to occupational terms in "the civilized languages." One would have to replicate Weber's effort in the crucial notes (204–210, notes 1 and 2) and demonstrate that the terms *Beruf* and *calling* alone carry a divine sanction, a sense of obligation going well beyond everyday utility.[34]

Tatsuro Hanyu has provided an important review of Weber's scholarship with respect to this etymological question. Weber's conclusion was that Luther's unique formulation "speedily took on its present meaning in the everyday speech of all Protestant peoples." Weber's extended footnote reviewed the usages of many non-English Bibles to show that they had not used any equivalent to *calling*, but, oddly, Weber did not report the content of any English texts. Hanyu reviewed six major English-language Bibles, from Coverdal's 1535 version to the Authorized (King James) Version of 1611. Weber's case is based on two lines from Sirach, 11:20 and 21. In Luther's translation the key passages are given as "beharre in deinem Beruff" and "bleibe in deinem Beruff." The term used in all six translations of the first passage, Hanyu shows, was *worke*. For the second, we have "byde in thine estate," used three times, that followed by "abide in thy labour," "tarie in thy place," and again "abide in thy labour." None of the English Bibles used the word *calling* in this context. None of the commonplace English-language terms conveys the unique meaning argued by Weber, the suggestion of God-given tasks.[35]

Most social science commentators pass over an important methodological point here. Weber focused on a single term used in a few passages selected from an enormous range of content. He then invested the term with world-historical significance. The attention paid this notion in Weber's monograph exceeds, by far, another central Lutheran concept, that of salvation by faith alone (that is, independent of "works"). Few social scientists are likely to realize the larger context of Luther's oeuvre. Martin Luther was one of the most prolific writers of the entire modern era. The Reformation that he stimulated was, for all practical purposes, the first of the media wars. At one point, one-tenth of all published material in Germany originated from Luther's pen. The American edition of his works contains fifty-four volumes (plus supplements) and fills three library shelves, a nineteenth-century German edition fills seven library shelves, and the contemporary Weimar edition, which is not yet complete, has well over a hundred volumes. The most important single publication within this corpus would be Luther's translation of the Bible.

The New Testament contains many admonitions to give up worldly goods. The most striking example involves a wealthy young man who asked Jesus what he must do to gain eternal life. Jesus replied first that he must keep the commandments. In addition, if he wished to be perfect, he was told to "sell that which thou hast, and give to the poor, and thou shalt have treasure in heaven: and come follow me." The man, who had great possessions, "went away sorrowful." It was in this connection that Jesus said that it is "easier for a camel to go through a needle's eye, than for a rich man to enter into the kingdom of God." The anxious Christian, accordingly, should dispose of worldly goods (as was the case in John Bunyan's novel, *Pilgrim's Progress*), rather than zealously accumulating them. Weber's reading gives extraordinary weight to "the calling" and to capital accumulation and, in contrast, treats the opposite biblical commandments as somehow without impact. The unintended consequences of the idiosyncratic translation of a key concept, presumably, had more impact than the many explicit "anti-Mammon" injunctions found in the same central text. Weber might be correct in his assessment but, at minimum, further justifying arguments and evidence are required.[36]

The second step of the argument deals with the predestination doctrine as it appeared in the Calvinist tradition. This discussion differs from Weber's consideration of Luther in that the Geneva reformer John Calvin (1509–1564) is neglected, the concern instead being with "Calvinism" per se. This focus is signaled in the opening sentence: "Now Calvinism was the faith over which the great political and cultural struggles of the sixteenth and seventeenth centuries were fought in the most highly developed countries, the Netherlands, England, and France" (98). A note is appended to remove any lingering doubt: "I may here say definitely that we are not studying the personal views of Calvin, but Calvinism, and that in the form to which it had evolved by the end of the sixteenth and in the seventeenth centuries in the great areas where it had a decisive influence and which were at the same time the home of capitalistic culture" (220 n7). For purposes of his exposition, Weber declared, "We can best learn its content [the predestination doctrine] from the authoritative words of the Westminster Confession of 1647, which in this regard is simply repeated by both Independent and Baptist creeds." Two pages of quotation follow (99–101).

This Confession provides the basis for his subsequent arguments, for what Weber terms "judgments of historical imputation." Little is said about the context of the Confession, the circumstances of its origin. A sentence, early on, signals some controversy about whether predestination was "the most essential dogma" or "only an appendage" to the Calvinist movement. A note (220 n7) reports that the doctrine "had evolved" since Calvin's time. These were (and are) problems that require attention. In Weber's account, however, the problems are mentioned, then passed over.

Still another difficulty appears in this connection. Weber treats the "authoritative words" as having a direct, unambiguous impact—as if artisan, yeoman, and peasant all accepted the words of the Confession without question. One alternative is that the doctrine might be rejected, and Weber quotes John Milton on this very point: "Though I may be sent to Hell for it, such a God will never command my respect" (101). But again, although the possibility is signaled, the problem is then ignored. The next sentence announces that "we" are concerned not with "the evaluation" but with "the historical significance of the dogma."[37]

One important fact about the English context is missing from Weber's account. With the restoration of the monarchy in 1660, the Westminster Confession "lost its official status in England." That point is obviously of more than passing interest; it is a fact the reader (then and now) should be told. That point, moreover, was not fugitive information. The quotation comes from a standard encyclopedia account. When that Confession lost its official status, *The Book of Common Prayer* once again provided the "authoritative words" for members of the Church of England, which included communicants of the Puritan tendency. The Westminster Confession provided a doctrinal standard for Presbyterianism in Scotland and, with modifications, in the United States. It also provided the basis for confessional statements of some Congregationalist and some Baptist denominations.[38]

The third and fourth steps in the argument, the question of transmission or of "delivery" to the followers is bypassed, as we have seen. Weber initially dismissed such questions with his declaration that "we are naturally not concerned" (97). His initial argument, accordingly, moves directly from doctrinal exposition to the psyche of the follower. "Content," however, does not move from the printed page to the minds of the followers without some agency. Some media of communication are required, some consideration of the transmission process (together with some documentation) is needed.

On the subject of the calling, the third step of the argument, Weber was actually on firm ground. It was an important doctrine, no marginal or peripheral concern. It occupied a central place in Luther's catechisms (of 1529 and 1530), in the later compromise, the *Formula of Concord* (1577), and, in a work for theologians, *The Book of Concord* (1581). Subsequent scholarship has also, according to Marshall, noted the centrality of this doctrine. Weber errs, however, in his narrow reading of the calling, in his almost exclusive focus on economic roles, specifically on those involving gainful employment. The "Table of Duties" in the *Small Catechism,* however, gives a wider reading to cover clergy, teachers, students, rulers, subjects, husbands, wives, and children. Where Weber argues an irrational discipline, a commitment to task without evident goal or purpose, those texts indicate utility and mutual support in conjunction with a corporatist view of society."[39]

In the revised version, Weber made frequent references to the works of his close friend Ernst Troeltsch, most often to his *Die Soziallehren der christlichen Kirchen und Gruppen*. Among other things, Weber writes, the book contains "a very welcome confirmation of and supplement to this essay," but Weber avoids specific page references, commending this large work only "for general comparison" (188 n1). On Luther and the calling, one is told to see "the relevant parts of his *Soziallehren*" (211 n4). The extended meaning of calling is clearly indicated in Troeltsch, who refers, for example, to "the calling of a house-father, or of marriage, the calling to be a paternal ruler." One's calling "is regarded as a service to the whole community."[40]

What of the dissemination of Calvinist teachings? Has Weber's account with respect to this fourth claim been supported? On one key point, his representation of the Westminster Confession, the account is misleading. Weber has presented English "Calvinism" in its moment of triumph but failed to report that its "official status" lasted only a dozen years. In his final chapter, he shifted from "the original body of ideas" to the pastoral level, again in the English context. The chapter opens with a declaration that it is necessary to examine "with especial care" those writings derived from ministerial practice. This is Weber's most serious attempt at delineation of the transmission process, the movement of ideas from theologians and synods to the congregations and communicants. For the purposes of this chapter, he announces, "we can treat ascetic Protestantism as a single whole." And, he continues, "we shall, following our previous method, place one of its representatives at the centre of the discussion. Richard Baxter stands out above many other writers" (155). An entire page is given to justifying the choice.

Calvinism, however, is best seen as a social movement. As such, it was subject to many impulses and, accordingly, was continuously changing. The movement had its greatest impact over nearly two centuries, beginning in the 1540s. It began as an aggressive radical force, as a "church militant," this phase culminating in the Thirty Years' War, a devastating struggle to determine among other things, the position of Calvinism within Europe. The war ended with the Peace of Westphalia in 1648. In the same year, Spain accepted the independence of the Netherlands, ending almost a century of struggle. In England, Calvinism was represented by the Puritans, a reform movement within the Church of England that began in the Elizabethan period. The struggle between the orthodox Anglicans and the reformers centered on questions of ritual, church governance, moral standards, and the royal prerogative. The attempted repression of this movement under Charles I and Archbishop William Laud led to the English Civil War (also called the Puritan Revolution), 1642–1648, and to the deposition and execution of the monarch. The short-lived Commonwealth followed; it was the period of Calvinist triumph. In 1660, Parliament ended that experiment and the monarchy was restored. The Puritanism of the Restoration period differed from its predecessors—sober, temperate, and restrained, it was no longer a "militant" church.

Over those two centuries, Calvinism was in continuous flux with many factions and many theological emphases. Weber has frozen this movement in two snapshots, one showing passages of the Westminster Confession, the moment of triumph, and the second showing some works of the exemplary figure Richard Baxter. Arnold Eisen has reviewed this aspect of Weber's procedure. Puritanism, he reports, was not a constant throughout the seventeenth century, and the use of the "ideal type" method based on a single writer led Weber to miss the changes. The basic problem, Eisen notes, is that "the Revolution had altered Puritanism." The doctrine of the calling existed before and after the Civil War, but before, the Puritan writers counseled "activism, warfare, vigilance, and intolerance," whereas afterwards the emphasis was on "meekness, humility, chastity, tolerance, etc." The earlier attempt to "transform the earthly order" gave way to an encouragement of the "lower class" in their "obedience to the new order by then produced." Baxter's ideal type, Eisen writes, "cannot be Weber's, for the personality moulded is different: in place of mastery, we find resignation, and in place of the accountable believer, a belittling of man's ability to decide the right for himself." Weber picked up and emphasized (Eisen says he "exaggerated") the denial of pleasure, the asceticism of Puritanism. But the portrait of driven men aiming to master the world is a "distortion" of the later formulations. Puritanism, in the second half of the seventeenth century, had adopted the quietism Weber attributes to Lutheranism.[41]

Richard Baxter lived from 1615 to 1691. Few specialists would question his importance in seventeenth-century Puritanism. An *Encyclopaedia*

Britannica account, for example, describes him as "one of the greatest English Puritan ministers . . . famous for his preaching, learning, writing and his pastoral counseling. His influence on English Protestantism was more profound than that of any other 17th century Puritan minister." Weber describes Baxter as "a Presbyterian and an apologist of the Westminster Synod," but then added a qualifying phrase—"at the same time, like so many of the best spirits of his time, [he] gradually grew away from the dogmas of pure Calvinism" (156). Few readers of *The Protestant Ethic* would sense from that vague phrase the direction and significance of the man's influence. Michael R. Watts writes that Baxter "modified Calvinism in a way which opened him to the charge of Arminianism" and that "among the next generation of Presbyterian ministers were those who insisted on free will as well as free grace to an extent which made nonsense of the Calvinist scheme." Kaspar von Greyerz writes that the man "was obviously not a predestinarian theologian, and to that extent, Weber's use of Baxter and of his prominent pastoral work, *The Christian Directory,* was indeed not at all well chosen." Baxter rejected, among other things, "the predestinarianism of the Westminster confession." The admonitions contained in his *Christian Directory* do stress asceticism and diligence but those demands would have had some other "sanction."[42]

What of the fifth step? The Calvinist doctrine of predestination produced extreme salvation anxieties, which, necessarily, were dealt with in isolation. Did the Calvinists (as opposed to other religions) suffer an "unprecedented inner loneliness?" Weber argues this point at some length, but he is confronted with the serious difficulty that little information exists on the psychological state of Lutherans, Calvinists, Sectarians, or of Catholics in the early modern period. The reading of the Calvinist response (the discussion of the psychological dynamics and the weighting of the sanction) is a logical construction or, another expression for the same thing, a read-in.

Any research in this area, any investigation of psychological states in the seventeenth century, faces almost insurmountable problems. Some sense of the difficulties is provided by Kaspar von Greyerz, who, making first a comparative judgment, reports that appropriate documents from seventeenth-century England are "relatively numerous," meaning "about 100 autobiographies and up to 300 diaries." Some of these, however, did not address the questions at issue. Greyerz's summary reads: "A fair number of these extant documents are spiritual accounts. I have looked at sixty

of them, spiritual and nonspiritual alike, and I have been struck by the relatively minor role played by explicit direct or indirect references to the
double decree of predestination. Covenant theology is not missing, but
likewise it is not very prominent." Greyerz then provides a positive statement, a report of the most frequent theological views: "What is striking
about seventeenth-century English autobiographical accounts—and the
many examples among them prove the point especially well—is that the
overriding concern of the great majority of primarily religiously motivated authors was not with predestination or with the covenant but with special providence, in other words, with God's presence in their daily lives.
Belief in special providence generally presupposed the universality of
grace. The God of Providence was not the distant and inscrutable God of
the doctrine of predestination, but rather a kind of father figure who intervened in one's life."[43]

Covenant theology, the second view mentioned, was the main successor to predestinarianism among the clerics. It allowed some role for individual choice; the believer, in effect, made a contract with God. Malcolm
H. MacKinnon reviewed pastoral sources on this change and, making an
inference, argued that the extreme salvation anxieties therewith disappeared. David Zaret, in a response based largely on formal texts, held that
the salvation anxieties remained even with the changed theology. Some
sense of the difficulties involved in establishing claims about the formal
theologies may be gained from Zaret's observation: "By invoking the
contrasting principles of contract and grace, Puritan clerics elaborated an
ambiguous doctrine whose inconsistent mixture of determinism and vol-
untarism was variably presented in different contexts."[44] Weber missed
these complexities. He described the predestination doctrine "in the fateful
epoch of the seventeenth century" as having "magnificent consistency"
(125).

Greyerz's evidence shows Weber's entire discussion to be off the point.
While theologians and pastors were grappling with the intricacies of predestinarian and convenant views, the general population was moved by
other considerations. Many of the accounts (the exact number not indicated by Greyerz) did not report any spiritual concerns. They said nothing
about salvation anxieties and offered no support for Weber's claim of "unprecedented inner loneliness." Some persons (again the number is not indicated) were moved by the notions of special providence, a view that
Greyerz thinks "resulted in as much rigorous self-control as that presuma-

bly brought forth by predestinarianism." Providentialism, moreover, unlike predestination, he added, "clearly had both individual and collective implications." The theologians, it seems, argued their formal systems. Neither of the two major competing views, however, was prominent in popular consciousness of the period and thus driving behavior. The general populace, showing remarkable independence, developed their own views. Some revealed no spiritual concerns; the "great majority" of the "religiously motivated" authors were moved by another theology, by special providence. Weber's claim about the central importance of the predestination doctrine in seventeenth-century England, in short, is not supported in this evidence. A straightforward reading of Greyerz's research requires rejection of that specific claim. This odd-lot "sample" of sixty accounts, it should be noted, provides probably the best available evidence we have about popular outlooks in that period.[45]

In the social science literature, the discussions of salvation anxieties have been limited. Particular interpretations during the period could have either enhanced or alleviated those fears. If pastors gave a generous reading of God's will, that might reduce anxieties. Or, another possibility, pastors might have offered some easily interpreted sign of assurance. When the Westminster Confession lost its brief official status, *The Book of Common Prayer,* which contains the "Thirty-Nine Articles," again held that position. Article XVII, entitled "Of Predestination and Election," opens with a suggestion of a wide embrace before it spells out the doctrine—"Predestination to Life is the everlasting purpose of God." Then, providing an easily read sign, the second paragraph begins as follows: "As the godly consideration of Predestination, and our Election in Christ, is full of sweet, pleasant, and unspeakable comfort to godly persons, and such as feel in themselves the working of the Spirit of Christ." A wide range of estimates of the chances of salvation has been provided. Lodowick Muggleton thought half might be saved, John Donne thought one in three, John Spittlehouse thought maybe a quarter. Arthur Dent's estimates ranged from one of a hundred to one of a thousand; Thomas Shepard also thought one of a thousand. John Bunyan, the most pessimistic of all, thought the chances of election were "perhaps one out of 1,000 men and one out of 10,000 women."[46]

The sixth step involves the claim of worldly success as a sign of salvation: for the desperate seeker, a clue, a way out had been provided. This is also a crucial step in Weber's argument. Unlike the claim about psychological states, this argument could be supported by textual evidence. It should accordingly be accompanied by appropriate references.

Weber's extended discussion focuses, for the most part, on the need for diligence, for unrelenting labor in one's calling (156–163). This culminates in a discussion of profit. He argues that "the faithful Christian must follow the call by taking advantage of the opportunity." A passage from Baxter follows, which raises the question of relative advantage. Baxter declares that "if you choose the less gainful way, you cross one of the ends of your calling, and you refuse to be God's steward." Addressing the ever-present threat of Mammonism, the theologian declares, "You may labour to be rich for God, though not for the flesh and sin." Weber elaborates on the point: "Wealth is thus bad ethically only in so far as it is a temptation to idleness and sinful enjoyment of life." He adds a biblical reference: "The parable of the servant who was rejected because he did not increase the talent which was entrusted to him seemed to say so directly." The commandment to be diligent in one's efforts seems amply documented. The correlated claim, however, that "worldly success" is also commanded, receives only fugitive support in the Baxter passage and in the biblical reference (162–163). Neither statement explicitly states that worldly success may be taken as a sign of salvation. Given the decisive importance of this step of the argument, Weber's sparse documentation for it is especially striking.[47]

A comprehensive review of Calvinist theological writing in the Netherlands has been undertaken by J. H. Van Stuijvenberg. On viewing work as a sign, he reports as follows:

> It will be recalled that in Weber's view only restless work in a calling and this alone would drive out the doubt about the elect and would give the certainty of grace. . . . Now, in this respect the result of our investigation thus far has been negative. Nowhere in the Calvinist theological literature covering the years 1650–1795 . . . have we found any trace of this view. None of the Calvinist theologians commends restless labour in a calling as the . . . only true means whereby the certainty of salvation may be attained. Nowhere does one read that this, and this alone . . . would destroy religious doubt. It may consequently be accepted as definitely established that there never was this theological hinge around which everything turns in Weber's thesis. On this point

the theological base which Weber lays under his thesis has never existed.[48]

Some sparse support for the success-as-a-sign viewpoint does appear in the English context. First is a brief discussion in the work of John T. McNeill, a leading historian of Calvinism. He addresses this precise notion, namely, that "worldly prosperity is evidence of the favor of God." He sees it as a belief that appeared first in the mid-seventeenth century. The key passage reads: "Certainly the bourgeois heresy of wealth as a mark of divine approval entered into later Calvinism, though always under the restraints of insistence upon charity and service. It may have broken in during the era of Puritan individualism, with the triumph of the Independents and the growth of foreign trading interests. Cromwell saw in his military victories the manifest favor of God and made of this something quite personal. In Charles II's reign [1660–1685] this view is out in the open." Instead of citing Weber's insistent focus on "the individual" and on reinvestment, however, McNeill focuses on the prudential use of wealth, on "the restraints of insistence upon charity and service." He cites several authors who have made this emphasis.[49]

The new prudential reading appeared also in the American colonies; Samuel Willard, president of Harvard College, wrote that "*Riches* are consistent with *Godliness,* and the more a Man hath the more Advantage he hath to do Good with it." This reading of "the sign" differs significantly from Weber's account. The new direction does not appear to stem from anxieties generated by the predestination doctrine, at least the authors cited do not make that connection. It is not even clear that those providing the new reading were predestinarians. The new view did make its appearance at a time when predestination was rapidly losing ground.[50]

Puritans were admonished to be diligent, but the demand was comprehensive; the requirement was for an insistent moral attentiveness in all matters. The onesidedness problem appears again in this connection: Puritan texts are examined to discover those admonitions to diligence, hard work, and so forth, the implication being that "the other side," Anglican orthodoxy, somehow encouraged or allowed laxity. Timothy Hall Breen reviewed the writings of both "sides" and found little difference between the two. On some points, he reports, the Anglicans made the more insistent demands.[51]

The seventh step involves the question of a response: Did Calvinists respond to anxiety and to the alleged sign with a prodigious work effort? Did Weber support this claim? Marshall argues that he did not; because of its importance, it is useful to have the entire text of Marshall's conclusion:

> Was the "psychological sanction" effective in changing peoples' orientation towards economic activities? This question may be answered only by investigating empirically the attitudes and everyday conduct of the Protestant business and labouring classes. Unfortunately this is something which Weber fails to do. For someone who is so explicitly interested in the practical consequences of theology, rather than theology itself, he is strangely unconcerned about documenting these consequences empirically as opposed simply to arguing them by assertion . . . all of Weber's data derive from Protestant theology. He provides no evidence whatsoever to substantiate his claim that the orientation towards economic conduct allegedly induced by the belief-systems of ascetic Protestantism was, in fact, subscribed to by the Protestant business community. His ideal-type of the spirit of modern capitalism, based entirely on the teachings of Franklin, remains but a "provisional description." It is therefore legitimate to claim, as several critics have, that Weber nowhere demonstrates that the average Protestant internalized and acted upon the ideas which he describes in his essays.[52]

Evidence on this point might well appear in those autobiographies and diaries. If the claim were accurate, the diarists should report salvation anxieties, note a recognition of "work" as the solution, and provide some information on their subsequent efforts. Probably the most extensive diary available from the period, next to that of Samuel Pepys (which is largely secular), is that of Nehemiah Wallington. A London Puritan and self-employed artisan, Wallington kept an extensive journal of which some two thousand pages have survived. For what it is worth, Wallington's diary evidences extreme salvation anxieties and extraordinary diligence in the recording of his moral behavior. In his economic affairs, however, he proved quite diffident.[53]

The eighth step involves capital accumulation and reinvestment. As a result of those remarkable work efforts, Calvinists generated extensive wealth. With self-indulgent expenditure forbidden, those ascetic Protestants reinvested their accumulated capital, which meant even greater returns. Evidence is generally lacking on this point, the conclusion being supported instead by the plausible logic. Even with the post-Restoration revision (taking success as a sign), the new reading did not command an "irrational" effort of continuous investment. It enjoined instead a prudential use of one's wealth. The question requires investigation: How much of "the Puritan's" wealth was invested and how much went to tithing or to charity? Did Puritans and Anglicans differ in their rates of investment? Were the differences large, medium, small, or nonexistent?

The ninth step of Weber's argument addresses the questions of location and impact. If ascetic Protestantism had appeared only in settings that were unfavorable for economic growth, such as Geneva and Scotland, the importance of the thesis would be rather limited. Were that the case, one might conclude that the thesis was valid but, because of the inauspicious circumstances, the economic consequences of the new beliefs were of no great importance. To make the case for world-historical significance, Weber must place "the ethic," the later "spirit," and the economic response in the Netherlands, in England, and in the United States. Crude comparisons of nations appear throughout the work, for example, in his reference to Geneva, Holland, and England, described as "those areas of high economic development." At one point, Weber draws a lesson from a comparison of the New England and southern colonies in North America. Weber's opening chapter is filled with such comparisons and illustration.[54]

A largely unrecognized problem is that of categorical readings. Entire populations are treated as either Lutheran or Calvinist, although the denominations were not clearly distinguished as of 1560, especially at the local level.[55] A ruler might convert or an accident of inheritance might change the "official" religion of the state (as with Frederick, the elector of the Palatinate, in 1559). The new ruler, typically, would purge the theological faculty of the university. Leading pastors would be replaced; they, along with prominent lay defenders of the previous established faith, would be expelled. It would take years for the new influence to reach "the masses" in town or country. In Brandenburg-Prussia, Calvinism remained a court religion, never reaching the general population. The process was further complicated by reversions. Inheritance might mean a return of Lutheranism. In the Palatinate, with Carl Theodor in 1743, it brought a Catholic ruler. By then, however, it had long-since been agreed that the imposition of a faith was unacceptable.

A glance at any historical atlas brings to light some further problems.[56] As of 1560, Lutheranism was well represented in Europe. It was the es-

tablished church in all of Scandinavia and in much of German-speaking
Europe. The lands facing onto the Baltic Sea were almost without exception Lutheran. The Lutheran presence may be seen in most of northern
Germany, north of Erfurt, Leipzig, and Dresden, and significant concen-
trations were found also scattered through the southern states (in Stuttgart and its environs, for example). Lutheranism was also present, mixed
in with other contenders, in the region that is now Hungary and Romania.
The Reformed churches (including here Calvinism and several others)
were most clearly represented in some of the Swiss cantons and in Scotland. Elsewhere that faith was present, again mixed with others, in the
Netherlands, in England, in France (Huguenots), and again in Hungary
and Romania. The mix in the Swiss case is often overlooked. Some cantons were Catholic, some were Calvinist, but others followed the Zwingli-
an direction (which Weber bypasses).[57] The casual listings and linkages
neglect a wide range of experience and "transform" others.

Following the basic outlines of Weber's argument, the best, the purest
cases would involve Scotland and the Calvinist cantons in Switzerland. It
would, at the outset, be difficult to make a world-historical claim out of
such limited experience. Much debate followed the original publication of
The Protestant Ethic, and between 1907 and 1910 Weber published four replies. In the second of these, Viner has pointed out, Weber acknowledged
that "the spirit of capitalism was not present in all Calvinist communities." He "expressly claimed the applicability of his thesis . . . only to England, southern France, Holland, New England, the Scotch-Irish, the
German diaspora (i.e. the Calvinist refugees in Germany), Friesland, and
a large number of German (non-Lutheran) communities." Viner notes
"the silent omission" of Geneva and Scotland, a decision he thinks was
not inadvertent; in his view, Weber was admitting that direct Calvinist
rule, the theocracy, restricted economic activity. If that was Weber's intent, it has had little impact since, with rare exceptions, Geneva and Scotland are regularly referred to in subsequent literature as relevant and
appropriate cases for his argument.[58]

Gordon Marshall has provided a detailed, sweeping review of relevant
evidence from the Scottish experience, covering both the Protestant ethic
and the capitalist spirit. The evidence on both points, and on the linkage
between the two, is very limited. Marshall's cautious summary conclusion
reads: "Notwithstanding the various problems pertaining to empirical
documentation in this matter, there are reasonable grounds for maintain-

ing that Weber's original thesis is vindicated by the Scottish data." That tentative conclusion holds for Scottish entrepreneurs, but not for laborers who, apparently, were not touched by Calvinist teachings. Marshall argues further that, because of the unfavorable conditions in Scotland, the ethic/spirit had a limited impact on economic development. Weber, of course, recognized the importance of "conditions"—the ethic/spirit alone was not a sufficient condition for capitalist development. Marshall's work is important for its "clarification of the nature of the evidence that is required in order to test Weber's thesis adequately." It makes eminently clear the difficulties involved in any historical test of the thesis.[59]

The Dutch and English cases are both mixed. Data are needed on the religious composition of those two nations and it must be established that the economic advance is distinctively linked with "Protestant" tendencies. In most discussions, that linkage has been assumed rather than established. Most social scientists will recognize the problem associated with such analysis. It involves the ecological fallacy—conclusions about individual behavior based on characteristics of mixed aggregates. Without further specification and investigation, it is entirely possible, in the Dutch case for example, that the economic growth was due to Catholic entrepreneurs (and artisans), or that Catholics and Protestants (of all persuasions) were equally zealous in their economic efforts.

This precise question was addressed by Samuelsson, who reviewed several historical sources. The Dutch commercial preeminence, he reports, antedated the appearance of Calvinism there. It was not until well into the seventeenth century that Calvinism "prevailed in Amsterdam, the most important mercantile city." Even then the change was "of an entirely political nature": Maurice of Orange changed his faith. The religion-statification linkage was not as it should be for Weber's argument. "More than two-thirds of the population of the Netherlands professed Catholicism" at the end of the War of Liberation (in 1648), Samuelsson writes, and "in the more important cities the preponderance was even greater." The Dutch historian I. W. van Ravesteyn, who studied "economic and social conditions in Amsterdam in the 16th and early 17th centuries," is cited, his conclusion being that "it was among the better-off sections of the community that Catholicism maintained its grip the longest." Calvinism, initially at least, drew its support "almost without exception from the lower strata of society." The "large merchants and industrial entrepreneurs," in contrast, "were generally indifferent." One would not suspect any of this from Weber's confident declarations about the impact of "Protestantism" in the Netherlands. Weber, however, knew the history; this is indicated in a late note where he reports "the relatively smaller extent to which the Calvinistic ethic penetrated practical life there." He adds that "the ascetic spirit began to weaken in Holland as early as the beginning of the seventeenth century. . . . Moreover, Dutch Puritanism had in general much less expansive power than English" (273 n67).[60]

Similar questions must be raised about the English case. The first line of Weber's text referred to "the occupational statistics of any country of mixed religious composition" and announced that "business leaders and owners of capital" there, in the late nineteenth century, were "overwhelmingly Protestant." In this context, following the logic of his argument, that would mean persons of the Puritan tendency, or later, those affiliated with the Nonconforming or Dissenting religious groups. While systematic investigation has been possible at all points in this century (and earlier), the most useful study of the question is the recent work of W. D. Rubinstein. He found the distribution of nonlanded wealth-holders bore no relation to "what one might have expected in light of the Weber Thesis." Except for "the dramatic overrepresentation of Jews and other migrants, the percentages bear a virtual random sample resemblance to the denominational percentages of the time. . . . The majority at each level of wealth were Anglicans, while Church of Scotland and dissenting adherents [were] almost precisely as one would expect on a purely random basis." Rubinstein's main conclusion is that "entrepreneurial success has little or nothing to do with *religion*. . . . the mechanism [for success] belongs to other realms than religion or theology."[61]

As with the Dutch case, Weber knew the English history and knew it to be problematic for his argument. Those difficulties are signaled only in notes appended to the last pages of the text. A brief note added in the revised edition reports: "At the present time the two parties of the Church are of approximately equal numbers, while in earlier times the Nonconformists were always in the minority" (279 n90). The formulation is vague: What was the size of that minority in those "earlier times"? Was it of sufficient size to generate or drive this world-historical movement, modern capitalism?

In 1715, a committee of London ministers undertook a survey of Dissenting congregations. Their findings, Michael Watts reports, provide "the most detailed and comprehensive survey we have of Dissenting strength before the religious census of 1851." In the early eighteenth century, the Dissenters formed just over six percent of the English population. David Little gives an even lower figure: "The Puritans never amounted to more than about 4 per cent of the population." The Nonconformist denominations increased in strength later in the eighteenth century, especially with the rise of Methodism, but even in the 1851 census, only about a fifth of the English and Welsh populations "attended non-Anglican (including Roman Catholic) services." Only about a fifth attended Anglican services at that point, but most of the rest, it appears, felt some sense of attachment to the Church of England. Four-fifths of the English and Welsh who married in 1851 "did so with the benefit of Anglican rites." Even in 1900, about two-thirds chose the Anglican rites, about one in eight married in one of the Dissenting churches, about one in eight had civil marriages. Weber's statement about the "approximately equal numbers" at the turn of the century is misleading. The two had approximately equal numbers of Sunday communicants, about two million each, but that statistic overlooks the problem of religious indifference, an issue facing all denominations. It was clearly much more serious in the Church of England.[62]

Were the Nonconformists in the right place? Were they located in the geographic centers of the later capitalist development? Or were they somewhere on the periphery of things? Drawing again on the 1715 survey, Watts reports that the Presbyterians "appear to have constituted more than 8 per cent of the population of Lancashire," that is, in the location of the later cotton industry. They were also strong in Devon, Somerset, and Dorset, areas not associated with later economic development. Watts provides several explanations for the geographic pattern. Some were areas of Puritan strength prior to the Civil War. Some active Presbyterian ministers were expelled from their pulpits after the restoration in 1662; they then carried their message out to other locations. The Church of England, like established churches elsewhere, was sluggish in its response to urban growth, producing an inadequate parochial structure in the cities. That archaic structure, established seven or eight centuries earlier, provided a remarkable opportunity for Dissenting clergy. Dissent also had greater success in urban areas also because the rural adherents were subject to social and economic pressures from the Anglican gentry. In addition, it was difficult for the Dissenting clergy to reach a clientele dispersed in the countryside.[63]

Another concern appears with respect to the social location of the Dissenting populations. Again, Weber knew there to be a problem. This is first signaled in a sentence late in the text: "With great regularity we find the most genuine adherents of Puritanism among the classes which were rising from a lowly status, the small bourgeois and farmers." (174). A footnote added to the revised edition developed this point. Petty, it seems, had noted this linkage (Weber gives no page reference). Then too, "all the contemporary sources without exception" report the Puritan sectarians "as belonging partly to a propertyless class, partly to one of small capitalists, and contrast them both with the great merchant aristocracy and the financial adventurers." Recapitulating, he states that it was from "just this small capitalist class, and not from the great financial magnates, monopolists, Government contractors, lenders to the King, colonial entrepreneurs, promoters, etc., that there originated what was characteristic of Occidental capitalism" (279–280 n93).

This argument carries an obvious implication: to sustain his case, Weber must show significant upward mobility among those "sectarians" (or among their immediate descendants). He provides a source at this point: "See Unwin, *Industrial Organization in the Sixteenth and Seventeenth Centuries*, London, 1914, pp. 196 ff." It is an unusual citation among the scores of works referenced: it is a scholarly work dealing with English economic history. The date of publication, a minor error, was 1904. The page he has given begins a chapter entitled "The Antecedents of the Trade Union." Some discussion of conflicts between small and large capitalists appears on that page. Nothing in the chapter describes "sectarian" versus Anglican differences, however, and nothing is said of the former rising from a lowly status. It is another false lead.[64]

A difficulty with Weber's casual use of selected cases is evident in his comparison of the Massachusetts and Virginia colonies. In the former, the Protestant ethic operated, presumably, with full force, and consequently the colony, did well economically. Virginia, founded for profit, was not as successful. But, Massachusetts was a mixed colony—again posing the ecological problem—and Virginia was hard hit by tropical disease. One possibility is that "other things" were not equal. Despite continuous generous references to many "other factors," Weber does not follow through to show that with those factors controlled, a decisive religious impact remained. Although lacking specific documentation, Edmund S. Morgan's account of the Massachusetts Bay Company provides a rich range of detail that goes far beyond Weber's superficial observations. In its first years, the company, "like most colonizing companies, did not prove a sound business investment." Puritan zealotry was a continuous problem facing the state's first governor, John Winthrop, whose key to success was his "realism in not seeking perfection." This portrayal begs a key question, that of actual economic performance. Gary Nash writes that pre-revolutionary New England, "especially in its transition to a market economy . . . may have been the least dynamic region of the British mainland colonies."[65]

The frequent casual correlations linking Protestantism with economic advance and Catholicism with economic backwardness are far from compelling. The Protestant nations typically discussed are all mixed cases. The alleged association and causal connection has not been clearly established in any of them. The available evidence tends rather to go against the Weber argument.

The tenth claim involves the assumption of a transformation: the driving work ethic has become detached from its ascetic Protestant origins and is now the secular capitalist spirit. This claim is probably the most weakly supported argument of all. One must assume, first, that the handful of passages from Benjamin Franklin accurately reflect the man's world outlook; second, that Weber's interpretation of those passages is accurate; and third, that this sample of one man's writing accurately represents the larger universe, all Americans, or all ascetic Protestant Americans. One must assume further that Franklin's homilies have Calvinist origins.

In the final pages of Weber's monograph, an even greater extension of impact is argued, the eleventh of the major claims. "The Puritan," Weber reports,

> wanted to work in a calling; we are forced to do so. For when asceticism was carried out of monastic cells into everyday life, and began to dominate worldly morality, it did its part in building the tremendous cosmos of the modern economic order. This order is now bound to the technical and economic conditions of machine production which today determine the lives of all the individuals who are born into this mechanism, not only those directly concerned with economic acquisition, with irresistible force. . . . In Baxter's view the care for external goods should only lie on the shoulders of the "saint like a light cloak, which can be thrown aside at any moment." But fate decreed that the

cloak should become an iron cage . . . the idea of duty in one's calling prowls about in our lives like the ghost of dead religious beliefs. (181–182)

The iron cage imagery is developed over three pages. The claims are total, comprehensive, all-embracing. Somehow, the driving force generated by those religious beliefs in several rather limited contexts have "today" taken on compelling force everywhere, or at least everywhere within the context of "victorious capitalism." (A minor point: Parsons's translation of the key expression, "iron cage," is not entirely accurate. The original is *stahlhartes Gehäuse*—the cage is as hard as steel.)

The process of diffusion from those early centers of Calvinism ought to be demonstrated. If that is a valid claim, one should be able to show the changing work ethic of all other groups in the course of, say, the eighteenth and nineteenth centuries. The Catholic populations of Europe and North America, along with those Protestants not previously moved by the demands of the ascetic branches, should show, unambiguously, the anticipated shift from traditional work attitudes to this now all-pervasive sense of "duty."

For many commentators, this conclusion has been accepted without question. Some of Weber's defenders have made use of the iron cage argument to counter Weber's critics, specifically those who have found no differences in the outlooks of contemporary Protestants and Catholics. The defense focuses on those final pages where Weber states that the original differences are no longer present. In the opening pages of the monograph, however, Weber had presented, an opposite argument. There he claimed sizable de facto differences in the attitudes and behavior of Protestants and Catholics in central Europe at the end of the nineteenth century. Weber put forth contradictory claims.

The acceptance of this second position, the invocation of the "no difference" claim, protects the Weber thesis from tests based on subsequent evidence, that is, from twentieth-century experience. While in principle an acceptable position, it ought to be used consistently, as applying equally to all parties. If Weber is allowed tests of difference, as with the Offenbacher data, and his "positive" results are accepted, then similar tests must be allowed other investigators and one should be open to any result.

The twelfth claim, that of Weber's opening discussion, was the assertion of significant Protestant-Catholic differences in outlook. The orientations formed in the seventeenth century had persisted through to the last decade of the nineteenth. Although accompanied by an array of bold declarations and many notes, this claim was not supported. The single instance of apparent support, that involving school choice, proved to be a spurious result. This argument, moreover, did not focus on Calvinism or ascetic Protestantism; it focused, effectively, on Lutheranism.

An assessment of claims may yield several possible outcomes: support or confirmation (evidence that sustains the original hypothesis); rejection or disconfirmation (evidence that goes against the original hypothesis); nonsupport (evidence on the point is unavailable, or so fragmentary as to allow neither confirmation nor rejection); mixed results (contingent findings; or, another possibility, the association is confirmed but the causal argument questioned). For the twelve claims, we have the following conclusions.

1. Luther and the calling. Supported but with an important qualification: Luther did give a special meaning to this term, one that was important in his theology. Weber, however, provided a miscue on this point. He focused on economic roles and gave an individualistic reading to the prescribed activity. But the term had much more general application and the activity was guided by a corporatist rationale. This was not an irrational effort; it was work for the collective good. Whether Luther's use of the term was unique, appearing in no other major language or tradition, is best viewed as an open question in need of confirmation.

2. Calvinism and predestination. Supported, but with an important qualification: the doctrine was central to "Calvinism" in all of its manifestations. As opposed to Weber's declaration that predestination was a doctrine of "magnificent consistency," an opposite conclusion, magnificent complexity, seems more appropriate. At all points the theological specialists had to grapple with an insoluble contradiction. The reconciliation of the eternal decree on the one hand, and free will, repentence, and God's grace on the other, brought diverse and ever-changing solutions.

3. Transmission: the calling. Supported, but with an important qualification: Luther's concept, not Weber's reading of the term, was built into Lutheran pastoral literature and widely communicated.

4. Transmission: predestination. Supported, but with important qualifications: this was an important Calvinist doctrine but there is some question as to its temporal and spatial extension. Weber portrays it as im-

portant in seventeenth-century England and suggests some continuity even into the eighteenth century, but the claims of extension are open to question. The use of Baxter as the exemplary representative was inappropriate. Weber's use of the Westminster Confession was seriously misleading. The predestination doctrine was being replaced by covenant theology before the Civil War. The collapse it seems, proceeded rapidly after the fall of the Commonwealth. Calvinism, at its strongest, had a limited presence in western Europe. Weber later discounted its importance in the Netherlands. He presents no clear evidence as to its incidence in England or in the American colonies.

5. Salvation anxieties stemming from predestinarian views. Not adequately supported by Weber; rejected in subsequent research. Greyerz's review of the limited evidence available for seventeenth-century England showed predestination playing a "relatively minor role." Claims about the psychological outlooks of "the masses" in previous centuries are close to untestable. To assess Weber's claim, for example, one needs information on the "anxiety levels" of Puritans and those of some appropriate control groups. Confirmation or disconfirmation of such claims, therefore, is extremely difficult, a problem clearly indicated in Greyerz's sample of diaries and autobiographies.

6. Work as a sign. Not supported by Weber; he presented no documentary evidence on this point. A recent review of relevant Dutch materials found no support for the claim, thus providing grounds for rejection. Unlike the question of salvation anxieties, this is a testable claim: if valid, one should be able to cite the documentary evidence.

7. Work as a response. Not supported: for this, one would have to establish that Puritans worked significantly harder than equivalent Anglicans. Such "outcome" differences are central to the validation of the entire Weber thesis. No evidence is presented to support this claim.

8. Reinvestment. Not supported: the argument assumes capital accumulation and reinvestment (as opposed to other uses, such as hoarding, tithing, philanthropy), for which no evidence is presented. This conclusion depends on deduction; it is an inference following from the strictures against self-indulgence. No serious evidence is presented to support the point.

9. The geographic correlations. Not supported. The most frequently presented correlations are, to say the least, somewhat crude. That the Netherlands and England showed outstanding economic performance

does not establish "Protestantism" as the cause. A more detailed examination shows an opposite relationship in the Netherlands (Catholicism in the higher ranks of Amsterdam; Calvinism in the lower classes or off on the Friesian fringes). The linkage of Puritanism (or Dissent) and economic success in England is not demonstrated.

10. The transformation from Protestant ethic to spirit of capitalism. Not supported. The support for this claim is extremely weak: one must assume that those few fragments of Franklin's writings do in fact represent the spirit of capitalism as defined by Weber. One must assume that the "spirit" is derived from Calvinist antecedents.

11. Generalization of the spirit: the iron cage. This too is unsupported. No evidence is presented to demonstrate the universal presence of the compelling work ethic; no evidence is presented to demonstrate the diffusion of that ethic in prior decades or centuries to those previously untouched by ascetic Protestantism.

12. The argument of persistence. The claim of significant Protestant-Catholic differences of achievement in the late nineteenth century was not adequately supported. The support seen in the Baden school attendance figures involved a copying error and a causal argument that proved to be spurious.

Weber's argument, in short, is badly flawed. The two claims about doctrinal innovation are supported but with important qualifications. The same holds with respect to the claims about their transmission. The remaining eight propositions are not adequately supported, at least not in Weber's text.

These conclusions accord with Jacob Viner's summary based on his review of relevant evidence: "I cannot find any reference in Weber to Calvinist correspondence and autobiographies, and neither my examination of a small sample of the available literature nor the writings of Weber's followers offer any persuasive indication that this literature would give significant support to Weber's thesis. Weber, like his followers, generalized freely about the actual economic behavior of Calvinists or 'Puritans' in the seventeenth century; but he seems to rely on common knowledge and gives no detailed historical evidence." These conclusions accord also with Gordon Marshall's summary judgment based on his extensive review. Weber's case, he wrote, "is empirically so thin that the only reasonable verdict for the moment would be one of 'not proven.' "[66]

Not proven is not the same as wrong. Most of the points of Weber's argument are, in principle, empirically testable. But for some, notably for the claims about psychological reactions, the possibilities for testing have long since disappeared.[67] The best available evidence for a test of the thesis would involve ecological correlation, a demonstration of significant economic growth in areas having a specific Calvinist presence as compared with some appropriate control cases. Without such systematic tests, the case remains an unsupported hypothesis.

The Protestant ethic thesis appears to be a social misconstruction. In a footnote, Weber refers to the argument as a "sketch," a term that seems entirely appropriate. In many confident statements in the text, however, Weber moves far beyond that indication of the tentative or of the hypothetical and treats the thesis as a well-documented conclusion. This misconstruction, the transformation of the hypothetical into a confirmed conclusion, is found also in the work of subsequent scholarly (and not-so-scholarly) writers, a tendency (as will be seen later) most pronounced among sociologists. Weber and his supporters have invested the *hypothesis* with validity and have accorded world-historical significance to "the Protestant ethic."

More than scholarly analysis is operating in such misconstruction. Scholarly analysis would mean criticism, analysis, and further research on the hypothesis. It would entail some cumulation, a drawing of lessons out of the long history of controversy. A scholarly analysis would recognize, cite, and deal with important criticisms. The complexities of the Dutch case, for example, should be indicated, especially the problematic relationship there of religious affiliation and social stratification. The complexities of the English case ought to be noted and its outright rejection in Rubinstein's research should be reported. This scenario, by and large, has not occurred, however; the criticisms, as will be discussed immediately, have been neglected.

The Reception of the Weber Thesis

Gordon Marshall's work opens with a play on a famous Crane Brinton sentence: "Who now reads *The Protestant Ethic and the Spirit of Capitalism?*" Marshall's answer: "Almost everyone it seems." The continuing controversy, he reports, is "one of the longest running and most vociferous in the social sciences. . . . Most students of sociological theory, the sociologies of religion, industry, and development, of theology, and of the economic and social history of industrialization in the West are required, at some juncture, to assess the relative strengths and weaknesses of Weber's case."[68]

To some academics, that conclusion will seem entirely plausible, but others know there are grounds for doubt. The attention paid the Weber thesis by specialists in religious studies may be seen in an appropriate citation index, *Religion Index One,* which covers approximately five hundred journals throughout the world. The four volumes for 1989–1992 contain a grand total of thirty-two citations of Max Weber, twelve of which, judging by titles, appear to deal in some way with the Protestant ethic. Under "Capitalism and Christianity" there were nine references that, again judging by titles, appeared to be on the Protestant ethic question, five of these repeating citations under Weber. In the four-year period then, sixteen articles were cited under those two headings. By this rule-of-thumb measure, the interest shown in the Weber thesis by the world's religion specialists amounts to about four articles a year.[69]

Philip Benedict has reviewed the treatment of the Weber thesis in the general historical literature. He concludes:

> Weber's ideas have provoked a considerable amount of comment and criticism from historians of Calvinism ever since they first appeared. A substantial literature has grown up around certain questions growing out of the Weber thesis debate. Nonetheless, when one surveys the broad range of writings devoted to the subject of early modern Calvinism, what is most striking of all is that the thesis in its broadest form has had remarkably little influence in stimulating and directing the main stream of research on the subject, except in England. Since the Weber thesis would seem to confer great importance on the history of Calvinism by suggesting that it played a particularly crucial role in moving European society down the road to modernity, this may seem surprising indeed. It points up the extreme compartmentalization of knowledge in the twentieth century and the considerable gulf between the concerns and training of those who have written about Calvinism, on the one hand, and those of Weber and of latter-day Weberians housed generally in departments of sociology, on the other.

The English exception, Benedict indicates, is due to the influence of R. H. Tawney, whose *Religion and the Rise of Capitalism* led to the development of an influential school.[70]

Many leading sources on the history of industrialization make no reference at all to the Weber thesis. Phyllis Deane's comprehensive study of Britain's industrial revolution has no index reference to Max Weber, to Protestantism, or to religion. Her chapters, incidentally, review and document the importance of a wide range of other factors that are neglected in most of the sociological literature. There is no reference to Weber in an older classic, J. H. Clapham's study of French and German economic development. T. S. Ashton's brief popular account of the Industrial Revolution, another of the older classics, contains no reference to Weber. A later scholarly work by Ashton makes a passing reference to the religious factor, touching on the Wesleyans for example, but includes no reference to Weber. Another noted economic historian, John Ulrich Nef, had little positive to say about the thesis; in a summary work on the Industrial Revolution, he reviewed Weber's claims but, for the most part, rejected them. Charles Kindleberger's study of France and Britain in the century after 1850 allots four pages to "religion" and there makes passing references to Weber and Tawney. His brief account is balanced (reviewing Samuelsson, for example) and is well documented. His last comment is negative: he has been "able to reject the hypothesis that changes in religious belief and practice played a major role in the course of British or French economic development after 1850." William H. McNeill's comprehensive study *The Rise of the West* has only one index reference to Weber, that to a footnote on page 590. There one finds a single noncommittal comment on the "famous thesis." Paul Kennedy's comprehensive study of economic change and military conflict from 1500 to 2000, *The Rise and Fall of the Great Powers,* contains no reference to Max Weber or to the famous thesis. David Landes provides the most favorable judgment (among the authors reviewed in this paragraph), but even there the Protestant ethic thesis is given little attention, only a few pages of his 550-page history.[71]

Carlo Cipolla, another leading economic historian, has edited an important collection of essays on developments in sixteenth- and seventeenth-century Europe. I found no reference to Weber in this nearly 600-page work. The closest to a confirmation is a brief passage in a chapter by Hermann Kellebenz, which tells of "a more thrifty attitude on the part of those of the nobility who had turned Protestant and had been influenced by the teachings of the Reformation." Some instances in which there is "exceptionally clear evidence" on the linkage of religion and technical innovation are provided. Several pages later Kellebenz reviews the secularization of Catholic church properties, noting one of the consequences—the classes that benefited "used their increased purchasing power, which in fact they often exceeded by obtaining credit, to demonstrate their new status by building houses and adopting a modern style of living worthy of them." A few pages later one learns that the social changes "brought about by the Reformation, especially secularisation, also stimulated consumer activity, as did fashion, particularly the vogue of the *nouvelle draperie*, Spanish fashions and, starting in the 1630s, the growing demand for French Fashions." No reference to Weber appears in his bibliography. Another article in the Cipolla volume, by Aldo De Maddalena, touches briefly on the Dutch experience. It too tells of the parcelling out of land that followed the Reformation, much of it coming into the hands of "the rich bourgeoisie." Modern and remunerative methods of farm management followed along with short-term leases, which allowed easier adaptation to changing economic conditions. As opposed to signs of asceticism, numerous "villas and gardens also grew up around the towns, representing not only a sop to their owners' social ambitions, but also a sensible policy of investment and agronomic innovation."[72]

The most positive reception of the Weber thesis, by a considerable margin, is found in sociology. Most introductory sociology texts are generous in their commendation of Weber, the man and the scholar. Most texts in the field review the thesis and give it credence. Some are noncommittal, providing only a report of its major claims. Neil J. Smelser's text, for example, introduces Weber as the "great German sociologist [who] used historical research to throw light on the link between religion and social change." Later, a biographical profile describes Weber as "a prodigious scholar" who "profoundly influenced" modern sociology. A brief account of the Protestant ethic thesis follows. Weber "showed that values can be a powerful force for social change." This is followed by statements about Calvinists and their work habits. The principal exposition of the thesis appears several pages later where a single long paragraph reviews the linkage of Calvinism, predestination, and the work ethic. The initial statement is a simple report: "Weber believed this ethic had a major influence on the growth of capitalism." A shorter second paragraph mentions that Weber "noted other factors," specifically "the military budget and high consumer demand." Smelser's final statement is an unambiguous confirmation: "Still, the Protestant Reformation changed not only the economic structure but also a variety of institutions, including science, law, and education. The changes brought about by Calvinism combined to transform the social order." Not one reference is provided to document the claim. There is not a single indication of any controversy about the thesis, nor any reference to the critics—none, for example, to Samuelsson or Marshall.[73]

A review of fifteen current sociology texts revealed that all provided brief summary reviews of the Weber thesis. Some authors accepted the basic claims, commending the argument to their readers. Others gave neutral descriptive accounts, saying that Weber had argued such-and-such but offering no comment on the validity of the claims. None of those texts reviewed the problems with Weber's evidence. None reported the inadequacy of Offenbacher's data or the copying error, none noted the misrepresentation of Franklin and Fugger; none mentioned the difficulties involved in the Dutch case. All of these problems, it will be noted, were signaled in the Samuelsson critique published in English in the early 1960s. Only eight of the fifteen texts indicated some controversy over the thesis. A couple of these were at best "trace" mentions; some others indicated unambiguous vindication for the thesis. Only three texts provided references to the book-length critical studies by Samuelsson and Marshall reviewed in this chapter. Two of these citations proved to be inadequate. One made reference to "Marshall, 1982" but did not list the book among the references. Another made reference to "Samuelsson, 1961," saying only that it was the source for a quotation, but not indicating that it provided a major critique; the critic's name in this case was misspelled in the references. VanderZanden's text signaled approval (Weber "marshalled evidence") but also cited Samuelsson accurately and listed four other critical studies. Those five citations were more than appeared in all of the other fourteen texts.[74]

Many of those textbooks introduced the possibility of an opposite causal direction—that the rise of capitalism stimulated the appearance of Protestantism. In some of them the counterthesis was given full credence even though no serious evidence was provided in its support. The documented account by Lewis A. Spitz (reviewed briefly earlier), makes this option implausible. The movement was led by theologians and clergy (that is, by intellectuals); their main support was from "the populace down below." Spitz does not assign any major influence to the rise of capitalism.

These university-level textbooks showed a near-complete indifference to evidence, both with regard to the original thesis and to this ad hoc alternative. Instead, glossing over the criticisms, most of the texts provided either enthusiastic approval or a brief unevaluated summary of Weber's thesis. For much of the 1980s, the best-selling sociology textbook in the United States was the work of Ian Robertson. He is a professional writer, not a professional sociologist, and his is the only textbook that signals doubt; he suggests that the Weber thesis is "probably unverifiable."[75]

The Samuelsson book makes many telling criticisms of the Weber thesis, as we have seen, but for the general social science audience the work has been lost from view. In 1976 Anthony Giddens wrote an introduction to *The Protestant Ethic* that appears both in the Scribner's and in the later Routledge editions. His four-page review of "the controversy" contains a brief mention of Weber's use of "a study of the economic activities of Catholics and Protestants in Baden in 1895," accompanied by an agnostic comment—"and the accuracy even of these figures had been questioned." Samuelsson is referenced at that point but few readers would be moved by that laconic statement to search out the source. Giddens could have easily pointed out the inaccuracy in the key row of percentages. Samuelsson received a second footnote mention, being cited as a critic who had questioned the Calvinism-capitalism relationship on the European continent.[76]

Evidence showing the "disappearance" of Samuelsson's work may be gained from the *Social Science Citation Index*, which covers a vast range of relevant literature. In the four years from 1989 to 1992, three articles referred to Samuelsson's critique. None of the three citations was accurate. All three misspelled the man's name; one, in addition, gave the English title but the date of the Swedish publication. Three references to Samuelsson appeared in the *Arts and Humanities Citation Index* in those same years. One article was listed in both sources, which means the grand total for both literatures comes to five citations. Only one of these citations, that in a specialized sociology of religion journal, was accurate. Both indexes in those same years list many references to *The Protestant Ethic*.

Marshall's critique fared somewhat better: a total of twenty-one citations were reported in the two indexes for the same four years. Five of these were repeated references, which means Marshall was cited in sixteen articles. None of those citations appeared in the three leading American sociology journals. One lesson is clear. The readers of social science and humanities literature are frequently told of the Weber thesis; it is regularly commended, but only rarely are they provided with references to works that challenge it. Those readers, typically, are told that Weber's many critics were mistaken, having failed to appreciate the basic argument, or have missed the "larger picture," or are attending to inessential details. In another context, however, a student of religious history might read the following: "The imaginative hypotheses of Weber and Troeltsch have been undermined by a winding procession of revisionist scholars: Sombart, Lujo Brentano, Tawney, Henri Hauser, Henri Sée, H. M. Robertson, Albert Hyma, George Harkness, Conrad Moehlmann, and André Sayous, not to mention the more recent contributors."[77]

A serious disparity has been shown in the treatments of the Weber thesis. It is highly regarded in sociology but is given little attention in the two fields most likely to have expert knowledge of the subject, Reformation history and economic history. This disparity points to a problem stemming from compartmentalization within the universities. The nonspecialist sociologists do not know what the specialists have said and done. The sociologists, accordingly, continue to present the thesis as well established, not recognizing its actual "hypothetical" standing. Weber's "sketch" remains a sketch some ninety years after its first exposition. The transformation of the hypothetical into the confirmed and the presentation of the argument in bold disregard of historical evidence (generated by two readily accessible groups of academic specialists) points to the operation of some extraintellectual factors or processes.

The operation of the extraintellectual may be seen in use of "saving" devices, of arguments to protect the theory from challenge. One of these points to Weber's larger enterprise. *The Protestant Ethic* is only a part of his world-historical project, one that reviewed the religions of China, India, and ancient Judaism. The suggestion is that one cannot assess the Protestant ethic "part" without consideration of those other components. But the argument is inappropriate; it is an obvious non sequitur. Claims about Luther's teachings, about Calvinism, or about Puritanism do not in any way require inquiry (or assessment) of claims about Taoism or Confucianism. Each part must stand on its own logic and evidence. Marshall reviews this line of defense and offers an appropriate conclusion: "Sociologists simply cannot escape the problems of historical counter-evidence, or more accurately . . . of the lack of substantiating evidence, by pleading for 'the big picture.'"[78]

Another "saving" procedure is to set stringent requirements for testing the thesis. If evidence on the psychological responses to specific doctrines were required, any test is effectively precluded, at least for historical experience. It is easy to locate centers of "Protestantism," but one cannot know with any certainty if predestination was accepted there, whether adherents felt a profound "inner isolation," whether they desperately sought a sign of their *certido salutis* (certainty of salvation), whether they, as a consequence, devoted themselves to their economic tasks, and whether they diligently accumulated and reinvested. The appropriate response, in the face of that historical problem, would be a conclusion of "not proven" or, more precisely, not known (or perhaps, hardly likely to be ever known). Yet in a remarkable declaration of faith, many sociologists, authors of sociology texts for example, have treated all of the hypotheses as proven.[79]

In the 1950s and early 1960s, a flurry of research activity designed to "test Weber" occurred, through the use of survey data from various American contexts. Most of those studies came up with negative findings. Those results were so persistently negative that one commentator, Andrew Greeley, appropriately called for a moratorium. Some of Weber's defenders objected to the entire operation, again on the basis of the stringent requirements. Instead of "examining the impact of specific beliefs," one commentator argued, "the researchers merely compared the members of two religious categories." Those researchers had not "made the proper Weberian analytical distinctions among types of Protestants." They did not check, for example, whether those Protestants "believed in predestination [or] viewed their jobs as a calling." Those studies are judged to be "poor-quality research." They did not "take seriously the rich analytical detail" of Weber's argument.[80]

This defense involves a double standard, since those later sociological studies are identical in form to the procedure Weber used in the opening pages of the monograph, that is, in his use of Offenbacher and others. He was examining behavioral correlates of religious affiliation, of Protestants and Catholics, with no investigation of "specific beliefs." Having established, to his satisfaction, a strong association between the two, Weber then read in his conclusion: "Thus the principal explanation of this difference must be sought in the permanent intrinsic character of their religious beliefs" (40). Weber is allowed a loose standard; his critics are held to a much more stringent requirement.

If a hypothesis is subjected to repeated test and not confirmed, a moratorium is one appropriate conclusion. If one argues that the tests are flawed, then more carefully designed tests are in order. But the common standard requires a recognition of the failed Weber-Offenbacher test. It calls for recognition of Weber's persistent failure to take seriously the implications of the "rich analytical detail" of his own argument. It was, and is, necessary to control for the many factors that could affect the religion–work ethic relationship. Without that necessary investigation of the relationship with *ceteris paribus,* one cannot be sure there is any "Protestant ethic" effect at all, let alone one that is "important." Consequently, until Weber's defenders work through those implications, the thesis will remain "not proven."

Another defense involves the claim of a termination date: the Protestant ethic was an important factor earlier, but later it no longer had any distinctive influence. Marshall argues this point: "By the eighteenth century, Weber maintains, the new capitalist mentality has . . . become wholly independent of its religious origins." Some supporting passages appear in Weber's original, the most compelling of which announces that "today . . . any relationship between religious beliefs and conduct is generally absent." One must, however, reconcile that pronouncement with his opening claim, that of "overwhelming" differences in Baden and elsewhere in the late-nineteenth century.[81] Again a double standard is involved: where later evidence appears to support the thesis, it is allowed and accepted, otherwise, the possibility is excluded a priori.

If Protestant and Catholic work efforts were substantially different prior to the eighteenth century, that point needs to be established. If a subsequent "conversion" occurred, with Catholics forced to assimilate and adopt the more demanding Protestant standard, that process too needs to be demonstrated. Otherwise, the claim is merely an easy out. One avoids a difficult problem—lack of support—by declaring a conversion, without any indication of when or where it happened and without any provision of supporting evidence.

Criticism is a normal feature of scholarly work. Where problems or outright errors are discovered, they should be signaled in subsequent comments and discussion, but that has not been the case with the Weber thesis. The work itself is canonized: it has become a "classic." In a parallel procedure, the author is described as a "prodigious scholar." Here too one sees the double standard. That adjective, *prodigious,* remarks on quantity or extent, but mention ought to be made also about the quality of that scholarship, about the erratic relationship between text and notes, about the implications of one-person "samples" for the depiction of world-historical movements, and about the absence of systematic evidence linking religion and economic development.[82]

Alternative Hypotheses

Marshall's summary conclusion, that the only reasonable verdict is "not proven," seems entirely appropriate. The implication for Weber's defenders is clear: provide the necessary proof. In the process, the serious researcher should also consider (and, if possible, test) alternative hypotheses to account for the rise of the West. Several alternatives will be reviewed here. All of these have appeared somewhere in previous literature. They are not ordinarily mentioned in discussions of the Weber thesis.

Carlo Cipolla, the noted economic historian, argued the importance of two technological innovations. England and the Netherlands developed ships that were larger and more seaworthy than those of other countries; they also developed superior cannons. The combination of the two innovations gave those nations a distinctive advantage. The large ship became a movable gun platform, allowing the concentration of unusual firepower on targets that could be approached by sea. Nations facing the Atlantic adopted the new techniques (with varying success and effectiveness). The two innovations made possible the "outreach program" known as the Age of Discovery. At the same time, however, Cipolla indicated, the new age began with a decisive defeat for "the West." The expansion of the Ottoman Turks disrupted the age-old trade routes to Asia, thus stimulating, in part at least, the search for Atlantic alternatives. The Turks moved into the Balkans, up the Danube, and into the heart of Europe, a movement that was not halted until the siege of Vienna in 1683. The technological advantages, the large ships and their guns, were of no use there.[83]

The Age of Discovery and the Turkish advances occurred simultaneously with the Reformation. Charles V, the Holy Roman emperor (and king of Spain), dealt with the conquest of the New World, with the Turks, and with Martin Luther. The New World provided a rich source of income for the Spanish treasury, but the large and complicated empire had to pay heavy costs to maintain its hegemony. The bullion that, with intelligent direction, might have gone into economic development, went instead to the creation and provisioning of armies and to the construction of vessels in Dutch shipyards.[84]

A peculiarity of the entire Weber controversy is an unwillingness to face up to basic economic facts. A nation with major expansionist ambitions, such as Spain (and later France), would have greater costs because of its sizable military establishment. Major continental powers, even if defensive in orientation, will ordinarily have more costly military requirements than nations on the periphery or those located behind natural barriers. Nations deriving much of their income through the sale of military services, mercenary nations, such as the German states, would also have high-cost government. The taxes required for the support of the military means a diversion of resources from other purposes, one of which could be investment for routine economic growth. Quite apart from the budgetary costs, men in the military are not producing goods. They are not developing productive skills. Officers are not learning entrepreneurial skills, at least not those required for economic development.

England (and later the United Kingdom), because of its insular setting, had distinctly lower military costs. Its army was ordinarily smaller, both in absolute numbers and in per capita terms, than those of its chief continental rivals. The naval costs were greater but still, on balance, total costs were lower, thus, "freeing," for the average citizen, a larger portion of household revenues for other purposes, either consumption or investment. Some tens or hundreds of thousands of men, moreover, were "freed" for productive economic activities (as compared to, for example, the many hours of infantry drill). Given the island location, surplus population could be "exported" to underdeveloped colonies where they could perform productive economic activities (versus idleness at home). England exported hundreds of thousands of its citizens; France, with its different concerns and incentives, kept men at home to fill those military needs. As of 1759, the date of Montcalm's defeat at Quebec, British North America had a population of 1.6 million, most of it of English, Scotch, or Scotch-Irish origin. New France, in contrast, had roughly 60,000 people. Those figures take on even greater significance when one recognizes the imbalance in the populations of the home countries, the United Kingdom having approximately 7.5 million and France about 23 million. The English colonies had a sizable, growing, and diversified trade with the United Kingdom, a trade that continued to grow even after American independence.[85]

Thus far, the discussion of the economic implications of military and geographic circumstances has treated only the "static" peacetime condition. Costs escalate dramatically in wartime. The outcomes also have economic implications. At the beginning of the seventeenth century, the Netherlands was part of the Spanish empire, but in a long and stubbornly fought struggle, the northern provinces gained their independence. After paying heavy wartime costs, Spain lost the Netherlands, its flourishing commercial center. The Dutch were also Europe's leading shipbuilders, a decisive fact for the outcome of the struggle. Because of the continued need for ships, Spanish silver continued to flow to Amsterdam even after independence.

The long military struggle in the Spanish Netherlands, according to one standard reading, stemmed from the underlying religious differences. Another reading was reported by Samuelsson. The Dutch historian Pieter Geyl, in 1955, argued the case for military determinants in the Netherlands outcome. The struggle with Spain did not involve an opposition of Dutch Protestants and Belgian Catholics. At the outset, according to Samuelsson's report, "the Protestants were no more numerous in the north than in the south." That geographic division was a result of the conflict, not a precipitating cause. The rivers that held up Field Marshal Montgomery's advance for months in 1944 had had the same impact centuries earlier. The rivers, it was argued, "enabled the rebellion to entrench itself in the North provinces while Spain recovered those situated on the wrong side of the strategic barrier."[86] Later, two large migrations occurred; Catholics moved south and Protestants moved north.

In the first half of the sixteenth century, Antwerp was the leading port city in the region, English merchants having chosen it as their major port of entry. The city "enjoyed a centrality in the economic activity of Europe that was nearly unique in history." But economic and political catastrophes followed. The settlement of the War of Liberation gave the Dutch control over the Rhine allowing access into the interior. The settlement blocked the mouth of the Scheldt, Antwerp's river, that city now being part of the Spanish Netherlands. That political fact "set the stage for" the subsequent advance of "Protestant" Amsterdam.[87]

A later major conflict began when Frederick of Prussia took Silesia from Maria Theresa of Austria. Tax revenues from Silesia (with a largely Catholic population) then flowed into the treasury of a "Protestant" nation. A series of wars followed, culminating in the Seven Year's War, in which Catholic Austria and Catholic France were defeated by Protestant Prussia and Protestant Britain. Britain acquired the entirety of New France. In 1763, France was left with a heavy debt burden, which had far-reaching implications for the nation's economy and political stability.

Another key consideration, one rarely given adequate attention, involves public finance. In the early sixteenth century, Spain looked to have a promising future, but a series of disastrous government decisions destroyed any possibility of a takeoff, producing instead four centuries of backwardness. Spain had the highest tax rates in Europe. A series of mistaken policies destroyed a flourishing woolen industry and ended some success in foodstuffs. France was favored with a large population, fertile lands, a central regime, and a powerful military establishment, but the government could not, or rather did not successfully organize its finances. The sale of offices was inefficient, costly, and socially corrosive. The system of tax farming had similar consequences. By contrast, the Netherlands and England had low-cost and efficient tax arrangements. While still problematic from the perspective of modern economics, those two nations, through trial and error, made unusual progress. Rondo Cameron traces this advancement to differences in the respective polities. The absolute monarchs of the age had little understanding of their developing, economies, and they had unchecked power to implement their policies. The greater pluralism in the Netherlands and, especially after 1688–1689, in England meant more effective input from people with a knowledge of business and commerce. The creation of the Bank of England made government borrowing easier and less costly than was the case in France or Spain. The lower interest rates that resulted also aided English commerce.[88]

Religions all have some kind of institutional apparatus which, depending on the size, could represent a significant or a modest charge for the supporting economy. Jacob Viner quoted Christopher Hill on this question: "The fact that Protestantism was a cheaper religion than Catholicism became a seventeenth-century commonplace." Viner noted that the observation "remained a commonplace in the eighteenth and nineteenth centuries," but Weber, he added, avoiding an obvious economic fact, "makes no reference to this theme in his explanation of . . . the relative economic backwardness of Catholic countries."[89]

Sociologists influenced by the Weber thesis have frequently noted the link of Protestantism and cities and, making unwarranted translation, think automatically of "the bourgeoisie." Spitz pointed up another option: "The clergy constituted a significant part of the population, in many cities, such as Worms, comprising at least 10 percent of the population." Six thousand of Cologne's 40,000 residents were clerics. Hamburg had 450 parish priests for a population of 12,000.[90] The total population figures would include children, hence the clerical presence among adults must have been much greater than even these figures suggest. With the Reformation and a dramatic shift of clergy into economically productive occupations, one would expect significant changes in economic growth quite independent of callings and predestination.

The confiscation and sale of church properties generated immense amounts of capital, which, presumably, was put to more productive use than was previously the case. If so, that too would have had some positive economic impact. How much weight, with ceteris paribus, should be assigned the calling? The "secularization" of church properties in Germany came at a relatively late point, in the early nineteenth century, an effort stimulated by the threat of Napoleon Bonaparte. This event, the *Säkularisation,* figures prominently in all serious histories of the period. With church income drastically reduced, many activities had to be abandoned, among them, the Catholic universities (eighteen of them) and church-sponsored primary and secondary schools. That shift had impacts for the Catholic population which, four score years later, appeared in Offenbacher's statistics.[91]

A reform movement within an established church would continue to be supported out of public funds. The same would hold for a breakaway movement which, as with Lutheranism or the Church of England, then became the established church. A reform movement that chose independence, however, had to be supported by its own members. For them, independence meant a new tithe to pay for the clergy, buildings, publications, transport, missions, and so forth. Those sums, obviously, were not available for reinvestment (at least not as conventionally understood). Those members choosing independence, moreover, were doubly taxed since ordinarily they were required to continue paying the costs of the established church.

The ethical teachings of any religion would also have some impact on the use of personal or household economic resources. Diligence in work, Weber's single-minded emphasis, is only one of many possible economic impacts of "religion." Daniel's discussion of Wenzeslaus Linck's activity in Nuremberg supports Weber on a key theme, the importance of the calling, albeit in conjunction with a notion of social responsibility. One relevant consideration in this connection is "last wills and testaments and the execution of legacies." Linck held that "gifts to the church, as endowments for the recitation of death masses . . . [entailed] was an exploitation of man by the church." The generous endowment, he argued, was stimulated not by freely willed choice, but by fear of damnation. He argued an opposite course: for economic and social reasons, it was "absolutely necessary" that goods be left to one's natural heirs "so that they would not be future burdens on society." His plea for "social justice and civic responsibility" was very popular and the sermon was reprinted and given wider circulation.[92] What weight, if any, should be assigned the calling and what weight given the change in inheritance patterns?

It is easy to make the purely logical case for asceticism: less drinking, smoking, and carousing would mean a greater "surplus" for capital investment. But have we seen a comparison of household accounts? Did the Puritans invest? Did they hoard their money? Or did they give it to the church in regular tithing? For poor people, the choice of asceticism as against wayward living would have considerable impact on a family's well-being. But what of the wealthy? How much difference would it make for them? The rather ascetic Baptist John D. Rockefeller had a large Euclid Avenue home in Cleveland and, later, a large home in New York City just off Fifth Avenue. How much difference did his—relative—asceticism make as compared, for example, with the luxury and extravagance of the Episcopalian J. P. Morgan? Again, have we seen the accounts? How much of their respective fortunes went into the household and idle consumption? How much did Morgan lose economically because of his art works, the library, and his famous yacht, the *Corsair*? Most of these questions are unanswered—most, in fact, are unasked.[93]

Apart from the Rockefeller and Morgan comparison, the hypotheses reviewed to this point touch on events occurring in the fifteenth to the seventeenth centuries, prior to what many scholars would count as the decisive development—the Industrial Revolution. Most accounts, for good reason, place the first of those transformations in the United Kingdom, basically in England. There is a longstanding struggle over the concept and the appropriate dates. Many scholars focus on the period from 1750 to 1850. Most accounts focus on the cotton industry and on Manchester and surrounding Lancashire. If the latter limitation is accepted, an even later dating of the revolution is appropriate. Cotton did not overtake woolens as the nation's leading export product until after 1800. The phenomenal growth of Manchester occurred in the 1830s and 1840s. These dates pose some problems for the Weber thesis. Almost two centuries intervened between the Puritan triumph in seventeenth-century England and this economic takeoff.[94]

Economic historians have provided a wide array of hypotheses to account for the development of "the West," only a small sample of which may be touched on here.[95] Early in the modern era England moved to eliminate internal trade barriers. Anticipating Adam Smith and the recommendations of liberal economics, a larger trade territory had been created. Geography also played a role, because the island location and navigable rivers made possible a coastal trade which also meant a larger economic base. In addition, in the eighteenth century, an extended infrastructure of canals and highways was built to link up that territory. The Industrial Revolution, moreover, was preceded by a series of innovations collectively termed the Agricultural Revolution. That development produced a healthier, longer-lived population, which, other things equal, would ordinarily mean a more productive population. The demographic revolution, which began in the middle of the eighteenth century, produced a demand for food, clothing, and housing, which, because of the prior innovations, could be met with reasonable success.

A series of inventions in the cotton industry—the flying shuttle, the carding machine, the spinning jenny, the water frame, and the cotton gin—made possible the breakthrough that most historians see as central to "the" Industrial Revolution. A parallel series of innovations led to the use of steam engines and coal as power sources and to the creation of the machine tool industry. The need for iron and steel, for frames in spinning and weaving, for steam engines, and later for rails, brought a third series of innovations and the development of another major industry. Some notion of the chronology is useful: the flying shuttle gained wide adoption in the 1750s and 1760s; the spinning jenny was patented in 1770; Whitney's cotton gin was introduced in the last decade of the century; use of the steam engine in textile manufacture "on a considerable scale" came only in the 1820s, 1830s, and 1840s.[96]

The explanations provided by economic historians focus on technology, on the sources of the innovations, and on social organization, the ability to adopt and use the inventions. It is striking that Phyllis Deane's account of the Industrial Revolution in Britain makes no mention of the Weber thesis. Rondo Cameron's economic history of the world, which of course deals with central Europe in the Reformation period and in the centuries thereafter, also makes no reference to Weber, to the calling, or to a Puritan work ethic. Deane and Cameron did not find it either necessary or useful to give so much as a paragraph to Weber's cultural and social psychological argument. David S. Landes's economic history of western Europe from 1750 provides a close parallel to Deane's and Cameron's in that his analysis centers on innovations and organization. It does, as noted earlier, give some attention to the Weber thesis, providing five paragraphs of exposition and two other paragraphs that give it some credence. The supporting evidence offered is very limited and scarcely compelling. In a work of 555 pages, the Protestant ethic does not appear to count for much.[97]

Weber and the "Ghost of Marx"

Many writers and commentators have portrayed the Weber thesis as an argument against Marx, a claim that seems immediately plausible. Albert Salomon, in 1945, wrote that Weber engaged "in a long and intense dialogue with the ghost of Karl Marx." That figure of speech appears frequently in the textbooks. Marshall cites five commentators who saw Weber's essay as a direct response to Marx. Marshall, however, reports an entirely different intellectual history. It developed out of themes covered in Weber's earlier work and was also a response to a controversy within the German universities, specifically between classical economics (rational, self-interested, calculating individuals) and the historical school (unique values associated with different training and traditions).[98]

A recent contribution supports Marshall's reading of the intellectual history and provides additional details. Friedrich Wilhelm Graf points to Weber's use of German theological sources and to Weber's concern with issues of Protestant church politics. "This heavy dependence on the theological discussion," Graf argues, "indicates that more value judgments, and specifically denominational ideology, are present in *The Protestant Ethic* than Weber himself realized or present interpreters are aware." Weber's argument, unexpectedly, is centered on the work of the Bern theologian Matthias Schneckenburger, who emphasized the differences between Lutheranism and Calvinism. He portrayed the former as generating passivity, the latter as generating activism. Schneckenburger also argued predestination as somehow the driving force. Another much-cited author in Weber's monograph is Albrecht Ritschl, the "most influential German-speaking Protestant theologian of the late nineteenth century." Ritschl played down the denominational differences, arguing that Protestantism generally was "the religion of progress" and that Catholicism was both backward and inferior. For Ritschl, Luther was "a true modernizer." In Weber's notes, Graf reports, no other author is "as frequently or contentiously [criticized] as Ritschl." Both theologians, clearly, assigned major importance to the "role of ideas" in human behavior. Their dispute was over the options—which ideas? Weber adopted the Schneckenburger argument for his purposes, taking Calvinism as the aggressive, driving force. For his argument about the development of capitalism, he had to focus on the English experience, on the role of Puritanism.[99]

It was the *Kulturkampf,* Bismarck's struggle against Catholicism, that provided the context for the controversy, not the *Sozialistenkampf.* Ritschl was arguing that Protestantism was a better religion than Catholicism. Along with many others, he was making a case that the social impacts of Protestantism were more desirable than those associated with Catholicism. Ritschl, who supported Bismarck in the "battle of the creeds," has been described as a National-Liberal theologian.[100] Weber carried this "battle" one step further, by making a crucial distinction within the Protestant camp.

Guenther Roth introduces his discussion of this issue with an unexpected observation: "The hatred [Weber] felt for his Lutheran heritage and the German authoritarian realities was so great that he modeled his notion of ethical personality and innerworldly asceticism to a considerable extent after an idealized image of English history, especially of Puritanism." In 1906, in a letter discussing *The Protestant Ethic,* Weber wrote: "The fact that our nation never went through the school of hard asceticism, in no form whatsoever, is the source of everything that I hate about it (and about myself)." The "radical idealism" of the Protestant sects, those of England and America, had produced the modern "freedom of conscience and the most basic rights of man," values he ardently defended. But that crucial formative experience was missing in Germany. In 1911, to another correspondent, he wrote that "a people which, as we Germans, has never dared to behead the traditionalist powers will never gain the proud self-assurance that makes the Anglo-Saxons and Latins (*Romanen*) ... so superior to us in the world." In her biography of her husband, Marianne Weber wrote that *The Protestant Ethic* "is connected to the deepest roots of his personality and in an undefinable way bears its stamp."[101]

The index to Marianne Weber's biography of her husband contains only six references to Marx, marxism, or marxists. Two of these are positive: "Weber expressed great admiration for Karl Marx's brilliant constructions and saw in the inquiry into the economic and technical causes of events an exceedingly fruitful, indeed, a specifically new heuristic principle that directed the quest for knowledge into entire areas previously unilluminated"; and "Weber suspected all political metaphysics up to that time as a kind of mimicry by which the privileged classes protected themselves against a rearrangement of the spheres of power. In this respect he shared Karl Marx's conception of the state and its ideology.[102]

The "ghost of Marx" claim, although not entirely without foundation, seems somewhat exaggerated, an overstatement. It appears to be still another social misconstruction. For marxists, it serves a useful purpose: that Germany's leading sociologist felt it necessary, supposedly, to mount such a challenge is proof of the importance of the marxian theory.

4

Hitler's Electoral Support

On 30 January 1933, Germany's president, Paul von Hindenburg, named Adolf Hitler as the nation's chancellor. The naming of Hitler was made possible by a remarkable series of electoral victories. Hitler's party, the National Socialist German Workers' Party (NSDAP), had gained less than 3 percent of the vote in May 1928. In September 1930, they took 18 percent of the total. Two years later, in July 1932, they jumped to 37 percent and became the nation's largest party. It was one of the most rapid electoral changes in the entire modern era.

The leading explanation for the National Socialist electoral victories, the dominant received paradigm, focuses on the lower middle class. That class, so it is said, suffered serious economic strains, faced a loss of status and, in desperation, reacted by abandoning the liberal middle-class parties in favor of Hitler and his party. The prime motive, again so it is said, was the party's promise to restore the lower middle class to its former position. That argument is a social misconstruction. Although widely accepted, the principal claims were put forth without any serious compelling evidence. At best, they were unsupported hypotheses. That agreed-upon reading misdirected our understanding of those world-historical events, for more than a half century. Some readily available evidence indicates other lines of analysis to be more appropriate.

This chapter will undertake five principal tasks. The first of these is to review some basic findings about the German elections of 1928, 1930, and 1932. The findings to be reported are sharply at variance with the lower-middle-class explanation. The initial review points to a range of new explanatory questions that should be at the center of our thinking and research; the statement of these new questions is the second task of this chapter. A third task is to provide an alternative explanation that accords with the evidence currently available. This provides a positive statement, focusing on a different and more appropriate range of causal factors operating in those elections. The fourth task is to provide some answers to that range of new explanatory questions posed as the chapter's second task. A more wide-ranging discussion follows, reviewing the experience of other nations and of other times. The aim of this discussion, the fifth task, is to provide additional tests of the original theory and of the alternative put forth here. The history of this social misconstruction, of its origins and perpetuation, is the subject of the next chapter.

This chapter summarizes and updates the arguments presented in my book *Who Voted for Hitler?* (1982).[1] There I reviewed the claims made about Germany's lower middle class. First, I concluded that the claims had been put forward without any serious supporting evidence. Second, I reviewed the then-available evidence (national, regional, and local) and indicated my arguments for considering another hypothesis—that the lower middle class did *not* provide exceptional support for Hitler's party. Third, to support that claim, I visited the archives of some major cities of Germany and examined the available voting records. No support for the lower-middle-class claim was found in those records; in most of the cities studied, the support for the NSDAP varied directly with class, it being greatest in the most affluent areas. The detailed findings and the alternative explanation of "the rise of Nazism" are summarized here.

Another researcher, Jürgen W. Falter, began work on Weimar-era voting patterns at about the same time as I did. He and his co-workers assembled a unique database, which contains comprehensive voting results for all of Germany's national elections from 1919 to 1933. For purposes of analysis, these researchers wished to have results for the smallest possible reporting units. Changes in district boundaries presented serious difficulties but these were overcome through painstaking efforts of combination. As a result, one can follow the voting (and nonvoting) patterns in 831 counties (*Kreise*) which, when combined, are identical with the national totals. In addition, Falter and his colleagues added data from other sources, mainly from the census, on the characteristics of the populations living in those districts (such as age, religion, occupation).

This extraordinary database allows a comprehensive detailed portrait of Germany's electorate over the fourteen-year period. It also allows systematic testing of a large range of explanatory hypotheses. There is, to the best of my knowledge, no comparable source available for any other nation in the world. The possibilities opened up surpass anything previously undertaken. With rare exceptions, all future studies of the German electorate in the Weimar period will have to begin with this set of data.

A score of articles by Falter and his associates dealing with Weimar voting patterns appeared in the eighties and early nineties. Falter's comprehensive book on the subject, *Hitlers Wähler* (Hitler's voters), was published in 1991. Key findings from his study will be reported in the following pages. As indicated, for their sweep and comprehensiveness (on the themes of religion and community size, two examples from among many), those results go far beyond my earlier effort. In one respect, the studies are complementary. Falter's study presents combined results for all of Germany's cities, for Berlin, Hamburg, Cologne, Munich, and so forth. My study provides evidence for subareas (upper class, upper middle class, mixed, working class) within a sample of the nation's largest cities.[2]

Hitler's Electoral Support

The National Socialists made their first electoral appearance, in coalition with another group, in the May 1924 Reichstag election only six months after Hitler's failed Munich *putsch*. Together they gained 6.5 percent of the vote. Their total fell to 3.0 percent in the second Reichstag election that year, in December. Four years later, no longer in coalition, the NSDAP total declined to 2.6 percent in the election of May 1928. That low figure, however, was deceptive. In 1929, prior to the onset of the Depression, the National Socialists began again to pick up votes in state and local elections. Then, in the Reichstag election of September 1930, they "exploded" onto the scene with 18.3 percent of the total. The gains continued: in July 1932, they received 37.3 percent of the votes cast.

The commentators of the age had a ready explanation—it was the reaction of the petty bourgeoisie gone mad. In another version, the key phrase was *Panik im Mittelstand,* panic in the middle class. The argument of an impoverished, proletarianized petty bourgeoisie has been the leading explanation for the rise of the NSDAP. From 1930 to the present it has appeared in countless repetitions. Among those scholars who have proclaimed this "truth" are Theodor Geiger, Harold Lasswell, Erich Fromm, Alan Bullock, Sigmund Neumann, C. Wright Mills, Seymour Martin Lipset, William Kornhauser, Joachim Fest, and Karl Dietrich Bracher. It would be easy to name dozens of others. That key phrase is the title of a famous article published in 1930 by the German sociologist Theodor Geiger, who extended the basic argument, again without supporting evidence, in an even more famous book published in 1932. In 1933, a young political scientist, Harold Lasswell, presented the basic claims of the position in English, in an article destined to have considerable influence. The best summary statement of the position in English is provided by Seymour Martin Lipset in a chapter published in 1960. That chapter, entitled " 'Fascism'—Left, Right, and Center," signaled some grounds for caution by challenging the general claim of a link between the lower middle class and fascism.[3]

A serious problem appears in these statements: the term *lower middle class* is rarely defined. In most instances only a listing of typical occupations is provided. The most important single occupation in such listings is "farmer" (or "peasant"). Small town and village middle-class populations, most of them shopkeepers, are also included as lower middle class, as petty bourgeoisie or *Kleinbürger.* The poorly paid salaried white-collar employees are also regularly counted as members of the class. A listing of occupations, however, the presentation of "typical" examples, is not a definition. The absence of definition points to a serious failing—absence of research on the subject. Much of the previous effort, in short, has been casual and imprecise, depending on assertion and mutual agreement rather than actual investigation.

The accounts of the lower middle class, moreover, are not typically accompanied by consideration of the logical counterpart, that is, of an upper middle class. Most writers in this tradition have settled for the crude distinction of bourgeoisie and petty bourgeoisie. In most accounts the "upper middle class" does not exist or, alternatively, is not worthy of attention. If, following Geiger, one assumes a tiny bourgeoisie, roughly 1 percent of the total, the entire remaining nonmanual rank would be lower middle class. But that would make little sense, at least not in terms of the

received paradigm, since many of that group would not be marginal, insecure, facing proletarianization, and so forth.

Still another problem with the received analyses stems from the categorical nature of the formulations. A division of haute bourgeoisie versus
petite bourgeoisie (or an upper-middle- versus lower-middle-class dichotomy) makes an arbitrary separation within a broad continuous range of experience. Unlike the "line" separating the manual and nonmanual
employees, no such sharp distinction runs through the nonmanual rank to
allow such easy judgments, that one position, for example, is unambiguously lower middle and another upper middle. Here one is dealing with a
continuum, a series of small variations based on income, education, job
security, or numbers under one's immediate supervision or control.

Although National Socialist electoral support has most frequently been
described and explained in terms of class, specifically in terms of lower-
middle-class concerns and susceptibilities, the party's following was, and
is, more appropriately described in terms of religion. Support for the
NSDAP was sharply differentiated by religion. Protestants, particularly in
villages and small towns, showed a marked attraction to Hitler's party.
Catholics, in equivalent settings, showed an equally marked aversion. In
July 1932, support for the party, overall, varied inversely with size of
place, the percentages in large cities generally being well below the national figure. But that overall result combines, and thus hides, two opposing patterns. The level of support for the NSDAP was very high in the rural
communities and small towns of Protestant Germany and fell off considerably in the larger communities. An opposite pattern appeared in Catholic communities at that point, National Socialist support being very low in
the villages and towns, then increasing somewhat in the larger cities.

The religion linkage, especially that seen in the villages and towns, is
one of the oldest and best established of all conclusions on the subject. An
illustration: in the Heidelberg area, among the small farm communities
were Catholic Dilsberg and Protestant Ochsenbach. In the second round
of the 1932 presidential election, those communities gave Hitler 16.3 and
94.1 percent, respectively, of the votes cast. Similar findings appeared
throughout rural Germany (a result, incidentally, that was immediately
evident in the voting figures published on the Mondays following each of
the elections of the early 1930s). One would have to look far and wide in
the literature on electoral behavior to find a disparity of that size and consistency anywhere in modern times. That finding, in the ordinary course

of things, should have led observers to consider the implications of the religious linkage. But most of them neglected that obvious task and instead proceeded to "explain" the not-yet-established lower-middle-class "finding."[4]

An article by Hermann Mulert stressed the importance of the religious factor in the elections of the period. It appeared in Germany's major political science journal in the early 1930s, but the article is rarely cited; the lesson provided has been ignored. Geiger's seventeen-page article contained only two passing mentions of the religious influence, and Lasswell's contained no indication of the Protestant-Catholic differences in NSDAP support. Karl Rohe, a leading social historian, has provided a useful summary statement: "From the beginning of mass politics up until the present religion has proved to be the most important influence in German electoral and party politics."[5]

Some commentators dismiss the religion finding, claiming that it has been noted and given due attention. Although "known all along," however, the implications are regularly neglected. The "most important influence" ought to be central to analyses of the rise of Nazism and, moreover, some explanation should be provided. Another problem requires attention—the general claim of a lower-middle-class reaction is challenged by this "known" finding. The class claim could possibly have been valid within Protestant Germany but that was not likely within Catholic Germany where "class" would have been of trivial importance. Apart from the basic problem (establishing the importance of the claim in any context), some specification, some additional argument is needed to account for the differences. Why did Protestants and Catholics who were engaged in the same lines of activity, facing the same markets, the same crisis, and threatened by the same fate, react in such markedly different ways?

The opposite correlations between religion and size of city in 1932 means that the differences by religion are attenuated in the larger cities. The comparison of Protestant Berlin and Catholic Cologne, for example, finds a difference in the July 1932 Reichstag election of only 5 percentage points, the respective figures being 29 and 24. Between Protestant Hamburg and Catholic Munich we find a similar result, those figures, respectively, being 33 and 29.[6] Religion, which was such a powerful factor in accounting for the NSDAP support in the small towns and rural areas, proves to be of minor importance in the cities. The two patterns of linkage with community size, like the religion tie, should also have been the subject of some effort at explanation. But again, having neglected the fact, the commentators had no incentive to provide an explanation.[7]

The urban context offers an important opportunity for research: it is perhaps the easiest setting in which to test the lower-middle-class hypothesis. Approximately one-third of Germany's population at that time lived in cities of one hundred thousand or more. Within that setting, for the reason just indicated, a discounting of the religious factor is justified. There, one may proceed directly to the claims of the lower-middle-class argument.

Until recently we have had no detailed analyses of voting patterns within the German cities. As a consequence, no systematic assessment of the lower-middle-class thesis in those settings had ever been undertaken. The principal finding of my review of voting records in fourteen of Germany's largest cities was a general tendency for NSDAP voting to increase with the class level of the neighborhood. In Hamburg, for example, where the party gained one-third of the vote in July 1932, the strongest support came from the three best-off districts, the percentages ranging from 41 to 48. The metropolitan area's most affluent suburban community gave the National Socialists 54 percent. With corrections, adjusting for the presence of Jews, Catholics, and working-class minorities, the levels for the remaining upper- and upper-middle-class voters would run well above those figures.[8]

Lower-middle-class families were not located in separate areas within those cities. Some appeared, as small minorities, in working-class districts, others were located in mixed districts with roughly equal numbers of manual and nonmanual families. The voting tendencies of urban lower-middle-class populations, therefore, cannot be established with any certainty. None of the mixed districts, however, provided majority support for the NSDAP. Those areas typically voted NSDAP at a level approximately equal to that of the city as a whole, at a level, in other words, that was not at all distinctive.

The only way the accepted claim could be valid in this context would be if workers in those districts had voted overwhelmingly for the parties of the Left. That, in turn, would have meant "opposite" overwhelming majorities for the NSDAP by the middle-class groups living there. No such divergence of preferences was established at the time, nor has such evidence been offered in the years since. On the contrary, some evidence points instead to an alternative conclusion, namely, a general similarity of political outlooks. A fair-sized minority of the lower middle class in the cities, possibly as much as 35 to 40 percent, supported the leftist parties, principally the Social Democrats. Another fair-sized segment would have supported the Zentrum (the Center, the Catholic party). And some, even in the late elections, would have continued to support the so-called middle-class parties. Some also, of course, supported the German Nationalists. Taken all together, the evidence suggests that the majority of the urban lower middle class did not support the NSDAP; only a minority responded to the suasions of the demagogues.[9]

These findings also show that "the lower middle class" was not all of a piece. The category contained three rather diverse segments, Protestants in villages and towns, Catholics in villages and towns, and a rather mixed urban group. Since each had a distinct voting tendency, separate and appropriate lines of analysis are required.

The working-class districts typically provided only minority support for the NSDAP on the order of 20 to 25 percent. However, because of the large number of such districts and their high population densities, those votes added up to a significant part of the NSDAP strength, in some cities providing roughly half of the party's total. In addition, those votes had a clear immediate antecedent; they were cast by persons who had previously voted for the liberal "middle-class" parties or, to a lesser extent, for the Nationalists. These votes, in other words, were cast by Germany's equivalent of the Tory workers. Any adequate theory of the rise of Hitler must recognize the quantitative importance of this working-class support and provide some explanation for it. The voting patterns of workers, of several component subgroups of the class, will be reviewed later in this chapter.

The conclusions reported to this point are summarized in Table 4.1, which provides data from the Falter project. One may see the inverse relationship with size of community in the largely Protestant and mixed districts, the modest reversal of that pattern in the largely Catholic districts, and, in the bottom line, the reduction of the religious differences in the larger communities. The difference in the smallest communities is less than was indicated earlier, this because of the low NSDAP percentage—44.6. That low figure stems from two methodological choices, first, from the use of the broad category—"less than 25 percent" Catholic—which means the result, to some extent, combines the two sharply opposed confessional tendencies. A "purer" category, less than 20 or less than 10,

Table 4.1   National Socialist Strength by Size of Community and Religion (July 1932)

Percent Catholic	Less than 2,000	2,000 to 5,000	5,000 to 20,000	20,000 to 100,000	More than 100,000
			Size of Community		
			(NSDAP Percentages[a])		
A. Less than 25	44.6	40.2	38.8	36.1	28.8
B. 25 to 75	34.2	35.3	28.2	30.1	26.1
C. 75 to 100	16.9	17.0	15.1	21.3	20.3
A − C Difference	27.7	23.2	23.7	14.8	8.5

[a]From Falter, et al., *Wahlen*, 178 (cited in note 7).
NSDAP = Nationalsozialistiche Deutsche Arbeiterpartei (National Socialist German Workers' Party).

would yield higher NSDAP figures. Second, Falter's percentages are based, for good reasons, on the eligible electorate including the nonvoters. This yields lower percentages for all parties. Nonvoting was slightly higher among Catholics; it was especially high in the Catholic villages.

For a brief synoptic portrait, three summary statements are required: that the NSDAP vote was generally high in Protestant Germany, the level in 1932 varying inversely with size of community; that the party's support was generally low in Catholic Germany, the level increasing somewhat in larger communities; and that in the cities the vote increased with the class level of the district. That "economical" account provides only a description; it does not explain the result. The three statements do, however, indicate which results need explaining.

Those summary statements do not accord with any of the current accounts of the National Socialist electoral victories—not with the lower-middle-class theory, nor with mass society claims, nor with the cultural argument, nor with the psychohistorical accounts.

The mass society theory begins with a sweeping assumption of breakdown. The traditional communal bases of modern society, it is claimed, have been destroyed through the corrosive impacts of urbanization, industrialization, increasing mobility, competitiveness, and so on. "Modern man," as a result, is left isolated and helpless. The corresponding high state of anxiety leaves "him" vulnerable to demagogic appeals, such as, for example, those provided by Adolf Hitler and his party. This theory, like the lower-middle-class argument, overlooks important evidence. That religion was the leading correlate of NSDAP voting demonstrates the continuing importance of one traditional communal base. The pathologies of the mass society are, typically, located in the large cities. The theory, however, overlooks the relative immunity of the large cities. The National Socialist infection was most serious in Protestant villages. Rudolf Heberle, in an important study, described one such area as follows: on the Geest, a region of small farms, "class distinctions are scarcely noticeable, and a spirit of neighborliness and true community prevails. . . . It was here that the Nazi party . . . scored its greatest successes."[10]

Dozens of works have argued the cultural explanation, essentially that Germany had a distinctively problematic intellectual and artistic tradition. The psychohistorical school focuses on the war, on the absence of fathers, the loss of fathers, as well as other the war-related deprivations. The basic problem with both positions is the lack of fit between the claims put forth and the actual voting results. The cultural argument must explain why the effects are so pronounced in Protestant as opposed to Catholic Germany and why, in the former regions, they are so strong in the villages and towns. The same locational questions have to be addressed by the psychohistorians. In addition, the same causes appeared in World War II without the equivalent effects.[11]

The Explanatory Questions

The explanatory questions that require consideration, the second of the present tasks, are very much altered by these results. One must ask, first, why there was such heavy support for the National Socialists in the Protestant towns and villages. In some villages, the support ran to 100 percent. Where their support went to "only" 70 or 80 percent, most of the remaining votes went to the Social Democrats. Since the latter were likely to have been working-class votes, the overwhelming majority of all other segments of provincial society, from the lower-middles to the upper-uppers (to borrow the now-antique terms of sociologist William Lloyd Warner), would have been voting heavily for the NSDAP, at levels in the middle or high eighties. The differences between any of these segments would have been of trivial importance. That being the case, even here the focus on the *lower*-middle-class segment seems misplaced.

The second explanatory question that must be addressed involves the Catholic towns and villages. The question is, Why was the response there so limited? Despite crisis, presumed status strains, and so forth, the voting patterns continued with little change. A third question needing attention involves the city-size relationship, the principal problem here being the lower susceptibility (or heightened resistance) of the Protestant cities in face of the NSDAP siege. What was it that limited the NSDAP success in these contexts? There is an obvious counterpart, a fourth question, namely, Why did the National Socialists have somewhat greater success in the Catholic cities?

One must consider the various class segments supporting the NSDAP within the cities, which poses the fifth question: Why was there such pronounced support for the party within the upper and upper middle classes? Recognizing the existence of some urban lower-middle-class support, we have a sixth explanatory question: What were the sources of the (probable) minority tendency? Was it the loss of position and the threat of proletarianization that moved this group, or was it something else?

A seventh explanatory question involves the voting of urban workers, particularly of the minority that "turned to the right." A standard cliché has it that "the workers" will move to the Left as a result of the economic disaster. The catastrophe will "remove the veil," destroying whatever remains of false consciousness. The growth of the Communist vote in the last Weimar elections, at first glance, appears to confirm that claim, but most of those gains came at the expense of the Social Democrats. The overall vote for the Left decreased in September 1930 and did so again in July 1932. The non-Left minority of the working class, as far as we can tell, shifted to the National Socialists.[12] An important question must be addressed here: Why did those workers shift to the Right rather than, as was so widely anticipated, moving to the Left?

An Alternative Explanation

The third task is to outline an alternative explanation. This begins with the assumption that individual political dispositions are the results of primary and secondary political socialization. One may think of voting decisions as the products of early training as modified by subsequent influences. Parents typically provide children with basic political values and teach them appropriate party preferences. Later in life, people come to be located in settings that, in most cases, reinforce those original dispositions.[13] The German experience, however, is complicated by serious discontinuities in these processes. Only two parties, the Social Democrats and the Zentrum, survived 1918. All others were new creations, although in most cases the links to a prewar predecessor were easily recognized.

Then too, numerous catastrophes had occurred in the two decades prior to Hitler's accession. There was the war, the revolution, the Treaty of Versailles, putsch attempts from the Left and Right, inflation, border struggles, and the worldwide Depression. This collection of events could easily loosen or break the tenuous party loyalties first formed in the early postwar period.

Many German voters could not have been guided by their early political socialization because the specific parties recommended by their parents (in most cases, by fathers) had disappeared. Weimar party loyalties do not appear to have been as fixed or committed as some present-day discussions of political socialization assume. Many voters were likely to have been guided by a general political direction or tendency rather than by a well-ingrained party loyalty. When a chosen party lost viability, the voter was stimulated to search for a next best alternative. The choice, in most cases, would have been limited to parties having the same general political direction.

Those choices were not made solely on the basis of "individual" factors (unique personal judgments of current political events). They would have been channeled by a range of guiding influences touching the voters. The most likely subsequent influences in Weimar Germany were, first, the direction provided by traditional notables, or opinion leaders. This category would include leaders of the "established" parties, religious leaders, employers, and, in general, persons of high status or reputation. There is a tendency to identify notables with parties of the Right or center, but parties of the Left also have their notables, August Bebel and Wilhelm Liebknecht being the classic examples in the Social Democratic Party (SPD).

The second guiding influence that might modify or change patterns of primary socialization would be the mass media, specifically the press. In the Weimar period newspapers constituted the only significant mass medium of communication; radio, mass-circulation magazines, and television came later.

The third influence in the late twenties was provided by the National Socialists, the principal new entry among the political actors of the era. The influences discussed to this point are all proximate in character, touching directly the various segments of the electorate. The possibility of two-step flows of influence should also be kept in mind; some voters would be influenced by the press or by the National Socialist activists and they, in turn, would pass on their newfound judgments to other voters.

Of the three influences—notables, the press, and militants—the last was probably the most important. The National Socialist militants delivered the message, bringing the party's offerings to the towns and villages. Without that organizational weapon, there was little chance for their appeals to be heard, let alone be heard with sympathy. The only other channel of communication would have been the press. Prior to the party's rise, the provincial press was either blandly neutral or supported the traditional parties of the Right and center. It was the NSDAP's direct communication, its use of militants as a "transmission belt," that brought about the dramatic voting shifts which in turn led to the changed orientations of the local notables and much of the press. Without the militants, moreover, there would have been no heroics for newspapers to report, no grounds for favor, and no reason for any sympathy or conversion. The militants appear to have been the decisive force, the key agency generating the electoral upsurge. The electoral victories would not have occurred without their efforts. For this reason, it is necessary to move back a step in the causal chain to account for both the numbers and capacities of these cadres.

We do not have precise figures on party memberships over the fourteen years of the Weimar Republic. Even more serious, we have no "hard" evidence on the proportions of activists (or militants) among the members. The NSDAP clearly had large numbers of devoted followers, both in the party itself and in its paramilitary force, the storm troops (*Sturmabteilung* or, for short, S.A.). These numbers showed rapid increases in the last years of the republic, beginning in 1929. Although the NSDAP aimed to break into the ranks of the "marxist" parties, its principal electoral gains came at the expense of the so-called middle-class parties. Although a massive shift in voter preferences occurred, the same does not appear to have been the case with party cadres. It appears that the "middle-class" party cadres retired, gave up, or were immobilized; the NSDAP cadres represented a mobilization from different social bases.[14]

An array of monographic studies attests to the high level of organizational ability demonstrated by these NSDAP cadres. One author describes them as possessing "energy, efficiency and virtuosity," traits certainly demonstrated in their electoral practice.[15] Unlike the four- or five-week campaigns of their competitors, they engaged in continuous electioneering. Their efforts were accompanied by a regular two-way flow of information; local units were required to report their experience with various themes and tactics to party headquarters in Munich. Those reports were then distilled and the lessons disseminated to local units across the land. The campaign effort, it should be emphasized, was self-financing. The party charged admission to meetings, which covered expenses and generated a surplus for subsequent campaign efforts. Campaigning, for them, was a paying business. A speakers' school trained and accredited orators, giving its trainees confidence, polish, and the appearance of a mastery of complex materials. A key question is how the party came to have such numbers and such high-level talent and capability.

The NSDAP cadres had their origins in World War I. Four years of combat had trained men in "energy, efficiency, and virtuosity"—and also in ruthlessness—all of these traits being necessary for battlefield survival. The November 1918 revolution and the Armistice provided material for a deleterious "misconstruction," for the "stab-in-the-back" myth, the claim that the troops in the field had been cheated out of victory (or at least cheated out of a stalemate and a negotiated settlement). In many cities, revolutionary mobs provided a hostile reception for the returning troops, the antagonism being directed especially toward the officers.

The Treaty of Versailles forced a major institutional change within German society with its requirement that the military establishment be drastically reduced. Some hundreds of thousands of professional military men were turned out of the ranks and forced into civilian careers. To those numbers must be added some other hundreds of thousands, the members of younger cohorts who aspired to careers in the military. Many of those reluctant civilians sought out analogous occupations in the new Germany, some finding a first opportunity in the Freikorps, in the hastily formed select military units intended to keep order at home and to secure the front in the border conflicts continuing in the east. With the dissolution of these units in 1920 the options remaining were a range of private paramilitary organizations. The S.A. proved the ultimate winner, being the toughest, the most "resourceful," the most aggressive of the various contenders. In the process, in this flow from one organization to the next, the "old fighters," with some system, enlarged their ranks by recruiting from among the younger cohorts, picking up and training persons who demonstrated the requisite aptitudes and talents.

The people who followed this career line were persons who in one way or another were very much committed to the military venture of

1914–1918. Recruitment for the Freikorps was heaviest among the lieutenants and, to a lesser degree, among noncommissioned officers (NCOs). Many lieutenants took positions as NCOs, preferring that to their next best option, civilian life. Those persons obviously had extensive combat experience, and, more to the point, experience in leadership roles. They would have supplied the initiative, organization, and direction in frontline combat, that is, in small-scale, tactical struggle. A social darwinist dynamic operates in such situations: survival depends on the development of commitment and the acquisition of tactical expertise. Given the select character of such units, given their recruitment of "war lovers," it should come as no particular surprise that they proved to be tough, aggressive, and ruthless.

Other soldiers, those not devoted to military careers or interests, were demobilized and, either again or for the first time, took up civilian careers. They came from all class backgrounds, upper and upper middle class, some from the lower middle class, and many from the working class. Given the close correspondence of military and civilian ranks, most of the latter groups would have served as privates or lower-level noncommissioned officers during World War I. The effects of sustained combat on a worker-turned-soldier would have been different from those experienced by the young officers. The ex-workers, on the whole, would not have developed the same commitment to the task. Foot-dragging, indifference, and pacifist sentiments would probably have been greatest in these ranks. Most important for the later "inputs" to civilian life, these soldiers were followers; they were not trained to lead, to plan, to show initiative, to make quick decisions in tactical struggles. When some of them were later organized in leftist paramilitary formations, their orientations, accordingly, were defensive in character. They protected their territory, the working-class neighborhoods, from outside incursions. They did not invade or push into new territory. The strongholds of the Left did, on the whole, successfully resist the National Socialist siege. But they did not gain new recruits within their territory, nor did they gain elsewhere. As noted earlier, the Left suffered some overall losses, mostly of Social Democratic workers located outside those urban bastions.[16]

The National Socialist cadres had their greatest success where they moved against traditional parties of notables that were poorly prepared to defend themselves against a formidable onslaught. This was most clearly the case in the Protestant towns and countryside. The parties there consisted only of a handful of elderly notables. Political power, typically, was passed on from father to son. Campaigning there had amounted to little more than coasting along with a routine of handed-down election procedures. The power of the notables would have been weakened by wartime losses; their sons, disproportionately, would have been among the fallen. Thus, in the late twenties, when the young, "tough," and "resourceful" NSDAP activists appeared on the scene, they were moving against a weakened coterie, persons with no staff, no bureaucracy, and no defense forces. At this time, as the economy deteriorated and the NSDAP attacks intensified, many notables began to distance themselves from their parties, this being especially the case with the two liberal parties. Reflecting the same circumstances, those parties experienced a disaffection of "their" newspaper support.

The argument delineated to this point may be summarized as follows. First is the social psychological component, the assumption of early political socialization as decisive for adult outlooks and party preferences. That primary socialization would, in all settings, be modified by subsequent experience. Four years of sustained frontline combat would, for many, result in significant transformations of those previous outlooks. Some additional "socialization" episodes were associated with the outcome of the conflict, yielding a sense of illegitimacy with respect to both the result and the new regime.

An important social structural change occurred at that point: the Treaty of Versailles required, among other things, a drastic reduction of the size of the armed forces. That transformation, in turn, forced a considerable amount of social mobility, injecting large numbers of unwilling "participants" into civilian roles. It proved possible, nevertheless, for the most devoted of the ex-military men to maintain their ranks, to develop and "refine" their talents, and to add to their numbers. The NSDAP proved the ideal agency for the harnessing of their energies. Created by men of the war generation, the party was a vehicle ideally suited for their aims, needs, and talents. The cadres, in summary, were created out of the wartime experience and the events accompanying its outcome—rather than being products of lower-middle-class life and circumstances.

Thus far, this account has sketched out the likely channels of social influence, both the routine or traditional ones and the newly arrived agency on the scene. It is necessary, in addition, to consider the content of the NSDAP's communications. The "message" had to have a logic, or at least the appearance of a logic. The NSDAP cadres had to provide some plausible solutions for the concerns felt by their listeners. To address this problem, some aspects of the party's efforts during the last years of the republic must be reviewed.

The party was outlawed after the November 1923 Munich putsch. After its refounding in 1925, the NSDAP achieved only a rather slow, erratic, and, on the whole, inauspicious growth. This was the case until 1929 when, just prior to the Depression, the party managed a remarkable take-off. This surge came in the course of the Anti–Young Plan Campaign organized by Alfred Hugenberg and his associates. Hugenberg, the owner of a major press empire and also chairman of the reactionary German National People's Party, had formed a coalition of national forces to halt further implementation of the Treaty of Versailles. The idea was to run an initiative to block the Young Plan (which revised reparations terms and payment schedules). In a decision that was fateful for the republic, Hugenberg brought the National Socialists into this coalition. His newspapers, wire services, and syndicated materials, throughout eight months of agitation, provided legitimation for Hitler and his party. Hugenberg consequently made the National Socialists *salonfähig*, that is, socially acceptable. It was the first time since the 1923 putsch debacle that they had such support, such sanction from "respectable" forces.

An informal division of labor developed in the course of the campaign. Hugenberg provided the press support; Hitler and his forces undertook the grass-roots campaigning. Local observers reported that the NSDAP militants used the occasion primarily to advertise the merits of their own party. It was in the course of the eight months of the Anti–Young Plan Campaign that the party, as indicated by state election results, made its breakthrough, this before the onset of serious economic difficulties.[17]

Given the occasion, NSDAP propaganda was very much focused on the Treaty of Versailles. The war guilt clause, understandably, came in for heavy attack. Reparations also, of course, figured prominently in the party's repertory of complaint. The "guilty" regime was also the object of considerable abuse. The unexpected calling of a Reichstag election in late summer 1930, so soon after the end of the Anti–Young Plan effort, meant that the enlarged and experienced NSDAP cadres could easily shift over to a general election campaign. With the Depression already at crisis level, the party could rerun the themes used in the Anti–Young Plan Campaign, pointing to the reparations as the source of Germany's economic disaster and, in the process, emphasizing the accuracy of their previous analysis.

The parties in power at this time, along with the SPD, were following a policy of "fulfillment" with respect to the Versailles obligations. For them, no simple response to the NSDAP attacks was possible. Guided by the best available economic thought of the day, the governing parties followed a strict laissez-faire economic policy, thus favoring deflation in the midst of what was already a serious deflationary crisis. On this issue too, therefore, they provided easy targets for National Socialist attacks. The governing parties had no plausible or politically palatable defense of their position. The NSDAP, was given a free field for its demagoguery.[18]

Two years later, in 1932, Germany experienced a series of five elections. The sequence was two rounds of the presidential election, state elections (in a collection of states covering almost the entire nation), and then, the culmination point, a Reichstag election on 31 July. A second Reichstag election was held in November, with a significantly different constellation of forces and choice of themes.

With the rising level of violence through to the July Reichstag election, much of it stimulated by NSDAP provocations, the party helped generate a sense of impending revolution. Through their street fighting, the NSDAP sought to communicate the lesson that they were the only force capable of countering the leftist threat. Other themes used in earlier campaigns were still invoked but now only in an ancillary role. Defense against "the marxists" was the central theme, as far as we can tell, in most National Socialist propaganda. It also figured prominently in the accounts of many bourgeois newspapers, particularly of those that had, in effect, adopted the party and were giving it supportive coverage. In the few studies directly addressing the question of voter motivations, antimarxism also figures as the leading concern.

An important variation on that theme appeared in the small towns and farm villages. There too, the NSDAP dramatized the revolutionary threat, but that distant struggle, alarming as it was for many, did not have immediate personal relevance. In this context the major problem was debt relief and that subject, together with the entire farm question, was given appropriate prominence. Debt forgiveness was one solution promised; freedom from taxation was another.

For workers, for any who might care to listen, the NSDAP had still another offering—a job-creation program. Although not likely to move supporters of the leftist parties (the Communists had a job-creation plan of their own), it is likely to have been important to workers who were not on the Left and supported the Nationalists or one of the liberal parties.[19]

This discussion of themes has necessarily been brief and summary in character. One further observation, however, must be added to this discussion of the party's use of issues. The NSDAP showed extraordinary flexibility or, a better term perhaps, opportunism, with regard to "the issues." The National Socialists have been described as a "feudal" organization; it was a collection of semiautonomous local units under the leadership of headstrong commanders, the barons of the system. The decentralized image is appropriate for the 1920s, but later, because of the problems posed by the diverse offerings, some efforts were made to coordinate the direction of their campaigns. Munich headquarters provided the guidelines, the basic themes and slogans for each campaign. Within that framework, the party allowed and encouraged invention with respect to themes and emphases. Munich headquarters, in general, did not impose close controls on the local units. A theme would be used if it proved successful; it was abandoned if no response or failure was the result. A theme might, at a given time, be used in some areas and be rejected elsewhere—because it "did not work" there. The architect of this thematic invention was Joseph Goebbels, who declared that a National Socialist must "be able to ride in all saddles." The party had declared its twenty-five-point program to be "unalterable." Complaining of the restrictions thus imposed, Goebbels said that if he had founded the party he would have had no program at all.[20]

The Explanatory Questions Reconsidered

The religious factor, whether voters were Protestant or Catholic, was of central importance, the leading "cause" explaining the electoral results of the period. But religion, curiously, in this context (as in many others) has suffered a distinct neglect in much of the relevant scholarly literature. Before addressing the explanatory questions posed earlier, some attention must be paid to the "missing agencies," the Protestant and Catholic churches.

The Treaty of Augsburg, from 1555, provided a settlement for the religious struggles of central Europe through the use of a simple formula, *cuius regio eius religio,* or loosely, "whose rule, his religion." Some modifications in the basic plan occurred as a result of the Thirty Years'

War. Other important changes developed after the "secularization" of 1803 (reviewed in Chapter 3) and later through mergers of territory arranged by the Congress of Vienna. Many German states, as a result, now had significant religious minorities. In most cases this meant Protestant royal houses and Catholic minorities. Austria and Bavaria were the principal "opposite" cases, having Catholic royal houses. An even more important merger, the "unification of Germany" in 1871, yielded a major "Protestant" state with a two-fifths Catholic minority. One of the first and most important political struggles in that new state was the *Kulturkampf,* a concerted assault on the minority's church. That led to the rapid growth of the Zentrum, a Catholic party devoted to the defense of the church and, more generally, of Catholic interests. For much of the period up to World War I, the Zentrum, when joined by Polish and Alsatian representatives, was the largest party in the Reichstag. In the Weimar period, the party joined with the Social Democrats (and other moderate parties) to form the national government. They remained in every government until Franz von Papen replaced Heinrich Brüning in June 1932. They also joined, with comparable success, in state government coalitions, the most important of these being in Prussia.

The Catholic church in Germany of 1930 was a strong and effective organization. Its leaders, the bishops, formulated policies and imposed them with a high probability of acceptance. Catholic communities were cohesive and, perhaps due to the struggles of the recent generations, had relatively high regular church attendance. One tends to forget that a church with a loyal following is, among other things, a mass medium of communication. Directives read from pulpits on Sunday would reach adherents and, unlike press or radio admonitions, those messages possessed considerable authority.

The religious question had, from the beginning, posed a problem for Hitler and his party. Erich Ludendorff's anti-Catholic statements at the trial of the Munich putschists gained wide attention. He and his wife, Matilde, later wrote anti-Catholic pamphlets, one of which sold more than four hundred thousand copies. Julius Streicher, known for his anti-Semitism, also made vehement anti-Catholic attacks. Hitler disavowed the Ludendorffs and indicated that for his party religion and politics were separate spheres. One important *Gauleiter,* Artur Dinter, challenged Hitler's policy and pressed for adoption of his plan for an "Aryan religion." Hitler expelled him from the party. These events alerted the Catholic hierarchy

to the threat. In 1930 Alfred Rosenberg, the editor of the party's newspaper, the *Völkischer Beobachter*, published *The Myth of the 20th Century*, a
book that brought criticism from Catholics and Protestants alike. Although the text was declared a statement of personal views and not a party document, the damage was done. The Catholic church reacted with a
policy of sharp condemnation.

This official position meant that Catholic priests were not present
within the NSDAP ranks, nor did they speak on its behalf. One "rebel
priest" was reprimanded by his bishop and future support was forbidden.
The NSDAP, innovative as ever, attempted to counter the hierarchy and
claimed they had support among the clergy. In one such instance, however, the party's claim was followed by an official statement: "We hereby
declare finally and emphatically that a Catholic priest, no matter what his
position, can never go along with a movement like that represented by
National Socialism." With the clergy, laity, and the Catholic press unambiguously opposed to their aspirations, it was difficult for the NSDAP to
make headway in the Catholic communities.[21]

The Protestant churches in Germany found themselves, in the late
twenties, in a very different situation. In contrast to the unity of German
Catholicism, "Protestantism" consisted of twenty-eight independent state
churches (*Landeskirchen*). In contrast to the unchallenged position of the
Catholic hierarchy, the Protestant churches provided for congregational
participation in decision making, through elected synods. The churches
were alike in one respect: as beneficiaries of the Augsburg settlement they
both had "their" territories, which meant large regions with religiously
homogeneous towns and villages. Still there was an important difference:
disaffection was a serious problem for the Protestant churches. It is a routine correlate for established or state churches. A large part of their clientele, consequently, could not be reached from the pulpit. For many of the
disaffected, that meant they were open to other influences.

The Protestant church leaders faced serious difficulties in developing a
policy with respect to Hitler and his party. In contrast to the consensus
present in the Catholic hierarchy, the Protestant leadership was divided,
the range extending from opposition to favor, sympathy, and direct involvement. Church leaders, according to J. R. C. Wright, disliked the violence and the racialism of the party. On the other hand, he reports, "they
were not as hostile to the 'national opposition' as they were to the socialist movement." Many church leaders saw the party as "basically sound

and blamed its 'faults' on the way Germany had been made to suffer by her former enemies." Some justified the sympathy in tactical terms: "The church would be isolated if it rejected a mass movement of 'national people' and, in addition, they saw in it a powerful defence against Communism." Wright concluded that "most Landeskirchen" did issue decrees in 1931–2 intended to keep party warfare out of the church and some condemned violence, but the church leadership deliberately avoided explicit condemnation of the NSDAP."[22]

It was relatively easy for the National Socialists to gain influence within the Protestant churches. They had outright supporters within the church organizations along with many members who were at least sympathetic. One source reports that as of 1931 "no more than 100" pastors (out of 18,000) were members of the NSDAP. Although a small part of the total, those members could be used effectively as speakers, giving testimony to the consonance of church and party purposes. Most state churches had some pastors willing to campaign for the party. In Württemberg, the party is said to have derived "great benefits" from such efforts before their prohibition. Such restrictions posed little problem for the party since they "could be evaded by bringing a pastor from another Landeskirche." The party could also gain influence within the churches through participation in synod elections, appropriately characterized as an effort for the defense of religion. William Sheridan Allen reports an episode in Northeim where the Social Democrats entered candidates in a church election. The local NSDAP organized against this threat and won an easy and, for them, important victory.[23]

The patterns of influence, the relative strength of the traditional notables, newspapers, and NSDAP activists, differed widely within the various cells of Table 4.1. The new explanatory questions raised in the second part of this chapter may be addressed in terms of the typical values and concerns present within each of those contexts and in terms of the conjunction of influences found there.

The first of those questions asked about the susceptibility of the Protestant countryside. The notables in Protestant villages and towns, typically, were affiliated with parties that, for many reasons, were discredited and losing support. Many notables, those of a conservative, nationalist persuasion, appear to have changed position, now either sympathetic to or supporting the new, active, and "dynamic" NSDAP. Those "converts" came from the higher ranks of the society, including factory owners, members of the nobility, and ex-officers. Among those ready to vouch for the NSDAP, to attest to its merits, were members of the Protestant clergy. No church hierarchy intervened, as in the Catholic experience, to take "authoritative" stands against Hitler's party. Indeed, some clergymen saw the party, with its promise of "national renewal," as a kindred agency, one with a great spiritual mission. In the Protestant towns, one found opinion leaders in all sectors who either directly recommended the NSDAP or, while recommending some other party, nevertheless spoke enthusiastically of the National Socialists.[24]

Some Protestant towns and cities had competing "bourgeois" newspapers, some of them with ties to one or another of the so-called middle-class parties. As the Depression worsened, some newspapers found themselves struggling for audience and advertising. Survival needs overwhelmed prior loyalties and some papers abandoned the middle-class parties, doing what they could to gain National Socialist favor or, more precisely, to gain advertising funds. For some editors and publishers these shifts were more than tactical; they were clearly true believers. Aided by the efforts of local notables and by the generous support of local newspapers, National Socialist activists, understandably, were able to make much headway in those communities. New recruits from among elites and masses were then able to sway the next groups of undecided voters. The continued erosion of the middle-class parties led to defections of still more tactical voters looking for a more effective political agency.[25]

One of the frequently mentioned issues in the literature is that of farm indebtedness. The combination of Depression-induced strains and National Socialist demagoguery led to substantial vote gains in the countryside. Falter's research on this question found substantial support for the claim. Indebtedness does appear to have had an important independent effect on the vote. This effect, however, like so many reported by Falter, appears in Protestant areas but not in equivalent Catholic ones.[26]

An especially important finding appears in this connection: Falter presents correlations between average farm size in the counties and support for the NSDAP. If the lower-middle-class thesis were valid, if the infection were most serious among small farmers, these correlations should be negative. In fact, however, the coefficients for the elections from 1930 to 1933 are all positive, +22, +21, +18, and +17 (the 1928 figure was −03): overall, NSDAP support tended to increase with average farm size.[27]

Falter next presented correlations by size categories, the first of these for share of farms with less than 20 hectares and NSDAP support. A hectare is equal to 2.471 acres, making the cutoff for the small farm category roughly 50 acres. These coefficients, again for 1930 to 1933, are negative, −14, −15, −11, and −17. The greater the share of small farms, the smaller the NSDAP vote, just the opposite of the predicted lower-middle-class tendency. In heavily Protestant counties, the correlations for the small farm category are more strongly negative, −24, −28, −21, and −27. Three larger size categories all show positive relationships with NSDAP support. This evidence, in short, does not confirm the lower-middle-class thesis. With exceptional consistency, it goes against the long-standing claim.

A third line of analysis dealing with average farm size and NSDAP support yielded regression coefficients for the five elections from 1928 to 1933 that are close to zero (the extremes are −08 for 1928 to +08 for 1930; the figures for the two key elections of 1932 are −01 and −02). These results are "net," that is, with the appropriate controls for farm indebtedness and religion. They again indicate that in the countryside, no support was found for the lower-middle-class thesis. These findings, it will be remembered, are based on the most comprehensive and detailed evidence ever assembled for these elections.

Some further insight into the voting shifts in the Protestant regions may be gained through consideration of the other voters there, that is, of those who did not choose the NSDAP. They might have been "traditional" middle-class voters, who even in mid-1932 remained with either the German Nationals or with the so-called middle-class parties. Most of those "others," however, favored the Social Democrats, which suggests they were workers (either commuters or perhaps farm laborers). That would mean the middle-class support for the NSDAP was even greater than is suggested in the overall figures. One example: in the July 1932 Reichstag election, the NSDAP gained 51 percent of the valid votes cast in Schleswig-Holstein. It was the party's best showing in any of the thirty-five large reporting districts. The SPD came in second with 26.2 percent of the total, and the Communists were third with 10.7 percent. The best showing for any of the bourgeois parties was the 6.6 percent gained by the German Nationals, and not all of that would have come from bourgeois voters.[28]

The Catholic villages and small towns (turning to the second of the explanatory questions) were characterized, typically, by near-monolithic support for the Zentrum (or in Bavaria, for the Bavarian People's Party [BVP]). Virtually every notable in those towns, clergy and laypeople alike, would have championed the Catholic party and, given the church's position, would have opposed any NSDAP aspirations. Those villages usually had only one bourgeois newspaper, which stood unambiguously behind the Zentrum (or BVP). Every influential (or "authoritative") person or political source in such towns (apart from a possible dissident working-class enclave) would have backed the traditional political direction and opposed the NSDAP insurgency. In such settings, campaigning NSDAP activists gained little or no positive response. They were not able to convert notables; they could not gain press support; they could not recruit activists; nor were they able to find followers to undertake routine political legwork. They faced a wall of opposition in those areas, a wall that, initially at least, seemed almost insurmountable.[29]

Falter shows some important changes in these relationships, which developed during the course of the crucial elections. The correlations between the farm population percentages and NSDAP voting in Protestant regions increased, growing from 25 in 1930, to 61, 57, and finally to 74 in 1933. In Catholic regions, there was a weakening of the initial strong negative relationship, −44 in 1930, to −15, then to −03, the pattern finally reversing, to +28 in 1933. This break with the original tendency appears to have been stimulated, in part, by a new direction signaled by the Zentrum. After the July 1932 election, that party, in an extraordinary reversal, undertook negotiations with Hitler and other NSDAP leaders to form a coalition government. The Zentrum leaders had a plausible rationale for the abrupt change. Fourteen years earlier, they had formed a coalition with another unlikely partner, the Social Democrats. The responsibilities of government, it was thought, would tame the otherwise unruly NSDAP. The negotiations, however, came to an abrupt end when Papen called another Reichstag election for November. Word of those negotiations probably influenced some of the party's voters, providing justification for a change to the NSDAP in November 1932 and again in March 1933.[30]

What may be said about the opposite city-size relationships for Catholics and Protestants? How can one account for those diverse patterns? The inverse relationship in the Protestant communities, the third of the delineated explanatory questions, may be explained in terms of the relative strength of the contending forces and in terms of newspaper content and recommendations. The National Socialists had their greatest successes where they faced weak or "soft" opposition. This was most pronouncedly the case with the classic parties of notables, the reactionary German Nationals, the two liberal parties, and a scattering of minor entries. Those parties had little organization to begin with and what little they had dwindled with the onset of the Depression. The absence of staff, speakers, and cadres was problematic enough, but in a struggle increasingly dominated by paramilitary organizations, parties without such forces were hopelessly outmatched.

In the larger communities the NSDAP faced parties with adequate defense forces, or at least with forces vastly superior to those of the middle-class parties. The leftist parties, Social Democrats and Communists (Kommunistische Partei Deutschlands, or KPD), were parties of integration, both attempting to create powerful, permanent, bureaucratic structures. Both had their own paramilitary forces; the Social Democrats controlled the Reichsbanner and the Communists had their Rotfront. In the larger communities, the NSDAP therefore faced an opposition that was better organized to defend its territory, its base. In the Protestant villages and small towns, the National Socialists could achieve the nearly across-the-board sweeps. The most serious opposition encountered in the Protestant countryside was provided by the Social Democrats, but, being poorly organized there, the party suffered serious losses to the NSDAP.

Most SPD and KPD newspapers were based in the cities, most of them probably having a largely working-class readership. The SPD journals were strongly and consistently opposed to the NSDAP. The KPD had few newspapers; in addition, that party's opposition to "the fascists" was not entirely consistent. No bourgeois newspaper in the fourteen large cities of my original study gave the National Socialists a direct recommendation (one rightist journal in Nuremberg gave an unambiguous indirect recommendation: "No Votes for Hindenburg!"). The large-circulation, prestigious liberal newspapers (in Berlin, the *Tageblatt* and the *Vossische Zeitung*; elsewhere the *Münchener Neueste Nachrichten*; in Stuttgart, the *Schwäbischer Merkur*; and the *Frankfurter Zeitung*) had influence in the home city and also had substantial outreach. Their recommendations were for the traditional bourgeois parties or, in the presidential election, for Hindenburg. As a result the bourgeois parties fared better in the cities, holding more of their previous strength than they did elsewhere. This also limited, in a small way, the extent of the National Socialist advance in those cities.[31]

Turning to the Catholic communities, to the fourth of the explanatory questions, we saw a modest opposite relationship, NSDAP strength increasing slightly with size of city. In general, of course, the larger the community, the more differentiated and heterogeneous the population. In the Catholic countryside, it is no problem at all to find villages that were 100 percent Catholic and, given the exceptional pattern of social controls there, ones that were also monolithic in their voting. But in the so-called Catholic cities, in Cologne, Munich, and Augsburg, for example, there were some Protestants, a small number of Jews, and some "unchurched" populations, people who, for one reason or another, had fallen away from the Catholic church. The defections were in two directions: workers fell away to the SPD and, even more, to the KPD; middle-class populations went to a wide assortment of non-Left parties. The NSDAP votes in the larger cities appear to have come from the Protestant minorities and from disaffected middle-class Catholics. The proportions of those groups open to the NSDAP appeals were greater in the larger "Catholic" communities, hence the greater relative NSDAP successes. The NSDAP found it easier to campaign there; they would find at least some resonance, some support from local notables, some response to their membership appeals, unlike their experience in the Catholic villages.

How may one account for the differentiated response within the cities? Why was there such pronounced support for the NSDAP in the upper and upper-middle-class ranks? What were the sources of that minority support in the mixed districts, those containing many "lower-middle-class" voters? And how may one account for the votes of the "Tory workers"?

National Socialist campaign strategies in the large cities necessarily involved a more complex range of tactics and of thematic offerings. Campaign efforts there were more differentiated, being tailored to the needs and interests of the diverse subcommunities. In the cities also, the party effort was aided by the testimonials of local and visiting notables, in this case, different notables for the different communities: upper-middle-class speakers for the well-off and/or educated, working-class speakers for the workers, and so on.

Outright recommendation of the NSDAP by bourgeois newspapers, as indicated, was a rarity in the major cities, but favorable comment, avuncular support, and assertions that the NSDAP was a worthy member of the "national" coalition were very frequent. Evidence attesting to the importance of the press appears consistently in the urban voting results. In a small city, Braunschweig, one leading newspaper was for all practical purposes a NSDAP party organ, giving Hitler a direct recommendation. There the party gained 60 to 70 percent in upper-middle-class neighborhoods, the highest percentages yet discovered in any German city. But where the leading bourgeois newspaper provided serious opposition to the National Socialists, as in Cologne, Munich, and Frankfurt, the voting did not show the general pattern of increased NSDAP support with class level; there the upper- and upper-middle-class districts were either average or even below average. Where a general-circulation popular newspaper opposed the party, as in Dortmund, the overall support for the NSDAP suffered accordingly.[32]

The cities were also the principal staging area for the party's basic provocative tactic. The procedure was very simple: the party announced meetings in the heart of working-class areas; there the storm troopers clashed with the forces of the Left and, the next day, accounts of NSDAP "heroism" appeared in the sympathetic press. With increasing "evidence" of an impending civil war, readers could easily conclude that the storm troopers provided the only effective barrier to the threat of a "marxist" revolution. This effort combined two types of influence—that provided by the militants and that by the newspapers. The provocative action "commanded" press attention. A relatively small effort by activists before an immediate "audience" of some hundreds or perhaps a few thousand could thus gain a secondary audience of tens or hundreds of thousands. On an active day in the early thirties, a newspaper might report a half dozen such confrontations from across Germany.[33]

The fifth of the explanatory questions posed earlier asked about the pronounced support for the National Socialists in Germany's upper- and upper-middle-class ranks. One plausible argument, based both on the party's thematic stresses and on the content of bourgeois newspapers, is fear of marxism, the fear of imminent revolution in Germany. Some voters apparently concluded that the NSDAP, or, more precisely, its fighting arm, the storm troopers, were the only force standing between them and Bolshevism. Some, no doubt, were true believers who accepted the party's claims of national renewal, of people's community, and of the Versailles *Diktat* as the source of all problems. Some others, possibly, may have given only tactical support—as their favored parties lost strength, they were led to this "second best" choice, to the NSDAP as the best "under the circumstances."[34]

The sixth explanatory question asked about the motives of the urban lower-middle-class NSDAP supporters. In 1965, William Sheridan Allen presented evidence showing real improvements in middle-class living standards as the Depression worsened. That conclusion was based on the experience of a single, largely Protestant town, Northeim. The explanation was that price levels fell more rapidly than salary levels. The purchasing power of savings, moreover, appreciates in a deflationary crisis. Although based on a small sample of experience, the finding indicated a need to rethink the motivational questions. Allen offered a plausible alternative: fear of marxism. That same motive may also have been present in the minds of some urban lower-middle-class voters. Like the classes above them, they may have feared a leftist takeover. Seeing their traditional parties as weak and helpless, they may have chosen the "tougher" and "more resourceful" alternative, the National Socialists. Other lower-middle-class voters in the cities would have maintained their previous party ties. The Zentrum and the SPD after all, were still viable parties. Allen's finding of middle-class economic gains has been neglected in most subsequent accounts. With few exceptions, it has not stimulated the appearance of follow-up studies. His finding has not been incorporated into subsequent accounts of the Weimar collapse, and where noted at all, it is treated simply as an "interesting" or "curious" exception to a still-unquestioned rule. A review of readily available evidence from statistical yearbooks of the period, however, showed that his finding had national applicability. This experience provides another instance of the "power" of a traditional paradigm.[35]

The nonmanual rank may be analyzed from another perspective, that is, by sector, whether independent, or salaried in private employment, or salaried in public employment. Falter finds support for the assumption about the relationship between "old middle-class" presence and NSDAP support, one which, for the most part, is limited to the Protestant districts. The relationships between white-collar employee percentages (private employment) and NSDAP support prove to be quite limited. A summary regression analysis controlling for religion, urbanization, and presence of blue-collar workers yields a series of modest negative correlations. Falter's conclusion is that those employees "on the whole did not by any means show a special NSDAP susceptibility" (my translation). On average, they were less likely to vote NSDAP than were other voters. As for the civil servants, the best summary is: a modest positive relationship. These results describe voting tendencies in what are essentially three vertical segments, which cut across the broad nonmanual (or middle-class) category. In each instance, the category includes all status levels—high, middling, and low. Those results, therefore, do not address the lower-middle-class thesis. Falter reports that his urban data do not allow exploration of that question.[36]

Most accounts of the "working class" in the modern period focus, understandably, on the dominant tendency, on the growth of the Left. The social and historical sciences have shown little interest in the remaining minority, that is, the "conservative" workers, who have been treated, typically, as cases of arrested development; time, it was assumed, would remedy the problem. There has been little analysis of their circumstances since they were expected to react like any other workers, only the pace of their maturation being different. That assumption might be accurate or, of course, it might not be. One may, at least as an exercise, take the lessons from the few available studies of "Tory workers" and think through the implications for Germany of the early thirties.

The working classes of all nations are drawn from the countryside. Migrants to the city ordinarily bring to their new urban locations the values, attitudes, and outlooks learned in their home communities. In addition to having an "inappropriate" party choice and unexpected economic views, some cultural conservativism is also likely, a commitment to the nation, respect for (or fond memories of) handed-down institutions (in some contexts, for example, the monarchy), and, in all probability, some religious belief and involvement. Much of that world view, unquestionably, is lost in the urban milieu. But for many, even in the heart of the mass society, it is possible to retain such "false consciousness," in some settings over generations. That is accomplished with the support of family members, friends, neighbors, and co-religionists. Within self-selected urban subcommunities, one can successfully protect traditional values from the secularizing influences present in the larger society.[37]

Another important ingredient was present in the German case. Conservative workers had retained those values in the face of persistent open hostility from Social Democratic and Communist activists, both in the shops and in the neighborhoods.[38] One would have to assume that those workers, in the midst of the crisis, would abandon the beliefs they had held and defended their entire lives; one must also assume the defectors would join a party that disparaged everything they previously stood for.

Given the histories, personal and social, a move to the Left" would seem unlikely.

A more plausible scenario is that, as the traditional parties dwindled in strength, those workers turned to the party that announced and "demonstrated" itself to be the only effective defender of their values. Conservative workers personally touched by the crisis may have found the NSDAP attractive by virtue of its job-creation program (in contrast to the steadfast laissez-faire orientations of the German Nationalists and both liberal parties). The four leading "bourgeois" parties all shifted to the Right at this point, telling their working-class followers that no aid would be forthcoming. Among these workers, as with other traditional or conservative segments of the society, one would also have found a kind of anti-marxism. The sources of such sentiments among the "Tory workers" would be substantially different from those of the middle-class citizenry.

To this point, the discussion of workers has focused on "backgrounds," on the political, social, or cultural heritage questions. One may also consider, however, the immediate determinants touching workers directly in the early 1930s. In this connection, Falter has provided several important and compelling findings. His study allows exploration of types of worker, whether farm laborers, artisans, or industrial workers. The correlations between farm laborer presence in rural districts and NSDAP percentages were modestly positive in Protestant regions. Some commentators had thought that the large estates, with their hundreds of farm workers, were centers of leftist voting. The results, however, suggest otherwise. The relationship with artisan worker presence was basically zero, and the correlation between industrial worker presence and NSDAP voting was modestly negative. Many commentators have assumed that industrial workers were largely immune to the National Socialist infection; it was believed they were solidly and firmly committed to the parties of the Left. Falter's results suggest that the assumption of extent is not justified. The relationship is negative, as anticipated, but no matter how approached—that is, regardless of statistical procedure—the relationship proves to be surprisingly modest.

One important specification appears frequently in the relevant literature: unemployed workers are said to have turned to the National Socialists. Falter's results do not support that claim. The relationship between unemployment levels and NSDAP voting proved to be consistently negative and was relatively strong. Unemployment levels were positively related to Communist voting and those relationships were quite strong. The received wisdom in this instance seems to have been very much mistaken. It appears to have been another social misconstruction, based initially on guesswork, then passed on and sustained through mutual agreement (backed by citation chains) for some three score years. The initial ready acceptance of the unemployment–NSDAP vote linkage poses something of a problem. Why did observers advance an unsupported claim with such confidence? One possibility is that the basic idea was similar to the Marx-Engels notion of the *Lumpenproletariat*, an unreliable segment easily mobilized for demagogic purposes. Perhaps intellectuals of the period had been "prepared" for acceptance of the unsupported claim.[39]

The handed-down analyses of the National Socialist electorate have stressed its class base, that argument centering on the plight of the lower middle class. That widely accepted conception assumed close linkages between classes and party choices. Workers, it was said, typically with little or no qualification, favored the parties of the Left, either the Socialists or Communists. The class-based idea has a "dialectical" opposite, that being the idea of a *Volkspartei*, a people's party that transcends any narrow class base. Such a party offers a diverse range of appeals and accordingly gains (or hopes to gain) a wide spectrum of support. Most liberal parties sought and, for a while at least, achieved such a following. The "class party" versus the "people's party" issue was at the heart of the revisionist struggle within Social Democracy at the turn of the century, that is, whether to emphasize a "Left" program so as to secure and increase worker support, or whether to develop "moderate" themes so as to gain support from the growing white-collar (new middle-class) populations. The struggle was resolved, six decades later, in favor of the volkspartei concept, this with the adoption of the party's Godesberg Program in 1959.

The use of the polar concepts and the either/or character of the discussior has been seriously misleading. Early in the century, two important studies pointed to a significant middle-class" presence within German Social Democracy, among both its voters and its cadres. Long before Godesberg, the party was, to some degree, a volkspartei. One should consider the alternative, that all parties are "people's parties"—they all draw support across class lines, that is, from more than a single, exclusive class base. The key question then is one of degree or extent: How much support from the principal base? How much from other segments? This reading would have been appropriate in Germany, at all times, for the

Conservatives (Deutschnationale Volkspartei, or DNVP), for Right and Left liberal parties, for the Catholic center, for the Social Democrats, and even, to a limited degree, for the Communists. At most times, it would have been next to impossible to measure the centrality or diversity of those party bases. Falter's estimates clearly support this alternative with respect to the Weimar parties. The "discovery" that the NSDAP was a people's party, in short, is truistic. It is "news" by virtue of the persistent misleads, the argument of distinctive, near-exclusive class-party linkages. By itself, the "new" description of the NSDAP voters provides no distinctive information; it gives no specifics as to the party's actual support. Unlike the lower-middle-class thesis, it provides no explanation.[40]

The Larger Experience

The fifth task of this chapter is to review and assess the alternative explanations in the light of a larger range of experience. Since the lower-middle-class argument is general in character, one should find a similar "reaction" in all countries. The socialization-personal influence argument, in contrast, assumes differences both within classes and between nations. Those differences would stem from an assortment of historical determinants. It would mean, for intellectual purposes, that the principal line of generalization would have to stress commonalities of historical experience—as opposed to the contemporary circumstances shared by a given class.[41]

The conventional arguments of "class" (or of "structure") assume both a direct and a powerful impact. Persons in a given class are subject to a set of determinants and, struggle as they may, they will ultimately be influenced. A time dimension is necessarily involved in any such statement, but that concern is usually handled rather cagily by the supporters of the class argument. The position argued here, in contrast, holds that patterns of interpersonal influence, principally those associated with religion, with the local notables, and with party activists, proved decisive in determining responses in the early 1930s.

Although Catholic and Protestant villages and towns, on the whole, were engaged in the same kinds of enterprise, had the same relationships to markets, faced the same crisis, and so forth, the populations reacted in distinctly different ways. Those reactions were determined, it appears, by the uniform opposition of notables in one setting and by the "permeability" of the same ranks to National Socialist influences in the other. In the one, National Socialists made little headway; in the other, they achieved their greatest victories. Put somewhat differently, outside of the cities, knowledge of "class position" predicted little about the political response; knowledge of social influences predicted a lot.

This point about the decisive role of interpersonal influences gains support also from another range of evidence. The economic crisis of the 1930s affected most Western nations, and yet the range of responses in democratic societies was about as diverse as one could possibly imagine. In England, the Conservatives increased their vote. In France and Spain, the electoral victories in 1936 went to the Common Front coalitions, joint efforts of liberal and leftist parties. In the United States the Democrats were the big winners. In Canada, it was a history of Conservatives followed by Liberals (in one province, Saskatchewan, a party of agrarian socialists made major advances, elsewhere very little changed). In Scandinavia, Social Democratic parties gained their greatest victories.

A brilliant analysis by Sten S. Nilson contrasts the experience in Schleswig-Holstein with equivalent farm areas in Norway. In the former region, the NSDAP, led by local activists, achieved its greatest support; in the latter, Vidkun Quisling's forces made only trivial gains, victory instead going to the Labor Party (that is, to the Social Democrats). Quisling, Nilson reports, had no activists in the field. Norway's Social Democrats did have activists and, not being hampered by marxian "theory" and its disdainful portraits of the petty bourgeoisie, they provided a sensible, attractive program for the nation's farmers.[42]

A similar proof of the role of the activists appears within Germany, also in the Schleswig-Holstein context. A group of National Socialist activists, members of the so-called Left (or Strasser) group, defected from the party and formed their own "purer" organization. The storm troopers quickly broke up their feeble attempts, after which some of the dissidents joined the Communists. Using the basic National Socialist grass-roots campaign techniques in the small farm communities, the defectors achieved a level of success in those petty bourgeois ranks that most "sophisticated" marxists would consider unthinkable. The experience has been lost from view, the superior wisdom provided by "advanced theory" presumably providing a better guide to praxis than this kind of evidence.[43]

One must consider the question of the weight given (or assigned to) the presumed causal variables. In the typical formulations of the tradition under review, class is portrayed as a powerful causal factor. The tenor of those formulations and the absence of any consideration of modifying, crosscutting, or extenuating factors mean that the authors expect strong correlations between "class position" and political attitudes and or behavior. Although using the language of correlation, it is instructive that such writing is never accompanied by research showing, for example, a Pearsonian coefficient of 0.89 for individual data. There is simple explanation: relationships of that strength have not appeared in social science research. Any summary of studies done in economically advanced nations over the last few decades must report modest relationships with class to be the typical result. Given the expectation of high correlations (or of "powerful" or "profound" linkages), it is striking that most discussion of research on class has such a distinctive opposite character. Most such discussion seeks to explain or account for the weakness of the linkages established in that research. Another procedure is always possible: one could reconsider the original theory and, for a variety of reasons, conclude that strong correlations of class and behavior are unlikely. That "paradigm shift" would have one distinctive advantage—consonance with available evidence on the subject.[44]

Given the difficulty involved, the proponents of class theories must adopt one or another theory-saving device. The ad hoc explaining away of low correlations is, of course, only one of many possibilities. Another tactic involves an exclusion of the time dimension. The advantage of the "revolution will come" hypothesis is that without a time specification it is always viable. It falls in the same category as the "it will rain" hypothesis. Ten, twenty, or even thirty years of drought in the Sahara are not sufficient to invalidate the claim.[45]

The revolution and rain hypotheses are not completely without merit. The class analyst can readily admit that "all the evidence goes against my claims," providing generous ad hoc reference to historical residues, false consciousness, mass media influence, hegemonic discourse, manipulation, and so forth. The bottom-line claim, however, is that the day of vindication shall come. Some questions must be raised: What does one want from a social science? Does one wish to "explain" events that are to occur some time in the distant future, at a point remaining forever unspecified? If so, the founders and defenders of such "theory" should recognize and state clearly that this 'science' has little relevance for events in the here and now and little for events in the foreseeable future. It is the science of the ultimate Saharan rain. It rather pointedly, stubbornly, and without explanation neglects the much more frequent and more obvious present fact—Saharan drought.

Another procedure involves what might be termed evidence recoding. One has a claim, for example, that the "history of all hitherto existing society is the history of class struggles." But that claim runs up against the evident problem of absent struggle, many epochs showing, for decade after decade, stable pacific relationships between the classes. The problem is handled with a gloss phrase—it is a "now hidden, now open fight." The "now hidden" argument, a marvelous Orwellian flourish, redefines the commonplace experience and declares peace (or perhaps passivity) to be merely hidden conflict.

The routine low correlation of class and attitudes and behavior has another implication, the previous paragraphs having spelled out only the "negative" case. If factor A is a poor predictor, given usual scientific assumptions, some other factor (or factors) must be better predictors. Given that assumption, those better predictors should occupy a central position in one's intellectual formulations. The core of the argument should focus on those factors.

It is useful to note the typical treatment of (or the weighting of) class in relation to the personal influence factor discussed here. The advocates of class analysis present embellishing comment that, without serious evidence, vouches for the merits of class and denigrates claims about the importance of other structures and of interpersonal influences. Class, so one is told, is a "big" factor; it is a larger concern. The analysis of the class structure (when properly understood) provides order, clarity, predictability. Other structures—most important, those provided by religious communities—are neglected entirely or are signaled in passing as having only minor and waning significance. Interpersonal influences, generally, are treated as "small" or, at best, epiphenomenal. Moreover, they are extraordinarily complex, highly idiosyncratic, and, as such, provide no basis for prediction. The concern with such influences is mere description, the tracking of a myriad of meaningless contacts, involvements, and so forth. In a more general formulation one finds the same legitimation/denigration in the preference for the privileged "structural" explanation as opposed to the (mere) social psychological, to the concerns with, for example, family and peer influences and associated political socialization.

In the social here and now, those non-class factors prove to be dominant. They are the best predictors of political outlooks and choices. Class may ultimately have some immense causal weight, but in the current research other structures and other sets of interpersonal influences outweigh the class factors by a heavy margin.[46] Nonclass influences define an "objective" situation and, also, prescribe appropriate responses. Those definitions and prescriptions are valued rather than "the objective conditions" or some mystical (that is, reified) "real" or "objective" interest. The focus on class, specifically on the linkage between fascism and the lower middle class, given the absence of evidence in its support, must be counted as an instance of stubborn theoretical prejudice. One may ask: Why continue to defend prejudice?

Should one reject the class variable entirely and focus exclusively on other variables? That would seem ill-advised since, as indicated, within the German cities there was a general tendency for the NSDAP vote to vary directly with class level. What then is to be said about this variable? What is the role of class? How does it work? How are the class-linked effects achieved?

It is useful, at the outset, to think of causal variables in terms of a simple dichotomy, active and passive. A social movement, a political party, a pressure group, or even a family, are normally active; they are agencies seeking to change or to stabilize some aspect of the human condition. Other variables, such as age, community size, income, home ownership, or that collection of events described with the expression "objective class situation," are passive—"they" do nothing. They provide a set of conditions or, put differently, provide an agenda of problems or concerns. The distinctive characteristic of such passive (or latent) variables, however, is that by themselves they carry no obvious or unambiguous political lesson. It is not the case, therefore, that time is the sole factor needed to "bring out" the import of such variables. To elicit the latent implications, an active or "educating" agency is required.[47]

The claims presented in this chapter assume the likelihood of what might be called an indeterminacy hypothesis. As opposed to the assumption of close and ineluctable connections, this argument sees the links between social structures and attitudes (or behaviors) as *not* narrowly determined. Phrased positively, this means that a given situation would ordinarily be open to a range of plausible readings or interpretations. Which of the readings comes to be accepted as valid would depend on the social influences present. Once accepted, that reading would then govern subsequent reactions and responses. There are, possibly, some "realistic" outer limits to this indeterminacy—it might be difficult to sell Communism to the haute bourgeoisie—but apart from such extreme cases, it would be difficult to establish any other limits. The diversity of national responses to the economic crisis of the 1930s attests to the openness of the crisis–political response linkage. That small farmers in Schleswig-Holstein supported fascism while those in Norway opted for socialism when faced with the same crisis attests to the limited impact of class position. In the latter comparison it was the activists who were decisive, who generated those diverse outcomes. One may assume that the economic stresses created an openness to new alternatives, making people willing to look for new solutions. But it did not predetermine the specific character of the options that would appear or the specific choices that individuals or groups would make.[48]

If class is a latent variable, if its import is dependent on some other fact, on the role of some mobilizing force(s), then the heart of one's analysis should deal with that other fact, with the mobilizing agency. That analysis should focus on the conditions giving rise to new opinion leaders, to social movements, to the innovating forces. A complete analysis also requires investigation and consideration of the "traditional" agencies, those that in a period of change, are seriously weakened or, as in the German case, entirely eclipsed.

One condition giving rise to a social movement, to a new set of "opinion leaders," is war.[49] The simple fact of war suggests a need for an expansion of the range of our thinking. Most contemporary discussions of class are peculiarly incomplete, because one class is missing—the military, the warrior class. Its development follows lines somewhat different from those affecting civilian classes. Normally that class is located apart from the civilian world. The support for the military and its activities usually comes from the "surplus" produced in the civilian economy. It recruits enlisted men and officers internally, from among its own offspring, as with any class, and externally, from the civilian population, providing a distinctive education or training for both segments. In addition to its task of maintaining (or possibly extending) national boundaries, the military was and continues to be the ultimate peacekeeping force within society. These propositions hold for capitalist and Communist societies alike.

Our thinking, as reflected in leading theoretical orientations, has little to say about the impacts of wars, the principal "dynamic" factor in the lives of the warrior class. Our thinking (like our statistical series) usually segregates or brackets wartime years, tagging them as exceptional or unusual breaks in the normal routines. That view, however, leads us to overlook possible spillover effects. Military defeats, most especially those seen as illegitimate, lead to the injection of "the military" into civilian affairs in new and different ways such that "normal" routines are disrupted.[50]

The basic lesson or need is for a reorientation of our thinking toward a focus on agencies, on the active forces seeking, in one way or another, to direct social affairs. This focus on the "voluntarist" components of social life requires some reworking of our research instruments so as to allow us to pick up information on personal influences, social movements, organizational initiatives, and, broadly speaking, "effort" and "ability" variables.[51] This is not to argue a neglect of class. The argument, rather, is to see the classes in conjunction with these active or directive agencies.

5

The Lower-Middle-Class Thesis

This chapter will review and discuss some of the larger issues posed by the lower-middle-class explanation for the rise of Nazism. It will consider, briefly, the origins of the argument and will review a range of subsequent presentations. Since the specific concern is with the social misconstruction problem, special attention will be given to the character of the support provided in the various formulations of the basic position. Most of the examples to be considered are based on the experience of Weimar Germany but, because the argument is a general one, some of the cases will involve applications of the thesis to experience elsewhere.

A Formula and Its Adaptations

In the *Communist Manifesto*, Marx and Engels provided a basic portrait of the "lower middle class," delineating its position and fate. This "lower strata of the middle class" was also referred to as the petty bourgeoisie (in French, *la petite bourgeoisie*, in German, *das Kleinbürgertum*). The reference is to the small independent businessmen, to the proprietors of marginal farm and nonfarm enterprises. No definition was provided; instead the authors offered a list of typical occupations: "the small manufacturer, the shopkeeper, the artisan, the peasant." Unable to meet the competition of the haute bourgeoisie, these people were destined to lose their middle-class position. They would "fall" into the proletariat. The lower middle class, Marx and Engels declared, "fight against the bourgeoisie, to save from extinction their existence as fractions of the middle class .... they are reactionary, for they try to roll back the wheel of history."[1]

Several decades later that formula had become problematic because the original class nomenclature was no longer comprehensive. A significant growth of salaried middle-class populations had occurred, a category that, for the most part, went unrecognized in the original Marx-Engels formulations. The tendency in much of the subsequent literature, marxist and nonmarxist alike, has been to portray the salaried employees as similar to the petty bourgeoisie. In English-language works, the term *petty bourgeoisie* has, by and large, been replaced by the term *lower middle class*. Both old and new middle-class segments, independents and salarieds, are generally counted under that heading.

Those persons, presumably, were poorly paid and could scarcely maintain their "middle-class" status. Relative to the workers, it was said, they were loosing position, coming to have the same income, or in some instances, earning even less than the better-paid skilled workers. Assuming marked differences at some time in the past, many commentators argued that the class now experienced a "status panic." Its members sought to restore their lost position or, at minimum, to maintain those few remaining signs of difference vis-à-vis the workers. In Germany, it is said, the loss of status made them susceptible to National Socialist appeals. The lower middle class, accordingly, voted overwhelmingly for Hitler and his party.

A typical formulation of the argument, from among scores of possible examples, is provided by the noted historian Geoffrey Barraclough: "We know today pretty accurately where Hitler found his main support. . . . his first great electoral successes were in rural Bavaria and then in the rural provinces of Schleswig-Holstein and Lower Saxony; [Hitler's] first allies were the farmers, deeply in debt and terrified of the impact of the modern capitalist and commercial state. His other main support, skillfully mobilized, was the anti-capitalism of the lower middle classes, shopkeepers, artisans and white-collar workers. These are well known facts, but they are nevertheless worth emphasizing."[2] Several problems appear in this statement. First, there is the matter of evidence, of the need for documentation. Barraclough refers his readers to a book by the eminent political scientist and historian Karl Dietrich Bracher. The work in question, *The German*

Dictatorship, is a popular account covering the entire Hitler era. The reader has not been directed to primary sources, which would provide evidence on voting tendencies or motives. Barraclough gives five page references to Bracher.[3] Three involve dateless restatements of the lower-middle-class argument, one deals with other topics. The final reference is to a discussion of the 1933 election, touching on party gains and losses, on nonvoters, on the working-class tendency, and on the religious factor (a subject to be covered here later). None of the references contains evidence to support Barraclough's claims about the lower middle class.

On the last of the pages referred to by Barraclough, Bracher refers his readers to another source, thus allowing the search to continue a step further. One is referred to "K. D. Bracher, W. Sauer, and G. Schulz, *Die nationalsozialistische Machtergreifung*, Cologne and Opladen, 1962, pp. 93 ff." The analysis there extends from page 93 to page 136. But most of those pages—95 to 133—contain mere listings of the March 1933 Reichstag election results, for thirty-five election districts and subdivisions thereof. A scattering of paragraphs appears throughout, drawing attention to noteworthy findings. No evidence appears there showing the results by class, that is to say, showing a distinctive lower-middle-class tendency.[4]

Bracher's unsupported statements in *The German Dictatorship* are preceded by claims about underlying motives. He refers to "the middle class's fear of proletarianization and Communism, and the added resentment and panic of a rural population threatened by the spread of modern technology. It should, therefore, not come as a surprise that National Socialism scored its greatest electoral successes first in rural Bavaria and then in the rural provinces of Schleswig-Holstein and Lower Saxony."[5] Barraclough has changed the motives attributed to both farm and nonfarm segments. Where Bracher refers to middle-class "fear of proletarianization and Communism," Barraclough reports the motive as "anti-capitalism." Bracher portrays the farmers as fearing the "spread of modern technology," Barraclough has them terrorized by "the modern capitalist and commercial state." Barraclough, in short, refers his readers to a blind source and, moreover, did not represent that source accurately.

One might withhold judgment about both authors' claims and put a prior question: How would anyone know the motives dominant within these two rather large collectivities, the rural and urban lower middle classes? No systematic surveys were done at the time, at least none that asked about voting or motives for the vote. If some informed source, say a journalist, social scientist, or ethnographer, had conducted unsystematic interviews (or engaged in "participant observation") in those ranks, those findings should long since have been referenced. Otherwise one should point out that the "conclusions" about motives are guesses, speculations, or imputations.

A third problem should be noted. Both quotations refer to regions of rural Germany, where the electoral lessons could be seen with relative ease. Neither author refers to evidence from German cities, from say, Berlin, Hamburg, Munich, or Essen, to show the distinctive lower-middle-class voting patterns. The absence of such evidence has a simple explanation: none exists.

There is also a fourth problem: Bracher refers to the electoral successes that came "first in rural Bavaria." That claim was then taken over intact by Barraclough. Detailed evidence is available on this point. It shows the claim to be, at best, a half-truth. Rural Bavaria contained a largely Protestant region in upper and middle Franconia. It also contained a (then) staunchly Catholic segment in upper and lower (or "old") Bavaria. The claim about the National Socialist electoral successes is valid for the former region but emphatically not for the latter.[6] The neglect of the religious factor, as seen in the previous chapter, has been persistent in discussions of the National Socialist electoral victories.

The election results published in German newspapers the day following any of the relevant elections showed clearly the centrality of religion. The treatment of this fact in these two sources proves instructive. Bracher's first explicit mention of the religious factor comes on the fifth of the pages cited, page 203, in a discussion of the March 1933 election. Even on that page, the reference might best be described as fugitive, two brief sentences: "In numerous Catholic and working-class strongholds, the National Socialists suffered clear-cut defeats. . . . Agrarian Protestant regions, small towns, and the lower middle class continued to furnish the majority of NSDAP votes."[7] Barraclough neglected the religious factor entirely.

Religion was easily the most striking factor linked to National Socialist voting. It was highly visible in any presentation of election results from at least September 1930. Any account purporting to explain "the Nazi vote" would have to, first, indicate the centrality of the religious factor and, second, give reasons for both the Protestant susceptibility and the Catholic immunity. The lower-middle-class propensity was not "visible" in those voting results. The claim was never backed up with evidence. Yet this thesis has been put front and center in some fifty years of subsequent "analy-sis." The immediately evident fact was neglected, whereas the fact that was neither evident nor subsequently established has been "explained" over and over again.[8]

Marx and Engels's discussions of the lower middle class were very "open" (or "flexible"), changing with the immediate analytical require-ments. The prediction of "reactionary" tendencies was only one of many options presented in their writings.[9] In subsequent treatment of the op-tions, however, first in the analyses provided by Social Democratic intel-lectuals, then in the analyses provided by journalists, literary figures, and academic intellectuals in Germany and elsewhere, there has been an ex-traordinary, single-minded convergence on *one* of the many predictions made by Marx and Engels, on the claim that the class was, and is, reac-tionary. The point is so well known as to scarcely deserve mention. One historian, David Blackbourn, in a dissenting statement, has provided a convenient summary of the tradition: "It has become customary for his-torians to stress the reactionary political potential of the lower middle class. Both the pre-industrial, independent lower middle class and the modern white-collar class have been cast as the natural prey of the ex-treme Right, the easily alarmed and defenseless victims of demagogues who have played successfully on the "classic" lower middle-class weak-nesses of economic insecurity, status anxiety, parochialism, and conserva-tive social morality. The susceptibility of the lower middle class to anti-modernist appeals has also become axiomatic."[10] In a supporting footnote, Blackbourn reported that this view "has now gained such wide currency that its appearance in particular studies would make a list too formidable to cite." Any informed reader could easily agree with that conclusion. Many readers, however, would not know the flimsy base of support for the claim.

In his discussion of the late Weimar-era years, Blackbourn declared that "a number of studies have indicated the particular attraction of NSDAP appeals to this group standing between organized capital and organized labour.[11] Two basic conclusions appear there: the situational claim, that the class was caught in the middle, being crushed by big business and big labor, and the motivational claim, that the lower middle class responded to the NSDAP appeals. Six references—one article and five books—are cited in support of this assertion.

The article referred to is the early and much-cited analysis by Charles P. Loomis and J. Allen Beegle, which focused on Nazism in selected rural areas (Protestant districts in Hanover, Catholic districts in Bavaria, plus some roughly comparable findings from Rudolf Heberle's study of Schleswig-Holstein, a heavily Protestant region). The findings are somewhat more complicated than Blackbourn suggests. The correlations of the percentages of small farms (less than two hectares) in the districts and the NSDAP percentages in the July 1932 Reichstag election are *negative* for Hanover and Bavaria ($-.55$ and $-.17$, respectively). Loomis and Beegle announce, without any evidence, that those small holders furnished labor for large estates or were industrial workers engaged in part-time farming. It is an easy theory-saving tactic: the nonconforming evidence is simply relabeled, and those small holders are no longer "lower middle class." The equivalent coefficients for the two- to twenty-hectare category for Schleswig-Holstein, Hanover, and Bavaria, respectively, are .85, .51, and .21, all positive, these providing strong, middling, and modest support for the received claim. In Bavaria, however, there is little justification for the emphasis on small farms (or lower middle class) since the correlations, as one goes from small to large, are: $-.17$, .21, $-.20$ (twenty to one hundred hectares), and .22 (one hundred hectares and over). An appropriate summary should note both the complexities and the regional differences.

A major finding reported by Loomis and Beegle is that "the larger the proportion of people who belonged to the Catholic faith . . . the smaller the Nazi vote," the figures for Hanover and Bavaria being $-.89$ and $-.90$. That conclusion is not mentioned by Blackbourn. It is another example of the procedure reported earlier: the strong and consistent finding goes unreported (and, of course, unexplained), the weaker and differentiated finding is given central attention and treated as a general result.[12]

Blackbourn's citation of the book-length studies also presents problems. To begin, no page numbers are indicated. That could be a rather formidable problem when, for example, checking into Karl Dietrich Bracher's monumental volume *Die Auflösung der Weimarer Republik*, a work of more than seven hundred pages. Blackbourn could easily have supplied the appropriate pages, but then the electoral data contained there prove to be rather crude, and they do not provide any specific or compelling support for the claim of lower-middle-class propensities.[13]

The work of William S. Allen is also cited. Allen lived in a German community for fifteen months, researching the documentary record and interviewing, beginning in 1956. His work is probably the best that will ever appear on the motivational question. Again Blackbourn's claim is not supported. Allen, first of all, did not focus on the lower-middle-class segments; his analysis dealt with general middle-class propensities. With evidence, as seen in the previous chapter, he rejected the claim of "impoverishment" or "proletarianization" as a determinant of NSDAP support. And he did not portray the middle class as "caught in the middle." Instead he declared, unambiguously, that it was "hatred for the SPD that drove [the town's voters] into the arms of the Nazis."[14]

To this point, none of Blackbourn's claims has been supported in the three sources reviewed. Examination of the remaining citations—three books is made difficult by the failure to provide specific page references. Rather than continuing the search for fugitive evidence, I offer the conclusion from my earlier review wherein all three works were discussed: "For all the emphasis and for all the certitude about lower middle class tendencies, the supporting evidence is either lacking entirely or, where present, of a rather tenuous character."[15]

The lower-middle-class thesis is put forward as a general argument. The problems, the stresses and strains, are said to affect the petty bourgeoisie everywhere. The following quotation applies the claim to the experience of five nations. It also provides another example of the persistent disparity between assertion and evidence, a problem that regularly accompanies discussions of "the lower middle class." The passage is by Seymour Martin Lipset, the eminent political sociologist, who introduces and quotes from the work of Mattei Dogan: "A review of the evidence dealing with the support of political tendencies in Italy and France, as of the mid-1960s, notes 'that, on the electoral level at least, Neo-Fascism, Poujadism, and the "activism" of Extreme Rightists are—as were German Nazism, Belgian Rexism, French *Croix de Feu*, Romanian Iron Guard of the 1930s—the expression of the petty bourgeoisie.' "[16]

Dogan's discussion and tables in the pages immediately preceding that summary conclusion deal only with France, not Italy. They address only the French legislative elections of 1956 and 1958, not tendencies "as of the mid-1960s." They deal with a short-lived protest party, led by Pierre Poujade, that made appeals to small businessmen and artisans. The first of Dogan's four tables contains a footnote that reads: "This estimate refers only to the 1956 elections," that is, to the occasion of the brief Poujadist success. His estimate has half of the independent businessmen voting "anti-Republican or Poujadist" in 1956 as opposed to only 11 percent voting for parties of the Left. That estimate differs from the figures contained in Lipset's *Political Man*, (based on an actual survey), which are, respectively, 43 and 28 percent. That support for the Left, moreover, is likely to be understated, Communist voters being especially hesitant to reveal their preferences. Three other tables presented by Dogan contain detailed breakdowns for four middle-class segments. All three tables, however, include the following statement just under the title: "conjectural estimates: to be interpreted as a scale of magnitude." The first seven syllables may be translated with a word of two syllables—*guesses*. Dogan's article, incidentally, contains no review of evidence bearing on the 1930s fascist movements.[17]

Lipset continues, in the same paragraph, with a second quotation: "And Mattei Dogan goes on to emphasize that 'surveys on the most diverse problems—economic, social, cultural, religious, and moral—show that the [main supporters of such movements] the so-called independent petty bourgeoisie manifest more sectarian, more 'misoneistic' (anti-novelty) opinions than the middle bourgeoisie, who in turn appear somewhat less liberal, less tolerant, than the upper bourgeoisie. And this is a fact not only in France and Italy, but in many other countries as well." Those conclusions, however, must be taken on faith since Dogan presents no evidence bearing on those claims, nor does he present a single reference to relevant sources. The conclusions presented with such confidence, with such assurance of backing, come with no evident support.[18]

Analysis versus Derogation

The accounts reviewed to this point might be described as neutral in tone. They merely describe the supposed position of the class and the supposed response. Other accounts inject an element of hostility scarcely matched anywhere in the entire social science or historical literature. The examples that follow show the "progress" of an idea across three intellectual generations.

In the mid-sixties, Ralf Dahrendorf, the eminent sociologist, provided a nomenclature and portraits of the classes in German society, which were derived in part from the earlier work of Theodor Geiger. The delineation of classes is a relatively easy task. If census materials allow, one can then establish the size of those classes and show their growth, stability, or decline, that being more difficult but still a relatively easy task. The next step, however, the description of the attitudes, outlooks, or behaviors of those classes, poses considerable difficulties. Dahrendorf first addresses this question hypothetically: "The notion of stratum or class mentality is plausible too: there are certain economic, political, and social attitudes that adhere to social positions just as role expectations do. Whoever becomes an entrepreneur is faced with these attitudes as a demand on him, and so is the clerical worker, the industrial worker, the peasant." Having argued the plausible case, he then provides a qualification, suggesting a central tendency with deviant or exceptional cases: "Class mentalities are never completely uniform. And not every member of a stratum displays the expected mentality at any given time; here, as with other role expectations, there are deviants, outsiders, marginal figures, and strangers."[19]

While a "class mentality" is certainly possible, one must still ask: What of the reality? A test of the mentality claim requires some specification of those "certain economic, political, and social attitudes." Once specified, the matter must then be researched. One must discover how much difference, if any, exists between the various "social positions." The sense of Dahrendorf's discussion is that a clear dominant (and distinctive) tendency is to be found within each of the classes; after discounting the exceptions, "class" should prove extremely useful in accounting for attitudes and behavior. Is that the case? An adequate answer to this question may be achieved only through investigation.[20] Dahrendorf neglected that option, proceeding instead with the following methodological comments:

> The picture of German social stratification that I would suggest . . . is not backed up by statistical analysis. In so far as quantitative statements are made, they are based on informed discretion, that is, reasoned estimate—a procedure that, in view of the fleeting boundaries between the strata, may be appropriate even in principle. So far as the description of mentalities is concerned, it is subject to Geiger's own reservation that it does not yield "any final results": "For an exact investigation of mentalities would require empirical material in great quantities." Since in social research such data have today become available at least in greater quantities than in 1932, it may be somewhat excusable if, contrary to Geiger, we venture "too far into the realm of interpretative construction."[21]

Dahrendorf's conclusions, as indicated in the first sentence, will not be "not backed up" by any evidence. "Informed discretion" and "reasoned estimate" are elegant ways of saying "I have no basis for these claims." "Interpretative construction" has a simple translation—a guess. The remainder of his chapter lays out, over several pages, a series of completely unsubstantiated claims about the "mentalities" of various classes. There was, perhaps, some justification for Geiger's "interpretive construction" because he was writing in the early 1930s, when there were few serious surveys or polls, but Dahrendorf was writing when a wide range of survey results were available from the Federal Republic.[22]

Dahrendorf delineated three nonmanual segments (apart from a tiny elite): a service class (basically the civil servants); a middle class (independent proprietors, farm and non-farm, owners of enterprises from giant to minute, plus salaried managers); and a "false" middle class (salaried persons in tertiary sector employment). He provided estimates of the size of the segments and described, in one or two paragraphs, their mentalities.

The description of the service class ("service to those in power"), which is embellished by quotations from Karl Renner and Theodor Geiger, focused on status. Modern society, he wrote, "provides the service class with many an occasion for displaying its social mentality: makes of cars and places of vacation, choir stools in the living room, and seven dwarfs in the front garden, the wife's coat and the children's toys. Members of the service class are the original status seekers." The self-employed middle class, one is told, "is not a seat of liberal convictions but, on the contrary, one of the main claimants for the protective hand of the state. As a group, it is not adventurous but anxious, not expansive but defensive, not liberal but protectionist, not an element of progress but a retarding force. . . . A propensity for estatelike closure, coupled with a temerity, if not resignation, from which only to demand for state protection occasionally awakens it, characterizes Germany's old middle class from the professions right down to small peasants and shopkeepers." The large entrepreneurs or dependent managers clamor "less noisily" for state protection. It would, nevertheless, "be an exaggeration to characterize them by initiative and daring." The false middle class consists of those in subordinate positions in service industries—"the waiter and the salesgirl, the conductor and the postman, the chauffeur and the gas station attendant." They are middle class only in "social self-evaluation." This portrait is the least flattering of the three:

Nobody defends middle-class rights and interests more noisily than the problematic members of this stratum, the workers of the tertiary industries. Moreover, the contradiction between social position and social consciousness makes this stratum a particularly unreliable category in political terms; no party that has won the support of this group can be very confident of its strength. It is no accident—and it has consequences for the mental make-up of professionals of these trades—that conversations at the hairdresser's, or across the counter, at gas stations and in restaurants, are stereotyped as few other social situations are.[23]

Dahrendorf's "interpretative construction" came more than a century after the original Marx-Engels exposition. In terms of method, however, little had changed. Dahrendorf too had announced the existence of an assortment of classes and provided an extensive description of their characteristics.

A near-exact repeat of the Dahrendorf performance appeared in the early 1980s. The following passage is from a book by historian Michael H. Kater: "What was this 'lower middle class mentality' that most of the Nazi functionaries shared with the petit bourgeois core of the rank and file and that constituted another normative criterion of their specific character as a cohort? It has already been suggested . . . that during the Weimar Republic a relationship existed between class and mentality. As Ralf Dahrendorf wrote in 1968 [*sic*], despite a lack of empirical evidence on which to base an exact examination of mentalities in terms of class criteria, a correlation between the two concepts did indeed exist."[24] Dahrendorf's "certain economic, political, and social attitudes" quotation then follows.

That "a relationship" between class and mentality existed during the Weimar Republic (or at any time) is certainly *likely*, but, since relationships can range all the way from trivial to enormous, one must also ask, How much difference? A relationship, moreover, can be positive or negative, that is to say, in accord or in conflict with any suggested claim. Kater's handling of the problem, absent evidence, does not improve on Dahrendorf's murky original. The difficulty is indicated in his curious no-but-yes formulation—despite the lack of evidence, a correlation did indeed exist. Use of the word *exact* does not avoid the difficulty; one cannot claim imprecise measurement to be the problem when nothing has been measured.

Kater does not stop with the declaration of a formal possibility. "Dahrendorf himself," the reader is told, "mentions industriousness or love of hard work; and for the German petit bourgeois of the 1920s and early 1930s other characteristics can be added—anti-intellectuality, ideological dogmatism, xenophobia, bureaucratic formalism, and authoritarian traditionalism. These inclinations and their extensions constitute a catalogue of values that may be said, on the one hand, to have been germane to the German lower middle class, and, on the other, to have possessed a special potential for breeding fascist proclivities."[25] Kater refers his readers to page 367 of Dahrendorf, where one does find references to industry and hard work. The chapter in question, however, is entitled "The German Character" and that page summarizes public opinion surveys from the 1950s and early 1960s. Dahrendorf was not discussing the "petit bourgeois" at that point nor was he dealing with Weimar Germany. He was describing the entire adult population of the Federal Republic of Germany.

Kater's list of ugly traits comes without any support whatsoever. The Dahrendorf reference proves a false lead. Kater adds a reference to another source: "The judgment on the petit bourgeois agrees with Mayer, 'Lower Middle Class,' page 432." On that page, Arno J. Mayer stated that "in certain conjunctures" besieged elites will cultivate the petite bourgeoisie, offering fulsome praise for their many positive traits. Some socialist ideologues, he added, denounce the "petit bourgeois" for "being pretentious and parasitic." Nowhere on that page, however, is any mention made of the unsavory traits listed by Kater.[26]

Mayer's frequently cited article provides another example of the dataless and derogatory portraits of the lower middle class. He reviews the Marx-Engels claims about the "swing" character of the petty bourgeoisie in 1848. This argument, the claim of vacillation, of unsteady direction, is probably the most frequent alternative to the claim of lower-middle-class reaction. Without any independent evidence, Mayer gives full credence to those claims. He recognizes the persistent deprecating treatment of the class—"Marxists and liberals," he declares, already by the early 1920s "had long since taken to using the term 'petit bourgeois' as one of denigration, abuse, and contempt." Mayer himself feels that constricting conditions "may well predispose [the class] to rally to a politics of anger, scapegoating, and atavistic millenarianism." He also cites, with evident approval, a comment by Engels about the "*mesquin* character . . . [and]

short-sighted, pusillanimous, wavering spirit" of the class.[27] Later he declares that "on the score of social contacts, job security, and advancement, the mixture of illusion and reality tends to be weighted in favor of the former." Writing again as the disinterested analyst, Mayer reports that "superordinate elites," in normal times, "see the lower middle class in a rather negative light." They look down on the petty bourgeois "for being mediocre, provincial, conformist, unambitious, parasitic, selfish, rigid, resentful, prudish, and moralistic." To this Mayer adds his own comment, indicating that even in times of stress "incumbent elites have little to fear from the lower middle class," because "the *Kleinbürger* is languid by habit." This claim is followed by the previously reported observation that in "certain conjunctures," when the elite is in need of allies, they are rich in praise of lower-middle-class virtues.[28] Some segments of the class, "those for whom a conjunctural threat of economic and social decline aggravates latent inner anxieties," Mayer declares, "are particularly prone to metapolitical appeals of a xenophobic and conspiratorial nature." Xenophobia is the only trait, incidentally, that also appears on Kater's list.

Mayer's final conclusion is that in times of severe crisis the lower middle class "develops considerable internal coherence." In the early phase of the crisis, it "may join" in support of "anti-establishment radicalism," but that "swing" is a phase, a passing episode. "Eventually" the lower middle class joins with "those higher social classes and governing elites on whom it never ceases to be dependent and for whom it feels envy exacerbated by resentment." In "the final analysis," it comes out "in favor of the ruling class." "It is this inner core of conservatism, ultimately revealed in moments of acute social and political conflict," Mayer tells us, "that is common to all segments of the lower middle class."

Because of these distinctive dynamics, Mayer declares, the lower middle class must be treated as "a significant historical problem." A judgment of significance, however, must depend on a prior assessment of the empirical adequacy of the claims that have been provided. But like the previous episodes of "documentation" reviewed here, this achievement also, to borrow Mayer's phrase, is weighted more in favor of the illusion than the reality.

Mayer offers an appearance of scholarship in that many books are cited. Knowledgeable readers, however, will recognize that many of them are of doubtful relevance. Nicos Poulantzas, for example, who only rarely engaged in research, certainly provided none showing trends in class differences.[29] To support a claim of "envy exacerbated by resentment," Mayer refers readers to Max Scheler's book *Ressentiment*, a work of speculative philosophy.[30] The portrayal contained in Hans Fallada's novel *Kleiner Mann—was nun?*, on the whole, challenges rather than supports Mayer's claims. A reference to Sinclair Lewis's *Babbitt* seems rather distant for a portrait of the lower middle class as "volatile in crisis." Much of Mayer's citation is not to evidence but rather to persons who have said essentially the same thing, such as George Orwell in *The Road to Wigan Pier*. Most of the books cited come without specific page references. Where pages are given, in approximately two-thirds of those instances, it is to the works of Marx, Engels, and Lenin.[31] The article, in short, proves to be a work of intellectual history, reporting what has been said about the lower middle class within a given tradition, rather than a contribution to social history, that is, one showing how the class actually behaved.[32]

Lest there be any doubt about this point, it should be noted that Mayer has not established (that is, with evidence) the outlooks of any lower middle class at any time. He has not shown its passage from the "polymorphous" state to one of "internal coherence" in so much as a single crisis. He has not established the alleged "swing" at any point in history. Nor has he shown that any segments (let alone "all" of them) reveal an ultimate "inner core of conservatism."[33]

Another work that without any serious evidence provides an insistently negative portrait of the lower middle class is C. Wright Mills's *White Collar*. The book received a scathing review from Dwight MacDonald, the noted social commentator. In response to a concerned letter from Mills, Richard Hofstadter, the noted historian, offered reassurance but, at the same time, reported some of his own reactions: "Look at your introduction: the words you apply to the white collar man: living out in slow misery his yearning for the quick climb, pushed by forces, pulled, acted upon but does not act, never talks back, never takes a stand, in a frantic hurry, paralyzed with fear, morally defenseless, impotent as a group, open to the focused onslaught of manufactured loyalties, turns to his leisure frenziedly, bored at work, restless at play, standardized loser, must practice prompt repression of resentment and aggression, etc. I don't totally reject this, but there is something else even in white collar life." At another point, Hofstadter declares that "there is a lot of human ugliness in the book—which is, I note, caught up in the jacket description of the book as a 'merciless portrayal' of a whole class. There are some people and perhaps even some classes in society that may call for merciless treatment, but why be so merciless with all these little people? If their situation is characteristically as bad as you say it is—which I doubt—that in a book which candidly seeks to express emotion as well as to analyze, why no pity, no warmth? Why condemn—to paraphrase Burke—a whole class?"[34]

The negative portraits of the lower middle class continue to appear. In a recent variation on the theme, the historian Christopher Lasch has provided some unexpectedly positive words, commending the class for its "egalitarianism, its respect for workmanship, its understanding of the value of loyalty, and its struggle against the moral temptation of resentment." That said, Lasch then offers his own statement of the familiar litany, referring to the "characteristic vices" of the class, "envy, resentment, and servility." Lasch writes, "I have no intention of minimizing the narrowness and provincialism of lower-middle-class culture, nor do I deny that it has produced racism, nativism, anti-intellectualism, and all the other evils so often cited by liberal critics." Liberals, he concludes, again turning to the neglected merits, have been blind to "the positive features of petty-bourgeois culture: its moral realism, its understanding that everything has its price, its respect for limits, its skepticism about progress."[35]

It is a peculiar history. Marx and Engels extemporized a series of claims—hypotheses—about the lower middle class. Within a few decades, most of their followers came to agree on a "consensus position," on the reactionary option, accepting it as the true, accurate, or "correct" line on the subject. Many nonmarxists, members of the liberal intelligentsia, also accepted that consensus, which came to be a standard element of the worldview of both the social and literary sciences in Europe and North America. While some of that "analysis" (deduction, or in some cases, mere declaration) might be counted as dispassionate, a mere delineation of the logic of the case, other accounts come heavily laden with derogation.[36]

That intellectual tradition appears to have been distinctively rooted within Germany, specifically within Social Democracy. The view appears to have been taken over by liberal journalists and, with time, was found also in German scholarship. The view provided a ready-made "explanation" for the rise of National Socialism. That line of analysis, particularly after 1933, was exported to other countries and gained acceptance there also, particularly in intellectual circles. It is understandable that eventually the outlines of that position would come to be applied to the experience of those other nations. Mayer's general account is only one of many attempting to "demonstrate" this wider application. Mills borrowed heavily from the German intellectual heritage for the framework he applied to the American experience. All of this effort, from its inception to the present, comes without benefit of any serious confirming research, without any competent investigation to validate the claims that are offered with such assurance. It is a most unusual performance for persons who ostensibly operate within a scientific tradition.

One might wonder about the impact of such efforts. What would be the effect of this kind of portrayal, of this condemnation of an entire class? That negative view, however, is not widely shared in the general population. The Opinion Research Corporation (ORC), beginning in the mid-seventies, has asked national samples of the American adult population how they would rate the "ethical and moral practices" of some eighteen occupations. One presentation of those results averaged the findings of four samplings from 1975 to 1981, showing physicians receiving the highest rating, 73 percent judging their practices as excellent or good. Two groups were tied for second with 71 percent ratings, small business proprietors and average workers. Similar results were found in 1983 and 1985 samplings.

Small business did not uniformly gain such high ratings. Another ORC question asked about the "trust and confidence" respondents placed in various institutions. "Small companies" (not quite the same as "small business") were ninth on a list of fourteen institutions. Although well down on the list, they were still ahead of the large companies, twelfth on the list. The most trusted institutions, by a wide margin, were the churches. A 1976 Harris survey asked whether twenty-five industries did a good or poor job "in serving customers." In this case, banks received the most favorable rating. In second place were the "small shopkeepers." Questions comparing the merits of big versus small companies (or big versus small business) found the public generally more favorably disposed to the latter. Small companies, for example, were viewed as "more likely to be honest" in dealing with the respondents. In contrast to the 71 percent rating of small business "ethical and moral practices" (reported in the text), corporate executives received a mere 33. Small business is generally viewed as powerless, in sharp contrast to the view of big business. Lipset and Schneider comment at follows: "Americans are acutely aware of the powerlessness of small business, and that perception seems to make small business more likeable."[37]

The attitudes of the West German population toward the petty bourgeoisie (kleinbürger) have also been explored. There too, public attitudes differ sharply from the positions adopted by many intellectuals. The Institut für Demoskopie interviewed two thousand persons early in 1982 for this purpose. Sixteen descriptive terms were presented and respondents were asked if they applied to the kleinbürger. The responses were generally favorable. Seventy-two percent associated the petty bourgeoisie with "family." Other positive descriptions were: thrifty, 71 percent; diligent, 66 percent; honest, 57 percent; convivial, 49 percent. The most agreement on a negative term, 38 percent, was on the often-heard *spiessig*—narrow-minded or stuffy. Perhaps the most noteworthy result was that only 8 percent associated the term "fascistic" with kleinbürger. One group in West Germany stands out for its "recognition" of this linkage, those who indicated support for the Green parties. One-fifth of that segment saw an undoubted link between "the" petty bourgeoisie and fascism, and another fifth saw "some" (*etwas*) linkage. The Greens, on the whole, have a young and highly educated constituency. The linkage that this minority senses is likely to be the result of recent "school training." As opposed to the portrait of petty bourgeoisie as villain, the general populace sees the class as composed of "nice people" (*nette Leute*), 44 percent of respondents making an unqualified choice of that option and another 28 percent seeing "some" tendency in that direction.[38]

These results make the performance of those intellectuals even more paradoxical. The majority of the population, people who doubtlessly have regular contact with "the petty bourgeoisie," portray the class in a generally favorable light. An important segment of the intellectual class, however, without any serious compelling evidence, *knows* them, the entire class, to be morally suspect.

The Social Misconstruction—A Note on Its Origins

In a 1984 review of several works on National Socialism, James J. Sheehan, a leading historian of Germany, wrote that "the most popular social interpretation of Hitler's success stressed his appeal to the 'lower middle class.' " After a brief review of the argument, Sheehan noted that my book *Who Voted for Hitler?* is a sustained attack on that thesis. "By the time he is through," Sheehan wrote, the argument "is very badly battered indeed. The best that can be said for certain versions of the argument is that they have yet to be corroborated; in fact, after reading Hamilton's examination of the argument and the evidence upon which it rests, one can't help but wonder how so many could have believed something for so long on the basis of so little."[39] Sheehan's concern may be addressed by posing two basic questions: How did this misconstruction come about? And how did it manage to persist?

To address the first question, it is appropriate to begin with the work of Theodor Geiger, author of the much-cited "Panik im Mittelstand" article from 1930. Geiger was probably Germany's leading sociologist at that point. Any doubt about that claim could be removed through the addition of a qualifying expression—he was Germany's leading empirically oriented sociologist.[40] His subsequent monograph, *Die soziale Schichtung des deutschen Volkes* (1932), was, and is, an important empirically based study in the field of social stratification. Rather than merely speculating on the subject, Geiger worked through German census materials to produce a documented quantitative portrait of Germany's classes. In the same monograph, however, Geiger inserted some accounts of class "mentalities" and these, as indicated, lacked any serious empirical foundation. His portrait of the lower middle class, not too surprisingly, matched his earlier account of the middle-class panic. The critical reader would have been justified in accepting Geiger's class nomenclature, but the same reader ought to have viewed the claims about "mentalities" with skepticism: they should have been recognized as unsupported hypotheses.

The Geiger argument just reviewed involves a two-variable relationship, that of class and mentality, with the former actually measured but the latter not. That particular focus, however, avoids the key consideration in "the" lower-middle-class argument, a specific behavior: votes cast for Hitler or his party. In this respect also Geiger had neglected the empirical task; he presented no evidence to demonstrate that distinctive lower-middle-class voting tendency.

For Geiger, the most easily accessible evidence appeared on the Mondays following those elections in the newspapers of his home city, Braunschweig. The aggregate national results told nothing of the lower-middle-class tendency, nor did the figures for the nation's thirty-five electoral districts. The detailed figures for Braunschweig, his best immediate information, carried an unexpected lesson. They indicated the greatest support for the National Socialists in the "best" areas of the city. Hitler's strongest showing in the presidential election, for example, came in seven upper-middle-class precincts, the range, in the second round of 1932, extending from 62 to 72 percent. The citywide results, moreover, provided no immediate, obvious, or compelling evidence showing a distinctive lower-middle-class tendency. If Geiger had explored that evidence, he would have seen the need for some revision of his analysis. That research would have been based on the experience of a single city, the thirty-fourth largest in the nation. But, lacking comparable evidence for more important urban centers, for Berlin, Hamburg, Cologne, and so forth, he should have recognized a need for caution. Had he investigated that most easily accessible evidence, Geiger would have been obliged to report nonsupport for the lower-middle-class argument in the only case for which he had evidence.

One extenuating circumstance is that discovery of the lessons contained in a given newspaper's report of the previous day's voting was not obtained without some effort. Typically, one was provided with a listing of votes for six or so parties for all of a city's precincts. In Munich, for example, one was faced with some eight hundred precincts. In Braunschweig, Geiger would have faced seventy-six precincts. One would have to calculate the percentages, for example, of support for the NSDAP and to know the city well (or undertake the needed research) to allow the conclusion, for example, that the votes cast in the Raabeschule were those of predominantly lower-middle-class voters.[41]

A study by Fritz Hasselhorn analyzed the 1930s election results from an important university town, Göttingen. His results, published a half-century after the events, provide another example of evidence "not seen" on its first appearance. In the early 1930s, the city had twenty precincts which Hasselhorn grouped into five segments: academic quarter, civil servant quarter, city center, railroad quarter, and worker quarter. The city center (Innenstadt) would be the most likely lower-middle-class district. In the September 1930 Reichstag election, 37.8 percent of the city's votes went to the NSDAP. By district, the respective percentages were: 33.5, 44.0, 39.8, 34.3, and 34.8. In the July 1932 election, a majority of the votes cast in the city, 51.0 percent, went to the NSDAP. The respective district percentages then were: 49.8, 58.6, 52.1, 46.8, and 46.4. Hasselhorn indicates that the NSDAP drew support from all segments. The city center, clearly, was not exceptional. The lesson in this case was easily seen, but the "research opportunity" was missed.[42]

One key aspect of the explanation for the origin of the lower-middle-class thesis in the German context must focus on the simple fact of the failure to research the claim. Theodor Geiger did not undertake the necessary task—and others, persons less committed to research, also avoided the task. If undertaken, that research would have yielded some striking instances of nonsupport in major urban contexts and, on the basis of what we now know, an absence of compelling supporting evidence.

That research failure was only one part of the problem. There was also a problem of prior disposition. The ready acceptance of an unsupported hypothesis points to some important previous "conditioning." Social scientists, journalists, and other commentators apparently had been trained to view this single logical case as sufficient to explain the new developments. They were, apparently, so thoroughly conditioned that they gave no serious consideration to any alternative logic, even when relevant evidence suggested the need.[43] The experience provides striking evidence of the power of a plausible paradigm. It would be a mistake, however, to see the convergence on the point as depending on "compelling logic" alone, as a victory of "pure reason." The acceptance of "the case" was not the result of individual assessments and judgments. It was a social construction, the product of initial training and subsequent interpersonal influences.

The Social Misconstruction—A Note on Its Persistence

How did the view come to persist? Since we do not know the thought processes of those many subsequent commentators, any answer to this question must be based largely on surmise. A trained disposition seems likely. Generations of students had been taught to believe the lower-middle-class thesis, their teachers having vouched for both diagnosis and conclusion. The subjects in Asch's conformity studies were provided direct, immediate cues by strangers. The "subjects" in university classes were provided with direct cues by leading professors, backed by the assurance that this "knowledge" was the work of many eminent scholars. But here one was dealing with an appearance of scholarly research which means the conclusions had been taken on faith, a faith that has been sustained with an impressive array of sources. Much of that effort, however, involved citation chains, or "sources" that are not sources. Some examples of the effort, although accompanied by "references," are more appropriately described as creative writing.

Additional insight into scholarly procedures may be gained through consideration of the lower-middle-class thesis in work that has appeared subsequent to the publication of *Who Voted for Hitler?*. The availability of relevant evidence provides an appropriate "experimental condition" for exploration of the responses to a challenge to a received paradigm.[44] Reporting relevant evidence (whether favorable, unfavorable, or "undecided") with respect to a given thesis is an important scientific norm. In an edited volume, a collection of articles published in 1986, this norm was not honored. The editor declared that the volume provided "a representative cross-section of the new research on the formation of the National Socialist constituency," offering "a useful guide to the methodological innovations of the past decade and presenting important findings of the most recent scholarship on the social bases of Nazism during its rise to power." Although the editor and contributors knew of my work, no report of the principal findings appeared anywhere in the collection.[45]

Some commentators raised a methodological objection to my study of voting patterns in German cities: it is based on a nonrepresentative sample of German cities.[46] The point is entirely accurate. For several reasons, from the start, the achievement of a representative sample seemed unlikely. At the time, many German cities were inaccessible, located in either the German Democratic Republic, Poland, or in one case, the Soviet Union. The state of the archival holdings also seemed likely to pose problems. Subsequent investigation showed this "hypothesis" to be amply supported. Much information was unavailable due to initial indifference or to subsequent loss in air raids. Due to the basic federal arrangements, German cities have quite diverse data collection and retention procedures. A given city might have "a lot" (as was the case with Hamburg); others had little (as with Munich); some had virtually none (as with Gelsenkirchen). Almost all cities had some voting records. Few, however, had any systematic evidence on the social character of subareas. Only two cities had data that in any away allowed a match of social characteristics and voting. While one might hope to see results for a "representative sample" of cities, that possibility, at the outset, struck me as an unrealizable aspiration.

My aim was to begin with the largest city, Berlin, and to work "down the list" as time and funds allowed. The most complete holdings, I thought, would be found in the largest cities. On the whole that judgment was supported in my subsequent experience. Given the diverse procedures in local statistical offices and municipal archives, I recognized the likelihood of uneven results, some good, some not so good, and hoped for the "lucky hit." Throughout the effort, I was assuming that some information was better than none. If we had results for Berlin, Hamburg, and Cologne, for example, that would be better than the previous situation—the absence of any serious urban results.[47] I also made another assumption: the findings presented could, at any time, be extended through the investigation of archival holdings in other cities. It was a possibility open to any researcher, but would, of course, be easiest for those "on the scene," for German social historians possibly or for their students.

A double standard appears in this connection, a direct parallel to one seen with respect to the Weber thesis. A weak standard is allowed for the original claim; a stringent one is set for the challenge. Although clearly unrealistic, the challenge to the lower-middle-class thesis is held to the strictest methodological requirement. That demand assumes, in effect, that "no evidence" is more compelling than "some evidence." A more appropriate reading perhaps would stress the conjunction: it is "no evidence" backed by a longstanding consensus that is "compelling." Again a simple question arises: Should scholars be guided by a consensus or by evidence? If the latter, then one must respect a second scholarly norm: there shall be no double standard.

Another procedure for "saving the case" involves a revision, a transformation of the original argument. That original, the longstanding claim, as noted earlier, is a causal argument dealing with the susceptibility of various classes to National Socialist appeals. The revision shifts to the question of composition, the proportion of National Socialist voters drawn from the various classes. The causal argument alleges a striking lower-middle-class tendency. The compositional statement asserts that a majority of the NSDAP votes came from the middle class (or that a disproportionate share came from the lower middle class). It is an important distinction, illustrated by two hypothetical possibilities: 70 percent of the lower middle class voted for Hitler (as opposed to 20 to 25 percent in other classes) versus 35 percent of Hitler's vote came from the lower middle class (which formed 25 percent of the electorate). If the former does not "work," the argument may be "saved" through the shift in focus.[48]

Still another procedure allows one, on the surface at least, to have it both ways. This process involves an argument of sequence or phases: the NSDAP began as a lower-middle-class movement and then, successfully, drew support from other classes to become a volkspartei. This position has been argued by Thomas Childers, who reports that the "hard core of the NSDAP's constituency was, indeed, drawn primarily from the lower middle class, just as the traditional literature assumed." Then, between 1928 and 1932, the NSDAP "attracted support of unprecedented social breadth. . . . What made the NSDAP's success so remarkable was its ability, in a period of severe economic distress, to reach beyond its lower-middle-class base to attract crisis-related protests [*sic*] voters from a wide variety of social backgrounds." Those statements alleging a trend or a transformation are not accompanied by supporting documentation. Relevant trend data is available for two major cities, for Berlin and Hamburg. The correlations between the socioeconomic status of subareas and support for the National Socialists were strong and positive at all points from 1924 to 1932. In Berlin, the coefficients were .69 and .63 in the 1924 elections. The figure increased in September 1930 to .81 and held at that level again in July 1932. In November 1932, the coefficient fell to .68, reflecting a decline in upper- and upper-middle-class support. In Hamburg, the coefficients were .82 and .80 in the 1924 elections and .84 and .83 in those of 1932.[49]

Several other authors have sought to rescue the lower-middle-class thesis by "having it both ways"—yes, there is new evidence, but no, nothing is changed, the handed-down claim is as valid as ever. They play down the importance of the new evidence, and, without presentation of evidence, new or old, reaffirm the validity and importance of the "ancient truth." Along with Caplan, Eley, and Childers, these authors argue "importance" without giving any indication of quantity. Since importance can range from much to little, from enormous to a jot, something more than the unspecified declaration is in order. If one recognizes the greater importance of other segments (of upper, upper middle, and working classes), it follows, like the night the day, that the importance of the lower middle class would be diminished. The key question is, How much diminished? Or, put differently, how much importance—if any—remains?[50]

As an aid to future scholarly efforts, a consideration of the kind of evidence needed to sustain the lower-middle-class thesis might prove useful. The sense of the argument is that "the lower middle class" provided strong support for Hitler's party and that other classes did not, that is to say, they gave the party rather limited support. Let us imagine we have a high-quality survey of the German electorate undertaken just before the key Reichstag election of 31 July 1932. To test the received line of analysis, we would first sort the nonfarm respondents by class into four segments: upper, upper middle, lower middle, and working. We would then examine the vote intentions reported. Let us imagine the following results: percentages supporting the NSDAP—upper class, 15 percent; upper middle class, 25 percent; lower middle class, 60 percent; and working class, 25 percent. Those figures would be "ideal" for confirmation of the hypothesis. One could imagine any number of variations, for example, 70 percent for the lower middle class and only 15 percent for the working class.

Testing the hypothesis in the farm population would require a different procedure. Again working with our imagined survey, we might divide the respondents by size of unit into equal thirds—small, middle, and large farm enterprises. If here, overall, some 60 percent had favored the NSDAP, the hypothesis would require differentiation, with small farmers "out front" at say 80 percent, the middle segment at 60 percent, and the large at 40 percent. Again one may imagine many variations on the theme. Basically, a confirmation requires a strong tendency in the indicated direction.

Those initial presentations of "survey results," those simple cross-tabulations of class and vote, would be problematic from the outset since they fail to consider the religious factor. Given the marked differences in their voting tendencies, one would have to examine the relationships separately for Protestants and Catholics. Confirmation of the original hypothesis would require the demonstration of a distinctive lower-middle-class preference for the NSDAP within each of the major religious communities.

A first observation to be made about these "results" is that we have never seen actual survey figures of this kind. The requisite contemporary survey was never undertaken. The next best procedure was (and is) the analysis of aggregate voting results. It is the only method available for the analysis of voting patterns in those elections. It is the procedure which has been used, in one way or another, now for more than sixty years.

Have aggregate voting studies provided results that approximate those of the hypothetical survey? The basic answer is no, they have not. The most comprehensive and systematic analyses, those of Jürgen Falter, indicate, as we have seen, a clear rejection of the basic hypothesis in Protestant farm areas. There the average size of holding and NSDAP support were positively related. My analyses of urban voting patterns showed either no difference or, with much greater frequency, a tendency for NSDAP support to increase with the class level of the district; nowhere was a pronounced lower-middle-class preference for the NSDAP found. Falter's data did not allow exploration of the basic question in the urban context. His analysis pointed in another direction: it showed distinctive susceptibilities of the independent (or "old") middle-class category. The only support for the basic hypothesis appeared, curiously, in the Catholic farm areas. Given the low level of NSDAP voting in such areas, however, that contribution would be modest, certainly not a "powerful factor" in explanation of the overall result.[51]

The lower-middle-class argument has had a long history. Many people have reported the "conclusion," but the agreement of hundreds, or even thousands, by itself, is nothing more than a social construction. Agreement is not evidence. Most recitations of the tale argue both the tendency and the weight (importance, explanatory power), but without evidence, the judgment of weight is every bit as fictive as the unsupported assertion of the tendency.[52]

6

Michel Foucault:
The Disciplinary Society

In his book *Discipline and Punish: The Birth of the Prison*, Michel Foucault offers a stunning revisionist account of the history of punishment. The
traditional reading, found in standard textbooks, saw the reforms institut-
ed over the last two centuries as progress. Liberals everywhere had condemned the entire array of old regime punishments, the torture and forced
confessions, the stocks, the lash, branding, cutting off of ears, and so on.
The sweeping use of the death penalty (Britain had 350 capital offences in
1780) was further proof of the moral bankruptcy of the old regimes, especially when grotesque tortures preceded the actual killing of the offenders.
The prison (called a penitentiary in some settings) was seen as a progressive step. The advanced nations thereby shifted from punishment as a
vengeance or retribution to punishment as correction, as reform of character, as a step toward eventual rehabilitation. The implementation of those
reforms was viewed as one component of the liberal victory. The change
in punishments, along with constitutions, guarantees of basic rights, elimination of legal privilege, and the gradual extension of suffrage, were all
aspects of the general defeat of the old regime.

Foucault purports to have found a distinctly different lesson in those penal reforms. In his portrait, the changes are driven by some undefined and unspecified "power." That power is always nefarious, never well-meaning, not even indifferent. Power, at one time, engaged in outrageous grotesque displays, literally ripping apart its opponents. But those efforts, allegedly, posed some functional problems: there was a threat of public intervention on the side of the victims. Hence, with supreme cunning, "power" substituted the prison and then extended its principles, an all-pervasive system of surveillance and discipline, to the entire society. The "essential techniques" of the new disciplinary institutions, Foucault tells us, were

> always meticulous, often minute . . . but they had their importance; be-
> cause they defined a certain mode of detailed political investment of
> the body, a "new micro-physics" of power; and because, since the sev-
> enteenth century, they had constantly reached out to ever broader do-
> mains, as they tended to cover the entire social body. Small acts of
> cunning endowed with a great power of diffusion, subtle arrange-
> ments, apparently innocent, but profoundly suspicious, mechanisms
> that obeyed economies too shameful to be acknowledged. . . . They are
> the acts of cunning, not so much of the greater reason that works even
> in its sleep and gives meaning to the insignificant, as of the attentive
> "malevolence" that turns everything to account. Discipline is a politi-
> cal anatomy of detail.[1]

Foucault's argument goes as follows. Early in the nineteenth century, the "great spectacle of physical punishment disappeared . . . the theatrical representation of pain was excluded from punishment." Drawing and quartering was replaced by the guillotine. The grotesque tortures gradual-ly disappeared and were replaced by the penal sanction. The "reduction in penal severity," Foucault notes, has long been regarded "as a quantitative phenomenon: less cruelty, less pain, more kindness, more respect, more 'humanity.'" Foucault is not sure there has been a "diminution of intensi-ty." He offers a noncommittal "perhaps" on this question. There was, however, a change in objective. In the former regime, punishments were addressed to the body; in the new, they are focused on the soul. "The ex-piation," he writes, "that once rained down upon the body must be re-placed by a punishment that acts in depth on the heart, the thoughts, the will, the inclinations." That was the underlying principle of the new prison. There, the soul could be surveyed, studied, controlled, and directed in minute detail. It was a new and cunning design, a masterful arrangement to serve the purposes of that anonymous power. "It was," he writes, "an important moment. . . . A new character came on the scene, masked. It was the end of a certain kind of tragedy; comedy began, with shadow play, faceless voices, impalpable entities. The apparatus of punitive justice must now bite into this bodiless reality."[2]

Foucault's work begins with a three-page description of the execution of Robert-François Damiens. It is one of the most grisly accounts to be found anywhere in the academic literature. It provides unambiguous support for one of Foucault's claims, that of "power" conducting an extraordinary assault on "the body" of an offender, in this case, a person who had physically attacked the king. On 5 January 1757, Damiens, an unemployed servant, had stabbed Louis XV with a three-inch knife and inflicted a superficial wound. On 2 March, the execution occurred. The event was a dramatic public display of the sovereign's power.[3]

With no break, with no transition, Foucault introduces the next episode, the subsequent change. "Eighty years later," he writes, "Leon Faucher drew up his rules 'for the House of young prisoners in Paris.' " A page and a half of rules follow, calling for detailed regulation of the lives of prisoners. The lesson appears in a brief sentence: "We have, then, a public execution and a time-table." This, presumably, provides a capsule summary of the transition. A key qualifying sentence follows, one that has been overlooked by most commentators: "They do not punish the same crimes or the same type of delinquent." This is a rather important point: the author has declared that he is setting aside the ceteris paribus assumption; he has signaled that he will not be "holding equal" the type of offense.[4]

If one were to compare similar events, it would be necessary to examine the reactions to regicide or attempted regicide in the eighteenth and nineteenth centuries, that is, before and after reform. One should also examine the reactions to assault, burglary, or robbery before and after the transition. Foucault's before-and-after comparison looks at the response to a major capital crime and then at the responses to commonplace felonies. What if one made the appropriate comparison? An instructive case, a useful example, occurred in France almost exactly a century after the Damiens affair.

On 14 January 1858, Louis Napoleon and his wife, Empress Eugénie, were entering the Paris Opera when a series of explosions shook the area. The couple escaped with minor cuts and continued on to the performance. The bombs left eight dead and more than a hundred wounded. The perpetrators, led by Félix (or Felice) Orsini, were quickly apprehended and brought to trial. Found guilty, three of them were condemned to death by decapitation. A fourth, because of "demonstrated mental incapacity," was sentenced to life at hard labor. One death sentence, at the last minute, was commuted to transportation for life in French Guiana. Here is Franklin Ford's account of the execution: "Early on the morning of March 13, 1858, [the two] were guillotined before a huge crowd surrounding the Place de la Roquette in Paris. Pieri went first, singing a Girondin anthem from 1791, Orsini after him, shouting 'Viva l'Italia! Viva la Francia!' "[5]

What is the lesson? In one respect, "power" had behaved exactly as it had a century earlier, that is, with an assault on the body of the offender—the blade "bit into" Orsini's neck. There was no surveillance, no timetable, no rehabilitation for Orsini. The execution was, as in the previous century, a grand public display. In one respect, however, there was a marked change. Rather than hours of torture, this execution was quick and expeditious. It proceeded as the liberal reformers wished and as the subsequent liberal histories of punishment have represented their case. If Foucault had reported the comparable event, there would have been no grounds for his skepticism about the reduction of cruelty and pain. There would be no room for his "perhaps" with respect to the intensity of pain.[6]

Several other features of Foucault's misleading before-and-after study deserve attention. He has not indicated the context of Damiens's execution or, to use current jargon, the event has not been properly situated. The suggestion is that this execution was typical of old regime procedures. In fact, however, due to the character of the offense, an assault on the monarch, the punishment dealt out was the most exceptional of the entire century. The concerned authorities had to reach back 150 years, to the assassination of Henri IV, for an appropriate procedure. The punishment meted out to Damiens had to be commensurate with that dealt out to François Ravaillac in 1610. Foucault has compared noncomparable experiences, taking a very exceptional case as the base-point for his argument. In the social sciences this is called a sampling problem: he has taken an outlier—a very extreme case—and suggested it to be typical.[7]

The Orsini case carries still another lesson. The man was a nationalist, a champion of Italy's unification. Louis Napoleon had undercut those aspirations in 1849 by sending in French troops in support of the pope. Orsini, something of a demagogue, pointed to this in his trial: "I acted as Brutus did. [The emperor] killed my country; I decided to kill him." He sent a letter to the emperor and, at his trial, read it to the court, calling on Louis Napoleon to now realize those aspirations. The emperor, much moved, "expressed an inclination toward clemency." Orsini, he said, unlike a common murderer of the period, "is a man and has my respect." But his ministers "were implacable." Public opinion in this case "seemed overwhelmingly opposed to forgiving the deaths of the eight innocent bystanders outside the Opera."[8] Power, it seems, is more complicated than is suggested in Foucault's brief and very selective report.

Prisons and Surveillance—The Panopticon

The new style of punishment in Foucault's argument centers on the prison, specifically on one designed by Jeremy Bentham in 1791. Called the panopticon, it was a circular structure with cells arranged along the circumference and an observation tower at the center, which allowed a maximum of surveillance, the warders being able to see into all cells. Foucault portrays the panopticon as the basic design for most subsequent prison construction. In the 1830s, he says, "it became the architectural programme of most prison projects." That design, it will be noted, is declared to have been a de facto accomplishment; it is not a metaphorical usage. The panopticon, he writes, "found in the prison its privileged locus of realization." Moreover, Foucault claims, the plan was incorporated in many other institutions. The point has been summarized by Alan Sheridan, Foucault's translator and enthusiastic advocate. There is, he writes, "an astonishing coincidence between the new prison and other contemporary institutions: hospital, factory, school, and barracks. It is no accident that Jeremy Bentham's famous 'panopticon' . . . was recommended and implemented for all these institutions."[9]

Nowhere in Foucault's work does one learn a simple and important fact about the panopticon. A leading criminology text by Harry Elmer Barnes and Negley K. Teeters, a work Foucault could have used, describes Bentham's effort as follows: "The plans were drawn up, but fortunately for penology this monstrosity was never built." The fact is clearly indicated in Foucault's original source, Bentham's *Works.*[10]

An extended discussion by L. J. Hume reviewing the administrative history of the panopticon reveals some other noteworthy features of Bentham's effort. The planning and negotiations extended over a period of more than two decades, that is, from "the early 1790's until he secured compensation for his losses in 1813." Although the scheme "finally collapsed" in 1801, Bentham tried later to revive it. After long negotiations, he was compensated for losses incurred over more than a decade. Bentham, from the first, one learns, "viewed the whole operation as a commercial undertaking." The plan called for the government to abandon direct management of convict labor. The government would transfer to Bentham "the responsibility to confine, maintain and discipline [convicts] . . . allowing him to extract what profit he could out of their labour." The government did provide money for purchase of the land, but then the project bogged down and came to a halt.[11]

As opposed to the portrait of plan (or cunning) offered by Foucault, the history as Hume reports it is more one of confusion and indifference. There were changes of government; officials and review committees had different opinions. Real estate developers did not wish to have a prison in the neighborhood. Costs had increased due to the Napoleonic War, and Bentham was asked to submit a new proposal reflecting that fact. That proposal was then rejected as too costly and he was asked to submit still another, this for a unit half the size of the original. But Bentham recognized it could not be profitable on that scale. Hume summarizes as follows: "To a large extent we can explain [Bentham's] frustrations as a product of the sheer muddle and delay that were still prevalent in British administration in the last quarter of the century, and that were exacerbated by the financial and administrative problems posed by the French wars of the nineties."

The government decision makers who finally untangled this web of complication saw another solution to "the crime problem." They had "a decided preference for, or commitment to, transportation and for imprisonment in the county gaols as modes of punishment." The panopticon was seen as a competitor to their preferred solution. To them, Hume notes, it was a matter of "Panopticon versus New South Wales." Power, it appears, was not interested in surveillance. Power preferred those prisoners to be far away; it wished them to be entirely out of sight.

One final point: The committee that worked out the settlement with Bentham was presided over by George Holford, a man "destined to become for the next two decades one of the ablest and most persistent of prison reformers." He was "unfriendly" to Bentham's recommendations. The committee report recommended a prison but "favoured a different kind of building and a different plan of management." Bentham was "dispossessed" of the land, which then was used for the new Millbank Penitentiary. It was not a panopticon.

Barnes and Teeters report that three "modified panopticons" were built in the United States. The first, built in Richmond, Virginia, in 1800, was designed by the architect Benjamin Latrobe, who in turn received some suggestions from Thomas Jefferson. The latter indicated his indebtedness not to Bentham but to a French architect, Pierre Gabriel Bugniet, who in 1785 had designed the Roanne prison in Lyons. Bentham's design, Barnes and Teeters report, was debated in New York in 1811 "but finally rejected." The second panopticon-style structure, actually a modified design, was the Western State Penitentiary in Pittsburgh, designed and erected in the 1820s by William Strickland, a disciple of Latrobe. The third use of the panopticon design was in Stateville, Illinois, where four structures were built between 1916 and 1925. A picture of one of these units appears in Foucault's book. No indication is given, however, that Stateville has the only existing panopticon-style prison in the United States.[12]

Another outstanding work on prison designs is that of Giuseppe di Gennaro and his associates. Bentham's proposals of 1787 and 1791 are described there, and again it is indicated that they were "never built." Of the Latrobe-Jefferson plan, this source reports it "was not, strictly, a panopticon." The Strickland design at Pittsburgh is described as a "distortion of the panopticon principle." It had back-to-back cells and poor lighting, and as a result "central supervision was impossible." Designed for solitary confinement, it proved inadequate for working prisoners and was torn down only a decade after its completion. Writing of France, these authors indicate that "no circular prisons were ever actually built." The Dutch, it seems, after a gap of about one hundred years, built three panopticons. They are "probably the only prisons of this type actually to be built which most nearly approached Bentham's ideas." All three, as of 1975, were still in use. The Stateville Penitentiary is described and illustrated. The comments, however, are unrelievedly negative. One summary conclusion: "Panopticon prisons are not, and can never be, successful institutions."[13]

Hollywood, in its many prison movies, has provided a more accurate portrait than that of Foucault's fiction. Most prison movies show cell blocks, not panopticons. The basic structure, called the Auburn plan, is rectangular, not circular. All of the cells back onto the inner wall, which bisects the building. Arranged in long rows along several tiers, the cells open onto a narrow gallery. Each cell faces the outside wall of the block. There is no observation tower; there is no central, continuous surveillance. In fact, except for the occasional guard on patrol, no one is in a position to observe the prisoners in the manner alleged by Foucault. Moreover, few hospitals, factories, schools, or barracks are based on the Bentham plan. In this case, an entire school of "social history" has been based on a patent nonfact.

Foucault, we saw, made an abrupt transition, jumping eighty years from Damiens's execution to Léon Faucher who "drew up his rules." Again Foucault has not "situated" this event properly. His bibliography indicates a work by Faucher, entitled *De la réforme des prisons*, from 1838, but that is all. Readers knowing anything of Faucher would find it unlikely that he was active as a prison reformer. The *Grande encyclopédie* account refers to him as a "journaliste, économiste et homme politique." A man of wide-ranging interests, Faucher wrote on many subjects and one of these, a topic of the day apparently, was prison reform. He was opposed to the use of cells, something not consonant with Foucault's case. He favored separation of offenders by type of offense, each category to engage in collective work as a measure to counter recidivist tendencies. Faucher then turned to other things. He worked for the formation of a French-Belgian-Swiss-Spanish trade area to counter Prussia's *Zollverein*. He wrote a work on England. He became a director of a railroad. Active in the opposition to the July Monarchy in 1847 and 1848, he was elected to the new Constituent Assembly and, eventually, the pinnacle of his career, became minister of the interior in Louis Napoleon's government. He seems to have been more interested in the organization of elections and in a plan for restricting suffrage than in prison reform. Faucher's 1838 rules appear to have been a plan, a proposal, something that remained on a library shelf. Like Bentham's panopticon, Faucher's rules do not appear to have had any impact.[14]

An important scholarly account of "the birth of the prison" was published in 1978, the same year Foucault's work appeared in the United States. This volume, by Michael Ignatieff, reviews the intellectual history (the plans, motives, and justifications), describes the various efforts of implementation (indicating successes and failures), and provides the larger context (conditions that aided or thwarted the various efforts). The idea for the institution came from John Howard, who has been described as "the father of the penitentiary." In 1777, he published a study, one based on his extensive research entitled *The State of the Prisons*. His ideas were incorporated in the Penitentiary Act of 1779, which provided for " 'fixed hours of rising, of reading a chapter in the Bible, of praying, of meals, of work etc.'—as well as uniforms, cellular confinement, and constant inspection." Howard, a devout Nonconformist, drew support from Quakers and from businessmen, professionals, and gentry moved by the man's moral mission. The Quakers were especially drawn "to the idea of using regimens of discipline to reform the confined." All of the elements of "surveillance and discipline," were discussed and built into law before Bentham's first exposition—all of the elements except the "specific form," the panopticon. A committee was formed to choose sites, approve the architectural plan, and oversee construction, but the implementation floundered. Howard's preferred architect won the competition, but then the reconstituted committee "became deadlocked in fruitless negotiations to buy land on Battersea Rise" and, as a result, in 1785, "plans for the penitentiary lapsed."[15]

It was a mistake, Ignatieff shows, to see the reform as driven by intellectuals and coteries of reformers. Wars proved to be the compelling events in history. Between 1770 and 1774, two-thirds of those sentenced at the Old Bailey were punished with either transportation or the hulks. One in six received a death sentence; one in seven was condemned to whipping, branding, or a fine. Only 2 percent were sentenced to prison. The American Revolution blocked off the principal option—transportation (a business, it seems: convicts were sold to employers in the colonies). The immediate result was a marked increase in imprisonment, up to 28.6 percent in 1775 to 1779 (between 1790 and 1794, with the French Revolutionary wars, imprisonment rose to 34.6 percent). Because the war in the colonies was expected to be brief, no new facilities were constructed. The county jails and all available hulks were soon overflowing, and death rates, always high, rose even further. The end of the war allowed a return, with one important modification, to the status quo ante. Since the American colonies were no longer "available" for the transported, another option was sought. A West African attempt ended in disaster. Nova Scotia and the Cape Colony both argued vehemently against the proposals. The new option, eventually, was to be Australia.[16]

The end of the Revolutionary War brought demobilization and a dramatic increase in crime; a public demand for action followed. George Onesiphorus Paul brought about the key institutional innovation at this point. After Howard, Ignatieff writes, Paul "was the most influential institutional reformer of his generation—a relentless, dictatorial administrator who singlehandedly made Gloucester penitentiary the model for prisons across the country." Opened in 1795, it had room for four hundred or five hundred prisoners. The plan called for cells and solitary confinement, one aim being to break the inmate subculture. But this too was a failure. The proper staff could not be found and discipline could not be enforced. The crime problem appears to have diminished with the Napoleonic Wars but then, after 1815 and demobilization, crime rates rose once again. The vast numbers of convicts put an end to any notion of solitary confinement in the Gloucester Prison. It was in this period that Bentham's plan was considered and rejected. Paul, among others, argued against it. The appropriate aim, he said, was reform of the prisoner; Bentham's aim, he indicated, was profit. The House of Commons agreed with Paul.[16]

To meet the new needs, the Millbank Prison was constructed. First opened in 1817, it could hold twelve hundred prisoners. The Pentonville Prison, another exemplary institution, was opened in 1838. Both Millbank and Pentonville incorporated elements of the initial Gloucester design. Like that original, Pentonville was intended for solitary confinement but again prisoner numbers soon made that "ideal" impossible. The use of physical punishments gradually diminished and was later abolished. The Australian authorities objected to transportation and that practice was suspended in 1853. The principal option remaining was imprisonment. Long-term sentences, those of more than three years, became frequent from this point and more prison construction followed.

Ignatieff provides a brief summary paragraph. As opposed to Foucault's linear history with "power" insidiously extending its control, Ignatieff sees "the history of reform as a cycle of good intentions confounded by unintended consequences." As opposed to Foucault's Bentham-centric portraiture, Ignatieff writes that "by 1860, most prisoners in Europe and North America marched to Howard's cadence." The basic elements of this narrative, the movement from John Howard's plan and "visions" to the penitentiaries as we know them today, may be found in almost any standard history. Ignatieff has added to that narrative, providing detailed information on the administrative history, the conflicting aims, the muddle involved, and the modification of plans or ideals by insistent realities. Foucault bypassed that history and in its place substituted a truncated account of Jeremy Bentham and his panopticon. That focus—on the rejected plan—has an "artistic" advantage: it allows Foucault to put the all-seeing eye of Power at the center of this portrait of the modern world.[18]

Foucault is equivocal about the place of the panopticon in the larger historical process. At some points, he sees it as the model for all subsequent disciplinary efforts. For Bentham, he writes, it was "a perfect disciplinary institution." It could "function in a diffused, multiple, polyvalent way throughout the whole social body." According to Foucault, "Bentham dreamt of transforming [his invention] into a network of mechanisms that would be everywhere and always alert, running through society without interruption in space or in time. The panoptic arrangement provides the formula for this generalization. It programmes, at the level of an elementary and easily transferable mechanism, the basic functioning of a society penetrated through and through with disciplinary mechanisms." No references are given, ones that might establish this as Bentham's program—as opposed to Foucault's reading of the reformer's intentions. At other points, Foucault sees a broad historical process that antedates Bentham and his work. There was a "gradual extension of the mechanisms of discipline throughout the seventeenth and eighteenth centuries." These spread "throughout the whole social body" creating what might be called "the disciplinary society." In this reading, the panopticon was a late innovation, one device among many (but clearly more useful, more insidious) at the disposal of the ever more menacing "power."[19]

The Disciplined Armies

In support of his claim about the tendency toward ever greater discipline, ever more insistent domination of individuals, Foucault provides a brief history of developments in the military. He focuses, not surprisingly, on the army of Frederick the Great, specifically on the Prussian infantry, an example, he says, that was imitated by "the whole of Europe." It is true that the Prussian infantry was highly disciplined; that was the key to its successes in the field. The experience was not imitated, however; an attempt was made in France but the effort was rejected. Then, within a couple of decades, the conduct of war shifted dramatically. The disciplined infantry ranks remained for another century or so but other less disciplined formations gained considerable importance.

France was the major loser in the Seven Years' War, having suffered repeated failures and defeats in the field and severe losses in the settlement. According to Hans Delbrück, a leading military historian, the French army "had never been disciplined in the same sense and manner as the Prussian army." France had known nothing "of the strictness and exactness of the Prussian drills, of the constant care that was applied there to this skill, day after day." The less demanding French discipline, he writes, had "just sufficed" for its purposes. After the defeat, however, St. Germain, the minister of war, "made a great effort to reestablish discipline in the army by introducing, in the Prussian manner, beating with the bare blade rather than the punishment of arrest." Both troops and officers opposed such changes. The troops, it was thought, would not accept beatings. Officers did not approve because, according to Delbrück, they were touched by "the spirit of humanity that emanated from the French literature of the period." The demand for enhanced discipline, Delbrück writes, "could not be accomplished through orders from the minister of war and references to the example of the glorious Prussian army." The attempt, by "power," to achieve "the disciplinary society" was defeated.[20]

Foucault's portrait is misleading also in that it focuses exclusively on the infantry. That perspective neglects the second major component of eighteenth-century armies, namely, the cavalry. The key development in that century, however, was a move in the opposite direction, away from "discipline." The ordered formation of the caracole gave way to the hell-for-leather charge. Foucault neglects also the growing third branch, the artillery. The appearance of lighter horse-drawn weapons gave that branch an ever-increasing importance. Because battlefield communication was so limited, decisions as to movement, targets, and firing were necessarily delegated, requiring extensive autonomy and initiative on the part of subordinate officers. Those decisions could not rest exclusively with a commanding officer.[21]

Where Foucault declares an insistent movement toward ever greater discipline and control, the subsequent experience showed some striking opposite tendencies. Within a generation of Frederick's death, in 1786, European armies saw the appearance of skirmishers (*tirailleurs*) as an important element in combat. These were harassing units operating more or less on their own, with soldiers firing at will rather than in ranks and on command. They formed a third of the French line infantry battalions and were an even larger proportion of the light infantry. The armies after Frederick's reign saw the development of the division, a self-contained unit capable of independent combat. Thus the new Napoleonic army was quite different from its predecessors. It involved significant decentralization of control and direction; it required independence and autonomy on the part of divisional officers, cavalry, and skirmishers. The disciplined firing by ranked infantry remained for several more decades as a necessary part of the operation. In that respect, Foucault is accurate. But accuracy on one point combined with a neglect of all nonconforming evidence yields a grossly misleading history.

Foucault's account is selective in still another way. It overlooks the existence of disciplined armies elsewhere in history—in ancient Sparta, in Alexander's army, in the Roman legions, in the Byzantine empire under Justinian and his general Belisarius, and also in the Mongol empire under Genghis Khan (who had "one of the best-organized, best-trained, and most thoroughly disciplined armies ever created"). Recognition of those other cases would damage Foucault's claim about the uniquely sinister tendencies of the modern period. His readers, if acquainted with that experience, would recognize that the historical processes were more diverse, the directions more complicated. The style of battle described by Foucault, linear warfare, was actually a rather brief episode in a continuously changing process. It was a style that reached its culmination during the Seven Years' War. Brent Nosworthy points out that the seeds of a new system, one "closely associated with the Napoleonic period," were already present. He refers to the new style as the "impulse system." As opposed to Foucault's "plot" theory, Nosworthy offers this eminently plausible alternative: "Most of the tactical and grand tactical systems used during the period . . . had their basis in the nature of the weaponry then in use, and as often as not, represented optimal solutions to the problems being faced."[22]

In an unusual demonstration of precision, Foucault gives a date and an explanation for this "new" move toward greater discipline. It began, he writes, at the "end of the seventeenth century." The causes given are "economic" and, more important, technical, namely "the invention of the rifle." The text declares, correctly, that the rifle was more accurate than its predecessor, the musket. It is grossly mistaken, however, in its claim about the rate of fire, that the rifle was "more rapid than the musket." It is also grossly in error in the dating of that innovation. A footnote declares: "The movement that brought the rifle into widespread use may be roughly dated from the battle of Steinkirk, 1699." Foucault's dating is rather "rough" since the battle was fought in 1692. John Fortesque's *History of the British Army* devotes twelve pages to the battle (also given as Steenkirk and Steenkerken) but his account makes no mention of rifles. Delbrück makes only a brief reference to the battle, linking it with two others of the period. They were "accompanied by much bloodshed," but otherwise, he reports, they "had hardly any effects."[23]

That conclusion is not surprising because, as any serious source makes clear, the musket continued as the basic infantry weapon throughout the eighteenth century. A musket, the Brown Bess, was the basic weapon of Wellington's regulars at Waterloo, more than a century after Steinkirk. Some skirmishers late in the eighteenth century used rifles, but their numbers were relatively small and, because of the weapon's slow rate of fire, they were at a severe disadvantage in close combat. The Brown Bess was not replaced until 1840.

In this instance, Foucault's bizarre history has an easy explanation: it stems from carelessness and a translation error. The English infantry did make serious use of a "new" weapon at Steinkirk. Foucault's original text describes it as a *fusil*, which could be translated as either musket or rifle, the choice depending on the specific details of the case. The actual innovation was a *fusil à pierre*; a flintlock musket. It replaced the more cumbersome and less reliable matchlock musket. The rate of fire was greater; any differences in accuracy were probably small. The impacts were not in any way as decisive as Foucault suggests. Basically, the number of steps involved in reloading was sharply reduced. The number of ranks necessary could be altered accordingly, shifting from as many as eight to the more familiar three and two. The innovation did not increase the need for "discipline." With the exact same discipline as before, the innovation allowed a given number of men to produce a much greater volume of fire.[24]

Foucault's Scholarship

Foucault's supporters are generally undaunted by such criticisms. The argument is that they have a new, a different, a "modern" epistemology or "way of knowing." One line of argument has it that the new way is superior to the old; it replaces an inadequate method. Another line has it that the "new" procedure is different; it is incommensurate with the old. The dominance of one over the other is a function of power, not of method-ological adequacy. The "positivists" are imposing, unfairly, an inappropriate, an unjust standard.

Foucault's methods are not easily summarized. Some sense of his procedures may be gained from a brief account provided by Hayden White. Foucault, he writes,

> rejects the authority of both logic and conventional narrative. His discourses often suggest a story, but they are never about the same characters, and the events that comprise them are not linked by laws that would permit us to understand some as causes and others as effects. Foucault's "histories" are as fraught with discontinuities, ruptures, gaps, and lacunae as his arguments . . . . he denies the authority which the distinction coherence-incoherence has enjoyed in Western thought since Plato . . . . Foucault sets the free play of his own discourse over against *all* authority . . . . [His] strategy is to work from texts or fragments of texts produced during a given period, without any concern for the biographies of the authors who wrote them, solely with the aim of identifying a distinctive "discursive mode" shared by all the important texts of an age or epoch.[25]

Examination of Foucault's actual procedures shows his "method" to be identical, in form at least, to its presumed opposite. In much of his work he is making use of documentary sources, presenting texts to support his claims. The problems faced are exactly the same as in traditional epistemology. There is the sampling problem, that of establishing the representative character of the texts cited. The author should accurately report both content and context. One should also establish the impact of the texts. Foucault's distinctive methodological innovation is a total indifference to these formal requirements. He does not attempt to establish the representative character of his texts. There are serious problems in the accuracy of his reports. He does nothing to establish impact—there is a hidden assumption in much of his writing which, if stated, would read "and the word became reality." But the specific claims are never established, only asserted.

These problems have long since been noted in Foucault's work. A 1974 discussion by George Huppert of an earlier work by Foucault reported arguments based on atypical texts and even those not represented accurately. In two instances, Huppert shows that Foucault, to sustain his case, "must do violence" to those texts. A critical essay by Pierre Vilar, also from 1974, refers to Foucault's "mixed-up dates . . . texts mistreated . . . historical absurdities . . . and errors so gross that we must believe them deliberate."[26] It is hard to see Foucault's discussion of the panopticon and its implications as the product of careless research. The deliberate-error hypothesis seems by far the more plausible option.

Critics and Commentators—The Reviews

We are speaking of a man who, despite such problems, has gained considerable renown. In the 1980s he was cited more than 200 times annually in the *Social Sciences Citation Index.* The attention paid him in the humanistic sciences has been even greater, the smaller *Arts and Humanities Citation Index* reporting more than 400 references per year in the 1980s, the peak coming in 1985 with 560 mentions. He is, according to Allan Megill, the twenty-fourth most-cited twentieth-century author in that *Index.*[27]

It is easy, of course, for a "school" to develop, to segregate itself, and to resist contact with "the outside world"—and that world's expertise. But any book given serious attention, it will be argued, would be reviewed in professional journals and there it would be subjected to careful, expert assessment. That might be the case, although, as always, investigation of such matters rather than a priori judgment proves useful. Examination of reviews of *Discipline and Punish* in twenty-four English-language sources addressed both to the intelligentsia and to academic specialists revealed that not one of them pointed out the fictive character of Foucault's "history" of the panopticon; not one pointed out the difficulties with his military history.

Several reviewers did recognize serious problems. Robert Brown, a philosopher, was the most skeptical. He pointed to the absence of evidence on key points, to problems of chronology, and to logical implausibilities. The negative comments generally came from the historians. Most of the reviews, however, indicated no serious doubts. Five of them were enthusiastic, another was strongly positive, and the rest favorable but indicating some minor reservations. Some of those enthusiasts vouched for both the framework and for the supporting scholarship. Robert Coles, writing in *The New Yorker,* declared that Foucault "knows his history, and is able to pinpoint chronologically" important shifts in behavior and sentiment. Robert Hoffmann wrote of Foucault's "elaborately articulated" conception which was "carefully tied to historical example." Another, Paddy

Hillyard, admired the "meticulous detail" found in the book—"there can be no doubt that it is the most important book ever to be written on the history of punishment." Roger Kaplan reports that Foucault is "a rigorous and shrewd historian." Another enthusiast, James Farganis, found "thorough detailed empirical inquiry," "empirical demonstration," and a "prodigious use of historical detail" in the work. Among the "best sections of the book," he found, was the discussion of panopticism. Peter Barham indicated some qualms (for example, that it is "difficult to maintain one's chronological bearings") but concluded that it was "structuralist writing at its best . . . a massive intellectual effort." Jan Goldstein wrote, appropriately, that Foucault "never marshals the concrete and specific evidence that historians crave." Donald Goodman wrote, inappropriately, that Foucault "marshals texts which indicate a similar shift in the military, in education, in medicine and in industry. The prison, in this book, becomes the body politic writ large." Stanley Cohen, who reviewed the book for America's sociologists, declared that it "must be the most stimulating and revealing history of prisons and punishment ever written." Richard Locke, in the *New York Times Book Review*, reported that *Discipline and Punish* "has won universal praise."[28]

These reviewers vouched for the work, accredited it, and effectively recommended it to the larger audience of intellectuals. Few of these reviewers, it would appear, possessed expert knowledge of the history of penology. This points to a problem for the book review editors of those journals: How did it happen that, with such system, expert judgment had been avoided? An extenuating circumstance, a hard fact facing any editor, is the shortage of knowledgeable reviewers, a problem that becomes especially acute with books on recondite subject matters. To assess Foucault's work, for example, one needs a specialist in the history of penology, preferably one well-versed in French experience. But penologists, practical people much concerned with current problems, typically show little interest in the history of their field. And few historians of eighteenth- or nineteenth-century France would have more than a passing interest in the treatment of criminals.

Even the competent area specialist would have difficulty checking Foucault's sources. Few libraries anywhere in the world, for example, would have a work by Colquhoun published in 1797. That source, Foucault reports, provided proof, "supported by figures," of the "urgent need" to check property theft. He gives the figures—£250,000 per annum taken from warehouses on the Thames, approximately £700,000 taken elsewhere in the city. But Foucault's account neglects a key figure and transforms the author's conclusion. Colquhoun estimated that approximately £220 million in property was exposed, hence the total amount of theft "sinks to a trifle . . . scarcely reaching one percent on the value of property passing in transit in the course of the year." It was not the loss, he felt, but the mischief, the destruction of morals, that was to be deplored.[29]

Given Foucault's portrait of savage punishments in the old regime, another of Colquhoun's observations is of interest. Calquhoun pointed to the "multitude of Crimes capital" but indicated a different consequence, namely that "Juries can never be made to believe [they] are of that nature in point of actual atrocity" and, as a result, refused to convict. Colquhoun is correct in his observation about British practice. Many commentators, Foucault among them, report the increasing harshness of English law but neglect the opposite tendency in English (later British) practice. The number of capital offences increased steadily from the fifteenth to the eighteenth century, but the proportion of capital penalties executed fell steadily, in one account from 52.6 percent in 1689–1718 to 4.1 percent in 1827–1833. By general agreement, other penalties also were moderated in practice. Bentham noted that branding in the late eighteenth century meant putting the red-hot iron to a slice of ham while, "to complete the farce, the criminal screams." Ignatieff reports that victims of crimes, knowing the viciousness of the punishment, refused to prosecute. Juries refused to convict or, frequently, found thieves guilty of stealing one shilling less than what would have been a capital offense, a procedure referred to as "pious perjury." After 1750, there was a rising rate of pardons.[30]

"Power," clearly, was being thwarted by "the people." This experience again challenges a basic truth of Foucauldian science. For Foucault, the solution is simple: he does not report the actual practice. But the difficulty was also missed by the critics. The combination of a lack of specialists and the fugitive sources gives rise to the problem of less than adequate reviewing.

One hardly expects such easy-going methods among the "tough" minds of academia, among those who regularly announce their critical tendencies. Scholars, so we are told, enjoy the clash of ideas. They take pleasure in confrontation. That "dialectical process," so it is said, leads to the detection and exposure of any false coinage. Yet that proudly announced critical propensity, for many at least, is little more than a pose. It is an approved stance, the way scholars are supposed to act, but it might be no more than another conformity and thus another appearance-reality problem.

An Explanatory Hypothesis

Some years ago, Richard Hofstadter, the historian, wrote an important and much-cited essay entitled "The Paranoid Style in American Politics." He carefully distinguished between the clinical case, the individual who feels persecuted, and "the paranoid spokesman in politics." They both, he indicated, "tend to be overheated, oversuspicious, overaggressive, grandiose, and apocalyptic in expression." The clinical paranoid, however, "sees the hostile and conspiratorial world in which he feels himself to be living as directed specifically *against him;* whereas the spokesman of the paranoid style finds it directed against a nation, a culture, a way of life whose fate affects not himself alone but millions of others. Insofar as he does not usually see himself singled out as the individual victim of a personal conspiracy, he is somewhat more rational and much more disinterested. His sense that his political passions are unselfish and patriotic, in fact, goes far to intensify his feeling of righteousness and his moral indignation." Hofstadter then applied this concept to interpret a wide range of social movements that had had some influence in American politics. The phenomenon, he noted, was not limited to the American experience: "Notions about an all-embracing conspiracy on the part of Jesuits or Freemasons, international capitalists, international Jews, or Communists are familiar phenomena in many countries throughout modern history."[31]

Although the tendency is evident throughout, not a single reviewer (of those listed in note 28) made mention of the paranoid style in Foucault's work.[32] The propensity may be seen in the long quotation that introduced this discussion: power is always at work, its techniques "always meticulous ... [characterized by] acts of cunning ... great power of diffusion, subtle arrangements, apparently innocent [but actually] too shameful to be acknowledged.... They are the acts of cunning ... of the attentive 'malevolence' that turns everything to account."

Power, the manifest source of this "malevolence," is so patently obvious to Foucault as to require no specification. People—kings, ministers, bureaucrats, powerful persons, decision makers—all effectively disappear.

Not the home secretary or the minister of the interior, but the "apparatus of corrective penality" (also termed "this punitive intervention") is the active agency. That apparatus works with sinister and insistent purpose. It "must rest on a studied manipulation of the individual." The "agent of punishment," one is told, "must exercise a total power . . . the individual to be corrected must be entirely enveloped in the power that is being exercised over him. Secrecy is imperative." The new "mechanics of power," this "calculated manipulation" is only gradually formed and extended, beginning in "a multiplicity of often minor processes." These are "of different origin and scattered location" but they "converge and gradually produce the blueprint of a general method." The processes "were at work in secondary education . . . later in primary schools; they slowly invested the space of the hospital . . . they restructured the military organization." Then there was "the insidious militarization of the large workshops." This power, Foucault declares, "had to be given the instrument of permanent, exhaustive, omnipresent surveillance, capable of making all visible, as long as it could itself remain invisible. It had to be like a faceless gaze that transformed the whole social body into a field of perception: thousands of eyes posted everywhere, mobile attentions ever on the alert." The overarching themes (or perhaps better, the subtext) may be expressed simply: they are watching us; they, somehow or other, are controlling us.[33]

Given these presumed facts, given the "studied manipulation" and the total envelopment of the individual, one serious problem remains that poses a decided challenge for those insistent claims. The prisons, Foucault indicates, are manifest failures. Rather than reforming the inmates, rather than producing "docile bodies," they appear to generate recidivism. The point is demonstrated by Foucault in an exercise best described as statistical malarky. Although undercutting his surveillance-manipulation-control argument, this presumed fact poses no problem for Foucault. "Is not the supposed failure part of the functioning of the prison?" he asks. This "encouragement of recidivism" must also be part of the larger conspiracy.[34]

Initially somewhat tentative, Foucault suggests that "perhaps one should look for what is hidden beneath the apparent cynicism of the penal institution." "Can we not see here a consequence rather than a contradiction?" He then moves to an if-then formulation—"If so, one would be forced to suppose that the prison, and no doubt punishment in general, is not intended to eliminate offences, but rather to . . . use them." The subsequent pages treat the insinuation as fact and spell out several possibilities, all of them sinister. One learns, for example, that this "production of delinquency" involves "tactics" to divide the lower strata of the population. Foucault's discussion leaves no doubt as to the intention or purpose: "It has been a long and arduous undertaking . . . specific methods were used to maintain the hostility of the poorer classes to delinquents. . . . In short, a whole tactic of confusion aimed at maintaining a permanent state of conflict."[35]

The reviewers, as suggested, appear to differ considerably in their expertise. The professional historians, generally, were the most likely to signal doubt about specific points of Foucault's argument. Not knowing the specifics of the many obscure nooks and crannies "investigated" by Foucault, they noted difficulties with chronology, lack of documentation, taking text for reality, and so forth, but otherwise providing an "agnostic" judgment. Not one of them, however, wrote even a single sentence of caution with regard to the paranoid style. Several of the reviewers showed no caution at all and, in fact, vied with Foucault in their depictions of the repressiveness of modern life. Casey Groves congratulated Foucault for his "marvelous job" in "demonstrating the ways in which social institutions increasingly function as elaborate parasitic mechanisms." D. W. Harding's review opens with a summary sentence describing the (modern) human condition: "A sinister feature of the regimentation that besets us now is our acquiescence in it as an inevitable process—a natural outcome of organised social life"; Foucault's book puts all this "into its context as a human invention with a history." Prisons, according to Louise Shelley, "are symbols of the present order of society." The "total regimentation" of the daily life of the inmates "epitomizes the form of social control exercised by today's disciplinary society." Modern society, she reports, "has acquired symbolic and actual control over the totality of the lives of its members through supervision of their daily activities in all major societal institutions." These reviewers showed unrestrained enthusiasm, on the whole accepting every claim put forth by Foucault. This reaction might be termed resonant paranoia.[36]

A Foucauldian Alternative

If Foucault's claims about the sinister intentions of "power" were accurate, one key aspect of the plot would require explanation. Why is "power" so careless, so indifferent about the activities of Michel Foucault? With power devoting so much time and effort to surveillance and control of "the society," how does it happen that Foucault is the world's twenty-fourth most-cited twentieth-century author? How does it happen that power, so intent on its secretive purpose, has allowed Foucault (and his faithful followers) to unveil those "shameful" practices and to disseminate that knowledge with such impunity? Why does power allow publication of his exposés? Was reviewer Harding "acquiescing" in power's regimentation when writing the review for the *Listener*? Given what reviewer Shelley has told us, one would have to believe that she was controlled by "power" when writing her review. The essay's publication in the *American Journal of Sociology* would also, of course, be part of that "actual control" over the totality of our lives.

This gap in Foucault's otherwise "implacable logic" (from Donald Goodman's review) requires further consideration. This discussion will follow, as much as possible, the broad outlines of Foucault's method (or *jeu*). One could argue, as Herbert Marcuse did a couple of decades ago, that the freedom to criticize was all a sham; it was "repressive tolerance," one more cunning device in power's repertory. It is to Marcuse's credit that he, unlike the Foucauldians, at least recognized the manifest fact—that to an amazing degree, probably more so than in all of hitherto recorded history, human behavior is not controlled; it is not regimented. Some members of the New Left, in the declining stage of that movement, eventually "recognized" the unsuspected truth, that Marcuse himself was a capitalist agent. His employment in the OSS during World War II led to the conclusion of persisting connections, at that point, with the CIA

Perhaps Foucault was also an agent of power. Several easily recognized elements of the case attest to the truth of this conclusion. One may note, first, his unhindered freedom to "expose" power. The publication and dissemination of his work in all major languages point to the same conclusion. Publication is one thing, gaining attention is another. The large numbers of positive reviews, beginning with the major media, again suggest a design or tactic. That the works are assigned widely in universities, for the edification of upper- and upper-middle-class children (those most likely to pose a threat), provides further evidence of this aspect of the new microphysics of power. Stanislav Andreski has given us the key to this cunning and necessarily secret arrangement: "If we convince the subjects that their ruler's power is irresistible, they will abandon all thoughts of rebellion."[37] That, surely, is the shameful intent accounting for the presence of those two apparently contrary facts—the domination of power and the freedom of Michel Foucault to "expose" that domination.

One further aspect of the microphysics of power needs explanation. A serious danger is inherent in this tactic, one that has been anticipated and successfully countered. Foucault's message, like that of Marcuse before him, is twofold, a dialectical combination of opposites. It contains, simultaneously, a call for liberation and a requirement, a need for self-imposed repression or, what amounts to the same thing, self-induced resignation. It is always possible, should the lesson reach a wider audience, that only a part of the lesson, that of liberation, might be heard. The lower classes might hear only one moment of the dialectical argument. To guard against this possibility, power recognized the need to "exclude a particular section." The message must be encoded so as to put it beyond reach of the general populace. This was easily achieved through its translation into an exotic language, one that can be understood only by those who have undergone a long (and expensive) apprenticeship or, to use the appropriate word, discipline. It is no accident that Marcuse's message also appeared in an encodified form. Although a different *specific* language was used, the purpose was doubtlessly the same, to distract the otherwise intelligent student from serious study of (or investigation of) social processes.

The same procedures have been used for some time, beginning with the work of Hegel and continuing with the arcane productions of Karl Marx. The latter's focus on economics, however, proved a mistake; it touched all too closely on the real interests of power. As a result, power saw to it that the hegemonic academic discourse was "re-philosophized." Perry Anderson has reviewed this remarkable transformation. He points to Georg Lukács, the son of a banker, and Karl Korsch, who along with Althusser were themselves bank managers, as the men who set the new direction. Their efforts, he writes, "marked the end of the phase in which Western Marxism was still at home among the masses. Henceforward, it was to speak its own enciphered language, at an increasingly remote distance from the class whose fortunes it formally sought to serve or articulate." Anderson describes the subject matter shift as follows: "The progressive relinquishment of economic or political structures as the central concerns of theory was accompanied by a basic shift in the whole centre of gravity of European Marxism towards *philosophy*." He then lists nine leading marxists who were professors (not possible without at least the consent of power, it should be noted) and adds that "in all cases, the discipline in which chairs were held was philosophy." Their language, he adds, "came to acquire an increasingly specialized and inaccessible cast." The minds (and activities) of many generations of otherwise dangerous intellectuals were thus safely neutralized. Their time and efforts were spent in "mastering" (a code word referring to a rigorous, time-consuming, self-imposed discipline) the details of labyrinthine systems. The specific content of those systems is unimportant. Whether Hegel, Marx, Adorno, or Poulantzas, whether Nietzsche or Foucault, Heidegger or Derrida, Sartre, Bourdieu, or even Talcott Parsons, the crucial concerns are that the possibly problematic intellectuals be distracted and that they "communicate" in a language that is unintelligible to the larger populace.[38]

Some Conclusions

In his book *Discipline and Punish,* Michel Foucault has provided an account of a shadowy "power" that successfully imposed a system of discipline and control on all aspects of modern society. This portrait is a misconstruction involving serious errors or, more precisely, gross misrepresentation of the events discussed. His account of the panopticon and its influence is a whole cloth fiction. As seen, his depiction of modern institutional history is based on Bentham's rejected plan. The Prussian infantry of the eighteenth century was certainly no fiction but, contrary to Foucault's bold declaration, it was not imitated by the whole of Europe. Military practice, within decades, was to follow an entirely different course. The Foucault "constructions" come with an appearance of scholarly support—that is, with footnotes, references, and the suggestion of documentation—but his own references tell another story. The most striking example, the day-to-night transformation, is his use of Bentham's *Works.* Foucault successfully took in scores of "gatekeepers," the critics and commentators, and presumably thousands of readers.

There is an easy alternative hypothesis with respect to the history of punishment. It is the traditional one found in the standard texts, namely that the prison and the associated reforms of punishment were all part of the liberal program. The reforms were intended, to borrow (and amend) Foucault's phrase, as a quantitative phenomenon to bring less cruelty, less pain, more kindness, more respect, and more humanity. That position, the claim of benevolent intent, on the whole is very well supported. Foucault's opposite case, that of malevolence, microphysics, acts of cunning, subtle arrangements, and shameful economies, comes with no serious supporting evidence.

Another possibility, as opposed to those of humane versus malevolent intentions, would be an indifference hypothesis. Offenders could be imprisoned but paid next to no attention. As opposed to minute scrutiny of behavior, "power" might just not care. The notion of indifference, of "power" too busy with other things, does not seem to occur to Foucault. The prison as warehouse with an accompanying throw-away-the-key philosophy might stem from malevolence. Or it might result from frustration, from the failure of other alternatives.

How did Foucault's misconstruction gain such resonance in the intellectual world? We have here an example of what, in Chapter 1, was referred to as the problem of failed controls. The review process did not function adequately. Reviewers did not know the subject matters covered, did not know the relevant literatures, and, more serious, did not investigate even small "samples" of Foucault's references. They had taken Foucault's conclusions on faith. Some reviewers indicated skepticism about Foucault's method, signaling reason for doubt. Others clearly resonated with Foucault's "findings," affirming them, enthusiastically elaborating on the possibilities.

Reviewers are only the "front line" of the reviewing process. They, in most cases, are selected by editors to render judgments. We know little about such decision making, that is, how editors choose reviewers. Editors could not, of course, be fully aware of reviewer dispositions at the outset and even after receipt of their contributions would be hard pressed to assess them for accuracy and fairness. Here too many judgments must be made on faith. Editors face a serious difficulty with this kind of book, which sweeps across time, place, and academic disciplines. Few specialists are prepared to assess the many facets of wide-ranging works. Such texts, accordingly, do not—cannot—receive the same kind of expert criticism that would be brought to bear on the specialized monograph in an area of general interest. Thus these works can more easily escape the "controls" of the review process.[39]

Allan Megill has pointed out that Foucault is not, as some might wish to believe, "an *inter*-disciplinary scholar, standing between and happily drawing from existing disciplines." He is "*anti*disciplinary, standing outside all disciplines and drawing from them only in the hope of under-mining them."[40] Given the peculiarities of Foucault's scholarly effort, Pierre Vilar's observation seems entirely appropriate—that the errors must be deliberate. It is as if Foucault were undertaking an experiment—to see how far he could go in purveying historical absurdities. There can be little question as to the validity of his underlying hypothesis. He has demonstrated, unambiguously, that one can travel a great distance in the academic realm (in the realm of "the scientific disciplines") dispensing mock scholarship without encountering any serious impediment. Foucault has replicated the Myron Fox experiment and confirmed the original finding, this time with astonishing, continuing, worldwide success.

7

Some Problems
of Intellectual Life

The previous chapters have reviewed and assessed three major theoretical statements. Each of the statements purports to be realistic, offering a documented, empirically supported account that describes and explains some complex events. On investigation, however, that support proved somewhat problematic.

Max Weber constructed an argument linking a religious ethic with a subsequent capitalist spirit. The argument was based on an enormous range of sources, the "density" of his documentation being among the greatest in all of modern scholarship. On closer examination, that evidence proved to be surprisingly weak. The bold claims of the opening pages, signaling the difficulty, prove to be based on a copying error and a spurious relationship. The linkage of text claims and supporting evidence may be appropriately described as flimsy. At best, the famous thesis is an unconfirmed hypothesis. Two groups of academic specialists, Reformation historians and economic historians, have not judged the thesis favorably. It has, nevertheless, been treated as a valid claim in sociology and also frequently in the humanities.

A broad range of commentators have vouched for the lower-middle-class thesis. For more than a half-century, it was the leading explanation for the rise of Nazism, the key to the electoral support for Hitler and his party. The claim has been invoked and accepted despite the absence, from the beginning, of specific compelling evidence. Even in the face of contrary evidence, some commentators continue to treat the argument as if it were entirely adequate.

Michel Foucault provided an account of punishment in the modern era that explains the "birth of the prison." The account was based on source materials that do not confirm his principal claims and, as a consequence, would require different lines of analysis. Some key elements of Foucault's "construction" appear to have been created in defiance of the sources he provided. And yet, the work has been widely accepted. Of special note perhaps, the enthusiasm is most intense among self-declared critical intellectuals.

All three cases point to a serious problem. Intellectuals regularly announce themselves as "critical." Unlike others, they challenge received wisdom. Unlike everyday conversation, the claims discussed in their realm are "put to the test" in the sense that both logic and evidence will be subjected to serious and insistent review. But in these instances at least, the critical stance has been remarkably absent. In some cases, in Foucault's history of the prison, in the Mozart and Columbus biographies reviewed earlier, many critical intellectuals have accepted day-to-night transformations of the actual histories. How does it happen? How is it that insistent critics, on occasion, let their defenses down and become so unexpectedly accepting? To address these questions it is necessary to review some of the fundamentals of intellectual activity.

Social Theories: Fact and Faith

A theory is a general simplification scheme, basically a set of statements that define and link events. Those statements indicate what is thought to be important (and what is not) and also how those important events are causally connected. To make "the world" at least intellectually manageable, we use simplifying assumptions. Since the world involves an infinitude of events, everyone must work with some kind of theory, with some simplifying arrangement, even when it is not explicitly recognized. Possibly the most widely used theory in economically advanced societies goes under the heading of "common sense," a viewpoint that in most instances involves orientations distilled from liberal social and economic theories of the eighteenth and nineteenth centuries.

Most social theories are derived, in one way or another, from experience. They are ordinarily synthesized out of various contributions of historical accounts, reports of contemporary events, and direct experience. Generally, apart from common sense, these theories are developed by intellectuals, by persons we might call professional theory makers. Most intellectuals, to be sure, do not actually make theories; most are users or disseminators. They apply the received theories in subsequent research or they teach the basic elements of those theories to a wider audience. Some intellectuals reach into the complexity of human experience and "distill its essence." Combining intuition, conceptualization, and research, they develop and justify a simplified scheme. Then, together with others convinced of its merit, they use the scheme in subsequent research and analysis. They also pass it on to others, upholding it, legitimating it, attesting to its merit, and training others to appreciate its special insights. Two processes are involved here: one is intellectual (people attempting to know or understand a complex reality), and one is social (people passing on and vouching for a given intellectual framework).

Underlying the effort, in both processes, is a concern for the adequacy, for the realism, validity, or truth of the schemes in question. The assumption—or hope—is that a theory will provide an accurate portrait, or reflection, of that "complex reality." Scientific theories go beyond mere intuition in the effort to assess adequacy. Some investigative procedures, some research operations are required to allow confirmation (or rejection) of the principal claims. It is this requirement of research, of the need for a validation procedure, that differentiates scientific theories from those produced by saints, shamans, and other purely intuitive theory makers.[1]

Unfortunately, scientific activity does not always follow the route outlined in introductory texts. The linkages between available evidence and the theoretical formulations are often surprisingly weak. In some instances, a theory is given primacy over "the facts." We have, for example, the statement of a prominent historical sociologist who, in defending a neomarxist theory, announced a unique methodological position: "Damn the facts! A good theory is hard to find."[2] Putting "the defense" of the theory ahead of its empirical adequacy has been called theory-saving. Such defenses have also been referred to as immunization strategies.

Some commentators have it that all intellectuals engage in theory-saving efforts. Everyone, presumably, has some strategy to protect or insulate favored notions. The underlying argument is one of relativism, basically, that all intellectual frameworks are "constructions" and that one is as good as the next. There is perhaps something to be said for these relativizing claims, but that "something" amounts to little more than a truism. For the sake of intellectual convenience, people hang on to cherished organizing principles. The Tocqueville passage (quoted in Chapter 1) points to this tendency, to the general acceptance, by everyone, of "many things" on faith or trust alone, essentially for reasons of "economy."

That said, moving beyond the truism, one may also note wide variations in actual behavior. People differ widely in their concern for "the facts." Some people give much time and effort to assembling evidence which is brought to bear on theoretical claims. At the opposite end of the continuum one finds data indifference, instances where people do not wish to be bothered by evidence or, the extreme case, where people would "damn the facts." One might, as an analogy, think of electoral behavior. Some voters wish to have "a lot" of information, fitting it into frameworks as an aid to assessment; others wish little information, finding "facts" troublesome, something of a burden. The former assume knowable differences between parties and candidates; the latter, oftentimes, make relativizing ontological and epistemological assumptions (such as politicians are all alike, they all lie to you). Persons with scientific commitments, one hopes, would be found clustered close to the former pole of the continuum. Other people would be found distributed along the entire range.

There are no "pure" cases. All scientists, or all "philosophers," depend in part on proofs and research findings and in part on faith. Our understanding of scientific knowledge, of the various results available to us, should therefore give consideration to both processes. The previous chapters have considered research findings. The discussion here will address the social influences that inspire trust.

The Social Psychological Components

This discussion is concerned with what might be called the social psychology of knowledge. Sociology treats human beings as formed by two processes, socialization and social control. Socialization refers to the training (or instilling) of values, outlooks, perceptions, and norms. Such efforts involve the teaching of the received, the handed-down, or approved "social constructions." Social control refers to mechanisms that somehow constrain outlooks and behavior; these might range all the way from a disapproving glance to the use of police. The observations and insights gained from thousands of social psychological studies are routinely applied to human behavior generally, that is, to "people." Only rarely are those same insights used to help understand the behavior of the subgroups studied here, that is, of scientists, speculative philosophers, intellectuals, or, a somewhat larger category, the intelligentsia. This discussion picks up and extends the observations put forth in the first chapter. It assumes that the lessons of the Asch and Milgram studies apply also to the intellectual enterprise. Some of these social psychological determinants provide constraints; they somehow limit responses to a restricted range of possibilities. Other determinants involve incentives or facilitating conditions; these encourage or reward the choice of recommended options.

Five themes will be explored here. These are: first, a trained concern with the "inner logic" of a paradigm; second, a trained attachment, loyalty, or cathexis, an unreasoning preference for given viewpoints; third, conformity, the acceptance of viewpoints regardless of evidence or cathexis; fourth, the role of gatekeepers in directing the flow of information; and fifth, a facilitating factor, the development of permissive standards for judgment.

The first of these themes involves a constraint on the direction of research efforts. Given a set of initial assumptions with high surface plausibility, researchers tend to work out and explore the "inner logic." It is the implications of the initial assumptions that are studied rather than the realism of the first principles themselves. Much valuable and useful work can be achieved within those constraints, possibly over some centuries, before it is recognized that the basic or axiomatic assumptions themselves require attention. Some kind of social influence, presumably, constrains the choices, directing attention to the former concern and to the neglect of the other.[3]

Second is the problem of psychological constraints. Many people, as a result of their prior training, develop psychological attachments to their preferred paradigm assumptions and are reluctant to see, hear, or accept contrary evidence. For some, that would mean a rejection of "dissonant" information. An illustration: a graduate student once undertook a study of an outpatient clinic. Knowing that the patients never saw the same doctor twice, that they were simply assigned to young and inexperienced student doctors, and knowing that they had to spend many hours "just waiting around" before being seen, this researcher "knew" that the experience must be degrading, humiliating, and dehumanizing. But in the interviews the outpatients began giving the wrong answers. They explained, at every point, why the clinic experience was better than the alternatives they had known previously. Instead of concluding that his original hypotheses were wrong or misleading, the student broke off the research. In effect, he suppressed the finding. In another case, a "concerned" graduate student wished to work on a "significant" topic. A professor suggested that he study the 1968 uprising in France, an appropriate survey of the adult French population being readily available. In this case the student "knew" that the reason for the rebellion was alienating work, the demanding pace, the bureaucratization of modern life, and a consequent lack of control over one's existence. He "knew" too that it was not a wage struggle. His initial investigation, however, revealed that workers, like the outpatients, were giving the wrong answers. They said their principal concerns were with wage and salary questions. Again, unwilling to hear (let alone transmit) this finding, the student broke off the research. In both cases, processes of self-censorship were operating. The professors involved opposed the positions taken, arguing that the students should respect the results and make them public, but in both cases, loyalty to the prior beliefs was given greater weight than professorial "authority."[4]

A related source of constraint, of intellectual misdirection, stems from the mixing of theoretical and practical concerns. Most theories have practical as well as cognitive implications. Some people become so attached to programmatic needs that they overlook or reject findings seen as detrimental to their cause. Some frameworks might be termed "theories of arousal," which aim to mobilize various segments of the society. This is certainly the case with liberalism in most aspects of its nineteenth- and twentieth-century variants. Marxism, Proudhonism, and Saint-Simonism are arousal theories, as are also the many varieties of anarchism. The "critical" versions of the mass-society theory (arguing manipulated or "narcotized" masses) also, presumably, aim at arousal. Other frameworks, however, might be termed "theories of restraint." They advise segments of the population to acquiesce, to accept, to consent (or at least to assent). Traditional mass-society theories carry this recommendation. Aroused masses following the lead of some demagogue could only make matters worse, this in an already fragile social order. Disorder, destruction, hunger, and death would surely follow such insurgency.[5]

The problem is that some intellectuals become advocates, putting "party" loyalties ahead of their intellectual concerns. They become missionaries or defenders of the faith. Their task is to protect the truths of a given position against any and all challenges, lest the interests of "the movement" be damaged. This support of party is, as one commentator put it, "the treason of the intellectuals."[6] In the extreme case, some "researchers" have chosen to fabricate the "evidence" needed to shore up their beliefs. They have sacrificed their intellectual obligation to the needs of a party or movement. Sociologist C. Wright Mills, addressing the same problem, the mixing of intellectual and practical tasks, argued for a clear separation of the two activities: "First, one tries to get it straight, to make an adequate statement—if it is gloomy, too bad; if it leads to hope, fine."[7]

A third kind of restraint has both internal and external components. Many people, so we have learned from the work of Solomon Asch and Stanley Milgram, are conformists. Many people will go along with almost any social environment. Although conformity is typically attributed to "other people," most especially to "the masses," the Dr. Fox study showed such behavior to be present also among academic intellectuals. Where a theory has been taught and vouched for by the leading figures of the age, many people, even many serious intellectuals, would find it difficult to challenge such a consensus. Like the rest of the human population, many intellectuals would feel discomfort, stress, or even some degree of angst at the thought of going against an established consensus or against "authority." That feeling would constrain them both in the choice of research topics and in the presentation of findings. In contrast to the previous hypotheses, which involve internalized norms or beliefs, this option focuses on behavior driven by the external cues (as in David Reisman's concept of the "other-directed" personality). In the pure case, one would have behavior (conformity) without belief or cathexis.[8]

Knowledge does not pass directly from producers to the ultimate consumers. It is passed along through many channels with many people along the way taking a position, vouching for claims, challenging or rejecting them, or urging postponement of judgment. Knowledge, in other words, passes through social networks with many "gatekeepers" in one or another manner directing the flow.[9] That direction might involve opposition on the part of persons who feel challenged or threatened by new, different, or unexpected findings. Given the conformist tendencies, it is likely that proponents of new and different findings would face some difficulties in getting a hearing for "challenging" results. At all stages, funding, review, and dissemination, there would be a bias in favor of the received wisdom.[10] This is not to argue insurmountable opposition, only some difficulty, some stickiness or reluctance in the dissemination process. While most people appear to be conformists, there are, to be sure, compulsive nonconformists, persons eager for any and all new and different ideas. Ahd there are others, the generally curious, people who are relatively open, willing to listen, appreciate, and defend the new and provocative.

These social psychological constraints have a conservative influence. They operate, independently of evidence, to keep "thought" within some restricted boundaries. Some social influences have an opposite impact. Some gatekeeper recommendations might best be described as enabling or facilitating. A permissive philosophy of science justifies the relaxation of, or indifference to, the constraints of evidence.[11] The requirement of validation, of confirmative procedure, is not universally accepted. There is some controversy over the requirement itself, although few would argue the pure "libertarian" (or latitudinarian) position. Many versions of social constructionism are strongly relativistic. They stand in opposition to the belief that our ideas and understandings derive ultimately from empirical investigation, from assessment of evidence. In its exteme form, as indicated, some proponents have declared that there is no objective reality, only these agreed-upon (or imposed) frameworks.

The extreme version, of course, is patently ridiculous. Hunger is not a social construction. It is signaled by a pain felt in the stomach and no amount of "discourse" will make it go away. If the extreme version were valid, one would have to fault its proponents for failing to make maximum use of this insight. The problems of poverty and want could be removed from this world by forbidding those problematic definitions. Human life would be dramatically improved if we did not have the words *hunger* and *pain* in our vocabularies. And what of heart disease, cancer, smallpox, and malaria? And what about death? Those so-called objective facts, after all, are merely imposed definitions.

The point here, to summarize, is that a range of extraintellectual factors are inherent in the scientific effort. Those factors, working separately or in combination, hinder the achievement of the primary intellectual goal, the production of empirically supported knowledge. In all three case studies reviewed here, some failure of scholarly procedures had been indicated; the critical apparatus did not operate as anticipated.

The explanation offered here consists of a series of hypotheses about the processes occurring at various points in the training of intellectuals and in the production, reception, assessment, and dissemination of scholarly knowledge. In part these hypotheses are supported with evidence provided in the previous chapters; in part they are backed up by independent studies of scholarly procedures. This account is, at best, a brief sketch with many empirical gaps. Few accounts, for example, report instances of self-censorship, that is, of researchers refusing to present uncongenial or dissonant findings. We will probably never know the frequency and impact of such decisions.

The Extraintellectual Factors

The most fundamental of the procedural problems seen in previous chapters is the failure to check text claims against original sources. A thoughtful review of source materials would have forced rejection of the Mozart "neglect and poverty" myth. It would have undone the portrait of Columbus versus the flat-earth theorists. Both myths have been sustained now for well over a century. The review of Foucault's sources would have cast serious doubts about his thesis of cunning and repressive purposes dominating the modern era. The review of Weber's source material shows the thesis to be a set of hypotheses with rather dubious empirical foundations. The problem is clearly a serious one. It means that for long periods, hypotheses or theories are sustained without any serious review of sources or, at minimum, without any successful challenge to the accepted misconstruction.[12]

This failure to check sources points to an underlying social psychological factor: large numbers of "critical" scholars have come to view those accounts as adequate, or worse, as commendable exemplary achievements. Faith, trust, acceptance, consent, any such terms signaling acquiescence or conformity, are social products. Students, professionals, and the "informed" public, have been trained to judge intellectual productions, some works being deemed worthy, some as unworthy of one's attention.

The role of such socialization and certification processes may be seen in patterns of paradigm dominance and in various paradigm shifts, these occurring without any special empirical, that is, scientific justification. For decades, at least in the English-speaking world, Herbert Spencer was the towering figure in the social sciences. The marxian framework, in contrast, was given little attention and even less approval at that time. In Germany, in the same period, the marxian categories, the class nomenclature and elements of the framework, were widely accepted as adequate and appropriate terms of analysis, within the universities and in journalistic accounts. Most of those commentators, to be sure, accepted the terms of analysis without in any way agreeing with the "larger purposes" of the theory.

By the 1930s, Spencer's influence was dwindling rapidly. In the United States, largely through the efforts of Talcott Parsons, sociologists shifted their attention to three important European scholars, Vilfredo Pareto, Emile Durkheim, and Max Weber. In the 1950s, Parsons's own abstract and general formulations were very much in the forefront of sociological thinking. By the late sixties, Pareto (along with other elitists) had been dropped from the sociological agenda. Parsons was also eclipsed, to be read and revered only by a small coterie of specialists. In the sixties, marxism gained attention and favor, the resonance occurring generally throughout the nations of the advanced captitalist world. In France, marxism had been certified in the early postwar period, but then, a few decades later, it was decertified. In the Federal Republic of Germany, the marxian framework was accredited first in the 1960s but, unlike in France, did not experience the same general decertification.[13]

These paradigm shifts suggest patterns of conformity (or obedience) similar to those seen in the studies reviewed earlier. The subjects in those experimental studies are often treated rather disdainfully, naïveté being a frequent suggestion, but, as seen, conformity is frequent also within the scholarly ranks, among those trained in the arts of criticism. More generous readings of such "unthinking conformity" may be easily provided. Every expert, all those one has read, heard, or talked with, has accredited or vouched for claim A. The few dissenting research articles could easily be discounted as exceptions to the rule, as deviant cases, or peculiar outliers. Such discounting comes all the easier when "guided" by that consensus among the experts. Then too, as Tocqueville argued, a question of economy is necessarily involved: How may one best use available time? When "the experts" have vouched for the conclusions, a check of the original sources, the work of Calvin, Baxter, or Bentham, would seem pointless. The acceptance (or conformity) would seem a rational choice, a reasonable estimate of probabilities.

In most instances those estimates would be a product of (or conditioned by) one's education or training. Teachers, texts, mentors, and peers have provided judgments of merit, claims that a work is worthwhile. As seen in the Dr. Fox experience, however, even highly trained educators are moved by appearances. In that case, the audiences judged the communication to be credible and worthy of attention on the basis of the social clues (proper credentials, a familiar style) alone. While that example is clearly an extreme case, some reliance on the social cues is likely to be present in all judgments of source credibility. The following paragraphs provide a brief sketch or outline of the social psychological processes as they might appear at various points in the academic career.

The first systematic knowledge of theories of the kind we have been discussing is ordinarily gained in undergraduate education. One learns about them from texts and from lectures. Textbook treatments of the Weber thesis, depending on the field, provide sharply divergent assessments. Texts in European history and economic history pay little or no attention to the thesis; they, in essence, dismiss it as without merit. The sociology texts are generally approving, many of them laudatory. The approval given in the sociology texts, moreover, is hortatory, based largely on commendation of the author rather than on consideration of argument and evidence. Some of those texts report controversy but suggest that expert judgment has supported the original claim. The criticisms provided, with rare exception, give little sense of the specific problems involved. Few texts provide references to appropriate critical studies.

Under such circumstances, a student's "knowledge" depends on an accident of fate. If course requirements or interest led to Introductory Sociology, Weber's argument would be taught as "a worthy thesis." If the same considerations led instead to Modern European History, the lesson would be "not worth your attention." In the ordinary run of things, neither student would be prepared to discuss the merits of Weber's arguments, that is, to give an informed account of their empirical adequacy.[14] In both settings the lesson provided would have been sustained through a social process. An authority signals either commendation or derogation, rather than providing a thorough review of evidence.

Weber's text, as noted, contains a copying error that enhances "support" for the author's thesis. Although pointed out by Samuelsson first in

Swedish in 1957, then in English in 1961, the error has never been either corrected or annotated in the many printings of *The Protestant Ethic* made available to students over the last thirty years. Samuelsson also pointed out that a key "finding" involved a spurious relationship. That too has not been signaled to readers. The key question then is, How many students have been told of those difficulties? And the related one, How many professors, of those who assigned the Weber text, knew of those difficulties, reported them, and reviewed the implications? In these respects, the science has not been cumulative: there has been a refusal to recognize and deal with important errors. The social clues, the regular commendations, have been given precedence over the evidential ones.[15]

One problem signaled both here and at various points in the previous chapters is compartmentalization. Some theories arise and flourish within a given academic specialization. In some instances those specialists neglect or avoid the relevant expert knowledge available in other fields. Foucault's history of penology has been favorably received in the humanities; his views, by and large, are neglected in criminology (which favors, for good reason, another reading of that history). The Weber thesis has been enthusiastically supported in sociology; but that enthusiasm has not been shared by specialist historians. Two complementary boundary-maintaining processes appear to be operating. The practitioners in one field, those developing or defending the social construction do not make systematic use of the relevant expertise of other fields. In an opposite process, the experts in those other fields do not intervene in any serious way to make correction. In both settings the focus of attention is internal; it is directed to the arguments and conclusions formulated and developed within that field.[16]

For many university graduates, the chance contacts with various theories in introductory courses are probably "the last word" they receive on the subject. Most who have been assigned Weber's monograph or Foucault's book would never come in contact with another reading of the Calvinist influence or the history of penology. Accounts of Hitler's rise to power appearing in popular sources continue to recite the lower-middle-class litany, confirming the version prevalent in textbooks.

For students taking relevant advanced courses, the situation would be little different. Students of history would gain some additional detailed knowledge of European history but, except for those specializing in the early modern period, would not be exposed to a detailed review of the Weber argument. Sociology majors might read *The Protestant Ethic* in its entirety, but detailed criticism and a systematic review of sources would ordinarily be missing. For most sociology students (and those among them who later become professors), Reformation history or European economic history would not be areas of active interest, hence the reliance on faith or on trust in the received wisdom.[17]

In casual usage, one often finds discussion of "the universities" and "the professors," as if further differentiation were unnecessary, as if the experience were all of a piece. But academic institutions differ in their principal tasks: some are designed for research and teaching, others for only teaching. Given the divergence of institutional goals, it follows that the activities of professors will also differ, in that some will be primarily researchers while others, again primarily, will be disseminators. The former category is much smaller but has greater visibility, that misperception providing the basis for quick generalizations. The research professors, to be sure, are also disseminators. They pass on knowledge in their choice of texts, in class lectures, in scholarly meetings, and in appropriate publications. The disseminators are not normally involved in the production of knowledge (in the sense of research and publication); they transmit knowledge through the choice of texts and in classroom presentations.

Those definitions of tasks are built into the organization of academia. Some institutions are constituted so as to further research; some are planned to maximize the teaching effort. The terms of employment typically specify that in the former settings one's time will be divided between the research and teaching obligations. In the latter, the teaching obligation is emphasized. The diversity of goals is seen most clearly in the different teaching requirements. The requirement in the research universities is usually about half that of the teaching institutions. Reflecting those diverse incentives (and reflecting also personal career choices), the specific intellectual efforts of the two categories of professor will also differ. These observations about the division of academic labor are all commonplace and scarely worth a mention, except for the persistent miscue in the "publish or perish" cliché.[18]

The producers, the active researchers, are more likely to be up to date about current research activity in their own specialties. They have to be knowledgeable, otherwise they would lose out in the competition for publication and funding. They would also be located in institutions providing the necessary resources, that is, library holdings, databases, computer facilities, and both intellectual and technical support from colleagues and staff. Those academics would ordinarily be well-informed about cutting-edge work in their fields, but in areas outside their immediate concerns, they would be less knowledgeable and, essentially, would act as disseminators. In those peripheral areas, they would also be inclined to take facts and theories on faith. Sociology, political science, and economics are present-oriented fields. Their major research problems, for the most part, arise from current trends and developments. Few active researchers would be reviewing the history of penology or linkages between religion and economic activity in previous centuries. In those areas, most research professors would be dependent on texts (Foucault or Weber) or on gate-keepers (reviewers) who vouched for those texts.

The professors in teaching institutions would, for the most part, be disseminators. The knowledge disseminated would originate disproportionately from texts (as opposed to original research). A heavier teaching obligation means a greater spread of attention and less in-depth knowledge. The relative lack of facilities (small libraries, for example) means professors and students would be unable to follow through on recondite questions (for example, the histories provided by Foucault or Weber). Textbooks in recent decades have deteriorated in quality, publishers requiring some "dumbing down" and authors assenting to that demand. Unless the professors undertook systematic correction of those deficiencies, students generally would be less capable, less prepared to make appropriate criticism of the works read.[19]

Different intellectual activities occur in these diverse settings. Professors in the major institutions would, typically, produce new, cutting-edge knowledge. In sociology in the 1990s, for example, they would be producing articles on organizational ecology, network analysis, rational choice theory, on the strength of weak ties, on neofunctionalism, resource-mobilization theory, feminist theory, gender studies, critical theory, and various kinds of structuralism. Those professors' articles would predominate in the leading journals, most of which are based in the major institutions. The editors, associate editors, and referees are drawn, disproportionately, from those same institutions.[20]

The major university presses are also located in the prestigious private institutions and in the leading state universities. They operate under separate management, that is, independently of the journals and the academic departments. They have full-time editors and supervisory boards that, officially at least, make final publication decisions. Board members are usually drawn from within the home institution. University presses typically publish works originating in only a few faculties in these institutions; most books deal with history, the humanities and the social sciences. The members of governing boards, accordingly, are generally drawn from those fields.[21]

The commercial presses, those producing textbooks, are located outside the universities and, unlike the previously discussed outlets, are basically profit-oriented enterprises. The principal decision makers there are publishers and editors. They contract with professors who write books according to publishers' specifications. With rare exceptions, the texts are "general"—they try to cover everything, attempting to please all and to offend few. A fair amount of imitation occurs, with new entries copying the format of previous successful offerings. Given those tendencies, it follows that such texts are rather dated. They also reflect preferences found in the heart of the market, which means the state colleges and junior colleges, not the leading or the most prestigious institutions. The received wisdom, the handed-down knowledge of previous decades dominates in these textbooks—as opposed to the latest research found in the journals and university presses. With only rare exceptions, the writers of commercial books in recent years have not been producers of cutting-edge knowledge.[22]

Professors (along with some advanced graduate students) are key decision makers in the determination of textbook quality. In both major and minor institutions, their gatekeeping choices, their assignment of manifestly inadequate texts, make the process work as it does. Their decisions would have varying impact. In the major institutions, textbook deficiencies might, to some extent at least, be overcome in higher level courses. Elsewhere, textbook knowledge, supplemented perhaps by some accessible, low-cost paperbacks, would be at the heart of the educational experience.

Gatekeeping decisions appear continuously in scholarly activity. Editors of journals, of university presses, and of commercial presses are all major gatekeepers. They are aided by inside and outside readers, who play ancillary roles in such decision making. Book publishers usually depend on a network of friends and associates who recommend manuscripts and likely referees. Teachers and professors, as noted, function as gatekeepers in their choices of texts. They also, in an ordinary week, would make dozens of relay-versus-discard decisions with regard to lecture material and discussions. In all of these judgments, there would unavoidably be some mix of faith (trust in the conventional readings) and of science (knowledge based on evidence).

Problems arise in the balance between the two. Editors, referees, and reviewers could give emphasis either to evidence and documentation or to a defense of a faith. One striking example of the latter appears in the career of Edwin Sutherland (1883–1950), who "has been widely acclaimed as the dominant criminologist of the 20th century." He developed a sociological theory of crime (called differential association) and trained a generation of students in this tradition, some of whom became leading criminologists. Sutherland was the author of a major text in the area, one that went through many editions. He also wrote two important monographic studies. Two other criminologists, Sheldon and Eleanor Glueck, produced a series of important pioneering research studies in the same period. These were based on four large, painstakingly assembled data sets. Their monographs contained a range of important empirically based findings. Initially Sutherland viewed those results favorably. Later, however, he changed his position and, in a series of reviews, declared the studies to be without merit. He adopted an idiosyncratic methodological standard that was not achieved in the Gluecks' work (or in that of most other social scientists). He insisted on an exclusively sociological reading of crime (basically on his reading), while the Gluecks' argued (with evidence) the importance of age, of maturation, and of diverse psychological factors.[23]

Sutherland was establishing and maintaining "boundary lines"—he "explicitly denied the claims of all other disciplines potentially interested in crime." The most serious charges against the Gluecks came in an unpublished review that was "circulated among colleagues [including the Gluecks] across the country." He implied that the Gluecks had "fudged their data," that key predictive judgments had been made after the fact. "When the data and methods are examined," Sutherland wrote, "they are found to be completely untrustworthy." The Gluecks responded with a detailed rebuttal.

Ultimately, Sutherland won out. In the struggle for influence, it was a complete rout. The best-selling criminology text in 1989 gives the work of the Gluecks a single, brief, deprecating, and misleading mention. That outcome is a comment on the social aspect of this contention. As for the intellectual contribution, the Gluecks appear to be "the winners." Sutherland's main objections to their work, from the outset, were of doubtful merit. The charge of manipulated results was groundless and not sustained in a subsequent replication. The Gluecks' principal conclusions are at the center, at the cutting edge, of current criminological research.[24]

The problems facing authors and editors may be described as follows. If a position is generally accepted, obtaining a fair hearing for dissenting views might prove difficult, since most eligible referees would favor the established position. Where there is contention, most knowledgeable referees would be aligned with one or the other of the opposing sides. The more technical the argument, the smaller the pool of qualified referees and the greater the likelihood of prior alignment. Even with the best will in the world, it is often difficult for editors to find referees who are both knowledgeable and disinterested.[25]

Editors are not always disinterested parties standing above the fray. They too have professional histories, identifications, and loyalties. If moved by those loyalties, an editor could determine outcomes through the choice of referees. If a veto were desired, the choice of two or three referees with known tendencies would ordinarily determine the outcome. Editorial favor may, on occasion, be seen in the treatment of dissenting contributions. Articles, normally, are free standing; they are published in rough order of acceptance with possibly some grouping by subject matter. On occasion, editors have altered those procedures, giving advantage to one side, to the received wisdom, in a controversy.[26]

Discussions of compartmentalization typically focus on, and lament, the effects of boundary lines within academia. The organization of knowledge by discipline means that researchers working in a given field will not know the research generated elsewhere. This does pose serious problems, as has been indicated repeatedly in previous chapters. Some problems appear also as a result of boundaries within fields. Textbooks do not reflect the current state of knowledge because cutting-edge research is not routinely reported there. When such topics do appear, it is after a substantial delay and then with much simplification. Serious difficulties, in short, appear in the transmission of knowledge from the producers to the disseminators.

Another important boundary line, one often overlooked, is found at the edge of the university. It is the line separating academia from "the outside world." Two questions arise here: What knowledge is "chosen" for transmission to a larger audience? And in what ways is that knowledge transformed when it is passed on to that larger audience? Both processes, selection and transformation, are shaped by various gatekeepers.

Only a small part of university-based knowledge ever appears outside the academic realm. It is not intended for the general public and, for good reason, no effort is made to monitor, digest, and transmit that information. Most of the work in the natural sciences, mathematics, and engineering departments experiences this understandable neglect. The more exotic productions of philosophy, literary criticism, and communications departments are seldom passed on. The highly technical statistical studies in the social sciences are also neglected. There is, again understandably, a marked bias in favor of accessible subjects. Selection favors the hot, topical, or less politely, the trendy subjects. If complex subject matters are passed on to the educated public, the presentations are radically simplified, omitting the details of argument and of method.[27]

Many people assume that the mass media presentations of social science findings will at least approximate the results contained in the scholarly literature. Popular reports might, for short periods, be off base with respect to some details but, making generous assumptions about the processes of correction, a close correspondence of source content and media content is taken for granted. As indicated in Chapter 1, however, in the process of transfer, day-to-night transformations are an easy possibility, whether by chance, indifference, or intent. Reference was made there to the automation scare of the 1950s, the rebellion-in-the-workplace flurry, and the white backlash claims of the early 1970s. One group of social science researchers have contrasted the productions of scientific experts and the popular journalistic renditions of that same knowledge. They found day-to-night transformations with respect to the safety of nuclear energy, educational impacts of school busing, and oil industry policies and profits. In another study a similar transformation was found with regard to I.Q. testing. The academic specialists, on the whole, report that intelligence can be reliably measured and that genetic endowment plays an important part (independently of environmental factors) in its determination. In both instances, the general public has been told the opposite.[28]

In 1968, Robert Rosenthal and Lenore Jacobson published a book entitled *Pygmalion in the Classroom,* wherein they reported the results of an unusual experiment. They gave I.Q. tests to students in a primary school and teachers were subsequently told of the "results." Actually the experimenters had, on the basis of random assignment, signaled some students as intelligent, as "late bloomers." When the same test was administered a year later, those who had been so labeled showed significant improvement in test scores. The study was picked up and widely reported; it also had impacts on policy in schools and in school districts (the Los Angeles school board forbade I.Q. testings). The experiment's conclusions rested on very slim evidence. The study was conducted in grades one through six, but only in the first and second grades were statistically significant gains registered. The number of students involved as "experimental subjects" in those grades were, respectively, seven and twelve. Some of the initial scores, moreover, were extremely low, such that the students would ordinarily have been classed as mentally retarded. Those results, one reviewer indicated, were not earned because of wrong answers but "because very few items were attempted by many of the children." The final result therefore could stem from "intellectual growth" presumably stimulated by teacher support, the Rosenthal-Jacobson reading, or from other factors, such as the students having learned how to take tests or through better test administration. Rosenthal's next four experimental efforts failed to replicate even this initial "mini" finding.[29]

Some of the journalists who passed on the Rosenthal-Jacobson findings may have been interested parties. Some, possibly, found the conclusion attractive and transmitted it without any further thought. For others, the reporting might have been of a more innocent character. A review of the small numbers, of confirming and nonconfirming cases, of tests of significance, and the meta-analyses of subsequent replications would not make exciting content. Wineburg, for example, commenting on one of Rosenthal's alleged confirmations, pointed out that "the mean is notoriously sensitive to extreme values when a distribution is skewed. The *median* effect size of Raudenbush's 18 studies is but .035; ten studies yielded positive differences and eight yielded negative differences." His conclusion would be understood by most readers: "What kind of phenomenon is it when nearly half the attempts to produce it yield results in the wrong direction?"[30]

The maintenance of boundaries, it was noted previously, is a two-sided arrangement. In this case, it appears, some interested journalists reported one side of a contentious issue and excluded contrary findings. Some journalists, apparently, "agreed" that that side was accurate and appropriate. Perpetuation of such misconstructions depends also on the behavior of "the experts." Few knowledgeable academic experts intervene with any system to challenge or correct journalistic misrepresentations. Some, rather disdainfully, reject any involvement in public controversy. Some view correction as a hopeless task. That choice, nonintervention, gives interested advocacy groups and supportive journalists a free field for their diverse constructions.[31]

8

Social Misconstruction, Validity, and Verification

As a counter to misconceived wisdom, one way of building the Cartesian principle, doubt or skepticism, into one's thinking is to assume the opposite.[1] On first hearing a claim, one should, as a didactic exercise, negate it and then ask, Can I defend, justify, or support the negation? The result might not be a full-scale confrontation, but a small-detail emendation, a specification, is itself an addition to our knowledge and understanding.

A second recommendation, a remedy for the groupthink problem, is to give more systematic attention to alternative theories. This is something that should be done by individual researchers themselves. They should think and review the "fundamentals" of major theories—those from the past, those with contemporary currency, and also any significant new arrivals on the scene. Part of the training of our students should be the exposition—and assessment—of all major social theories. Some academics, however, are advocates of a single all-purpose explanatory account or "system." In the process, the insights that might be derived from other perspectives are lost.[2]

Horace Miner, a noted anthropologist, studied a farm community in Quebec in the mid-thirties and built his analysis around the family and the church. He also made some use of the mass-society theory in the final chapters, which reviewed signs of community "breakdown." It is a high-quality study filled with insightful observations and intelligent analysis. It is difficult to see, however, that anything would have been lost by a consideration of questions drawn from the marxian framework. Most of the families in this community were "petty bourgeois" and would, presumably, have faced serious strains in the midst of the Great Depression. But those questions were all avoided: the families were not placed within the class hierarchy. There was no discussion of the markets for their produce, and not so much as a paragraph on farm indebtedness, on foreclosures, on the threat of proletarianization, or on possible fascist tendencies. The questions that dominate analyses of farming elsewhere in that period were entirely neglected.[3]

An opposite theoretical bias appears in much recent writing where the religious factor is neglected in favor of class. A particularly striking example appears in the work of the historical sociologist Theda Skocpol. Her account of the English Civil War (sometimes referred to as the Puritan Revolution) gives no indication of the central role of religion in that struggle; the entire analysis is framed in class terms. The religious factor, as was seen in two of the previous chapters, is overlooked entirely or figures only peripherally in analyses of National Socialist voting, where, again, primary attention has been given to the dynamics of "class." These twin biases appear repeatedly in the contemporary social sciences.[4]

One obvious need is for a greater effective theoretical pluralism. Researchers should carry with them a large repertory of theoretical orientations. They should be able to work with those theories, to think easily in those terms, and be able to apply them to any research materials at hand. One should pay special attention to theories that are no longer in favor, those that, possibly for the wrong reasons, have been rejected. Tocqueville, describing the "characteristics of historians in democratic times," said that they "attribute hardly any influence to the individual . . . but, on the other hand . . . assign great general causes to all petty incidents."[5] One senses an "instant truth" here, the generalization bias having been carried to its extreme not by historians but by economists, political scientists, and sociologists. Although not popular, although virtually heretical, the "role of the individual" is a hypothesis deserving attention and thought, rather than the instant dismissal that is so often the case.

A third recommendation involves the need for replication: claims should, in some way, be repeatedly tested.[6] Although regularly approved, replication is not a standard operating procedure in the natural sciences, in the social sciences, or in history. The absence of regular, systematic, detailed replication is the key to the scholarly problems reviewed here, to the uncritical acceptance of handed-down beliefs.

Very different problems arise with respect to replications, depending on the specific field and the kind of research one is considering. Given the frequency of polls and surveys nowadays, replication of claims about mass attitudes and behavior is a relatively simple matter. It is, unfortunately, still an infrequent practice. Replication of field studies, of participant observation studies, in contrast, proves to be more difficult. There the researcher in most cases has provided a guarantee of anonymity to the respondents. The original data exists only in the form of private field notes. Robert A. Dahl, the author of a famous study on New Haven politics, deserves credit for making his field notes available to G. William Domhoff, a known skeptic. The result was a significantly different portrait of New Haven, one that also allowed some demonstration of the constraints on the thinking of Dahl and his co-workers.[7]

Historical study involves still another kind of problem. Most studies will not be replicated, in the sense that a second researcher will cover the same ground within a decade or so of the original research. Most studies are based on a rather diverse range of materials. Published volumes are normally be found in the libraries of major universities, but there are also archived documents, private papers, newspaper accounts, and possibly interview notes or transcripts to be reviewed. The costs of replication, in such cases, are considerably greater than those involved in rerunning a survey. As a result, replication of historical studies occurs with even less frequency than in economics, political science, or sociology. The consequence, the other side of the coin, is that historians, more than their peers in the other social sciences, must have faith or trust in their fellow researchers.

We have some relevant cases. First, there is a David and Goliath story, the struggle of Chester M. Destler and Allan Nevins. Some fifty years ago, Nevins, in the course of his defense of John D. Rockefeller and the Standard Oil Company, made some denigrating comments about Henry Demarest Lloyd's scholarship. Lloyd was the author of *Wealth against Commonwealth*, a major attack on Rockefeller and the company. Destler came to Lloyd's defense in an impressive multiround exchange. As part of that defense, Destler checked 420 of Lloyd's footnote references and was able to vouch for 410 of them. In only ten cases, none of them of great import, did the citation "fail to support the narrative." Ten errors out or 420 would be viewed by most scholars as a very creditable record. Lloyd's work certainly stood the test in this replication.[8]

A second case involves a book published in the mid-1960s dealing with the tariff question in the 1880s. The text was based on a dissertation written under an eminent historian at a leading university. The work, it turned out, contained concocted sources, invented passages designed to supplement the author's argument, and faked quotations from archives the author had never visited. None of this was detected by the readers of the dissertation or by the readers for the publisher, all of whom should have had some expertise in the area. Exposure in this case was the result of a fluke conjuncture. A graduate student writing on one of the political leaders of the period knew the archival sources being cited and he, together with a couple of other young researchers, established the fradulent character of the work—just prior to the author's consideration for tenure at a major state university. The book was withdrawn and disowned by its publisher. Because it required an act of the state legislature to void a degree, the story ends there. The author of this fictional work, of this mock-scholarship, continued to be an accredited doctor of philosophy.[9]

A third case involves a book that has been described by one reviewer as "a stunning achievement . . . surely the most important single work on interwar Germany since Arthur Rosenberg's *Geschichte der Weimarer Republik*." Some historians, not quite so enthusiastic as that reviewer, discovered serious problems in this work, for example, a crucial discussion embellished with concocted quotations. One historian undertook a check of seventy references and concluded that only four of the seventy were found to present no problem. The author of the book conceded some of the errors and promised correction of others in a revised edition. A detailed review of the revised version yielded a severe negative judgment—given its failings and "the impossibility of repairing this project without reconceiving it," the critic, Peter Hayes, writes that he "can have no confidence in any of the professed contributions of this book. . . . [It] literally subtracts from our knowledge of the subjects it treats."[10]

In the latter two cases, many involved parties had failed to undertake even the most rudimentary effort of replication—checking the accuracy of at least a sample of footnote references. The work of replication is a dreary, and in some instances, a most unpleasant effort. The most agreeable outcome, that an author performed impeccably, yields little reward beyond that satisfaction. That finding, normally, might justify a footnote or at best a paragraph. Journal editors, on the whole, are not enthusiastic about replications—a report that the "gimcrack thesis" has been supported once again, now for the sixth time, would make an unexciting journal even less so. Not much advantage, in short, is to be gained through replication; it does little for a scholar's career. It can even be a detriment in that the discovery of serious errors yields a rather nasty result.[11]

Unpleasant as it may be, replication is still a necessary part of the scholarly effort and one that ought to be undertaken with more system. One possibility is to incorporate such tasks into the training of social scientists and historians. Students might be required to follow in the footsteps of Chester Destler. The requirement would, one hopes, be a more modest one, possibly samples of twenty-five or thirty references. In most instances, only published volumes could be assessed with this procedure. Archival documents and field notes, unfortunately, would be beyond the reach of most students.[12]

Compartmentalization is another aspect of the academic routine that stands in the way of confrontation. Members of one department do not routinely bring their expertise to bear on the contributions of another. Worse still, the members of other departments are not typically called on for their expert knowledge. Articles in historical sociology are not routinely sent to historians; in some instances, with intent, that option has been avoided. Articles on the Weber thesis are not routinely sent to Reformation historians or economic historians. Critiques of science are not routinely reviewed by knowledgeable scientists.[13]

One way to avoid confrontation is to form a new compartment. The devotees of a new position, let us call it New View, withdraw from their respective departments and create an interdisciplinary program. The arrangement can easily be justified by reference to historic precedents; virtually all of the established departments in our universities "broke away" at some point from their original base. In the healthy case, this leads to specialization; it advances knowledge in that area. In the unhealthy or pathological case, it provides protection against serious criticism. In one case, for example, a dissertation on the subject of demography produced within a communications department was successfully shielded from any contact with demographic experts elsewhere in the university.

The exponents of New View, typically, will found a journal. The members of the editorial board will, of course, all be New View adherents. The arrangement allows publication that would not otherwise be possible. At the same time, it ensures that the advocates of the position will not have to face the criticisms of experts in other fields. Most New View orientations contain, as part of the basic ideology, a strong claim for methodological relativism, and also share a pronounced hostility to something called positivism. The term is rarely defined but careful hermeneutical study makes the meaning clear: it refers to "'the bringing of evidence to bear on."

Openness is a fundamental rule of academia—one must be open to new ideas. For many, that rule is treated as a near absolute. But as near absolute, it runs up against another compelling rule, the demand for skepticism, for doubt, for the critical attitude. Where the latter rule yields to the former, the result is a reluctance, or for some, an inability to say no. Some academics, for example, would be unhappy with the unambivalent declaration by the little child in Hans Christian Andersen's fairy tale: "But he [the emperor] doesn't have anything on!" Some would object to the child's use of simple categorical alternatives. The child's statement represents merely one perspective on what is actually a rather complicated subject. The child is the prisoner of an outmoded (and imposed) mode of discourse. One would normally, of course, wish to question the claims of authority figures (especially those of an emperor), but some intellectual framework doubtlessly exists, some universe of meaning, within which, when properly understood, the emperor is entirely correct.

It is perhaps this trained inability to say no that made possible the reactions in the original Dr. Fox experiment. Rather than declaring forthwith that "it makes no sense," many academics have been conditioned to search for "meaning" in otherwise obscure material.[14] While from one perspective an admirable intention, from another it is rather problematic. It means that one hypothesis—no meaning—will be rejected a priori. Those who have uncritically accepted that training are thus vulnerable to the put-on, to the academic scam, to the big con. Where circumstances warrant, one should try expressing the thought, "It is nonsense." That harsh judgment could, of course, be balanced with the usual cautionary phrases; one could indicate the preliminary or tentative character of the conclusion. This procedure might serve as an academic equivalent to zero-based budgeting.

There is a clear need for regular affirmation of the evidential standard. Serious scholarship cannot be "open" on this question. A laissez-faire attitude toward free-and-easy methods yields "results" that discredit the entire scientific enterprise. Larry Laudan, who has undertaken such an affirmation, notes a difficulty he encountered: "The hardest task," he writes, was "that of finding a suitable voice for the relativist."[15] The suggestion is that the new relativisms present only an appearance of validity; they represent, like the emperor's clothes, a nothing.

There are some easy operational tests. What happens when serious illness occurs? Do the academic relativists turn to medical doctors, to certified specialists? Or do they follow some other strategy? How do they deal with money? How do they manage their savings? Do they turn to deconstructionist investment counselors? Do they put their money in postmodernist banks? And how do they feel about bridges and airplanes? Do they prefer the "constructions" of civil and aeronautical engineers? Or are they open to other possibilities?

The groupthink tendency is probably inherent in the human constitution. Some people are convinced, because of their training, that "institutional" solutions exist for all problems. If only we were to adjust the social structure somehow, the problem would be resolved. But the responsibility, initially at least, lies with the individual scholar. One must continuously ask the question: Am I doing my own thinking? Or am I drifting along with some groupthink notion? If we suspect the latter, then it is time to stop and think, a time to remember Dr. Myron Fox and his enthusiastic listeners.

Notes

Chapter One: On Social Misconstructions

1. See Stewart Richards, *Philosophy and Sociology of Science: An Introduction* (Oxford: Basil Blackwell, 1987), chap. 4.

2. See Derek L. Phillips, *Abandoning Method* (San Francisco: Jossey-Bass, 1973); Paul K. Feyerabend, *Against Method: Outline of an Anarchistic Theory of Knowledge* (London: Verso, 1978 [first published, 1975]); Steve Woolgar, *Science: The Very Idea* (Chichester: Ellis Horwood; London: Tavistock, 1988); Karin D. Knorr-Cetina, *The Manufacture of Knowledge: An Essay on the Constructivist and Contextual Nature of Science* (Oxford: Pergamon Press, 1981); and Stanley Aronowitz, *Science as Power: Discourse and Ideology in Modern Society* (Minneapolis: University of Minnesota Press, 1988).

Feyerabend's conclusion with regard to method reads: "The only principle that does not inhibit progress is: *anything goes*" (23). Before accepting any of the claims found in Knorr-Cetina's work one should read the review by Marion J. Levy, Jr., in *Knowledge: Creation, Diffusion, Utilization* 4 (1982–83): 147–154.

For useful criticisms of relativist arguments see: Larry Laudan, *Science and Relativism: Some Key Controversies in the Philosophy of Science* (Chicago: University of Chicago Press, 1990); Stephen Cole, *Making Science: Between Nature and Society* (Cambridge: Harvard University Press, 1992); Ernest Gellner, *Postmodernism, Reason and Religion* (London: Routledge, 1992); and Paul R. Gross and Norman Levitt, *Higher Superstition: The Academic Left and Its Quarrels with Science* (Baltimore: Johns Hopkins University Press, 1994), which gives a devastating critique of Aronowitz (50–55).

For an overview of recent discussion of "the objectivity question," see the collection of articles edited by Allan Megill, "Rethinking Objectivity," *Annals of Scholarship* 8, 3–4 (1991).

3. See Nicholas Abercrombie, Stephen Hill, and Bryan S. Turner, *The Dominant Ideology Thesis* (London: George Allen and Unwin, 1980).

4. Several works (from among a large literature) showing this decline in legitimacy are: James D. Wright, *The Dissent of the Governed: Alienation and Democracy in America* (New York: Academic Press, 1976), and, also by Wright, "Political Disaffection," in S. Long, ed., *The Handbook of Political Behavior* vol. 4 (New York: Plenum, 1981), 1–79, and Seymour Martin Lipset and William Schneider, *The Confidence Gap: Business, Labor, and Government in the Public Mind*, rev. ed. (Baltimore: Johns Hopkins University Press, 1987).

5. Possibly the most spectacular case of scientific malfeasance in modern times involved the psychologist Cyril Burt. For a review of that case see Steven Jay Gould, *The Mismeasure of Man* (New York: Norton, 1981), chap. 6. For two authors who, independently, later came to Burt's defense, see Robert B. Joynson, *The Burt Affair* (London: Routledge, 1989), and Ronald Fletcher, *Science, Ideology, and the Media: The Cyril Burt Scandal* (New Brunswick, N.J.: Transaction Books, 1991). For a brief, approving, review of the two books, see Arthur R. Jensen, "IQ and Science: The Mysterious Burt Affair," *Public Interest* 105 (1991): 93–106, but see also Raymond E. Fancher's review of Joynson's book in the *London Review of Books,* 9 November 1989, 19–20, and his review of Fletcher's book in *Science,* 27 September 1991, 1565–1566.
For reviews of other instances of data fakery, together with some consideration of the underlying motives, see William Broad and Nicholas Wade, *Betrayers of the Truth* (New York: Simon and Schuster, 1982), and Alexander Kohn, *False Prophets* (London: Basil Blackwell, 1986).

6. Pierre Bourdieu, for example, has discovered "logical logic" and, even more remarkable, found "structured structures predisposed to function as structuring structures" see Bourdieu, *The Logic of Practice,* trans. Richard Nice (Stanford: Stanford University Press, 1990), 267, 53. See also the comments in Richard Jenkins, "Language, Symbolic Power and Communication: Bourdieu's *Homo Academicus,*" *Sociology* 23 (1989): 639–643.

7. See Broad and Wade, *Betrayers,* and Kohn, *False Prophets,* for examples. On the partitive usage: one may, for example, commend many aspects of Broad and Wade's book but also note some problems. See the review by James D. Wright in *Society,* 28, 5 (July–August 1991): 81–84.

8. For a convenient introduction to a large literature, see S. E. Asch, "Effects of Group Pressure upon the Modification and Distortion of Judgments," in Harold Guetzkow, ed., *Groups, Leadership and Men: Research in Human Relations* (New York: Russell and Russell, 1963), 177–190. See also Stanley Milgram, *Obedience to Authority: An Experimental View* (New York: Harper and Row, 1974). Most introductory texts will provide a brief summary review of these studies: see for example, Jonathan L. Freedman, David O. Sears, and J. Merrill Carlsmith, *Social Psychology*, 4th ed. (Englewood Cliffs, N.J.: Prentice-Hall, 1982), chap. 9. For a comprehensive overview, see Serge Moscovici, "Social Influence and Conformity," chap. 20, in Gardner Lindzey and Elliot Aronson, eds., *Handbook of Social Psychology,* 3d ed., vol. 2 (New York: Random House, 1985).

9. David Halberstam, *The Making of a Quagmire* (New York: Random House, 1965), 12–14.

10. Timothy Crouse, *The Boys on the Bus* (New York: Random House, 1973), 12–13, 22. The notion of "sensing policy" has a long history. For an important early study, see Leo C. Rosten, *The Washington Correspondents* (New York: Harcourt Brace, 1937), chap. 10.

11. Irving Janis, *Groupthink: A Psychological Study of Policy Decisions and Fiascoes,* rev. ed. (Boston: Houghton Mifflin, 1982), chaps. 2, 4, and pp. 185–192. In addition to the three examples reported here, Janis reviews, either briefly or in detail, many other examples of groupthink among top-level decision makers. See also Elliot A. Cohen and John Gooch, *Military Misfortunes: The Anatomy of Failure in War* (New York: Free Press, 1990). For a study dealing with personal psychological dynamics and decision making, see Norman F. Dixon, *On the Psychology of Military Incompetence* (London: Jonathan Cape, 1976).

12. Donald H. Naftulin, John E. Ware, Jr., and Frank A. Donnelly, "The Doctor Fox Lecture: A Paradigm of Educational Seduction," *Journal of Medical Education* 48 (1973): 630–635. For a critical comment, see the letter by Robert M. Kaplan, *Journal of Medical Education* 49 (1974): 310–312. A fair-sized literature developed subsequently, most of it dealing with the relative impacts of content versus style (or appearance) factors.

13. One reader of this example offered an alternative hypothesis: the result was a function of the audiences involved. At the three universities where the reader had taught, Dr. Fox would have been "skewered ... in the first five minutes of the question period. Of course, I'm not talking about colleges of education or about a spew-and-listen model of learning, but about research universities where intelligent give-and-take was demanded." While an important alternative hypothesis, the question should not be solved by fiat.

    In a suggestive discussion, one certainly relevant to the Dr. Fox study, Stanislav Andreski reviewed some writing of Claude Lévi-Strauss and argued, plausibly, that it had no discernible substantive content. See his *Social Sciences as Sorcery* (New York: St. Martin's Press, 1972), 129–136, and, for another example, 128–129. Another example involves Talcott Parsons, once a leading figure in sociology. C. Wright Mills translated some of Parsons's prolix writing into straightforward English; the exercise demonstrated that little worthwhile substance remained. See Mills, *The Sociological Imagination* (New York: Oxford University Press, 1959), chap. 2.

14. Asch, "Effects of Group Pressure," 181. See Stephen Perrin and Christopher Spencer, "Independence or Conformity in the Asch Experiment as a Reflection of Cultural and Situational Factors," *British Journal of Social Psychology* 20 (1981): 205–209, and Marie-France Lalancette and Lionel Standing, "Asch Fails Again," *Social Behavior and Personality* 18 (1990): 7–12. The quotation is from Lalancette and Standing, 10–11.

15. The same tendencies appear also among business elites. In one notorious case, a forger and confidence man produced "the Hitler diaries" and sold them to one media chain which, in turn, sold the rights to several other major enterprises. No serious doubts appear to have been expressed by any of those decision makers prior to the exposure. See Robert Harris, *Selling Hitler* (New York: Penguin Books, 1986), and Charles Hamilton, *The Hitler Diaries* (Lexington: University Press of Kentucky, 1991).

16. From William L. O'Neill, *The Last Romantic: A Life of Max Eastman* (New York: Oxford University Press, 1978), chap. 6. The quotations are from 108–109.

17. Alexis de Tocqueville, *Democracy in America* (New York: Knopf, 1963), vol. 2, 8–9. Throughout this work I have "taken on trust a host of facts and opinions." In Chapter 2, for example, I have not checked the sources of Braunbehrens, Landon, Stafford, Bar, or Kraemer.

18. Philip D. Curtin, *The Atlantic Slave Trade: A Census* (Madison: University of Wisconsin Press, 1969), chap. 1, "The Slave Trade and the Numbers Game: A Review of the Literature." Curtin's work stimulated further research on the question and led to a major revision of the previous "understandings." For reviews of that later work, see James A. Rawley, *The Transatlantic Slave Trade* (New York: Norton, 1981), 17–19, and David Levering Lewis, *W. E. B. Du Bois: Biography of a Race 1868–1919* (New York: Holt, 1993), 583–584 n13.

19. Jeffrey Burton Russell, *Inventing the Flat Earth: Columbus and Modern Historians* (New York: Praeger, 1991), 26–27.

20. Morison, quoted in Russell, *Inventing,* 53–54. Russell gives several pages to a review of Irving's sources and to his use of them. Of one key source, Irving wrote: "Wherever I found a document published by him I was sure of its correctness, and did not trouble myself to examine the original" (55).

21. Ibid, 36–46. The "captured the imagination" quotation, on p. 46 in Russell, is from David C. Lindberg and Ronald L. Numbers, "Beyond War and Peace: A Reappraisal of the Encounter between Christianity and Science," *Church History,* 55 (1986): 338–354, specifically 338–340.

22. Russell, *Inventing,* 70–71, 75.

23. These examples, along with several others, are reviewed in Richard F. Hamilton and James D. Wright, *The State of the Masses* (New York: Aldine, 1986); see especially chaps. 1 and 2 and, for an earlier discussion of groupthink, 417–420. On the "white backlash" theme, see Richard F. Hamilton, *Restraining Myths* (New York: Sage-Halsted-Wiley, 1975), chap. 4, "Black Demands and White Reactions." For a comprehensive review of attitudes over the last forty years, see Howard Schuman, Charlotte Steeh, and Lawrence Bobo, *Racial Attitudes in America: Trends and Interpretations* (Cambridge: Harvard University Press, 1985). Although white attitudes have, on the whole, continued to improve, that evidence, like "the bulk of the evidence" on sphericity, is neglected in most popular accounts.

George B. Morris, Jr., in 1973 General Motors' vice president in charge of industrial relations, recognized the dynamics involved in both the automation and the workplace rebellion scares. Pointing to a citation chain problem, he declared that the "academics started talking about it and pretty soon they were quoting each other," (Hamilton and Wright, State of the Masses, 29).

Chapter Two: Mozart's Poverty, Wellington's Epigram

1. Volkmar Braunbehrens, *Mozart in Vienna, 1781–1791,* trans. Timothy Bell (New York: Grove Weidenfeld, 1990), 1. For convenience, I have quoted from the English edition. All passages have been checked against the German original, *Mozart in Wien* (Munich: Piper, 1986).

For one example from among the many works of the kind described by Braunbehrens, see the popular biography by Marcia Davenport, *Mozart* (New York: Scribner's, 1960 [original, 1932]).

2. Braunbehrens, *Mozart*, 124–132, 119, 138–141. The description of Mozart's dwelling is from Else Radant, "An Illustrated Study of Mozart's Apartment and Wardrobe," which appears as appendix A, 201-208, in H. C. Robbins Landon, *1791: Mozart's Last Year* (New York: Schirmer, 1988).

3. See Landon, *1791*, and William Stafford, *The Mozart Myths: A Critical Reassessment* (Stanford: Stanford University Press, 1991). The quotations are from Stafford (257) and Andrew Steptoe, "Mozart and Poverty: A Re-examination of the Evidence," *Musical Times* 125 (1984): 196.

4. Braunbehrens, *Mozart*, 362–363, 400. On the opera commissions, see 50–51 of Carl Bär, " 'Er war kein guter Wirth': Eine Studie über Mozarts Verhältnis zum Geld," *Acta Mozartiana* (1978): 30–53.

5. Braunbehrens, *Mozart*, 355–359; 388–395; Landon, *1791*, chap. 9.

6. Carl Bär, *Mozart: Krankheit-Tod-Begräbnis*, 2d, enlarged ed. (Salzburg: Schriftenreihe der Internationalen Stiftung Mozarteum, 1972), 22, 31. Bär provides the most detailed account of Mozart's funeral and of the prevailing burial practices of the time (126–157).

7. Landon, *1791*, 153; Braunbehrens, *Mozart*, 404–405, 419, 421; Stafford, *Myths*, 50–51. Sophie Haibel's account of Mozart's last days must be viewed with some caution. The account was written thirty-three years after Mozart's death and, moreover, was edited by Constanze; there seems little reason, however, to doubt her statement about the crowds of mourners. For this problem, see Stafford, *Myths*, 9, and Wolfgang Hildesheimer, *Mozart*, trans. Marion Faber (New York: Farrar, Straus and Giroux, 1982), 360.

8. Braunbehrens, *Mozart*, 406.

9. Ibid., 367. Braunbehrens, Landon, and Stafford summarized and added to prior research on these questions. In 1980, prior to publication of those works, Donal Henahan, music critic of the *New York Times*, reviewed the state of Mozart studies and complained of the inaccessibility of many new works. Among others he referred to "Uwe Kraemer's fascinating study of Mozart's financial dealings in his final years, which shows convincingly that the composer was anything but the pauper of Romantic myth. Mozart, it seems, had fairly large sums at his disposal and simply could not hold onto money" (*New York Times*, 20 July 1980). The reference is to Kraemer's article, "Wer hat Mozart verhungern lassen?" *Musica*, (1976): 203–211. Braunbehrens thinks Kraemer exaggerated (making him "a Croesus") and recommends instead Bär's account, "Mozarts Verhältnis." Stafford declares Kraemer's estimates to be "absurdly inflated" (*Mozart Myths*, 105).

More than a decade after Henahan's review, the music critic of a midwestern metropolitan daily newspaper wrote that "we can't help wondering why the world treated Mozart so badly during this lifetime. Must genius be recognized, and rewarded, only in retrospect?" (*Columbus Dispatch*, 27 January 1991). This appeared on the same page with another article on Mozart, reprinted from the *New York Times,* which bore the headline: "Viennese seeking to stop lingering myths."

In early December, just before the bicentennial of the composer's death, the *New York Times* published an article by Christoph Wolff, author of a book on the Mozart Requiem. The article appeared under the following headlines: "A Requiem for Mozart: Some Myths Dispelled; Why did musical Vienna neglect Mozart at his death? The mystery is finally explained: It didn't." Two days later a *Times* critic reviewed Stafford's just published book under the headline "Debunking Some Myths about Mozart" (*New York Times*, 1 and 3 December 1991). Several days later, the *Columbus Dispatch* music critic, relying on a doubtful source, reported that "the Austrian genius died in poverty . . . as every Mozart lover—and anyone who ever saw the movie *Amadeus*—well knows" (6 December 1991). On the Mozart-Salieri misconstructions, see Volkmar Braunbehrens, *Maligned Master: The Real Story of Antonio Salieri*, trans. Eveline L. Kanes (New York: Fromm, 1992), chaps. 5–7.

10. On the Jahn influence, see Braunbehrens, *Mozart*, 1. Stafford shows the distortions to be more pervasive; the mythmaking was not uniquely dependent on Jahn's contribution. For the romantic influence, see Stafford, *Mozart Myths*, chap. 6, where he writes that in the decades following Mozart's death, "the mainstream of criticism assimilated Mozart to Romanticism, judging his music to be expressive and passionate," although Jahn, to his credit, stood apart from that tradition, recognizing Mozart as a classical composer.

11. See Stafford, *Mozart Myths*, chap. 1 ("Melodrama and Evidence"), especially 88 and 11 (which contain the quotations), but see also 95–97, 118–119.

12. Steptoe, "Mozart and Poverty," 198, and Braunbehrens, *Mozart in Vienna*, 310–316. For a brief account of the Turkish War and its domestic implications, see Saul K. Padover, *The Revolutionary Emperor: Joseph II of Austria* (Hamden, Conn.: Archon, 1967 [original, 1934]), chap. 15, especially 267–276. The war, of course, affected all musicians; see Braunbehrens, *Maligned Master*, 162. The winter of 1788–89, was exceptionally bitter, according to some commentators the worst of the century; that too might have had an impact on Mozart's fortunes.

13. Further discussion and evidence on these points appear in Richard Hamilton, *The Bourgeois Epoch* (Chapel Hill: University of North Carolina Press, 1991), 200–205.

14. All of the particulars recounted here are from Elizabeth Longford, *Wellington: The Years of the Sword* (New York: Harper and Row, 1969), 15–17. The duke's paternal grandfather, Richard Colley, changed his name to Wesley in 1728, adopting the name of his benefactor. Some years after Arthur's Eton experience the name was changed to the Wellesley, that of one prominent line of ancestors.

    A minor point still deserves a mention: there is no definitive proof that Wellington either said or thought the epigram. Longford's review amounts to an estimate of likelihood, hence the careful formulation, "probably he never said."

15. Ibid., 15.

16. Borrowing another frequent usage, it might be said that the epigram had "taken on a life of its own." But that analogical usage also has no clear and evident meaning. As such, it avoids direct inquiry—what has happened? What process is operating? The cliché suggests an explanation when in fact it is no more than a glissade. Inquiry has been avoided, or, to use a less flattering expression, the problem has been covered up. George Orwell, an Eton graduate, offered some useful advice: "Never use a metaphor, simile or other figure of speech which you are used to seeing in print." (from "Politics and the English Language," in *The Collected Essays, Journalism and Letters of George Orwell* [New York: Harcourt, Brace and World, 1968], vol. 4, 139).

17. From Orwell's essay "England Your England," in *A Collection of Essays* (Garden City, N.Y.: Doubleday Anchor Books, 1954), 274. Orwell, it should be noted, accepted the famous cliché: "Probably the battle of Waterloo *was* won on the playing-fields of Eton, but the opening battles of all subsequent wars have been lost there" (272). For confirmation of Orwell's main point, see Byron Farwell, *Queen Victoria's Little Wars* (New York: Harper and Row, 1972), and Denis Judd, *Someone Has Blundered: Calamities of the British Army in the Victorian Age* (London: Arthur Barker, 1973).

18. See A. L. Kennedy, *Salisbury 1830–1903: Portrait of a Statesman* (London: John Murray, 1953), 6–9. A recent study argues that these schools have had a "gentrifying influence," training their charges in values that are more or less useless for the modern age. See Martin J. Wiener, *English Culture and the Decline of the Industrial Spirit, 1850–1980* (Cambridge: Cambridge University Press, 1981), 13, 16–22, 35–37, 132–141.

19. Bentley Brinkerhoff Gilbert, *David Lloyd George: A Political Life* (Columbus: Ohio State University Press, 1987), 27–30; and W. R. P. George, *The Making of Lloyd George* (London: Faber and Faber, 1976), chaps. 4, 5.

Chapter Three: *Max Weber and the Protestant Ethic*

1. *Die protestantische Ethik und der "Geist" des Kapitalismus* was published in two parts in the *Archiv für Sozialwissenschaft und Sozialpolitik* 20 (1905): 1–54 and 21 (1905): 1–110. A revised version appeared (with the quotation marks removed) in Weber's *Gesammelte Aufsätze zur Religionssoziologie* (Tübingen: J. C. B. Mohr [Paul Siebeck], 1920), vol. 1, 17–206. The English-language edition, *The Protestant Ethic and the Spirit of Capitalism*, trans. Talcott Parsons, was first published in 1930 (London: George Allen and Unwin; New York: Scribner's); the quoted sentences appear there on 35–36.

    Weber wrote an introduction for the three volumes of essays on the sociology of religion (the *Gesammelte Aufsätze*). To give "some of the general background of ideas and problems," Parsons included it as the first chapter of his translation of *The Protestant Ethic*. This has given rise to occasional misunderstandings, the introduction being taken as a part of the original monograph.

    The title page of the *Archiv*, vol. 20, bears the date 1905. In the revised version Weber gave the original publication dates for the two parts as 1904 and 1905. Talcott Parsons, Marianne Weber, and many others have also taken 1904 as the publication date for vol. 20. Part 1 appeared also in an undated separate printing (*Separat-Abdruck*) which was circulated late in 1904.

2. Martin Offenbacher, *Konfession und soziale Schichtung: Eine Studie über die wirtschaftliche Lage der Katholiken und Protestanten in Baden* (Tübingen and Leipzig: J. C. B. Mohr [Paul Siebeck], 1900). The two references given by Weber in his footnote 3, dealing with "the Catholic press and literature," were taken directly from Offenbacher. The latter made several trivial citation errors (23–24) which were taken over by Weber. Another minor error was added in Parsons's translation.

    Offenbacher's work was published twice, once in 1900 and again in 1901 (Tübingen: H. Laupp). The first edition, the one I have used, was part of a series entitled *Volkswirtschaftliche Abhandlungen der Badischen Hochschulen,* edited by Carl Johannes Fuchs, Gerhard von Schulze-Gävernitz, and Max Weber. The second, the one Weber cited, is identified as an inaugural dissertation and, as is customary, contained a brief biographical statement. A note indicates that it is taken from the *Abhandlungen* series. Apart from the title page and the biography, the two versions appear to be identical.

3. A few passing references to Jews and their economic activity appear elsewhere in the monograph. Weber indicated he had omitted any discussion of "the problem of the Jews" in this monograph but promised a subsequent consideration (187). For a detailed review and commentary, see Gary A. Abraham, *Max Weber and the Jewish Question: A Study of the Social Outlook of His Sociology* (Urbana: University of Illinois Press, 1992).

4. For an overview and appropriate references, see Lewis W. Spitz, *The Protestant Reformation, 1517–1559* (New York: Harper and Row, 1985), 164–165, 180–191; the passages quoted appear on 182, 184.

5. The initial error appears in Offenbacher, *Konfession*, 16. Kurt Samuelsson's work, *Ekonomi och religion*, first appeared in Sweden in 1957, and the English translation was first published by Basic Books in 1961. A paperback edition, the version cited here, appeared a few years later: see Samuelsson, *Religion and Economic Action: A Critique of Max Weber*, trans. E. Geoffrey French (New York: Harper Torchbooks, 1964); the error and his correction are noted on 140. The English-language versions were long out of print, a situation remedied with a reprint (Toronto: University of Toronto Press, 1993).

Two transcription errors, it should be noted, appear in Samuelsson's critique, yielding a row of percentages adding to 103 percent (139). For George Becker's reanalysis, see his "Educational Choice of Catholics and Protestants in Nineteenth-Century Germany: A Challenge to Weber's and Merton's Interpretation," forthcoming.

Offenbacher clearly stated that his figures covered the ten school years from 1885 to 1895 (16–17). Weber made a minor transcription error, reporting the years as 1885 to 1891, this appearing in both the 1905 and 1920 versions. The dates are not given in the Parsons translation. Offenbacher's education statistics, incidentally, are for males only. A question might arise as to the appropriate comparison. One could compare the religion of school attenders (e.g., those in the gymnasium) with the religious distribution of the entire population of a state or region. Or one could compare that same group with the entire secondary school population. Both comparisons are relevant to the claim of a distinct religious orientation. If group A is over- or underrepresented in secondary schools, that is a useful datum. The choice of a specific type of secondary school is another useful datum, one best interpreted, however, against figures for the entire secondary school population, that is, for those who have continued beyond the primary school.

6. Offenbacher, *Konfession*, 17–19.

7. Given Weber's basic argument, one should expect a sizable Protestant underrepresentation in the Latin schools and a considerable overrepresentation in the commercial schools. Protestants, however, were overrepresented in both, by 4.1 and 3.7 points, respectively.

It should be noted that in Württemberg Offenbacher was comparing all students for the years 1872–1879 and 1883–1898 with the population of 1880 (*Konfession*, 18).

8. Ibid., 16. Offenbacher's procedure is not clearly indicated in his text. The first footnote appearing after the crucial table, the table taken over by Weber, is to "Gemss, Statistik der Gymnasialabiturienten im Deutschen Reich," but that is the source for his subsequent observations, not for the Baden figures. The full reference is Gustav Gemss, *Statistik der Gymnasialabiturienten im Deutschen Reich während der letzten drei Schuljahre* (Ber-

lin: Wissenschaftliche Beilage zum Jahresbericht des Königlichen Luisen-Gymnasiums zu Berlin, 1895). In other contexts, Offenbacher does reference statistical yearbooks (e.g., Baden, Bavaria). No source is indicated for his statistics on Prussia. His Hungarian figures are from an independent analysis.

Samuelsson provides no further information on the questions of sources or on the aggregation. He makes no mention of Gemss. He went directly to the Baden statistical yearbook for the 1895–96 result. He also reviewed the figures for 1884, just before the aggregation, to address (and reject) the possibility of a trend. The Catholic percentage in the realgymnasium in that year was 36, again higher than Offenbacher's aggregate (Samuelsson, *Religion*, 140). For further discussion of the trend question, see Becker, "Educational Choice."

The entire Offenbacher-Weber analysis involves compositional as opposed to causal treatment of the data. As indicated here in Table 3.1, the rows add to (or should add to) 100. Had Offenbacher followed the alternative procedure, having the columns add to 100, one would have seen the importance of the gymnasien and the realschulen, the respective percentages of total secondary school enrollment being 37.3 and 26.4. Only about one in eight students were enrolled in the realgymnasien. The respective figures for Protestant and Catholic attendance in the latter institutions were 13.5 and 11.1 (recalculated from Samuelsson's figures for 1895–96 [139]). For discussion of the direction of percentages question, see Hans Zeisel, *Say It with Figures*, 4th rev. ed. (New York: Harper, 1957), chap. 2.

9. Samuelsson, *Religion*, 139.
10. Offenbacher, *Konfession*, 54–55.
11. The figures are from ibid., 43–44. The clearest example of Protestant overrepresentation in Offenbacher's high-status occupational category is in the military, i.e., officers. Overall, the figure is 72.7 (versus 37.0 in the Baden population). This "overwhelmingly Protestant" tendency is most striking in the heavily Catholic Constance region, where the respective figures are 68.3 and 9.6 (ibid., 89).
12. See ibid., 20–21, and Samuelsson, *Religion*, 142–144. Offenbacher establishes, in his first pages, that the Catholic population in Baden is located in small towns and rural areas. Their capital, accordingly, would tend to be in land. Any conclusions about Protestant and Catholic propensities based on the tax figures would require an appropriate control.
13. Offenbacher, *Konfession*, 17 and 18n. In Baden, in the three school years, 1891–1893, 42 percent of the Catholic gymnasium graduates ($N = 533$) wished to study theology, as against only 14 percent of the equivalent Protestants ($N = 375$). The percentages for Prussia, respectively, are 42 and 19 (my calculations from Offenbacher's figures). The results for Baden and Prussia are based on data in Gemss. This finding would justify an alternative focus, that is, on "the Catholic ethic"—why were Catholics more likely to choose clerical careers? Becker, "Educational Choice," reviews this entire question and provides supporting evidence.

Offenbacher and Weber treat the religion-education figures as constants. The Gemss data for Prussia (14), covering the school years from 1887/88 to 1893/94, show many changes in process. There was a slight decline in the proportion of Protestant graduates (69 to 64 percent) and a slight increase in the proportion of Catholics (22 to 28 percent). There was a steady decline in the numbers intending to study Protestant theology and a steady increase in the numbers intending to study Catholic theology. Offenbacher, neglecting those changes, reports only the last years in the series. Important shifts occurred in other fields as well.

For discussion of the religion-education relationship in the Prussian context, together with evidence and sources, see Konrad H. Jarausch, *Students, Society, and Politics in Imperial Germany: The Rise of Academic Illiberalism* (Princeton: Princeton University Press, 1982), 93–104.

14. One row of Samuelsson's percentages, as already seen, added to 103 percent. One realgymnasium is said to be located in Billingen; that should read Villingen.

15. See Becker, "Educational Choice," for further details.

16. See, for example, Stephen Cole, *The Sociological Method*, 2d ed. (Chicago: Rand McNally, 1976). These requirements are merely a formal statement of causal rules that have been understood for millennia.

For a study that deals with religion and achievement in Germany and follows this basic methodology, see Ursula Hoffmann-Lange, "Katholiken und Protestanten in der deutschen Führungsschicht: Ausmaß, Ursachen und Bedeutung ungleicher Vertretung von Katholiken und Protestant in den Eliten der Bundesrepublik," in Hans-Georg Wehling, ed., *Konfession—eine Nebensache?* (Stuttgart: Kohlhammer, 1984), 75–93. Hoffmann-Lange establishes the Protestant advantage (the first study cited dates from 1971) and then explores the causal possibilities. Social psychological investigations, she reports, find no difference in the aspirations of Protestants and Catholics, hence the outcome must be due to "other factors" which are also explored. She takes that "no difference" result as a confirmation of Weber's argument of assimilation and convergence (to be discussed later)—but that assumes, without evidence, significant differences at some previous point.

17. Jacob Viner's critique appears in his *Religious Thought and Economic Society* (Durham, N.C.: Duke University Press, 1978), chap. 4, "Protestantism and the Rise of Capitalism." The parts discussed appear on 181–182, and 187–189. Viner tracked down the relevant passages in the work of William Petty and found Weber's usage to be, at best, misleading. Weber claims to have found support there for his thesis. Petty, however, argued that heterodoxy favors trade and "that trade is not fixed to any species of religion" (Viner, *Religious Thought*, 167–168, 174–175). Some of this ground was covered in an earlier discussion by Reinhard Bendix, "The Protestant Ethic—Revisited," in Reinhard Bendix and Guenther Roth, *Scholarship and Partisanship: Essays on Max Weber* (Berkeley: University of California Press, 1971), chap. 16.

Emile-Louis-Victor Laveleye, a Belgian economist and publicist (1822–1892), was the author of *Le Protestantisme et le Catholicisme dans leur rapports avec la liberté et la prospérité des peuples* (1875). English and German translations of Laveleye's work appeared in the same year (Viner, *Religious Thought*, 181, and Bendix, "Protestant Ethic," 300). On Laveleye, see *La grande encyclopédie* (Paris: Lamirault, 1886), vol. 21, 1056–1057.

The comments on Macaulay are from David Thompson, *England in the Nineteenth Century* (London: Penguin, 1978), 104. For passages that support both Weber and Thompson, see Thomas Babington Macaulay, *The History of England from the Accession of James the Second* (New York: Riverside Press, 1866), vol. 1, 52–53.

18. The C. A. Hanna volumes were published in 1902. The passage cited is from vol. 1, 52. Viner reported he could find "no particularly relevant material" in Hanna's work; see his *Religious Thought*, 175 n60.

19. See James G. Leyburn, *The Scotch-Irish: A Social History* (Chapel Hill: University of North Carolina Press, 1962), 175, 190–192.

20. Gordon Marshall, *In Search of the Spirit of Capitalism: An Essay on Max Weber's Protestant Ethic Thesis* (London: Hutchinson, 1982), 152. Marshall touches on Samuelsson's work at several points but does not review his arguments in detail. Marshall provided another important comprehensive review of the Weber argument in an earlier work, *Presbyteries and Profits: Calvinism and the Development of Capitalism in Scotland, 1560–1707* (Oxford: Clarendon Press, 1980), chaps. 1, 2. Marshall points out that Weber's later writings do discuss modern capitalism and its institutions (as opposed to the earlier and more restricted focus on the "capitalist ethos"). Marshall refers to these as "Weber's two theses," adding that the two concerns, unfortunately, have been conflated in many discussions.

Another useful critique and review of evidence is that of Luciano Pellicani, "Weber and the Myth of Calvinism," *Telos* 75 (1988): 57–85. For a comprehensive overview, a rich treasure of information and documentation, see the collection of essays in Hartmut Lehmann and Guenther Roth, eds., *Weber's "Protestant Ethic": Origins, Evidence. Contexts* (Washington, D.C.: German Historical Institute–Cambridge University Press, 1993).

21. Marshall argues, with considerable justification, that Weber's real concern in *The Protestant Ethic* is with the sources of economic growth or development as opposed to the origins of "modern western capitalism," which suggests structures, institutions, and so forth. Weber deals with a distinctive work ethic rather than with "rational structures of law and administration . . . industrial processes and technology" (*Search*, 64). In part at least, Marshall suggests, the misunderstandings of Weber may have been generated by Parsons's insertion of Weber's 1920 essay at the beginning of the monograph, with the heading "Author's Introduction." That essay addresses the wider and different range of issues.

The Samuelsson quotation is from his *Religion*, 92. The book's central flaw, the expanded definition of capitalism, was noted in an early review by Edmund S. Morgan, *William and Mary Quarterly* 20, 1 (1963): 135–140. See also David Hackett Fischer, *Historians' Fallacies: Toward a Logic of Historical Thought* (New York: Harper and Row, 1970), 275–276.

22. Samuelsson, *Religion*, 58. The maxims quoted by Weber come from two brief pieces, "Necessary Hints to those that would be rich" and "Advice to a Young Tradesman." Weber was citing from the Jared Sparks edition of *The Works of Benjamin Franklin* (Boston: Hilliard, Gray, 1840). The articles are in vol. 2, 80–81, 87–89. To speak with such authority about "all [Franklin's] works without exception," Weber would have had to read ten volumes. A somewhat different orientation is suggested by one of Poor Richard's sayings: "Wealth is not his that has it, but his that enjoys it," quoted in Esmond Wright, *Franklin of Philadelphia* (Cambridge: Belknap Press of Harvard University Press, 1986), 115, and see also 219, 216.

For a brief review of earlier comments on Weber's portrayal of Franklin, see Roth, Introduction to Lehmann and Roth, *Weber*, 16–20. Werner Sombart argued that Franklin's advice is a "word-for-word repetition" of the counsel given by Leon Battiste Alberti, a Florentine businessman, written around 1450. Weber wrote a four-page note rejecting the claim (194–198). Alberti's advice, he argued, was not based on religion, hence lacked the important noneconomic "psychological sanctions (197). See Malcolm H. MacKinnon, "The Longevity of the Thesis: A Critique of the Critics." in Lehmann and Roth, *Weber*, 227. For a recent comprehensive critique, see Tony Dickson and Hugh V. McLachlan, "In Search of 'The Spirit of Capitalism': Weber's Misinterpretation of Franklin," *Sociology* 23 (1989): 81–89.

23. From Franklin, *The Autobiography of Benjamin Franklin*, Max Farrand, ed. (Berkeley: University of California Press, 1949), 147, 53, 84, 98–99.

24. Ibid., 98. Standing before kings, given Weber's views, would not seem a highly approved aspiration for the strict Calvinist. Franklin writes with evident pride that "I have stood before five, and even had the honour of sitting down with one, the king of Denmark, to dinner" (98). The omitted footnote appears in Weber, *Gesammelte Aufsätze*, 36, n1.

25. Franklin, *Autobiography*, 9–10, 70, 99. Weber missed a telling passage in *The Autobiography*, one he could have used to his advantage. Franklin placed a marble stone on his parents' grave which commended them for fifty-five years of loving wedlock, for their constant labor and industry, and for their maintenance of a large, comfortable, and reputable family. "From this instance, Reader," he added, "Be encouraged to diligence in thy calling, And distrust not Providence" (14).

26. Samuelsson, *Religion*, 65 n52. Weber did not provide an original source for the Fugger quotation. He reports, rather obliquely, (192 n4), that Sombart had used the quotation in his *Der moderne Kapitalismus*. A brief Fugger quotation does appear on the page indicated, but there is nothing on the context and the source given is imprecise. Samuelsson reports that the "story is derived from" the work of Richard Ehrenberg, *Das Zeitalter der Fugger: Geldkapital und Creditverkehr im 16. Jahrhundert*. He cited the third unaltered edition, my source also (Jena: Gustav Fischer, 1922, vol. 1, 118). The first edition was published in 1896. Ehrenberg reports that it was a nephew, Georg Thurzo, not a "business associate," who advised giving up the threatened Hungarian business activities. Ehrenberg reports, as opposed to retirement, that Fugger was near death (*in seinen letzten Lebenstagen*).

27. Marshall, *Search*, 45, 67–68. Marshall reviews Weber's "spirit of capitalism" argument at length in chap. 3 and the historical evidence on entrepreneurial and worker attitudes in chap. 5.

28. Ibid., 19–20.

29. Viner, *Religious Thought*, 182, 185.

30. Marshall, *Search*, 72. If Weber had intended the limited reading, the expression "Protestant ethic" in the title would have been inappropriate. Some restriction, ascetic Protestantism, for example, would be necessary. Even more telling, the first chapter, with its evidence from Baden and other central European regions, would make little sense because the "Protestantism" there was overwhelmingly Lutheran. For further discussion of the weight of Lutheran versus Calvinist doctrine in moving adherents, see Weber, *Protestant Ethic*, 125–128.

31. Even the sentence from Dowden is problematic. Weber gives it in English and, through his insertion of the parenthetical—"with God"—provides a context. The pre-

ceding passage in Dowden, however, reads: "Let any man record faithfully his most private experiences in any of the great affairs of life, and his words awaken in other souls innumerable echoes." The "deepest community" is with "other souls," a point confirmed by the reference, in the following sentence, to "our common humanity." This is based on the third edition, which has the same pagination as the edition Weber used; see Edward Dowden, *Puritan and Anglican: Studies in Literature* (London: Kegan Paul, Trench, and Trübner, 1910), 234.

32. On Franklin's relationship with Whitefield, see the *Autobiography*, 128–133; Wright, *Franklin*, 48–49; and David T. Morgan, "A Most Unlikely Friendship—Benjamin Franklin and George Whitefield," *Historian* 47 (1985): 208–218.

33. Franklin's utilitarian view of religious ethics appears at many places in his writings, for example, in the *Autobiography*, 71, 99. A Franklin biographer writes that the "theme of doing good to man is a constant in *Poor Richard* and throughout Franklin's correspondence" (Wright, *Franklin*, 5, 364 n7). Franklin could have enhanced his fortune by securing a patent on his inventions (e.g., the famous stove), but chose not to, a decision that seems relevant to the "spirit of capitalism" argument. On the *Almanack*, see Wright, *Franklin*, 53–55.

Whitefield's theology has been described as follows: "Although adhering to a Calvinist doctrine of predestination, he did not hesitate to offer Christ to everyone. The experience of new birth was all-important. By that experience a man might be assured of salvation and enabled to progress in holiness" (*The Westminster Dictionary of Church History* [Philadelphia: Westminster Press, 1983], 864). For more detail, see Harry S. Stout, *The Divine Dramatist: George Whitefield and the Rise of Modern Evangelicalism* (Grand Rapids, Mich.: Eerdmans, 1991), 95, 117, 126–127, 136, and Frank Lambert, " 'Pedlar in Divinity': George Whitefield and the Great Awakening, 1737–1745," *Journal of American History* 77 (1990): 812–837.

34. Lujo Brentano, one of the earliest critics of the Weber thesis, addressed this question (in *Die Anfänge des modernen Kapitalismus* [Munich: Verlag der Akademie der Wissenschaften, 1916]). Weber responded to these criticisms in his notes to the revised edition. One of the "second generation" critics, H. M. Robertson, devoted an entire chapter to these issues; see his *Aspects of the Rise of Economic Individualism: A Criticism of Max Weber and His School* (Cambridge: Cambridge University Press, 1933), chap. 1.

35. Tatsuro Hanyu, "Max Weber's Quellenbehandlung in der 'Protestantischen Ethik' Der Begriff 'Calling,' " *Zeitschrift für Soziologie* 22 (1993): 65–75. It is impossible in a brief space to cover all of the central points contained in this important article. Two other Bible passages are cited by Weber: I Corinthians 7:20, "Let each man abide in that calling wherein he was called," and the one discussed earlier, Proverbs 22:29, "Seest thou a man diligent in his business? he shall stand before kings." Weber disclaimed the former passage, arguing that there the term *calling* had a different meaning, not relevant to his task (209). The latter passage was problematic since Luther had used the secular term *Geschäft*.

At one point Weber referred to a nonexistent Bible, "Geneva von 1557," an error that Hanyu shows stemmed from his dependence on a secondary source, *A New English Dictionary on Historical Principles* (1893). The word *calling*, as noted previously in the text, has several meanings. Hanyu argues, plausibly, that Weber erred in his interpretation of the *New English Dictionary* and assigned the definition most useful for his argument, that is: "Ordinary occupation, means by which livelihood is earned, business, trade." This overlooks, among others, the following alternatives: "Position, estate, or station in life; rank," and "The summons, invitation, or impulse to God to salvation or to his service; the inward feeling or conviction of a divine call; the strong impulse to any course of action as to the right thing to do."

36. Between 1517 and 1520, Luther published some thirty items and these sold over 300,000 copies. In the course of his lifetime, he wrote about 450 treatises. Spitz writes: "There are 3,000 sermons and 2,580 letters extant, and the scholarly Weimar edition of his works runs to well over 100 folio volumes or 60,000 pages" (*Protestant Reformation*, 89). Luther's translation of the New Testament (with its Lucas Cranach woodcuts) was published in September 1522 and was "a runaway best-seller." About 5,000 copies sold within two months. There were fifty printings in four years and over 200,000 copies sold in the next twelve years. The eye-of-the-needle passage is from the Bible, American Standard Version (New York: Thomas Nelson, 1901), Matthew 19:16–26.

37. This discussion is embellished, as indicated earlier, with an extensive array of notes. In this connection Weber allowed himself a whimsical remark—"I have condemned the reader as well as myself to the penitence of a malignant growth of footnotes" (220 n5). The notes, however, do not address the problems of the context or the impact of the Westminster Confession. Milton is dismissed as an isolated figure who "must remain outside our investigation" (220 n10). A dramatic instance of rejection of the doctrine, by a rather shy and deferential weaver (also an isolated figure), is recounted in Joseph Frazier Wall, *Andrew Carnegie* (Pittsburgh: University of Pittsburgh Press, 1989), 34.

38. *New Encyclopaedia Britannica*, 15th ed., 1987, s.v. "Westminster Confession." Another account reports that the *Book of Common Prayer* "has been in continuous use since the sixteenth century, except for the years of the English Commonwealth (1645–1660), when it was proscribed in public and private use. It is the only vernacular liturgy of the Reformation period still in use" (*Encyclopedia of Religion* [New York: Macmillan, 1987], vol. 1, 287); see also *Westminster Dictionary*, 861–862. For further comment on Weber's use of the Confession, see MacKinnon, "The Longevity of the Thesis," especially 218–220. For a brief discussion on its fate in the American colonies, see Daniel Walker Howe, "The Decline of Calvinism: An Approach to Its Study," *Comparative Studies in Society and History* 14 (1972): 307–327, especially 313–314.

39. All of these documents named here are contained in *The Book of Concord: The Confessions of the Evangelical Lutheran Church,* trans. and ed. Theodore G. Tappert (Philadelphia: Muhlenberg Press, 1959); for discussion of the calling, see especially 65, 219, 275. For an instructive example of the corporatist notion, see Charles E. Daniel, Jr., "Hard Work, Good Work, and School Work: An Analysis of Wenzeslaus Linck's Conception of Civic Responsibility," in Lawrence P. Buck and Jonathan W. Zophy, eds., *The Social History of the Reformation* (Columbus: Ohio State University Press, 1972), 41–51.

40. Ernst Troeltsch's *Die Soziallehren* was first published in Tübingen, 1912. It has been translated, by Olive Wyon, as *The Social Teachings of the Christian Churches* (New York: Harper Torchbooks, 1960 [original, London: Allen and Unwin, 1931]). Luther and the calling are discussed briefly in vol. 2, 473–474, 561–562. The passages quoted appear on 473 and 474.

Weber refers to one article on "Beruf" as "valueless" and adds some further denigrating comment (214 n16). This article also focuses on the corporatist implications of the term. See L. Lemme, "Beruf," *Realenzyklopädie für protestantische Theologie und Kirche,* 3d ed. (Leipzig: J. C. Hinrichs, 1897), vol. 2, 652–657.

41. Arnold Eisen, "Called to Order: The Role of the Puritan Berufsmensch in Weberian Sociology," *Sociology* 13 (1979): 203–218, especially 208–210. Weber depended on a ten-volume collection, *Works of the Puritan Divines,* published in 1845–1848. Apart from Baxter and Bunyan, the collection explicitly aimed to present writing of "less well-known" authors. Except for one author, the works contained there postdate the Civil War and are from "relatively minor figures."

For a useful overview, see G. R. Cragg, *From Puritanism to the Age of Reason: A Study of Changes in Religious Thought within the Church of England, 1660 to 1700* (Cambridge: Cambridge University Press, 1950), especially chap. 2, "The Eclipse of Calvinism." "Seldom has a reversal of fortune been so complete," Cragg writes; "Within fifty years Calvinism in England fell from a position of immense authority to obscurity and insignificance" (30). Robertson reviewed these problems earlier in his 1933 publication, *Aspects of the Rise of Economic Individualism.*

42. *Encyclopaedia Britannica,* 14th ed., 1973, s.v. "Baxter, Richard"; Michael R. Watts, *The Dissenters: From the Reformation to the French Revolution* (Oxford: Clarendon, 1978), 376–377; and Kaspar von Greyerz, "Biographical Evidence on Predestination, Covenant, and Special Providence," in Lehmann and Roth, *Weber,* 273–284. (the passage quoted appears on 273). Weber recognized the problem, as is evidenced by his equivocal discussion, 258–259 n1. David Zaret dissents from this view: he finds "Baxter the Calvinist" the more compelling reading (from Lehmann and Roth, *Weber,* 258). This question is discussed further in note 44 of this chapter.

For a brief overview of the stages of Puritanism and the implications for Weber's argument, see Hartmut Lehmann, "Ascetic Protestantism and Economic Rationalism: Max Weber Revisited after Two Generations," *Harvard Theological Review,* 80 (1987): 307–320, especially 314–315. See also Howe, "Decline of Calvinism": he reports that most "remaining traces of Anglican Calvinism evaporated quickly after 1660" (310). It took longer among the Presbyterians, but the tendency was unmistakable. Watts reports that in 1732, nineteen of the forty-four Presbyterian ministers in London were said to be Calvinists. By 1750, one clergyman described himself as "almost the only London minister who continued to regard himself as both a Calvinist and a Presbyterian" (Watts, *Dissenters,* 464–465). Weber, it will be remembered, argued that Whitefield, who worked in the eighteenth century, had prevented the "premature collapse" of the predestination doctrine, but the collapse had begun decades earlier—Baxter's "Middle Way" was key to the transformation.

The literature on the struggle within the Church of England is enormous. Some sense of the dynamics may be gained from the following: John F. H. New, *Anglican and Puritan: The Basis of Their Opposition, 1558–1640* (Stanford: Stanford University Press, 1964); Michael Walzer, *The Revolution of the Saints: A Study in the Origins of Radical Politics* (Cambridge: Harvard University Press, 1965); David Little, *Religion, Order, and Law: A Study in Pre-Revolutionary England* (Chicago: University of Chicago Press, 1969); and David Zaret, *The Heavenly Contract: Ideology and Organization in Pre-Revolutionary Puritanism* (Chicago: University of Chicago Press, 1985).

43. Greyerz, "Biographical Evidence," 275–276. For more detail, see his *Vorsehungsglaube und Kosmologie: Studien zu englischen Selbstzeugnissen des 17. Jahrhunderts* (Göttingen: Veröffentlichungen des Deutschen Historischen Instituts London, 1990), vol. 25.

44. The Zaret passage appears in Lehmann and Roth, *Weber*, 263. One could substitute "special providence" for "predestination" and argue the same subsequent economic effect, thus perhaps saving the larger position. But the "spirit of capitalism" is a different question, one Greyerz chose not to address in his chapter.

    See Malcolm H. MacKinnon, "Part I: Calvinism and the Infallible Assurance of Grace: The Weber Thesis Reconsidered," *British Journal of Sociology* 39 (1988): 143–177, and "Part II: Weber's Exploration of Calvinism: The Undiscovered Provenance of Capitalism," ibid., 178–210. For Zaret's response, see "Calvin, Covenant Theology, and the Weber Thesis," *British Journal of Sociology* 43 (1992): 370–391. See also the MacKinnon and Zaret contributions in Lehmann and Roth, *Weber,* chaps. 10 and 11. Zaret has explored the dynamics of Puritanism and the coming of covenant theology in his *Heavenly Contract.*

45. Greyerz, "Biographical Evidence," 283, 276.

46. *The Book of Common Prayer* (London: William Pickering, 1853), pages not numbered. The estimates are reported in Christopher Hill, *A Tinker and a Poor Man: John Bunyan and His Church, 1628–1688* (New York: Knopf, 1989), 171.

47. Winthrop S. Hudson reviewed Weber's use of this passage from Baxter. He described it as "a perfect illustration of the distortion involved in isolating the concept of 'the calling' from its context"; see his "Puritanism and the Spirit of Capitalism," *Church History* 18 (1949): 3–17. Both Weber and R. H. Tawney, he writes, "failed to realize that [their] interpretation not only isolated the doctrine of the calling from its larger context in Calvinist thought, but it completely subverted the fundamental theological structure of Calvinism." One aspect of the relationship of calling and that larger context is described by Baxter as follows: "When two callings equally conduce to the public good, and one of them hath the advantage of riches and the other is more advantageous to your souls, the latter must be preferred." The passages cited are from 11, 7, and 12; for further comment on the larger context see especially 7–8. Hudson reviewed some of the same themes in a subsequent article, "The Weber Thesis Reexamined," *Church History* 30 (1961): 88–102. He again disputed Weber's reading of the calling: "Far from being a means to accumulate financial gain, one's calling was the normal channel through which love of neighbor was to be expressed and his welfare sought" (93).

48. J. H. Van Stuijvenberg, " 'The' Weber Thesis: An Attempt at Interpretation," *Acta Historiae Neerlandicae* 8 (1975): 50–66. The quotation is from 63.

    In a note, Weber declares that "we" are "naturally not so much concerned with what concepts the theological moralists developed in their ethical theories, but rather, what was the effective morality in the life of believers—that is, how the religious background of economic ethics affected practice" (267 n42). An adequate account would provide evidence with respect to all aspects of the presumed sequence—the theology, its transmission, the conditions of its reception, and the possible responses. Weber has treated none of these issues satisfactorily.

49. John T. McNeill, *The History and Character of Calvinism* (New York: Oxford University Press, 1954), 418–420; see also W. A. Speck and L. Billington, "Calvinism in Colonial

North America, 1630–1715," chap. 9 in Menna Prestwich, ed., *International Calvinism, 1541–1715* (Oxford: Clarendon, 1985), especially 268–269.

50. The Willard quotation appears in Stephen Foster, *Their Solitary Way: The Puritan Social Ethic in the First Century of Settlement in New England* (New Haven: Yale University Press, 1971), 111. Zaret, in a brief discussion touching on this issue, provided a quotation from Calvin in which the reformer declares that "all who are of God are regenerated and made new creatures. . . . In this way they make their calling sure, and like trees, are judged by their fruits." Zaret adds, "Treating works in this manner, as the 'fruitful' consequence of faith, subsequently became a rhetorical hallmark in pastoral writings by Puritans" (from Lehmann and Roth, *Weber*, 260). No specific citations of pastoral writings are provided. It seems unlikely that any Puritan pastor would have made the unqualified recommendation announced by Weber, that is, "intense worldly activity" as "the most suitable means" to gain assurance of salvation (112).

51. Timothy Hall Breen, "The Non-Existent Controversy: Puritan and Anglican Attitudes on Work and Wealth, 1600–1640," *Church History* 35 (1966): 273–287. Breen's analysis points up an important methodological flaw in much of the literature on the Weber thesis. Many accounts report changes in the "experimental case" but say nothing about change, or the lack thereof, in appropriate "control groups."

52. Marshall, *Search*, 95.

53. For a brief overview, see Paul Seaver, "The Puritan Work Ethic Revisited," *Journal of British Studies* 19 (1979–1980): 35–53. For an extended overview, see Seaver's *Wallington's World: A Puritan Artisan in Seventeenth-Century London* (Stanford: Stanford University Press, 1985).

54. Weber, *Protestant Ethic*, 37, 38, 39, 43, 44. On the American colonies, see 55, 278 nn85 and 86, and 279 n92.

55. Lehmann writes that "in late sixteenth- and early seventeenth-century Europe, confessional boundaries [within Protestantism] were only slowly coming into existence. Produced by the disciplinary measures of secular and religious authorities, confessional allegiance was a matter of educating and indoctrinating several generations. The peace treaty of Augsburg in 1555 was only the first step in this direction. Contrary to Weber's view, clear-cut confessional boundaries had not been achieved even by 1648 and were not enforced until the second part of the seventeenth century" ("Ascetic Protestantism," 315). See also Lehmann's *Das Zeitalter des Absolutismus* (Stuttgart: Kohlhammer, 1980), especially part 2, and Ernst Walter Zeeden, *Die Entstehung der Konfessionen: Grundlagen und Formen der Konfessionsbildung im Zeitalter der Glaubenskämpfe* (Munich: Oldenbourg, 1965).

Jan Rubens, the father of the famous painter, was an advocate and alderman, a leading citizen of Antwerp. In the "spirit of the times," he had become a Calvinist, which brought persecution from the Spanish authorities. His first response was a "specious pleading of his Catholic orthodoxy." Exile, however, seemed a more prudent course and he fled to Cologne. In that Catholic city his religious beliefs again proved problematic and, threatened with expulsion, he returned to his original faith. Later, for almost a decade, the family lived in Siegen, where the family "belonged of necessity to the Lutheran Church." Still later, after their return to Cologne, they "returned to the Catholic faith, which became the religion of their children." Christopher White, *Peter Paul Rubens: Man and Artist* (New Haven: Yale University Press, 1987), 1–3.

56. See, for example, Henry Chadwick and G. R. Evans, eds., *Atlas of the Christian Church* (London: Macmillan, 1987), 100, 94, 108, the maps showing the distributions in, respectively, 1560, 1618, and 1648. Or see Josef Engel and Ernst Walter Zeeden, eds., *Grosser Historischer Weltatlas* (Munich: Bayerischer Schulbuch-Verlag, 1981), part 3, 8–11. The greatest extension of Protestantism was in 1618. The entirety of eastern Europe, from the Baltic to the Ottoman territories, had a mix of Lutheranism, Calvinism, and Catholicism. By 1648, most of the Protestantism there had disappeared.

57. The first note in the ascetic Protestantism chapter opens with this sentence: "Zwinglianism we do not discuss separately, since after a short lease of power it rapidly lost in importance" (217). Ulrich Zwingli is neglected by Troeltsch also, whose second volume makes only three minor references to the reformer and his influence. For a useful overview see J. Wayne Baker, "Zwinglianism," in *Encyclopedia of the Reformation,* forthcoming.

58. See Viner, *Religious Thought,* 155, 157, 170 n48, 186–189. Weber's listing of the appropriate contexts appears in his "Bemerkungen zu der vorstehenden Replik [by Karl Fischer]," *Archiv für Sozialwissenschaft* 26 (1908): 275–283, specifically 277.

59. Marshall, *Presbyteries,* 272, 262.

60. Samuelsson, *Religion,* 104–105. For more detail on the religion-commerce relationship there, see Albert Hyma, "Calvinism and Capitalism in the Netherlands, 1555–1700," *Journal of Modern History* 10 (1938): 321–343, especially 339–343. "During the days of greatest prosperity for the Dutch Republic as a whole," Hyma reports, "the provinces in which Calvinism was the strongest [Friesland and Groningen] shared the least in the process of capitalistic growth" (342). Also citing sources, Ephraim Fischoff reports "no proof to sustain [the] theory of a connection between Calvinism and capitalism among the Netherlanders"; see his essay "The Protestant Ethic and the Spirit of Capitalism— The History of a Controversy," *Social Research* 11 (1944): 53–77, especially 70–71. For another review, see Pellicani, "Weber," 71–73.

61. W. D. Rubinstein, *Men of Property: The Very Wealthy in Britain since the Industrial Revolution* (New Brunswick, N.J.: Rutgers University Press, 1981), 145–163. The quotations are from 155, 163. Similar results were found in David J. Jeremy's study of the religious backgrounds of chairmen and managing directors of Britain's one hundred leading firms, in those of 1907, 1935, and 1955; see his *Capitalists and Christians: Business leaders and the Churches in Britain, 1900–1960* (Oxford: Clarendon, 1990), 102–104.

62. The sources and quotations are from Watts, *Dissenters,* 267–270; Little, *Religion,* 259; and Rubinstein, *Men of Property,* 146–147. The turn-of-the-century figures for England and Wales are from J. Scott Keltie, ed., *The Statesman's Year-Book, 1903* (London: Macmillan, 1903), 29–32. For a more detailed review, see E. D. Bebb, *Nonconformity and Social and Economic Life, 1660–1800* (London: Epworth, 1935), chap. 4.

63. Watts, *Dissenters,* 271–289.

64. The work in question is by George Unwin, an eminent economic historian. It was first published by the Clarendon Press, Oxford. T. S. Ashton provides a brief account of him in a prefatory note to the second edition (actually reissue) of the volume in 1957. Few commentators pick up on this point, that is, on the need to demonstrate substantial amounts of upward mobility among the ascetic Protestants. Tawney and his followers agree with the Weberians on this point; for them, the Puritans were the "rising bourgeoisie," a conclusion requiring no demonstration.

65. See Weber, *Protestant Ethic,* 55–56; 278 nn85 and 86, 279 n92, and Edmund S. Morgan, *The Puritan Dilemma: The Story of John Winthrop* (Boston: Little, Brown, 1958), 51, 184. For additional details, see Rex A. Lucas, "A Specification of the Weber Thesis: Plymouth Colony," *History and Theory* 10 (1971): 319–346. For an overview of the problems in the Virginia Company, see James West Davidson and Mark Hamilton Lytle, *After the Fact: The Art of Historical Detection* (New York: Knopf, 1982), especially 10–22. The Gary Nash passage is from his "Social Development," in Jack P. Greene and J. R. Pole, eds., *Colonial British America: Essays in the New History of the Early Modern Era* (Baltimore: Johns Hopkins University Press, 1984), 236. See also Pellicani, "Weber," 73–78.

66. Viner, *Religious Thought,* 156, and Marshall, *Search,* 13.

67. Viner notes also that even the grammatical form of Weber's argument signals a problem: "In common with some of his most important followers Weber relies heavily on the results which particular beliefs 'might have had' on practice. This device entails the use of what has been called 'the conjectural preterite'; i.e., what a writer might 'logically' have gone on to say if he had extended his remarks or, as applied to behavior, what a person might have done if he had acted out the 'logical' conclusion of his beliefs. It is a species of argument from ignorance which is extremely difficult to answer except by drawing attention to its inherent subjectivity or by asking why the historian should have found it necessary to have recourse to such methods" (*Religious Thought,* 156).

68. Marshall, *Search,* 9. Rubinstein writes along the same lines: "It is safe to say that virtually every economic and social historian of Britain writing in the last 30 years has accepted that there is at least some merit to the Weber Thesis in its post–1760 British context" (*Men of Property,* 145). Both statements, those of Marshall and of Rubinstein, are mistaken, as will be seen immediately.

69. *Religion Index One: Periodicals* (Evanston, Ill.: American Theological Library Association), vol. 21–24, 1989–1992. One of the sixteen references was to an article in a sociology journal, and one appeared in a general history journal.

70. Philip Benedict, "The Historiography of Continental Calvinism," in Lehmann and Roth, *Weber;* the passage quoted is from 306. An important history published in 1954, Benedict writes, gave six pages (of 454) to discussion of Weber's argument. Some thirty years later, a collective volume written by specialist historians gave more pages, but less favor, to Weber's ideas, suggesting that they have "become more marginal yet." The two books (with the relevant page references) are: McNeill, *History and Character of Calvinism,* 221–223, 418–421, and Prestwich, *International Calvinism,* 9–10, 269, 369–390 (a chapter by Herbert Lüthy based on a 1965 work).
The index to a collection of articles by Reformation historians, a collection focused on social history, contains one reference to Weber and that to a fugitive, nonsubstantive comment; see Buck and Zophy, *Social History,* 31.

71. The works discussed are: Phyllis Deane, *The First Industrial Revolution,* 2d ed. (Cambridge: Cambridge University Press, 1979); J. H. Clapham, *The Economic Development of France and Germany, 1815–1914,* 4th ed. (Cambridge: Cambridge University Press, 1936); T. S. Ashton, *The Industrial Revolution. 1760–1830* (London: Oxford University Press, 1948), and, also by Ashton, *An Economic History of England: The 18th Century* (London: Methuen, 1955); John Ulrich Nef, *The Conquest of the Material World* (Chicago: University of Chicago Press, 1964), chap. 5; Charles P. Kindleberger, *Economic Growth in France and Britain, 1851–1950* (Cambridge: Harvard University Press, 1964), 94–97;

William H. McNeill, *The Rise of the West: A History of the Human Community* (Chicago: University of Chicago Press, 1963), 590n; Paul Kennedy, *The Rise and Fall of the Great Powers: Economic Change and Military Conflict from 1500 to 2000* (New York: Random House, 1987); and David S. Landes, *The Unbound Prometheus: Technological Change and Industrial Development in Western Europe from 1750 to the Present* (Cambridge: Cambridge University Press, 1969), 21–23, 160.

The following works of economic history contain no index references to Max Weber: Rondo Cameron, *A Concise Economic History of the World: From Paleolithic Times to the Present*, 2d ed. (New York: Oxford University Press, 1993), a leading economic history textbook; Roderick Floud and Donald McCloskey, eds., *The Economic History of Britain since 1700*, 2 vols. (Cambridge: Cambridge University Press, 1981); R. M. Hartwell, ed., *The Causes of the Industrial Revolution in England* (London: Methuen, 1967); Peter Mathias, *The First Industrial Nation: An Economic History of Britain, 1700–1914* (London: Methuen, 1969); Joel Mokyr, ed., *The Economics of the Industrial Revolution* (Totowa, N.J.: Rowman and Allanheld, 1985); E. A. Wrigley, *Continuity, Chance and Change* (New York: Cambridge University Press, 1988).

The three volumes of the second edition of Floud and McCloskey's *Economic History* (Cambridge: Cambridge University Press, 1994) contain one index reference to Weber, that to a single deprecating sentence. Mathias has two brief discussions of the role of religion, neither of which makes explicit reference to Weber (160, 164). The first of these does, however, contain an oblique denigrating comment. A fugitive mention of Weber appears in Mokyr; it reads, in its entirety, as follows: "A well-known and highly controversial theory of entrepreneurship is the one somehow linking businessmen to religion. Originally proposed by Weber, the argument is more successful in explaining the differences between Western Christianity and the rest of the world than in explaining differences within the West" (17). No references to Weber appear in Cameron's extensive annotated bibliography; it does contain a reference to Robertson's critique of Weber and his school (415).

Three index references to Weber appear in Peter Kriedte, *Peasants, Landlords and Merchant Capitalists: Europe and the World Economy, 1500–1800*, trans. V. R. Berghahn (Leamington Spa, England: Berg, 1983). None of those references touch on the Protestant ethic thesis. The thesis is reviewed and discussed in Nathan Rosenberg and L. E. Birdzell, Jr., *How the West Grew Rich: The Economic Transformation of the Industrial World* (New York: Basic Books, 1986), 129–134. These authors note that Weber's thesis has been "hotly debated" since first publication and they review some of the major arguments. Reference is made to a wide range of commentators, including Robertson, Tawney, Nef, and Landes. E. L. Jones, *The European Miracle: Environments, Economies, and Geopolitics in the History of Europe and Asia* (Cambridge: Cambridge University Press, 1981), contains four fugitive references to Weber, none of them approving "the thesis." The bibliography refers only to his *General Economic History*.

72. Carlo M. Cipolla, ed., *The Fontana Economic History of Europe: The Sixteenth and Seventeenth Centuries* (Glasgow: Collins, 1974), 240, 247, 260, 296.

73. From Neil J. Smelser, *Sociology*, 4th ed. (Englewood Cliffs, N.J.: Prentice-Hall, 1991), 14, 294, 300, 309. Smelser's text has been singled out for attention because he is one of the most eminent of all current authors of introductory sociology texts. He has written many wide-ranging works, several of them dealing with economic history and eco-

nomic sociology. He has edited a comprehensive review volume, *Handbook of Sociology* (Newbury Park, Calif.: Sage, 1988). He would then, more than most such authors, be conversant with the entire Weber controversy. Smelser is also the author of a relevant scholarly monograph, *Social Change in the Industrial Revolution: An Application of Theory to the British Cotton Industry* (Chicago: University of Chicago Press, 1959). Weber is given very little attention in this 400-page scholarly work; the thesis is discussed on 67–77.

74. The "sample" of texts reviewed consists of all those that were both current and available within the Sociology Department of the Ohio State University (OSU) in 1992–93. The OSU Columbus campus is the largest in the nation, with 38,958 undergraduates in the autumn quarter of 1992. At some point in their academic careers, approximately half of the undergraduates take introductory sociology. Publishers' representatives routinely contact the instructors and provide them, and the department, with examination copies. Instructors may also request copies. The texts reviewed here, while clearly not a random selection, would probably be those with the greatest circulation.

In addition to Smelser (see previous note), the introductory sociology texts reviewed were: David B. Brinkerhoff and Lynn K. White, *Sociology*, 3d ed. (St. Paul, Minn.: West, 1991); Gordon J. DiRenzo, *Human Social Behavior: Concepts and Principles of Sociology* (Fort Worth, Tex.: Holt, Rinehart, and Winston, 1990); John E. Farley, *Sociology*, 2nd ed. (Englewood Cliffs, N.J.: Prentice-Hall, 1992); James A. Inciardi and Robert A. Rothman, *Sociology: Principles and Applications* (San Diego, Calif.: Harcourt Brace Jovanovich, 1990); Allan G. Johnson, *Human Arrangements: An Introduction to Sociology* (San Diego, Calif.: Harcourt Brace Jovanovich, 1989); Kenneth C. W. Kammeyer, George Ritzer, and Norman R. Yetman, *Sociology: Experiencing Changing Societies,* 5th ed. (Boston: Allyn and Bacon, 1992); Donald Light, Suzanne Keller, and Craig Calhoun, *Sociology,* 5th ed. (New York: Knopf, 1989); John J. Macionis, *Sociology,* 3d ed. (Englewood Cliffs, N.J.: Prentice-Hall, 1991; David Popenoe, *Sociology,* 8th ed. (Englewood Cliffs, N.J.: Prentice-Hall, 1991); Ian Robertson, *Sociology,* 3rd ed. (New York: Worth, 1987); Richard T. Schaefer and Robert P. Lamm, *Sociology* (New York: McGraw-Hill, 1992); Rodney Stark, *Sociology,* 4th ed. (Belmont, Mass.: Wadsworth, 1992); George and Lucille Theodorson, *Sociology: Principles and Applications* (St. Paul, Minn.: West, 1990); and James W. VanderZanden, *The Social Experience: An Introduction to Sociology,* 2d ed. (New York: McGraw-Hill, 1990).

None of these texts referred to Jacob Viner's work. Marshall's critique is mentioned (without the citation) in Light, Keller, and Calhoun, *Sociology,* 529. The inadequate citation of Samuelsson is in Farley, *Sociology,* 453. Smelser's text does not include *The Protestant Ethic* in its listing of references; it was also omitted in the third edition.

Many of these problems were found also in an earlier study based on a comprehensive review of sociological works published between 1930 and 1960. See Richard L. Means, "Weber's Thesis of the Protestant Ethic: The Ambiguities of Received Doctrine," *Journal of Religion* 45 (1965): 1–11. His conclusion: "An analysis of samples of research monographs, textbooks, and articles indicates an almost complete lack among sociologists of a critical discussion of Weber's thesis. The historians have directed a number of criticisms against Weber, but there are few attempts, if any, for the textbook and monograph writers in sociology to recognize the existence of the growing source material on the history of Protestantism," (9).

75. Robertson, *Sociology,* 407.

76. Giddens, Introduction, in Weber, *Protestant Ethic* (London: Routledge, 1992) , xxiv.

77. Both citation indexes are from the Institute for Scientific Information, Philadelphia. The social sciences index covers approximately 2,800 journals. The arts and humanities index covers approximately 1,800.

    The quotation commending Weber's critics is from New, *Anglican and Puritan,* 96.

78. Marshall, *Search,* 140.

79. Jonathan Turner, a sociologist, has indicated some understandable concern about those who "genuflect at the sacred works of St. Marx, St. Durkheim, and St. Weber"; see his *Herbert Spencer: A Renewed Appreciation* (Beverly Hills, Calif.: Sage, 1985), 7.

80. Andrew M. Greeley, "The Protestant Ethic: Time for a Moratorium," *Sociological Analysis,* 25 (1964): 20–33. The other quotations are from Gary D. Bouma, "Beyond Lenski: A Critical Review of Recent 'Protestant Ethic' Research," *Journal for the Scientific Study of Religion* 12 (1973): 141–156. Marshall, *Search,* 165–166, and Zaret, in Lehmann and Roth, *Weber,* 245, also argue along these lines.

    In a rare investigation of the sort Bouma recommends, Harold B. Barclay studied an ascetic Protestant sect, the Holdeman Mennonites, and found their beliefs impeded capitalist development; see his "The Protestant Ethic versus the Spirit of Capitalism," *Review of Religious Research* 10 (1969): 151–158. Another insightful case study is provided by Randall G. Stokes. Afrikaner Calvinism, he reports, was "theologically identical to European Calvinism of the 18th century" but had "a highly conservative impact on economic action." His explanation: this group dealt with the predestination doctrine and the resulting anxieties in a very different way, See Stokes's "Afrikaner Calvinism and Economic Action: The Weberian Thesis in South Africa," *American Journal of Sociology* 81 (1975): 62–81.

81. Marshall, *Search,* 129, and Weber, *Protestant Ethic,* 54–55 and, for the quotation, 70.

82. Another argument has appeared in recent sociological literature. This direction, which is *not* a defensive response, points to a later Weber formulation. One may always provide an improved or extended framework; it is a routine expectation in scientific work. If the later version is the "real" or "final" Weber position, then it is that case that should be presented, beginning with the sociology texts, not the flawed, or preliminary version of *The Protestant Ethic.* See Randall Collins, "Weber's Last Theory of Capitalism," chap. 2 of his *Weberian Sociological Theory* (Cambridge: Cambridge University Press, 1986). The chapter originally appeared in the *American Sociological Review* 45 (1980): 925–942. The key text in this connection is Weber's *General Economic History,* trans. Frank H. Knight (New York: Collier, 1961 [original, 1927]). The work was out of print for many years but was reissued in 1981 by Transaction Books. Few of the sociology texts reviewed here make reference to this "later theory" option; few of them cite the *General Economic History.*

    It is not possible to cover all of the many arguments dealing with the Weber thesis in a brief chapter. Readers interested in the earlier controversies involving Lujo Brentano, Albert Hyma, Henri Pirenne, Felix Rachfahl, H. M. Robertson, Amintore Fanfani, R. H. Tawney, and many others might begin with Ephraim Fischoff's review, "The Protestant Ethic."

    Another strand of the controversy has focused on scientific and technological innovations in the British context, the emphasis typically being on the dissenting churches. Much of this literature has been quick to invoke Weber and the Protestant ethic but conflates two distinct subject matters, a general work ethic and scientific aptitudes. Again, typically, much of that research has been indifferent to the ceteris paribus requirement and has failed to explore other possibilities, e.g., discrimination, disabilities due to the Test Act, and the simple matters of geography. For a brief discussion of this problem, see Rubinstein, *Men of Property,* 146–149. For more detail, see the important study by George Becker, "Pietism and Science: A Critique of Robert K. Merton's Hypothesis," *American Journal of Sociology* 89 (1984): 1065–1090. Merton's reply (same issue: 1091–1121) does not address the issues raised. For further relevant detail and discussion, see Becker's response in a later issue, 91 (1986): 1203–1218. For another important contribution, see Becker's article "The Merton Thesis: Oetinger and German Pietism, a Significant Negative Case," *Sociological Forum,* 7 (1992): 641–660. On science in Geneva under Calvin and afterwards, see Viner, *Religious Thought,* 186–187.

83. Carlo M. Cipolla, *Guns, Sails, and Empires: Technological Innovation and the Early Phases of European Expansion* (New York: Minerva Press, 1965).
84. For some sense of the difficulties facing the Habsburgs, see Geoffrey Parker, "Spain, Her Enemies and the Revolt of the Netherlands 1559–1648," *Past and Present,* 49 (1970): 73–95. Parker has written several books dealing with Spain's problems.
85. For a summary overview of army and navy expenditures, see John Brewer, *The Sinews of Power: War, Money and the English State, 1688–1783* (Cambridge: Harvard University Press, 1990), chap. 2. The figures on population, all rounded off, are from: A. Goodwin, ed., *The New Cambridge Modern History,* vol. 8, *The American and French Revolutions 1763–93* (Cambridge: The University Press, 1965), 714; Evarts B. Greene, *American Population Before the Federal Census of 1790* (New York: Columbia University Press, 1932), 6; and C. P. Stacey, *Quebec, 1759: The Siege and the Battle* (London: Pan Books, 1973), xviii–xix. The climate and soil conditions in New France, to be sure, were not such as to encourage migration. For the problems of settlement, development, and defense, see Mason Wade, *The French Canadians, 1760–1967* (Toronto: Macmillan, 1968), vol. 1, chap. 1.
86. Samuelsson, *Religion,* 106. He was drawing from Pieter Geyl's essay "National State and the Writers of Netherlands History," chap. 9 of Geyl, *Debates with Historians* (The Hague: Nijhoff, 1955), especially 182–184.
87. Spitz, *Protestant Reformation,* 28–30, and Cameron, *Concise Economic History,* 97.
88. See Cameron, *Concise Economic History,* chap. 6.
89. Viner, *Religious Thought,* 164. Several eighteenth-century authors commented on the number of holidays: "Because Catholics had 120 per year and Protestants only 60, the latter were thus able to record a profit from the extra 60 work days"; see Paul Münch, "The Thesis before Weber: An Archaeology," in Lehmann and Roth, *Weber,* chap. 2, especially 64–65.
90. Spitz, *Protestant Reformation,* 50–51.
91. See James J. Sheehan, *German History: 1770–1866* (Oxford: Clarendon Press, 1989), 243–246, 269–272, 355. The change, Sheehan reports, was "one of the greatest territorial rearrangements in all of European history" (243). See also Rudolf Morsey, "Wirtschaftliche und soziale Auswirkungen der Säkularisation in Deutschland," in Rudolf Vierhaus and Manfred Botzenhart, eds., *Dauer und Wandel der Geschichte: Aspekte europäischer Vergangenheit* (Münster: Verlag Aschendorff, 1966), 361–383.
92. Daniel, "Hard Work," 45.

93. It is not clear that those luxuries should be counted as losses or as "wasteful" expenses. Morgan concluded a major business agreement on board the *Corsair*. "Appearances," the show of wealth or of "solidity," can have real economic consequences. Again, one should not beg questions.

94. See N. F. R. Crafts, "British Economic Growth, 1700–1831: A Review of the Evidence," *Economic History Review*, 2d ser. 36 (1983): 177–199. For more detail see N. F. R. Crafts, *British Economic Growth during the Industrial Revolution* (New York: Oxford University Press, 1985).

95. The "new economic history" (sometimes called the new institutionalism) focuses on the long term, on facilitating conditions developed in the centuries prior to 1800. Europe had a system of states, as opposed to the empires of the Ottomans, of India, and of China. Other things equal, competing states encourage innovation and some transfer of procedures follows. Private property, eventually, came to be more secure in the West than elsewhere. The incentive to hoard capital was reduced and interest rates fell accordingly. The European states on the Atlantic built large ocean-going ships and mastered the intricacies of navigation; the empires, in contrast, "stayed home." See especially Douglass C. North and Robert Paul Thomas, *The Rise of the Western World: A New Economic History* (Cambridge: Cambridge University Press, 1973); Jones, *European Miracle;* and Rosenberg and Birdzell, *How the West Grew Rich.*

96. On the Industrial Revolution, see Deane, *First Industrial Revolution;* Cameron, *Concise Economic History;* and Landes, *Unbound Prometheus.* The expression "Industrial Revolution" is problematic; for the details, see Cameron, 165–167.

97. Landes provides the following: a brief exposition of the Weber thesis along with several other explanations (22–23); a paragraph-length exposition of the English experience, giving credence to the Weber claim of a Dissent-entrepreneurialism linkage, accompanied by other explanations (73–74); and a paragraph discussion of the Calvinism-entrepreneurialism link in the Mulhouse region of Alsace (160). The English case is based on the crude ecological relationship ("surely no coincidence that Dissenters were more numerous in the North and Midlands" [73]) and a study that has been successfully challenged by Rubinstein. On those points, see Watts's *Dissenters*, 271–289, on the frequency and location of dissent (reviewed earlier in the text), and Rubinstein, *Men of Property,* 146–149. For the Mulhouse experience, see David S. Landes, "Religion and Enterprise: The Case of the French Textile Industry," in Edward C. Carter II, Robert Forster, and Joseph N. Moody, eds., *Enterprise and Entrepreneurs in Nineteenth- and Twentieth-Century France* (Baltimore: Johns Hopkins University Press, 1976), 41–86.

    Wolfgang Schivelbusch has advanced still another hypothesis in an important chapter entitled "Coffee and the Protestant Ethic." Prior to the seventeenth century, he reports, alcoholic beverages were standard fare for most European populations. English families began the day with a breakfast of beer soup. That was followed, in the course of the day, by the drinking of beer or ale which, on the whole, was healthier than water. The subsequent widespread use of coffee transformed a generally begrogged population it into a sober, alert, and active force. This change, understandably, brought about a dramatic improvement in work habits. See Schivelbusch, *Tastes of Paradise: A Social History of Spices. Stimulants, and Intoxicants,* trans. David Jacobson (New York: Pantheon, 1992), chap. 2.

98. The Albert Salomon quotation appeared first in the essay "German Sociology," in Georges Gurvitch and Wilbert E. Moore, eds., *Twentieth Century Sociology* (New York: Philosophical Library, 1945), 596. Guenther Roth cites the passage and questions it in his account, "The Historical Relationship to Marxism," in Bendix and Roth, *Scholarship and Partisanship,* 228. References to Marx's ghost appear also in the sociology textbooks by Macionis, *Sociology,* 107; Robertson, *Sociology,* 15; and VanderZanden, *The Social Experience,* 20. For Marshall's comments, see *Search,* 203 n44, 22–40, 150.

99. See Friedrich Wilhelm Graf, "The German Theological Sources and Protestant Church Politics," chap. 1 of Lehmann and Roth, *Weber,* 31, 42. Graf writes that "*The Protestant Ethic* demonstrated that Weber became involved in theological discourse more than any other sociologist of the century" (48–49). Two other chapters in the Lehmann and Roth volume provide important information on the "theological" and political background of the monograph, those of Paul Münch, "The Thesis before Weber," and Thomas Nipperdey, "Max Weber, Protestantism, and the Context of the Debate around 1900."

100. On Ritschl as National-Liberal theologian, see Graf, "German Theological Sources," 43.

101. Guenther Roth wrote that "Weber greatly sympathized with the Puritan and liberal traditions of England. Sometimes he sounded as if he were half English"; see his "Weber the Would-Be Englishman: Anglophilia and Family History," in Lehmann and Roth, *Weber,* 83, 85, 86. Philip Benedict commented on the extent to which "Weber's essay was a product of the confessional rivalries and prejudices of the specific time and place in which it was written, not to mention Weber's own critical attitude toward Germany's Lutheran inheritance, to which the Reformed tradition constituted in his eyes a superior alternative"; see Benedict, "Historiography," 325. The Marianne Weber quotation is from her *Max Weber: A Biography,* trans. Harry Zohn (New York: Wiley, 1975), 335.

102. Marianne Weber, *Max Weber,* 335, 587. Fischoff writes that Weber "was an admirer of the Marxian hypothesis, only objecting that it should not be made absolute and universal, a summary philosophy"; in "Protestant Ethic," 67.

Chapter Four: Hitler's Electoral Support

1. Richard F. Hamilton, *Who Voted for Hitler?* (Princeton: Princeton University Press, 1982). This chapter draws heavily on my later account, "Hitler's Electoral Support: Recent Findings and Theoretical Implications," *Canadian Journal of Sociology* 11 (1986): 1–34.

2. Jürgen W. Falter, *Hitlers Wähler* (Munich: C. H. Beck, 1991). Most of that "score of articles" are cited in the book. For the present purposes, the following are of special importance: Jürgen Falter, Andreas Link, Jan-Bernd Lohmöller, Johann de Rijke, and Siegfried Schumann, "Arbeitslosigkeit und Nationalsozialismus: Eine empirische Analyse des Beitrags der Massenerwerbslosigkeit zu den Wahlerfolgen der NSDAP 1932 und 1933," *Kölner Zeitschrift für Soziologie und Sozialpsychologie* 35 (1983): 525–554; Jürgen Falter and Dirk Hänisch, "Die Anfälligkeit von Arbeitern gegenüber der NSDAP bei den Reichstagswahlen 1928–1933," *Archiv für Sozialgeschichte* 26 (1986): 179–216; Jürgen Falter and Reinhard Zintl, "The Economic Crisis of the 1930s and the Nazi Vote," *Journal of Interdisciplinary History* 19 (1988): 55–85; and Jürgen Falter, "Arbeiter haben

erheblich häufiger, Angestellte dagegen sehr viel seltener NSDAP gewählt als wir lange Zeit angenommen haben," *Geschichte und Gesellschaft* 16 (1990): 536–552. Other articles relevant to the concerns of this chapter will be referenced later.

In the late seventies, Falter and I discovered that we were working on the same subject. We were both reaching out for "new" election data and, independently, had both developed considerable skepticism with regard to the received readings of National Socialist support. I wish to indicate my thanks and appreciation for his many helpful comments and suggestions on my subsequent chapters, this one included, and on my later articles.

3. For a brief account of these elections, see Hamilton, *Who Voted*, appendix A, 475–484. The works mentioned are: Theodor Geiger, "Panik im Mittelstand," *Die Arbeit* 7 (1930): 637–654; Theodor Geiger, *Die soziale Schichtung des deutschen Volkes: Soziographischer Versuch auf statistischer Grundlage* (Stuttgart: Ferdinand Enke Verlag, 1932), especially 109–122; Harold Lasswell, "The Psychology of Hitlerism," *Political Quarterly* 4 (1933): 373–384; and Seymour Martin Lipset, *Political Man: The Social Bases of Politics* (Garden City, N.Y.: Doubleday, 1960), chap. 5. For a review of other statements of the position, with citations, references, and some initial discussion, see Hamilton, *Who Voted*, chaps. 1 and 2; Falter, *Hitlers Wähler*, 194–198; and Chapter 5 herein.

The lower-middle-class thesis clearly involves a causal question. Something about the circumstance of people in the class induces strain and moves them to a given reaction, e.g., to vote for party A. One could take the same data, on class and voting, and address a different question, a compositional one. The causal question asks about the sources of the response by a given class; the compositional question asks about the distribution among groups making the response. To address the causal question one must first ask: How did various classes vote? The compositional question asks: What part of the vote for a given party came from class X and what part from other classes? The answers to these questions could diverge considerably. Three-quarters of class X might vote for party A but, because of the class's small size, it is possible that only a fifth of party A's votes would come from that class. Both are legitimate questions, but it is important to keep them separate in order to avoid confusion of the two distinct concerns. When one speaks of "the bulk" of the NSDAP voters being lower middle class, one is addressing the compositional question, not the causal thesis. For a straightforward discussion of this point, see Hans Zeisel, *Say It with Figures*, 4th ed. (New York: Harper, 1957), chap. 2.

4. The Ochsenbach-Dilsberg figures given in the text were arbitrarily chosen for the dramatic contrast. Falter's comprehensive result for Hessen-Darmstadt and Baden (which would include those two villages) showed 72 and 23 percent support for the NSDAP in Protestant and Catholic villages in the July 1932 election, still a sharp contrast (*Hitlers Wähler*, 185). For a more detailed review, see Hamilton, *Who Voted*, chap. 3, and for a comprehensive portrait, Falter, *Hitlers Wähler*, 169–193. Strong summary statements on the primacy of the religious factor appear in the latter work 187, 193, 259–260, 278, 325. Falter also notes the neglect of religion and the emphasis on class in the analyses from the early thirties (194).

5. Hermann Mulert, "Konfession und politische Parteistellung in Deutschland," *Zeitschrift für Politik* 21 (1931–1932): 334–345, and Karl Rohe, "German Elections and Party Systems in Historical and Regional Perspective: An Introduction," in Rohe, ed., *Elections,*

Parties and Political Traditions: Social Foundations of German Parties and Party Systems, 1867–1987 (New York: Berg, 1990), 3.

Some commentators make note of the Protestant tendency but then drop all further reference to it, turning immediately to the class analysis. Lipset, for example, recognizes the religious linkage at several points (e.g., "The ideal-typical Nazi voter in 1932 was a middle-class self-employed Protestant who lived either on a farm or in a small community" [*Political Man*, 149]. The point is clearly and forcefully stated in a footnote: "All the studies agree that religion affected support of the Nazis *more* than any other factor. The Nazis were weak in Catholic regions and cities, and secured majorities in many Protestant small communities" (146) The subsequent footnote restates the point and contains also the appropriate methodological conclusion: "Catholic affiliation constantly overrides class or other allegiances as a major determinant of party support in practically all election data for Germany, in both the Weimar and Bonn republics." The conclusion drawn is that ecological analyses of mixed regions that do not hold religious affiliation constant are "relatively useless." The lesson of the footnotes, however, is not incorporated into the text.

For a recent example of this neglect, see Peter Baldwin, "Social Interpretations of Nazism: Renewing a Tradition," *Journal of Contemporary History* 25 (1990): 5–37. The otherwise uninformed reader would never guess the importance of the religious factor from Baldwin's passing reference to "Protestant peasants" seeking to "recapture lost social status" (8). Another fleeting reference to the subject appears in his note 40.

6. For details on Berlin, Hamburg, Cologne, and Munich, see Hamilton, *Who Voted*, Chaps. 4–6, and appendix B, 485.

7. Falter, *Hitlers Wähler*, 163–168. The overall inverse relationship between size of community and National Socialist voting appeared first in 1932. No differences of note were found in 1928 and 1930 (165). Falter's presentation of results by religion divides into only two community-size categories, predominantly country and predominantly urban (more than 5,000 inhabitants). Results are also presented from communities in Hesse-Darmstadt and Baden (the five categories range from "less than 250" to "more than 2,000 inhabitants"); see 180–186. For more complete results see Jürgen W. Falter, Thomas Lindenberger, and Siegfried Schumann, *Wahlen und Abstimmungen in der Weimarer Republik: Materialen zum Wahlverhalten 1919–1933* (Munich: C. H. Beck, 1986), 178.

One important new finding appears in Falter's research: in the Catholic regions, the size of community pattern reversed in the March 1933 election. Support for the NSDAP in the smallest of those communities went from 14.9 percent in November 1932 to 33.4 percent in the following March. Although still below equivalent figures for Protestant communities, the National Socialists made substantial gains in all categories of predominantly Catholic communities (Falter et al., *Wahlen*, 178). In Hesse and Baden, the correlations between NSDAP support and size of the largely Catholic communities had been slightly positive. In Baden, in the Reichstag election of March 1933 the coefficient was − 18 (Falter, *Hitlers Wähler*, 185).

8. Hamilton, *Who Voted*, chap. 5. The positive relationship between socioeconomic status of the urban districts and NSDAP support was, as noted, the most frequent pattern. There were, however, three clear exceptions: in Cologne, Munich, and Frankfurt. Those exceptions appear to be a result of media impacts. Important newspapers in

those three cities were, in one way or another, strongly opposed to the National Socialist aspirations. The findings in two cities, Wuppertal and Düsseldorf, did not allow
unambiguous conclusions. My summary conclusion was that none of the fourteen cities
showed results consonant with the lower-middle-class hypothesis; in none of them did
the lower-middle-class districts show exceptional support for the NSDAP (218–219).
The cities studied were, in order of size, Berlin, Hamburg, Cologne, Munich, Essen,
Frankfurt am Main, Dortmund, Düsseldorf, Hanover, Duisburg, Stuttgart, Nuremberg,
Wuppertal, and Mannheim. Wuppertal was, in 1933, the sixteenth-largest city in the
nation, Mannheim, the twenty-third. My original intention was to start with the largest
city, Berlin, and work down the list. The omissions among the top sixteen were then
all located in "the east," Leipzig and Dresden in the German Democratic Republic
(GDR), Breslau in Poland. The seventeenth city, Chemnitz (Karl-Marx-Stadt), was also in the GDR. I visited the City Archive in Gelsenkirchen, the eighteenth city, but
found no usable election data (ibid., 542 n59). Someone else, I was told, had researched Bremen, the nineteenth city. An accident of personal biography made it easy
to add Mannheim.

9. See Hans Neisser, "Sozialstatistische Analyse des Wahlergebnisses," *Die Arbeit* 7
(1930): 654–659, and Hamilton, *Who Voted*, 45–50. Middle-class support for the Social
Democrats was noted early in this century, for example, in a work by R. Blank that
analyzed the elections of 1893 and 1897; see his "Die soziale Zusammensetzung der
sozialdemokratischen Wählerschaft Deutschlands," *Archiv für Sozialwissenschaft und Sozialpolitik* 20 (1905): 507–550. Blank, however, appears to have exaggerated the extent of
that support; see the criticisms by Gerhard A. Ritter, *Die Arbeiterbewegung im Wilhelmis-
chen Reich* (Berlin: Colloquium Verlag, 1963), 77–78.
Two-thirds of the employed residents in one Hamburg harbor district, a unique free
port area, had nonmanual occupations, most of them as white-collar employees or civil
servants. Given the location, it is likely that they were lower middle class. In July
1932, only 23 percent of the votes cast there were for the NSDAP, a level 10 percentage
points below the citywide figure. Most of the district's votes went to the Socialists or
Communists; see Hamilton, *Who Voted*, 116.

10. Rudolf Heberle, *From Democracy to Nazism* (Baton Rouge: Louisiana State University
Press, 1945), 39. For the mass society claims, see Emil Lederer, *The State of the Masses*
(New York: Norton, 1940); Hannah Arendt, *The Origins of Totalitarianism* (Cleveland:
Meridian Books, 1958), chap. 10; and William Kornhauser, *The Politics of Mass Society*
(Glencoe, Ill.: Free Press, 1959). For brief critiques of this position, see Richard F.
Hamilton, *Class and Politics in the United States* (New York: Wiley, 1972), 44–49; Hamil-
ton, *Who Voted*, 433–437; and Bernt Hagtvet, "The Theory of Mass Society and the
Collapse of the Weimar Republic: A Re-examination," in Stein Ugelvik Larsen, Bernt
Hagtvet, Jan Petter Myklebust, eds., *Who Were the Fascists: Social Roots of European Fascism* (Bergen: Universitetsforlaget, 1980), 66–117.
Mass society theorists have made much of the mobilization of previous nonvoters,
pointing to the increased participation in the last Weimar elections. Falter's analysis
suggests that approximately one-quarter of the 1930 NSDAP support came from previous nonvoters. In the July 1932 election, approximately one-eighth were previous
nonvoters. For Falter's discussion and estimates, see *Hitlers Wähler*, 98–101, 110–113
(estimates are from table 5.9, 111).

11. Three leading works dealing with the cultural argument are Hans Kohn, *The Mind of Germany: The Education of a Nation* (New York: Macmillan, 1961); George Mosse, *The Crisis of German Ideology: Intellectual Origins of the Third Reich* (New York: Grosset and Dunlap, 1964); and Fritz Stern, *The Politics of Cultural Despair: A Study in the Rise of the Germanic Ideology* (Garden City N.Y.: Doubleday Anchor, 1965). For a critique of this position, see Richard F. Hamilton, "Some Difficulties with Cultural Explanations of National Socialism," H. E. Chehabi and Alfred Stepan, eds., *Politics, Society, and Democracy: Comparative Studies* (Boulder: Westview, 1995), chap. 12. For the psychohistorical position, see Peter Loewenberg, "The Psychohistorical Origins of the Nazi Youth Cohort," *American Historical Review* 76 (1971): 1457–1502. These arguments have focused on the German case. A glance at the other "fascisms" indicates a wide variety of social bases, which in turn poses problems for the general arguments, those focusing on the lower middle class, the mass society, and the wartime deprivations. See the comprehensive review by Juan J. Linz, "Some Notes toward a Comparative Study of Fascism in Sociological Historical Perspective," in Walter Laqueur, ed., *Fascism: A Reader's Guide* (Berkeley: University of California Press, 1976), 3–121, and also, an abridged version, Linz's "Political Space and Fascism as a Late-Comer," in Larsen et al., *Who Were the Fascists*, 153–189.

12. The combined Social Democratic Party of Germany (SPD) and Communist Party of Germany (KPD) percentages for 1928, 1930, and July 1932, respectively, were 40.4, 37.6, and 35.9. In November 1932, there was a slight recovery, the combined Left figure increasing to 37.3. The major shifts among the workers, as far as we can tell, were first, within the "marxist" camp, a move from the SPD to the KPD, and second, among the "Tory workers," a shift from the Right and center "bourgeois" parties to the NSDAP. Corresponding to the overall decline of the Left, we have the following estimates from Falter: that 14 percent of the NSDAP vote in 1930 came from 1928 SPD voters and 3 percent from former KPD voters. In July 1932, 10 percent of the NSDAP voters were 1930 SPD voters and 2 percent former KPD voters; see *Hitlers Wähler*, 111.

13. The basic presentation of this position appears in Bernard R. Berelson, Paul F. Lazarsfeld, and William N. McPhee, *Voting: A Study of Opinion Formation in a Presidential Campaign* (Chicago: University of Chicago Press, 1954), chap. 6. For a summary, discussion, and criticism of the position, see Hamilton, *Class and Politics*, 49–63. Although the Berelson-Lazarsfeld-McPhee position is frequently referred to as an "interpersonal influence" model, it is an influence-plus-logic (or rationale) model. A shift from one milieu to another brings a new range of social contacts. Those persons, typically, would be the bearers of a new and different "logic" or reading of social events and experience.

14. For information on the NSDAP membership, see Michael H. Kater, *The Nazi Party: A Social Profile of Members and Leaders 1919–1945* (Cambridge: Harvard University Press, 1983). For information on the S.A., see Conan Fischer, *Stormtroopers: A Social, Economic and Ideological Analysis 1929–1935* (London: George Allen and Unwin, 1983). For the collapse of the Right and Left liberals and of the conservatives, see Hamilton, *Who Voted*, chap. 10. For a comprehensive account, see Larry Eugene Jones, *German Liberalism and the Dissolution of the Weimar Party System, 1918–1933* (Chapel Hill: University of North Carolina Press, 1988).

15. For a review and documentation of the claims made about the NSDAP cadres, see Hamilton, *Who Voted*, 310–328. The quotation is from Jeremy Noakes *The Nazi Party in Lower Saxony 1921–1933* (London: Oxford University Press, 1971), 211. Efficiency and virtuosity are matters of degree. Although the party, in its self-indulgent portraiture, repeatedly emphasized its exceptional organizational achievements, evidence of inefficiencies and outright failures is also available. It would be astonishing if, in a period of rapid growth and much turmoil, that were not the case. The key question, as in any struggle, is that of relative efficiency—in this case, How well did the NSDAP function as compared to its competitors?

16. For discussion of the wartime experience, the demobilization, and the moves to the Freikorps, to various paramilitary units, and ultimately to the S.A., see Hamilton, *Who Voted*, 329–355; and Fischer, *Stormtroopers*, 4–5, 56–57.

17. For this history and for data on state elections of the period, see Hamilton, *Who Voted*, 234–237. For details of this history in one state, see Ellsworth Faris, "Takeoff Point for the National Socialist Party: The Landtag Election in Baden, 1929," *Central European History* 8 (1975): 140–171

The Reichstag election of 20 May, 1928 was the low point in the party's fortunes. Many commentators have pointed to the September 1930 election as the occasion of the breakthrough and link that success with the economic collapse. But the party was making significant gains already in 1929 during the anti–Young Plan Campaign. The party's upward course was evident even earlier, in the May 1928 election. The overall result, the NSDAP's 2.6 percent in that election, hides two opposed tendencies. The party increased its percentage share, over December 1924, in nineteen of the thirty-five large districts (*Wahlkreise*), most of these in southern and western Germany. In the eastern and central districts they lost badly; see Hamilton, *Who Voted*, 236. These largely unrecognized "findings" point to different causal dynamics: as opposed to "the Depression" as key cause, they suggest the importance of activists and party organization. It was the linkage of the two, the activists' use of the economic catastrophe, that generated the electoral breakthrough. In other nations the catastrophe had markedly different political outcomes. The results for the nation and for the thirty-five large districts of Germany may be seen in Alfred Milatz, "Das Ende der Parteien im Spiegel der Wahlen 1930 bis 1933," in Erich Matthias and Rudolf Morsey, eds., *Das Ende der Parteien, 1933* (Düsseldorf: Droste Verlag, 1960), 743–793 (particularly 782), and Falter, et al., *Wahlen*, 70–71.

18. The best account of the Anti–Young Plan Campaign themes and the carryover of those themes to the 1930 election appears in David Andrew Hackett, "The Nazi Party in the Reichstag Election of 1930," (dissertation, Department of History, University of Wisconsin, Madison, 1971), chaps. 2 and 4. The best recent account of the NSDAP electoral organization and campaign themes is by Gerhard Paul, *Aufstand der Bilder: Die NS-Propaganda vor 1933* (Bonn: Dietz, 1992), Chaps. 2 and 3.

19. On the themes and motives for support, see Hamilton, *Who Voted*, 374, 376, 389–393, 413–419. On the party's antimarxism, see 314–315, 325, 374. See also Paul, *Aufstand*, 91, 100–101, 113, 220. The Social Democrats, Paul shows, were the principal target of this "antimarxist" effort; the Communists received much less attention.

Many NSDAP leaders wrote memoirs in the mid-thirties, accounts of their "years of struggle." These focus on the wartime origins of the party cadres and have "antimarxism" as their central organizing theme; see, for example, Hermann Okrass, *Das Ende einer Parole—"Hamburg bleibt rot"* (Hamburg: Hanseatische Verlagsanstalt, 1934). For a memoir based on small town experience, see Franz Buchner, *Kamerad! Halt aus! Aus der Geschichte des Kreises Starnberg der* NDSAP (Munich: Zentralverlag der NSDAP, 1938). Buchner, incidentally, continuously emphasized the military linkages. The founders of the 1925 *Ortsgruppe* are described as "all three, front soldiers, Freikorps fighters . . . all SA, and marchers on November 9, 1923" (6, and also, for similar statements, 237, 319).

20. From Karl Dietrich Bracher, *Die Auflösung der Weimarer Republik*, (Villingen/Schwarz-wald: Ring-Verlag, 1964), 108. The party's efforts to centralize campaign organization are reviewed in Dietrich Orlow, *The History of the Nazi Party: 1919–1933* (Pittsburgh: University of Pittsburgh Press, 1969), 37–38, 82–83, 116, 148, 205, 238. See also Paul, *Aufstand*, chap. 2.

    Anti-Semitism was used in the party's electoral efforts, but here again it was a theme used where advantage was seen. Those appeals appeared with greater frequency in small towns, especially in areas with some previous anti-Semitic history. Where unsuccessful, or where the response was negative, the subject was dropped; see Hamilton, *Who Voted*, 366–367, 370–371, 377, 605–607, n46. Paul's content analysis of 124 NSDAP placards from 1928 to 1932 found six that targeted Jews; three of the six were from the 1928 campaign (*Aufstand*, 220).

21. See Hamilton, *Who Voted*, 371–373; and Klaus Scholder, *Die Kirchen und das Dritte Reich*, vol. 1, *Vorgeschichte und Zeit der Illusionen 1918–1934* (Frankfurt: Propylaen Verlag, 1977), or, trans. John Bowden, *The Churches and the Third Reich*, vol. 1, *Preliminary History and the Time of Illusions* (Philadelphia: Fortress Press, 1988), part 1, chaps. 9–10, part 2, chap. 2. See also Geoffrey Pridham, *Hitler's Rise to Power: The Nazi Movement in Bavaria, 1923–1933* (New York: Harper Torchbooks, 1973), chap. 5, and especially, 162, 170–171. The quotation is from 155.

22. On the situation of the Protestant churches at this point, see J. R. C. Wright, *"Above Parties": The Political Attitudes of the German Protestant Church Leadership 1918–1933* (London: Oxford University Press, 1974), especially chaps. 5 and 6; the quotations are from 74, 89–90, 104. See also Scholder, *The Churches*, part 1, chaps. 8, 9, 11, 12, and part 2, chap. 1.

23. The number of pastors in the NSDAP is from Scholder, *The Churches*, 193. On the contested synod elections, see Wright, *"Above Parties"*, 92–98, and Scholder, *The Churches*, 214–216. For the Northeim episode, see William Sheridan Allen, *The Nazi Seizure of Power: The Experience of a Single German Town, 1922–1945*, rev. ed., (New York: Franklin Watts, 1984), 45–46. See also Kurt Nowak, *Evangelische Kirche und Weimarer Republik: Zum politischen Weg des deutschen Protestantismus zwischen 1918 und 1932* (Göttingen: Vandenhoeck and Ruprecht, 1981).

    For a portrait of one Protestant clergyman, a true believer, and of his involvement in the political events of the age, see Dietrich Kuessner, *Landesbischof Dr. Helmuth Johnsen 1891–1947: Nationaler Lutheraner und Bischof der Mitte in Brauschweig* (Büddenstedt: Evangelisches Pfarramt Offleben, private printing, 1982). For another portrait of an ex-front fighter, clergyman, and NSDAP activist, see Scholder, *The Churches*, 204.

24. For review and documentation of circumstances in the Protestant villages and towns, see Hamilton, *Who Voted*, 364–371, 373–382. For a portrait of the community notables in one Protestant town, Northeim, see Allen, *Nazi Seizure*, 84–87.

25. For supporting evidence, see Hamilton, *Who Voted*, 208–209, 375, 546–547, 607–608; see also Paul, *Aufstand*, 185–186. This paragraph restates, with somewhat greater caution, the points made in my earlier account (see note 1 of this chapter). Jürgen Falter and a co-worker, Torsten Schneider, have undertaken a systematic study of newspaper recommendations and explored the possible effects on voting (reported in *Hitlers Wähler*, 327–337). Among the findings reported by Falter, we have the following: in small towns (those with two thousand to twenty thousand inhabitants) roughly half of the newspapers reported no political direction, that is, declared themselves neutral; roughly two-thirds of the National Socialist newspapers were published in larger communities; some newspapers shifted "to the right" but perhaps not as many as was suggested in my earlier formulation. Schneider's sample, for example, found thirty-seven "liberal" newspapers in 1928. By the spring of 1932, roughly one-fifth of them had moved to the right, one-sixth described themselves as "neutral," and 5 percent no longer published. Going by their self-reports, three-fifths had kept the liberal faith. Falter reports a very modest but statistically significant correlation between a "rightist" newspaper climate and NSDAP voting. For further discussion, see note 31 following.

26. Falter, *Hitlers Wähler*, 317–324, especially 321, and 437. A somewhat stronger relationship between indebtedness and NSDAP support appears in urban settings, 437. See also, Jürgen Falter, "Economic Debts and Political Gains: Electoral Support for the Nazi Party in Agrarian and Commercial Sectors, 1928–1933," *Historische Sozialforschung* 17 (1992): 3–21.

27. On the relationship with size of farm, see Falter, *Hitler's Wähler*, 259–261, 437. An opposite relationship, positive coefficients between small average farm size and NSDAP voting, appears in heavily Catholic regions. Given the low overall support for the party in those areas, even this confirmation of the thesis would be of limited importance.

28. Falter et al., *Wahlen*, 73.

29. For discussions of the Catholic villages and towns, see Hamilton, *Who Voted*, 371–373, 382–385. A useful vignette, showing the strength of the personal influence factor is reported in Edward N. Peterson, *The Limits of Hitler's Power* (Princeton: Princeton University Press, 1969), 411. In the March 1933 Reichstag election, when the NSDAP vote was increasing almost everywhere, a capable and charismatic priest in Warmisried (Bavaria) managed to reduce their votes to less than half of the already low previous level. This experience, it should be noted, is exceptional. For another portrait of a Catholic village, see Walter Rinderle and Bernard Norling, *The Nazi Impact on a German Village* (Lexington: University Press of Kentucky, 1993).

30. For evidence and discussion of the late NSDAP gains in Catholic areas, see Falter, *Hitlers Wähler*, 176, 260–261. On the Zentrum-NSDAP negotiations, see Hamilton, *Who Voted*, 256–260, and Detlev Junker, *Die Deutsche Zentrumspartei und Hitler, 1932/1933* (Stuttgart: Ernst Klett Verlag, 1969), chap. 3.
    Although not dealing directly with German villages in the early 1930s, two studies provide suggestive findings from parallel experience elsewhere. Maurice Pinard gives a detailed account of the breakthrough of a third party to major party status; see his *The Rise of a Third Party: A Study in Crisis Politics* (Englewood Cliffs, N.J.: Prentice-Hall, 1971). Chap. 11 has a discussion of the facilitating conditions in the smaller communities. Guenter Golde gives a detailed study of the social characteristics of two adjacent

German villages, one Protestant, one Catholic, this based on work done in the early
1970s. It is the kind of study that should have been done in the 1930s or, at the latest,
in 1950 or 1960, before the surviving participants had disappeared from the scene. See
Golde's *Catholics and Protestants: Agricultural Modernization in Two German Villages* (New
York: Academic Press, 1975).

31. Falter reports (*Hitlers Wähler*, 327–339) the results of a systematic sample of newspapers (from 1928 and 1932) in communities of two thousand or more inhabitants. A majority of the ten Communist newspapers published in 1932 were issued in large cities
(those of one hundred thousand or more). Only a fifth of the thirty-four SPD papers
were published in the large cities. Approximately half of them came out of "middle cities," those of twenty to one hundred thousand. This sample showed the NSDAP (or related agencies) publishing a similar number of journals ($N = 30$) in 1932. The place of
publication of those journals was similar to the SPD pattern, roughly a quarter appearing in large cities and two-fifths in middle cities. My guess is that the NSDAP papers had
a fair-sized circulation in the smaller communities. They were either delivered to members there or were carried out by activists in the course of routine campaigning. Probably neither the KPD nor the SPD had comparable small town or rural "outreach."
The question of media impacts in these campaigns, unfortunately, has been seriously
neglected. The Falter-Schneider study is an important contribution but, as Falter makes
clear, much of the result must be viewed as preliminary. The newspapers studied include dailies and weeklies. Some information was not available, such as circulation
(many journals did not report that key information) and the location of a newspaper's
audience.
The political orientation of the newspapers is based on self-reports. In the course of
my research, I checked several of these against actual press performance and found
some to be inaccurate. Those reports, moreover, were dated, having been made some-
time between the fall of 1931 and the spring of 1932. Some newspapers would be hard
to classify as of July 1932. Many bourgeois (or conservative, or national) newspapers
recommended a range of rightist parties, seeing them as a coalition of forces that
would stand behind Hindenburg and Papen. On the limitations of the survey, see Falter, *Hitlers Wähler*, 328–329, and nn 384 and 387. The key source is: Deutsches Institut
für Zeitungskunde, *Handbuch der Deutschen Tagespresse*, 4th ed. (Berlin: Carl Duncker
Verlag, 1932); for the methodology of this survey see 6–8.

32. Accounts of newspaper treatments of the NSDAP and of their election recommendations
appear throughout Hamilton *Who Voted*: for Berlin, see 92–98, for Hamburg, 123–127,
and also the subject index; see also note 25 in this chapter. For a review of the Braunschweig experience, see Richard F. Hamilton, "Braunschweig 1932: Further Evidence
on the Support for National Socialism," *Central European History* 17 (1984): 3–36.
Many accounts have focused on the high level of NSDAP support in Schleswig-Holstein,
a region characterized by small farm agriculture and, overwhelmingly, Protestant
affiliations. Overlooked in this discussion is the high percentage of NSDAP supporters in
Kiel, the Provincial capital. The 46 percent share received there in July 1932 was the
highest of the thirty largest cities of the nation. It too was a city with a pro-NSDAP
newspaper, the *Kieler Zeitung*, described in one source as the most prestigious and important of the region; see Horst Seidel, *Kieler Zeitungs-Chronik: 200 Jahre Zeitung in der
Landeshauptstadt* (Kiel: n.p., n.d. [after 1949]).

33. The prototypical case (presumably) of the provocative tactic is the Pharus Hall Battle. In 1927, Joseph Goebbels, recently appointed as Gauleiter of Berlin, marched his S.A. units across the city into working-class Wedding to the Pharus Hall, where, as advertised, he would make a public address. A brawl ensued and as a consequence, so it is said, Goebbels had "all the headlines he wanted." I checked this claim in Berlin newspapers and found it to be misleading—the event gained very little attention. Subsequent scholars and popular writers were so taken by the "good story" that they overlooked the doubtful record of credibility of their source. See Hamilton, *Who Voted*, 99–100, 521–522 for details. For the most recent version, see Ralf Georg Reuth, *Goebbels* (Munich: Piper, 1990), 115–116. Although the key fact in this specific instance has been erroneously reported, the basic mechanism was practiced successfully on countless subsequent occasions. For portrayals of violence by the Berlin press, see Hamilton, *Who Voted*, 93–99.

34. For discussion of the motives of upper- and-upper-middle-class voters, see Hamilton, *Who Voted*, 393–419.

35. Allen, *Nazi Seizure*, 13–14, 24, 73, 108–109, 140. The national evidence showing real improvements, for some people, is reviewed in Hamilton, *Who Voted*, 376–377, 605 n45. Falter also picked up on this theme and has provided additional relevant evidence; see *Hitlers Wähler*, 243, nn301 and 302.

36. Falter, *Hitlers Wähler*, 230–266, 419 n420, and appendix tables, A7–A10. The quotation is from 238.

37. See Hamilton, *Who Voted*, 35, 57, 171, 264, 387–389. The best studies of Tory workers are those of Robert T. McKenzie and Allan Silver, *Angels in Marble* (Chicago: University of Chicago Press, 1968), and Eric Nordlinger, *Working Class Tories* (Berkeley: University of California Press, 1968)

38. See Hamilton, *Who Voted*, chap. 10. It is often thought, because of our training, that the social struggle in the Weimar period was one of workers versus bourgeoisie. But much of the actual struggle pitted one group of workers against another, the Socialist-Communist confrontations being the most obvious example. In some instances, workers joined with employers in efforts to keep the firms open, in opposition to leftist strike efforts. See ibid., 169–170, 287–308 (especially 295), 386–390.

39. See Falter, *Hitlers Wähler*, 198–230, 292–314. In my study of German cities, the poorest districts, those most likely to have had the greatest unemployment, provided the lowest percentages for the NSDAP; Hamilton, *Who Voted*, 111–112, 433–434.

40. The two early studies of middle-class SPD support are those of R. Blank, "Die soziale Zusammensetzung," and Robert Michels, 'Die deutsche Sozialdemokratie: I. Parteimitgliedschaft und soziale Zusammensetzung," *Archiv für Sozialwissenschaft und Sozialpolitik* 23 (1906): 471–556.

The lower-middle-class formula, clearly, does not begin to describe the actual results in Germany. One writer, recognizing the difficulty, has sought to make do with a substitute formula—that the NSDAP was "a catch-all party" see Thomas Childers, *The Nazi Voter: The Social Foundation of Fascism in Germany, 1919–1933* (Chapel Hill: University of North Carolina Press, 1983), 118, 127, 268. This new formula exchanges the spurious precision of the lower-middle-class claim for a nebulous statement (indifferent to number or proportions) about support from all classes. Although often cited, the statistical aspects of Childers's work are seriously flawed. Falter reports "so many statistical blunders that [Childers] virtually invalidates the results of his considerable computational efforts." The problems are reviewed in three detailed paragraphs of criticism. Falter's conclusion is that Childers's quantitative analysis "must be totally reworked before his conclusions can be incorporated into the body of accepted historical knowledge." See Falter's review of *The Nazi Voter* in the *Journal of Interdisciplinary History* 16 (1985): 138–140.

It comes as something of a surprise that Falter, in one summary statement, should find Childers's formulation "most adequate." Falter then claims that in terms of the backgrounds of its voters, the NSDAP, "already from 1930, stronger than any other large party of the time, bore a people's party character" (*Hitlers Wähler*, 289). That conclusion is based on work reported by Falter elsewhere, in "The First German Volkspartei: The Social Foundations of the NSDAP," in Rohe, *Elections, Parties and Political Traditions*, 53–81; for a slightly different German-language version, see "War die NSDAP die erste Deutsche Volkspartei?" in Michael Prinz and Rainer Zitelmann, eds., *Nationalsozialismus und Modernisierung* (Darmstadt: Wissenschaftlicher Buchgesellschaft, 1991), 21–47. Falter worked with a "catch-all party index" based on correlation coefficients of sixteen selected social variables. This procedure differs from most discussions, which typically focus on a single factor, that is, on the class bases of support. The values of the index range from 100 (least socially distinct) to 0 (the most distinct). As of 1928, when the NSDAP gained 2.6 percent of the votes cast, the party had the highest score, 93, well ahead of the next contender, the Conservatives (DNVP) with 83. In subsequent elections, the NSDAP lost its exceptional standing, falling to 83, 76, 77, and finally, in 1933, to 68. At that point, the DNVP had the highest score with 78. Four other parties matched the NSDAP with 69, followed by two at 65 and one at 62. The Communists were "more distinct" at all points, ranging from 50 to 54.

41. See Seymour Martin Lipset and Stein Rokkan, "Cleavage Structure, Party Systems, and Voter Alignments," in Lipset and Rokkan, eds., *Party Systems and Voter Alignments* (New York: Free Press, 1967), 1–64.

42. Sten S. Nilson, "Wahlsoziologische Probleme des Nationalsozialismus," *Zeitschrift für die gesamte Staatswissenschaft* 110 (1954): 295–311. See also Timothy Alan Tilton, *Nazism, Neo-Nazism, and the Peasantry* (Bloomington: Indiana University Press, 1975), chap. 2.

43. Hamilton, *Who Voted*, 450–451. Much of the scholarly literature assumes, without evidence, that "activists" (or "militants") have positive impacts. One should give consideration to the opposite possibility, however, that some "activists" might repel otherwise willing followers. The aggressive, hostile style, so favored by many on the Left (at least from the time of Marx), is clearly not intended to convince, as with a reasoned argument. It would be easy for many observers, on hearing such "appeals," to conclude that things might be worse under the direction of such people. The influence of such "negative" advocates might help to explain the modest predictive power of class, the existence of so much "false consciousness," and, in some measure at least, the "failure of the revolution." This line of argument points to the need for still another line of investigation, that of the psychology of the self-defeating activist. For a useful beginning, see Herbert E. Krugman, "The Role of Hostility in the Appeal of Communism in the United States," *Psychiatry* 16 (1953): 253–261.

44. For evidence showing the modest and diminishing class differences see Terry Nichols Clark and Seymour Martin Lipset, "Are Social Classes Dying?" *International Sociology* 6 (1991): 397–410. Three subsequent articles appeared in the same journal: for dissenting argument and evidence, see Mike Hout, Clem Brooks, and Jeff Manza, "The Persistence of Classes in Post-Industrial Societies," 8 (1993): 259–277; for a comment and respecification, Jan Pakulski, "The Dying of Class or of Marxist Class Theory?" 8 (1993): 279–292; and for further comment, Terry Nichols Clark, Seymour Martin Lipset, and Michael Rempel, "The Declining Political Significance of Social Class," 8 (1993): 293–316. For another dissent, see John H. Goldthorpe and Gordon Marshall, "The Promising Future of Class Analysis: A Response to Recent Critiques," *Sociology* 26 (1992): 381–400.

45. One may, of course, change the prediction as the need arises, that is, after each failure. For a partial listing of Marx's revisions, see Fritz J. Raddatz, *Karl Marx: Eine politische Biographie* (Hamburg: Hoffmann und Campe, 1975), 220–222, 303.

46. In 1961, Gerhard Lenski published a work entitled *The Religious Factor* (Garden City, N.Y.: Doubleday). He established therein, with data, the greater importance of religion (as against class) in predicting a wide range of attitudes and reported behaviors (293–294). This central finding has been neglected in much of the research and study done in later decades. Some subsequent evidence on the importance of the religious factor appears in Hamilton, *Class and Politics*, chap. 5; and Hamilton, *Restraining Myths: Critical Studies of U.S. Social Structure and Politics* (New York: Sage-Halsted-Wiley, 1975), 116–120.

   A comprehensive review of data for eight countries from 1970, one enquiring about "predictors of political party preference ranked according to relative strength in additive model," found the best predictor in six of the eight to be "parents' party," that variable in most cases holding a commanding lead over the next best predictor. In most instances church attendance and religious denomination placed high on the list of predictors. Only well down on the list and making only a modest contribution did one find a familiar class variable "occupation, head of household." From Ronald Inglehart, *The Silent Revolution: Changing Values and Political Styles among Western Publics* (Princeton: Princeton University Press, 1977), 246–249. This is not to suggest that those findings are the last word on the subject. There are difficulties with the samples and also, doubtlessly, difficulties with the definitions of class. Nevertheless, the study does provide an empirically based result one with a clear lesson. The study, however, would stand among the best available researches on this subject and therefore should figure prominently in our theorizing. For a review of the difficulties, see Richard F. Hamilton and James D. Wright, *The State of the Masses* (New York: Aldine, 1986), 95–100.

   An earlier comparative study shows the effects of three variables on partisanship, giving the percentage of variance explained by occupation, religion, and region. This analysis deals with fifteen countries, including, in addition to the Common Market countries of Inglehart's study, the Scandinavian countries, and three that were once linked to the British empire; see Richard Rose, ed., *Electoral Behavior: A Comparative Handbook* (New York: Free Press, 1974), 17. The contributors found that occupation outweighs religion in five nations: Sweden, Norway, Finland, Great Britain (a small difference), and Australia. Data for religion were not available for Denmark but one suspects it too would show the north European pattern. In the other nations, in eight of the total, religion was the stronger predictor. This result would indicate that some specification of the general claims about the importance of class is in order. The Rose volume does not contain information on parents' party, hence the primary socialization factor cannot be assessed there. For another important contribution, see Arend Lijphart, "Religious vs. Linguistic vs. Class Voting: The 'Crucial Experiment' of Comparing Belgium, Canada, South Africa, and Switzerland," *American Political Science Review* 73 (1979): 442–458.

One of the studies in the Rose volume provides a classic example of denigration and reconstitution of empirical findings. Discussing the Canadian case, the author states that "of all the indicators of origin in our survey, religion is the greatest source of polarization for political parties." One also learns that: "occupational class turns out to be a poor predictor of class-based voting in Canada." The final discussion of the "relations among variables," nevertheless, focuses on class and mentions religion only in passing. "None of this," one is told, "means that class cleavages, at least in the sense of economic differences, are not important. . . . Given the confused place of class in Canadian voting behavior, is it really worth the effort to continue to analyze voting data along this dimension? The answer is decidedly yes" (from Mildred A. Schwartz, "Canadian Voting Behavior," chap. 11 of Rose, *Electorial Behavoior*, see specifically 579, 592–593. The variance explained by occupation in Canada is 1.7 percent, that explained by religion is 8.0 percent (Rose, (*Electoral Behavior*, 17).

For reviews of evidence showing the continuing importance of the religious factor in Germany, see Karl Schmitt, "Religious Cleavages in the West German Party System: Persistence and Change, 1949–1987," in Rohe, *Elections, Parties, and Political Traditions*, 179–201. This chapter opens with a review and commentary on the failure of many historians and social scientists to deal with the religious factor. See also Juan Linz's discussion of religion, "Some Notes," 81–86, and Hans-Georg Wehling, ed., *Konfession— eine Nebensache? Politische, soziale und kulturelle Ausprägungen religiöser Unterschiede in Deutschland* (Stuttgart: Kohlhammer, 1984).

47. See Richard F. Hamilton, *Affluence and the French Worker in the Fourth Republic* (Princeton: Princeton University Press, 1967), chaps. 6, and 7, where, with data, this point is discussed in some detail. Even where some significant variation is found associated with the categories of a passive variable, with community size or income, for example, that result is likely to be spurious, hiding the effect of some active variable (political socialization, that is, family influence, being the most likely agency).

48. One may easily accept the logic of these limiting cases, but even here it is instructive to consider some fragmentary evidence. Upper- and upper-middle-class students at Bennington College in the 1930s, children of well-off Republican parents, shifted their political loyalties under the tutelage of liberal and leftist professors. The percentages indicating Socialist or Communist preferences increased with every year in the institution; see Theodore M. Newcomb, *Personality and Social Change: Attitude Formation in a Student Community* (New York: Dryden, 1943), 28.

Waldorf Astor, one of Britain's richest men, has been described as "not antipathetic" to "the movement for intense socialism" that grew during World War II. The *Observer,* a leading intellectual journal owned by the Astors and edited by Waldorf's son, reflected these sentiments; see Christopher Sykes, *Nancy: The Life of Lady Astor* (London: Collins, 1972), 451, 490, 508. Abby Rockefeller, daughter of David Rockefeller (head of

Chase Manhattan Bank), has been described as "a professed Marxist"; see Kathleen
Teltsch, "The Cousins: The Fourth Generation of Rockefellers," *New York Times Magazine,* 30 December 1984, 16, and, for more detail, Peter Collier and David Horowitz,
The Rockefellers: An American Dynasty (New York: Holt, Rinehart and Winston, 1976),
589–606.

49. There are obviously other kinds of mobilizing conditions. The cadres of the Labor Party in Norway (discussed by Nilson) did not have wartime origins. Nor were the efforts
of Cooperative Commonwealth Federation activists in Saskatchewan in the thirties and
forties generated out of wartime experience or resentments; see Seymour Martin Lipset, *Agrarian Socialism: The Cooperative Commonwealth Federation in Saskatchewan* (Berkeley: University of California Press, 1950).

50. For a review of relevant experience, see Hamilton, *Who Voted,* 444–447.

51. This kind of analysis is also possible in historical studies. For a brilliant, data-based reanalysis of the June Days in Paris of 1848, focused on the organizational histories and
dynamics of the two opposing "armies," both of which were recruited from the same
class, see Mark Traugott, *Armies of the Poor: Determinants of Working-Class Participation in
the Parisian Insurrection of June 1848* (Princeton: Princeton University Press, 1985). For
another outstanding study of agencies from the same period, see Peter Amann, *Revolution and Mass Democracy: The Paris Club Movement in 1848* (Princeton: Princeton University Press; 1975).

Chapter Five: The Lower-Middle-Class Thesis

1. Karl Marx and Frederick Engels, *The Manifesto of the Communist Party,* in the Marx-
Engels *Collected Works* (New York: International Publishers, 1975), vol. 6, 494. A
slightly different list of occupations appears there on 491. "The lower strata of the
middle class—the small tradespeople, shopkeepers, and retired tradesmen generally,
the handicraftsmen and peasants—all these sink gradually into the proletariat." These
are the formulations as they appear in the Engels-approved English translation. The
English expression "lower middle class" (494) appears as *die Mittelstände*—middle estates—in the German original, Marx-Engels *Werke* (Berlin: Dietz Verlag, 1964), vol. 4,
472. The phrase "the lower strata of the middle class" (491) appears in German as
"Die bisherigen kleinen Mittelstände," or the former small middle estates (*Werke*, vol.
4, 469).
Marx and Engels provided a wide range of "positions" on the petty bourgeoisie. For a
review, see Richard F. Hamilton, *The Bourgeois Epoch: Marx and Engels on Britain, France,
and Germany* (Chapel Hill: University of North Carolina Press, 1991) , chaps. 3, 4; for
a summary, see table 2, 161. The position stated here, judged by frequency of appearance, is the dominant or "consensus" position in subsequent literature.

2. Geoffrey Barraclough, "The Social Dimensions of Crisis," *Social Research* 39 (1972):
346. For early influential formulations of the position, see those of Theodor Geiger
and Harold Lasswell, cited in Chapter 4, note 3.

3. Karl Dietrich Bracher, *The German Dictatorship: The Origins, Structure, and Effects of National Socialism* (New York: Praeger, 1970), 47, 155, 159, 178, 203.

4. For a more extended review of what one might call the "literature of claims," a literature filled with false leads, see Hamilton, *Who Voted for Hitler?* (Princeton: Princeton
University Press, 1982), chap. 2.

5. Bracher, *German Dictatorship,* 47. Barraclough was restating Bracher on the developments in Bavaria and Schleswig-Holstein, but Bracher presented no evidence and, as will be seen, his statement does not accurately summarize the Bavarian experience.

6. See Mainrad Hagmann, *Der Weg ins Verhängnis: Reichstagswahlergebnisse 1919 bis 1933, besonders aus Bayern* (Munich: Michael Beckstein Verlag, 1946), 17–18; or Jürgen Falter, Thomas Lindenberger, and Siegfried Schumann, *Wahlen und Abstimmungen in der Weimarer Republik: Materialien zum Wahlverhalten 1919–1933* (Munich: C. H. Beck, 1986), 69–79. Those results appeared earlier, of course, in daily newspapers and in Bavarian and national government publications. See also Jürgen Falter, "Der Aufstieg der NSDAP in Franken bei den Reichstagswahlen 1924–1933," *German Studies Review* 9 (1986): 319–359.

A precautionary note: the criticisms made here apply only to the sources reviewed and discussed. Some recent histories, breaking with the handed-down view, now clearly indicate the importance of the religious factor and report the differentiated support for the NSDAP by class; see for example, Dietrich Orlow, *A History of Modern Germany: 1871 to Present,* 2d ed. (Englewood Cliffs, N.J.: Prentice-Hall, 1987), 187, and Mary Fulbrook, *The Divided Nation: A History of Germany 1918–1990* (New York: Oxford University Press, 1992), 55, 60.

7. Earlier Bracher reported the party's "largest electoral gains in *all* agrarian regions" (155, emphasis added). Catholic farm regions, as seen in the previous chapter, voted overwhelmingly for the Zentrum or for the Bavarian People's Party; the NSDAP had less success there than in urban working-class areas.

8. Every empirical analysis of the voting patterns points to the importance of the religious factor. See, for example, Heinz Herz, *Über Wesen und Aufgaben der politischen Statistik* (Waldenburg/Sachsen: E. Kästner, 1932), and Charles P. Loomis and J. Allan Beegle, "The Spread of German Nazism in Rural Areas," *American Sociological Review* 11 (1946): 724–734. The point was reviewed at length in the previous chapter; see especially the work of Mulert and of Falter cited there in notes 4 and 5.

9. Hamilton, *Bourgeois Epoch,* especially 161.

10. David Blackbourn, "The *Mittelstand* in German Society and Politics, 1871–1914," *Social History* 2 (1977): 409–433. The quotation is from 409. Blackbourn indicates skepticism about the received claim and devotes the entirety of the article—except for the last paragraph—to a review of evidence showing the complexity of mittelstand responses during the years indicated. In the final paragraph, however, without providing any evidence, he accepts the standard claim about the middle-class reaction after 1929. His explanation, to be sure, is different from that provided by Barraclough, Bracher, and others. He sees the middle-class response as a result of tactical failures. The Left had shunned the supposedly conservative mittelstand, "using it as an alibi for the failure of socialism," and the Right had taken the class for granted and had sought to exploit it politically (433). For book-length elaborations of the "axiomatic" position, see Annette Leppert-Fögen, *Die deklassierte Klasse: Studien zur Geschichte und Ideologie des Kleinbürgertums* (Frankfurt: Fischer Taschenbuch Verlag, 1974), and Berthold Franke, *Die Kleinbürger: Begriff, Ideologie. Politik* (Frankfurt: Campus, 1988).

11. Blackbourn, "*Mittelstand,*" 409.

12. Loomis and Beegle, "Spread of German Nazism." The correlations are found in table 3, 730; the quotation on 732.

13. For Bracher's analysis of election results, see his *Die Auflösung der Weimarer Republik* (Villingen: Ring-Verlag, 1964 [original, 1955]), 645–656.

14. For the Allen references, see William Sheridan Allen, *The Nazi Seizure of Power: The Experience of a Single German Town, 1922–1945* (New York: Franklin Watts, 1984), 140, also 296.

15. Hamilton, *Who Voted*, 33–34. The three books are: Rudolf Heberle, *Landbevölkerung und Nationalsozialismus: Eine soziologische Untersuchung der politischen Willensbildung in Schleswig-Holstein 1918 bis 1932* (Stuttgart: Deutsche Verlags-Anstalt, 1963); Jeremy Noakes, *The Nazi Party in Lower Saxony 1921–1933* (London: Oxford University Press, 1971); and Heinrich August Winkler, *Mittelstand. Demokratie und Nationalsozialismus: Die politische Entwicklung von Handwerk und Kleinhandel in der Weimarer Republik* (Cologne: Kiepenheuer and Witsch, 1972). The Heberle and Noakes books are used and discussed at many points in Hamilton, *Who Voted*; for a comment there on the limitations of the Winkler book, see 498.

16. From Seymour Martin Lipset, "The Revolt against Modernity," in Per Torsvik, ed., *Mobilization, Center-Periphery Structures and Nation-Building* (Bergen: Universitetsforlaget, 1981), 451–500. This quotation and the following one appear on 480. The article also appears in Lipset's *Consensus and Conflict: Essays in Political Sociology* (New Brunswick, N.J.: Transaction Books, 1985), chap. 7. The quotations appear there on 276.

17. Mattei Dogan, "Political Cleavage and Social Stratification in France and Italy," in Seymour M. Lipset and Stein Rokkan, eds., *Party System and Voter Alignments: Cross-National Perspectives* (New York: Free Press, 1967), 129–195. Dogan's discussion, "The Two Faces of the Petty Bourgeoisie," appears on 150–159; the passages cited by Lipset appear on 159.

   The survey reporting the 1956 voting of French Independents appears in Lipset's *Political Man* (Garden City, N.Y.: Doubleday, 1960), 225. The 43 percent figure just given here combines the support for Poujade, de Gaulle, and the Independents (Conservatives) in order to approximate Dogan's combination "anti-Republican or Poujadist." The percentages—respectively, 19, 3, and 21—are calculated on a base of 81 respondents. Support for de Gaulle or the Independents, it should be noted, did not necessarily indicate "anti-Republican" sentiment.

   It might be pointed out too that Lipset himself recognized that the various 1930s fascisms could not be seen as a mere "expression of the petty bourgeoisie" (as shown in chap. 5 of *Political Man*, entitled " 'Fascism'—Left, Right, and Center"). Additional evidence on the disparate social bases of fascist movements may be found in Walter Laqueur, ed., *Fascism: A Reader's Guide* (Berkeley: University of California Press, 1976), especially chap. 1, Juan J. Linz's sweeping review entitled "Some Notes toward a Comparative Study of Fascism in Sociological Historical Perspective." Another important data-laden source is Stein Ugelvik Larsen, Bernt Hagtvet, and Jan Petter Myklebust, eds., *Who Were the Fascists: Social Roots of European Fascism* (Bergen: Universitetsforlaget, 1980). Again, Linz's contribution to that volume, "Political Space and Fascism as a Late-Comer" (153–189), is especially important on the question of the social bases. Jens Petersen has reviewed claims and evidence from the Italian context. Adriano Tilgher, late in 1919, first applied the lower-middle-class thesis, invoking all the standard themes. There too, the "conclusions" ran well in advance of any serious evidence. Petersen refers to those widely accepted notions as "rather intuitive insights." The worsened psychological and material condition of some middle-class groups, he reports, has often been described, but, in a footnote, he mentions that the literature on the problems of the Italian middle classes "is meager." The data he presents point in different directions. Students and veterans were heavily represented among Mussolini's followers. See Petersen, "Wählerverhalten und soziale Basis des Faschismus in Italien zwischen 1919 und 1928," in Wolfgang Schieder, ed., *Faschismus als soziale Bewegung: Deutschland und Italien im Vergleich*, 2nd ed. (Göttingen: Vandenhoeck and Ruprecht, 1983), 119–156, especially 140–141, 145, 149–151, n42. See also Hamilton, *Who Voted*, 454–457. For a dataless application of standard lower-middle-class arguments in connection with Italian fascism, see Alan Cassels, *Fascist Italy* (New York: Crowell, 1985), 34–35.

In Canada, the Social Credit movement, which governed in Alberta from 1935 to 1971, was portrayed as another instance of the petty bourgeois tendency, the view argued in the leading work on the subject, C. B. Macpherson's *Democracy in Alberta* (Toronto: University of Toronto Press, 1953). A recent investigation, by Edward Bell, reports that "no study has provided empirical evidence substantiating the received claim." See Bell, "The Petite Bourgeoisie and Social Credit: A Reconsideration," *Canadian Journal of Sociology* 14 (1989): 45–65, and his book *Social Classes and Social Credit in Alberta* (Montreal and Kingston: McGill-Queen's University Press, 1993).

18. This is not to say the conclusions are erroneous, only that in Dogan's chapter they are unsupported. Independent businessmen in France in 1956 did give considerably greater support to the Poujade movement than did any other segment, but that is perhaps to be expected for a *Union de défense des commerçants et des artisans*. More of those businessmen supported the Socialists and Communists than Poujade; see Lipset, *Political Man*, 225.

19. Ralf Dahrendorf, *Society and Democracy in Germany* (Garden City, N.Y.: Doubleday, 1967), 93. This is a translation of the German original published in 1965. The Poujade data referred to in the previous footnote shows only one petty bourgeois in five displaying the "expected mentality." The rest, the "deviants, outsiders, marginal figures, and strangers" supported parties of the Right, center, or Left.

20. Many people, following the received assumptions, assume significant differences in the outlooks of independent businessmen (the classical petty bourgeoisie) and blue-collar workers. For an empirical assessment of the independent businessmen and their outlooks that does not support the conventional assumptions, see Hamilton, *Restraining Myths* (New York: Sage-Halsted-Wiley, 1975), chap. 2. Ronald Inglehart's study of "materialist" values, based on samples from nine European Community nations from 1976 to 1979, found a difference of three percentage points between younger self-employed businessmen and the equivalent manual workers. In the middle-aged and older categories the differences between the two class segments were only one point. Ronald Inglehart, "Post-Materialism in an Environment of Insecurity," *American Political Science Review* 75 (1981): 893.

21. Dahrendorf, *Society and Democracy*, 93–94.

22. A major effort of this kind was already in existence. Juan Linz's 950-page dissertation had appeared six years prior to publication of the original German-language edition of Dahrendorf's essays. Based on surveys from the early postwar period, it contained a vast amount of information relevant to the "class mentalities" question. It is not men-

tioned in Dahrendorf's volume. See Juan J. Linz Storch de Gracia, "The Social Bases of West German Politics," unpublished dissertation, Columbia University, 1959. Linz shows one-third of lower-white-collar men supported the Social Democrats (527). A majority of those lower-white-collar men came from blue-collar families. For that subset, the Social Democratic support was 43 percent (535).

23. Dahrendorf, *Society and Democracy,* 96, 97-98, 99–100. A comprehensive investigation of white-collar employee attitudes was undertaken in West Germany in the summer of 1961 by the German Trade Union Federation. Dahrendorf's claims gain little support in those findings. Those results, unfortunately, have not received any serious attention in German social science publications. See the report by the Institut für angewandte Sozialwissenschaft, "Angestellte und Gewerkschaft" (Bad Godesberg, 1964). For a review of lower-middle-class political orientations based on evidence from the United States, see Hamilton *Restraining Myths,* chaps. 2 and 3.

24. Michael H. Kater, *The Nazi Party: A Social Profile of Members and Leaders, 1919–1945* (Cambridge: Harvard University Press, 1983), 184. See also my review of Kater's book, in *American Historical Review* 89 (1984): 469–470.

25. Kater, *Nazi Party,* 185.

26. The reference is to Arno J. Mayer, "The Lower Middle Class as Historical Problem," *Journal of Modern History* 47 (1975): 409–436. The quotations in the two following paragraphs are from 422, 423, 426, 428, 431–432, 436.

27. *Mesguin,* a French word, means shabby, paltry, mean, niggardly, illiberal. A similar portrait is provided by Mihaly Vajda, *Fascism as a Mass Movement* (London: Allison and Busby, 1976). It too is dateless; it too depends on the agreement of "authorities." Antonio Gramsci, for example, is quoted: he wrote that fascism "made use of and organised the irresponsibility of the petty bourgeoisie, as well as its cowardice and stupidity" (29).

28. The argument is not fully explicated but would develop as follows. Elites, in normal times, treat the petty bourgeoisie with sovereign contempt. They show no decency, humanity, or good will. In time of need, however, for purely tactical purposes, they make a remarkable about-face and lavish praise on persons formerly treated with contempt. The elites must be ultimately cynical; the lower middle class, in contrast, must be ultimately gullible. The dynamics are unclear. Does the lower middle class not recognize the cynical practice? Are their memories so short? Or are they so psychologically bound, all of them, that they feel "compelled" to accept such treatment? There is, of course, an alternative—that Mayer's scenario does not have even surface plausibility.

29. For an assessment of his performance in one rare research effort, see Jane Caplan, "Theories of Fascism: Nicos Poulantzas as Historian," *History Workshop* 3 (spring 1977): 83–100.

30. Max Scheler, *Ressentiment* (New York: Free Press of Glencoe, 1961) . For readers unfamiliar with this work, a quotation may give something of its flavor: "The *ressentiment* of cripples or of people of subnormal intelligence is a well-known phenomenon. Jewish *ressentiment,* which Nietzsche rightly designates as enormous, finds double nourishment" (50–51).

31. Another book that comes with specific page references is Mayer's own *Dynamics of Counterrevolution in Europe, 1870–1956* (New York: Harper and Row, 1971,). Rather surprisingly, Mayer does not refer to 41–42, those pages containing his discussion of the

petite bourgeoisie. Perhaps it is because another example of careless scholarship appears there, on 42. Mayer has taken over the *Manifesto* description of the lumpenproletariat, all the relevant terms—"dangerous class," "social scum," and "bribed tool of reactionary intrigue"—and applied them to the petite bourgeoisie. On the same page, Mayer refers to some unnamed "social and behavioral scientists" who, he tells us, "missed the ultimate interconnection of these insecure and vulnerable social layers with the superordinate cartel of anxiety." For the Marx-Engels text, see the *Collected Works*, vol. 6, 494.

32. Early in the article, Mayer reports that "the lower middle class generates and keeps generating a separate culture, ethos, life-style, and world view" (411). He lists, without any supporting references, fourteen characteristics. In the same connection, Mayer declares that, although perhaps lacking class consciousness, the lower middle class "does have a sharply defined class awareness." For support here, one is referred to Anthony Giddens, *The Class Structure of the Advanced Societies* (London: Hutchinson, 1973), 111–114, 185. Only two paragraphs (on 111) prove relevant to the claim and they do not support Mayer's unambiguous empirical declaration. Giddens provides a general hypothetical statement as to how events are likely to be related, his key sentence reading: "We may say that, in so far as class is a structured phenomenon, there will tend to exist a common awareness and acceptance of similar attitudes and beliefs, linked to a common style of life, among the members of the class." Giddens's page 185 repeats the "class awareness" claim, this time referring us to "a number of fairly recent . . . studies" that have "demonstrated" the point. Many of the by now familiar documentation problems appear also with respect to his sources.

A variant reading of the same tradition is provided by Jonathan M. Wiener, "Marxism and the Lower Middle Class: A Response to Arno Mayer," *Journal of Modern History* 18 (1976): 666–671. Wiener reports, erroneously, that Marx "sees the petty bourgeoisie consistently struggling against the forces of reaction (however ineffectively or half-heartedly), in alliance with the proletariat" (668). The principal claim of the *Manifesto*, it will be remembered, was that of reaction—the class was trying to "roll back the wheel of history."

33. One of Mayer's pageless book references is to my *Class and Politics in the United States* (New York: Wiley, 1972). But there, on 206, after a discussion and presentation of relevant evidence, one will find the following conclusion: "In short, the familiar lines of analysis about the small independent businessmen simply do not apply to them." An earlier article, dealing with many of the same themes, showed roughly half of U.S. clerical and sales employees identifying themselves as working class, a finding that should give pause to those arguing an across-the-board fear of proletarianization. See Richard Hamilton, "The Marginal Middle Class: A Reconsideration," *American Sociological Review* 31 (April 1966): 192–199.

In 1941, Alfred Winslow Jones published a commendable study, investigating attitudes toward property in a moment of "acute social and political conflict." This rarely cited study also provides no support for the received claims. See Jones, *Life, Liberty, and Property* (Philadelphia: Lippincott, 1941). For a brief review, see Hamilton, *Restraining Myths*, 61–62.

34. The quotations are from Irving Louis Horowitz, *C. Wright Mills: An American Utopian* (New York: Free Press, 1983), 249–252.

35. Christopher Lasch, *The True and Only Heaven: Progress and Its Critics* (New York: Norton, 1991), 17. The work differs substantially in emphasis from the others considered here in that all the negative claims appear on that one page. The remainder of the work focuses on the lower-middle-class virtues. Lasch does not provide specific references to support either set of claims, that is, the positive or negative ones. Instead, he has a general "Bibliographical Essay" (533–569). If any of the works listed there provide evidence showing the distinctive lower-middle-class vices, e.g., envy, resentment, and servility, he could have cited author, title, and, where necessary, appropriate pages.

36. For a particularly striking example involving both distortion and derogation, see the case reviewed in Hamilton *Who Voted*, 471. For an important critical discussion of the entire syndrome, see Michael Lerner, "Respectable Bigotry," *American Scholar* 38 (1969): 606–617.

37. The ORC data are reported in Seymour Martin Lipset and William Schneider, *The Confidence Gap: Business. Labor, and Government in the Public Mind* (New York: Free Press, 1983), 78, 83, 88. For the later results, see Lipset's "Unions in Decline," *Public Opinion* 9, 3 (September–October 1986): 52–54.

38. These figures are taken from Wolfram Fischer, "Auf dem Wege zum Kleinbürger?" *Frankfurter Allgemeine Zeitung*, 24 July 1982.

39. James J. Sheehan, "National Socialism and German Society: Reflections on Recent Research," *Theory and Society* 13 (1984): 851–868. The quotations are from 852–853.

40. See the brief biography by Paul Trappe, "Theodor Geiger," *International Encyclopedia of the Social Sciences* (New York: Crowell Collier and Macmillan, 1968), vol. 6, 83–85.

41. See Richard F. Hamilton, "Braunschweig 1932: Further Evidence on the Support for National Socialism," *Central European History* 17 (1984): 1–36. The figures reported appear on 10. Hitler received 42.4 percent of the valid votes cast in the city on that date.

42. Fritz Hasselhorn, *Wie wählte Göttingen? Wahlverhalten und die soziale Basis der Parteien in Göttingen 1924–1933* (Göttingen: Vandenhoeck and Ruprecht, 1983), from tables 18 and 20.

43. See the articles by Blank and Neisser, Michels, and Mulert (cited in Chapter 4, notes 9, 40, and 5, respectively).

44. Although the groundless claims about the lower middle class continue to appear and to be given credence, there are of course exceptions. Thomas Childers provides a more differentiated picture in *The Nazi Voter: The Social Foundations of Fascism in Germany, 1919–1933* (Chapel Hill: University of North Carolina Press, 1983), discussed earlier in Chapter 4, note 40. See also, for another example, Stanley Suval, *Electoral Politics in Wilhelmine Germany* (Chapel Hill: University of North Carolina Press, 1985), chap. 11. Christopher Lasch, although still giving credence to many of the received claims, has made a major shift in emphasis. Although National Socialism and fascism are mentioned at many points in his book, *The True and Only Heaven*, none of those discussions argues the conventional claim about lower-middle-class voting tendencies.

45. Thomas Childers, ed., *The Formation of the Nazi Constituency 1919–1933* (Totowa, N.J.: Barnes and Noble, 1986), 2. Another work neglected is Henry A. Turner's *German Big Business and the Rise of Hitler* (New York: Oxford University Press, 1985); although cited at several points, no report was made of its principal findings. See my review of Childers's volume in *American Historical Review* 93 (1988): 1072–1074. Alan Bullock, a

leading specialist, described Turner's book as "the most impressive and original contribution to the study of Nazism in years," (*New York Review of Books*, 7 November 1985). Jane Caplan, one of the original reviewers of *Who Voted*, reports that the work "devastates the plausibility of much of the received literature" dealing with the lower-middle-class thesis. In the end, however, she claims to find support for that thesis in the work of Childers and Kater. Her initial conclusion reads: "What we have, then, is neither a class party nor a stable *Volkspartei*, but a doughnut-like combination of the two." This is referred to as a "palliative conclusion." Caplan's final judgment is that "the traditional wisdom about the social location of support for National Socialism was not wide of the mark, even if it was unproven." See her "Class and Class Structure: Recent Works on the Sociology of National Socialism," *Queen's Quarterly* 92 (1985): 66–76; the quotations are from 74 and 75. Caplan was a contributor to the Childers's collection, and her final conclusion there gives credence both to the Childers's formula and to the lower-middle-class argument—the NSDAP had become "a relatively broad-based protest party" although "it was most durably located on a lower-middle-class base, the old petty bourgeoisie of town and country" (*Formation*, 199). Caplan's final note refers to *Who Voted* but without indication of its major findings.

I do not find support for the received thesis in either Childers's or Kater's work. See my review of the Kater volume (cited here in note 24). The statistical analysis in Childers's work, it will be remembered, is severely flawed (see Chapter 4, note 40).

46. Thomas Childers, "Who, Indeed, Did Vote for Hitler?" *Central European History* 17 (1984): 49, and Peter Manstein, *Die Mitglieder und Wähler der NSDAP 1919–1933* (Frankfurt am Main: Peter Lang, 1988), 175–178.

47. Of all the cities I visited, Hamburg provided the richest array of evidence. A brief study of the 1930 election showed, in a map, the pattern for the city's precincts. It indicated substantial NSDAP strength in the well-off districts. For anyone knowing the city, the pattern "was such that one could hardly miss it." See *Who Voted*, 122–123. The brief study appeared in a local municipal publication but, clearly, received little attention; see *Aus Hamburgs Verwaltung und Wirtschaft* 8, 5 (1931): 177.

48. See the discussion of this point in Chapter 4, note 3. An example of this revisionism appears in Geoff Eley, "What Produces Fascism: Pre-Industrial Traditions or a Crisis of the Capitalist State?" chap. 10 of his *From Unification to Nazism: Reinterpreting the German Past* (Boston: Allen and Unwin, 1986). Commenting on Larsen et al., *Who Were The Fascists*, Eley writes that "while the aggregate effect of around 800 pages is hard to assess, it seems to confirm the received assumptions. There have been attempts to suggest that other social groups were ultimately more important in the fascists' makeup, or that class was less important than 'generational revolt.' But on the evidence of *Who Were the Fascists* the fascist movements' social composition seems to have been disproportionately weighted toward the petite bourgeoisie" (263). Confirmation of Eley's "seems to confirm" claim would require specific page references. The well-documented Juan Linz article contained in Larsen et al. (153–189) does not confirm that claim; it points to a wide diversity of social bases. It also points to, and documents, the importance of World War I and of the subsequent revolutions (158–161, 173–176). Eley passes over Linz's contributions with this odd comment: "Personally, though there are many valuable insights to be culled discretely from his work, I find

[his] general argument obscure, inconclusive and confusing in the density of its culti-
vated empirical complexity" (278, n3).

49. See Childers, "The Middle Classes and National Socialism," chap. 11 in David
Blackbourn and Richard J. Evans, eds., *The German Bourgeoisie: Essays on the Social History of the German Middle Class from the Late Eighteenth to the Early Twentieth Century*
(London: Routledge, 1991). The passages quoted are from 322 and 333. For the Berlin
and Hamburg evidence, see Hamilton, *Who Voted*, 82, 112. This ground was covered in
a previous discussion; see my reply to Childers's comments, in *Central European History*
17 (1984): 77. The "unprecedented social breadth" claim assumes a knowledge of the
social bases of German parties in the nineteenth and early twentieth centuries. That
claim too comes without support.

50. In his introduction to *The German Bourgeoisie*, David Blackbourn reported that the new
research of Hamilton, Falter, and Childers "has enlarged the picture" but that the "importance of the lower middle class to the mass base of Nazism is undeniable" (29). Another example is provided by Peter Baldwin, "Social Interpretations of Nazism:
Renewing a Tradition," *Journal of Contemporary History* 25 (1990): 5–37. He recognizes
the doubts and the new evidence on the subject, but passes quickly to a reaffirmation
of the previous truths—"The petty bourgeois fascism of the pre-power phase was
gradually conquered by the fascism of big capital. . . . Coming close to power on the
backs of the lower middle class" (13). The article is poorly argued and, although richly
embellished with citations, is poorly documented. See also Heinz-Gerhard Haupt,
"Mittelstand und Kleinbürgertum in der Weimarer Republik: Zu Problemen und Per-
spektiven ihrer Erforschung," *Archiv für Sozialgeschichte* 26 (1986) : 217–238. In his first
sentence, Haupt assures readers of the truth of the standard claim ("das bis heute gül-
tige Bild vom Mittelstand," the picture of the middle class, valid up to the present day).
Toward the end of his essay, he recommends that future research should pay more attention to "the political heterogeneity" in the class (236). Manfred Kuechler also bypasses the dual problems of present and absent evidence to reach his conclusion: "In
essence, then, there is no need for a major revision of the traditional thesis that the
lower middle classes provided the major support base for the Nazis," in Kuechler's
"The NSDAP Vote in the Weimar Republic: An Assessment of the State-of-the-Art in
View of Modern Electoral Research," *Historische Sozialforschung* 17 (1992): 22–52.

51. The major theses reviewed to this point, Weber's and the lower-middle-class position,
contain opposite constructions. Weber and his followers assign a powerful role to religion, despite the absence of compelling evidence. Those arguing the lower-middle-
class case pay little attention to religion, effectively assigning it a negligible influence,
despite unambiguous evidence of its importance.

52. Arno Mayer, reacting to the Los Angeles riots, wrote the *New York Times* to alert that
newspaper's readers to "the spiraling frustrations and resentments of a vast but powerless lower middle class that spans the full ethnic spectrum" (8 May 1992). That sentence, by my count, contains five groundless judgments of quantity.

Chapter Six: Michel Foucault

1. Michel Foucault, *Discipline and Punish: The Birth of the Prison*, trans. Alan Sheridan (New
York: Vintage, 1979), 139. The work was first published in France as *Surveiller et punir:
Naissance de la prison* (Paris: Gallimard, 1975). The first American edition was issued by

Pantheon, 1978. The literature on Foucault is enormous. For an overview, a portrait of the man and his works, see James Miller, *The Passion of Michel Foucault* (New York: Simon and Schuster, 1993).

2. Foucault, *Discipline,* 14–17. For a useful overview of the French experience, covering much of the same ground as Foucault but reaching markedly different conclusions, see Gordon Wright, *Between the Guillotine and Liberty: Two Centuries of the Crime Problem in France* (New York: Oxford University Press, 1983).

3. For a detailed scholarly account, see Dale K. Van Kley, *The Damiens Affair and the Unraveling of the "Ancien Regime," 1750–1770* (Princeton: Princeton University Press, 1984).

4. Foucault, *Discipline,* 6–7. Many reviews of Foucault's book reported an overall change from one kind of punishment to another instead of the appropriate focus—punishments associated with specific offenses.

5. Franklin L. Ford, *Political Murder: From Tyrannicide to Terrorism* (Cambridge: Harvard University Press, 1985), 223.

6. Like the swallow and the prediction of summer, the "sample" reported here consists of a single case. The appropriate procedure would be to review the reactions in all relevant cases found in, say, the eighteenth and nineteenth centuries. Eight attempts at assassination were made during the reign of Louis Philippe (1830–1848). At least six attempts were made on the life of Queen Victoria and two on the life of Kaiser Wilhelm I. Empress Elisabeth of Austria, wife of Franz Joseph, was killed by an anarchist. Relevant cases may be found also in Russia and the United States.

7. Van Kley, *Damiens,* 94.

8. Ford, *Political Murder,* 223.

9. Foucault, *Discipline,* 249, and Alan Sheridan, *Michel Foucault: The Will to Truth* (London: Tavistock, 1980), 135–136. A later publication contains an interview with Foucault, who again treats the panopticon as an actuality rather than as a rejected plan. He declared that the panopticon "has in fact been widely employed since the end of the eighteenth century." His two interviewers, both enthusiastic supporters, raised no question on this point. See Michel Foucault, *Power/Knowledge: Selected Interviews and Other Writings, 1972–1977* (Brighton, England,: Harvester Press, 1980), chap. 8, "The Eye of Power," 148.

10. Jeremy Bentham, *Works,* ed. John Bowring (Edinburgh: William Tait, 1843), vol. 4, 171–172, and, Harry Elmer Barnes and Negley K. Teeters, *New Horizons in Criminology,* 3d ed. (Englewood Cliffs, N.J.: Prentice-Hall, 1959), 335.

11. L. J. Hume, "Bentham's Panopticon: An Administrative History," *Historical Studies* 15 (1973): 703–721, and 16 (1974): 36–55. Some brief discussion appears also in Mary P. Mack, *Jeremy Bentham: An Odyssey of Ideas* (New York: Columbia University Press, 1963), 204, 367, 403–404. Bentham offered to build and manage a panopticon in Paris. The proposal was well received in the new National Assembly but, Mack reports, "no prison was built" (417). For a detailed review of the history, see Janet Semple, *Bentham's Prison: A Study of the Panopticon Penitentiary* (Oxford: Clarendon, 1993).

12. Barnes and Teeters, *New Horizons,* 335n; for the New York experience, see their second edition (1951), 389–390. For an interesting sociological account, see James B. Jacobs, *Statesville: The Penitentiary in Mass Society* (Chicago: University of Chicago Press, 1977). The modified Bentham architectural plan receives little attention there. The diverse

seesaw history of "discipline" reported by Jacobs shows little correspondence with Foucault's predictions. Three of the four Statesville units, incidentally, were removed in the early 1980s and replaced with other types of structures. The fourth unit, because of some earlier expensive renovation, could not be similarly replaced.

13. Giuseppe di Gennaro ed., *Prison Architecture: An International Survey of Representative Closed Institutions and Analysis of Current Trends in Prison Design* (London: Architectural Press, 1975), 18–19, 29–30; the generally used Auburn plan is described (with floor plan and picture) on 20.

14. On Faucher, see *La grande encyclopédie*, (Paris: Lamirault, 1886–1902), vol. 17, 38–40. The account in the *Biographie universelle*, (Paris: Louis Vivès, 1843–1865), 2d ed., vol. 13, 414–416, suggests his work on prisons was a minor passing interest. It is again a puzzling performance. Prisons everywhere have rules; they are referred to in all texts and in all major sources. Why does Foucault present an unrealized plan as opposed to one of the many de facto realities?

Gordon Wright has reviewed the waves of attention and neglect regarding prisons in France. One prison inspector "grumbled in 1846 that everybody in France had his own ideas on the subject and was thinking of writing a brochure about it." A prison doctor "counted up the works on prisons published between 1818 and 1840 and reached a total of 142." In a brief footnote reference, Wright, commenting on the 1844 article, refers to "the alarmist reaction of the journalist Léon Faucher." (*Between*, 48–49, 230 n2). A book-length study of French prisons makes only three fleeting references to Faucher (there referred to as a "penal critic" and a "reformer"). All three references are to an 1844 article; no mention is made of the 1838 book. See Patricia O'Brien, *The Promise of Punishment: Prisons in Nineteenth-Century France* (Princeton: Princeton University Press, 1982), 46, 297, 301. O'Brien has high praise for Foucault but makes only a few passing references to him and his work (and several of them note deficiencies). There is no mention of Bentham or the panopticon in O'Brien's book. She writes that "the French eventually adopted the modified Auburn system of confinement" (23).

Karl Marx makes a brief mention of Faucher in the initial pages of his *Class Struggles in France*. His account of the man and his activity, like Foucault's, is not quite accurate. See Richard Hamilton, *The Bourgeois Epoch: Marx and Engels on Britain, France, and Germany* (Chapel Hill: University of North Carolina Press, 1991), 55–56, 92.

15. Michael Ignatieff, *A Just Measure of Pain: The Penitentiary in the Industrial Revolution, 1750–1850* (New York: Pantheon, 1978). On Howard and the reform effort, see 47–79.

16. Ibid., 80–84, 91–94.

17. Ibid., 98–108. For the rejection of Bentham's plan, see 109–113.

18. Ibid., 170–171, 200–204. A small detail: Ignatieff writes that the panopticon design "exerted a profound influence on the circular forms adopted for Millbank penitentiary" (113), but in a later description, he reports it consisted of seven pentagons, linked blocks apparently. "In theory," Ignatieff writes, "the prison was modeled on Bentham's inspection principle, but in practice the prison was a maze of endless corridors" (171). The penultimate paragraph of Ignatieff's book addresses a theme raised by Foucault. He rejects the latter's notion that the social sciences "exclusively define the modes of public perception or that they have driven from our cognitive field any possibility of alternative vision." Foucault's own work, he writes, "is a triumphant demon-

stration of the falsity of his own fatalism" (220). His final paragraph, curiously, treats Foucault's history as accurate even though Ignatieff's own account demonstrates its falsity.

19. Foucault, *Discipline,* 208–209.

20. I am indebted to David Shewchuk for the observations contained in this and the following four paragraphs. They appeared in an unpublished and undated seminar paper, "A Look at Foucault's Use of Military History." For the discussion of France and Prussia, see Hans Delbrück, *History of the Art of War within the Framework of Political History,* vol. 4, "The Modern Era," trans. Walter J. Renfroe, Jr. (Westport, Conn.: Greenwood Press, 1975), 390–391. This volume was first published, in German, in 1920.

21. Delbrück reviews the caracole in *History,* vol. 4, book 2, chap. 1, "The Transformation of Knights into Cavalry," see especially 123–125 and, for his discussion of the artillery, 284–285, 407–408. Two other useful sources are those of Richard A. Preston and Sydney F. Wise, *Men in Arms: A History of Warfare and Its Interrelationships with Western Society,* 4th ed. (New York: Holt, Rinehart and Winston, 1979), chaps. 7 and 9, particularly 108–112 for their discussion of the caracole, and R. Ernest Dupuy and Trevor N. Dupuy, *The Encyclopedia of Military History* (New York: Harper and Row, 1970), 457.

22. Brent Nosworthy, *The Anatomy of Victory: Battle Tactics 1689–1763* (New York: Hippocrene, 1990), xvi, xv. For a comprehensive treatment of the Prussian military achievement, see Delbrück, *History,* vol. 4, book 3, and Gordon A. Craig, *The Politics of the Prussian Army, 1640–1945* (London: Oxford University Press, 1955), chap. 1; for a brief review of the shift away from eighteenth-century discipline, see 27. See also Preston and Wise, *Men in Arms,* chap. 12; Dupuy and Dupuy, *Encyclopedia,* 732–737; Trevor N. Dupuy, *The Evolution of Weapons and Warfare* (New York: Bobbs-Merrill, 1980), chaps. 17, 18; and Alfred Vagts, *A History of Militarism,* rev. ed. (n.p.: Meridian, 1959), chap. 4.

Some of the moves toward more flexible military formations came earlier. General Braddock was routed by irregular French and Indian forces in 1755 near Fort Duquesne. On 19 April 1775, General Gage marched his disciplined units to Lexington and Concord. American irregulars inflicted serious losses on the return march. The odds against the disciplined units had so shifted that no further marches were attempted. In a second engagement, on 17 June 1775 at Breed's Hill, the British gained the ground but suffered far heavier losses than the Americans. For brief reviews, see Walter Millis, *Arms and Men: A Study in American Military History* (New York: Putnam, 1956), chap. 1, and Preston and Wise, *Men in Arms,* chap. 11.

Discussions of those other disciplined armies may be found in Dupuy and Dupuy, *Encyclopedia*: on Byzantium, 184–188; on Genghis Khan, 340–345 (the quotation is from 340).

Many of the British reverses in the nineteenth century were due to the continued use of the old disciplined procedures. For examples, see Byron Farwell, *Queen Victoria's Little Wars* (New York: Harper and Row, 1972), and Denis Judd, *Someone Has Blundered: Calamities of the British Army in the Victorian Age* (London: Arthur Barker, 1973).

23. Foucault, *Discipline,* 162–163, 316 n11. See J. W. Fortesque, *A History of the British Army* (London: Macmillan, 1935), vol. 1, 362–369, and Delbrück, *History,* vol. 4, 302.

24. On the flintlock musket, see Delbrück, *History,* vol. 4, 270–271, and Nosworthy, *Anatomy,* 4–5, and, for discussion of its use in Steinkirk, 41. See also Dupuy and Dupuy, *En-*

cyclopedia: on the flintlock, 523; on the rifle and skirmishers in the Braddock episode, 664–665, 706, 734. Preston and Wise review the flintlock and the linear tactics, in *Men in Arms*, 140–141. Because of the complications involved, they report, the old system required "at least two years" to train an infantryman. Mass mobilization along with Napoleon's mode of operation changed all of this. His campaigns brought heavy losses which resulted in a need for easily trained replacements. The two-year drill, according-ly, yielded to a simpler procedure. For overviews, see Vagts, *History*, 112, and Geoffrey Parker, *The Military Revolution: Military Innovation and the Rise of the West, 1500–1800* (Cambridge: Cambridge University Press, 1988), 17–19, 24.

25. Hayden White, "Michel Foucault," in John Sturrock, ed., *Structuralism and Since: From Lévi-Strauss to Derrida* (Oxford: Oxford University Press, 1979), 85, 98–99. White's con-clusion is also worth noting: "Foucault uses rhetorical notions of language to project a conception of culture as magical, spectral, delusory. Strangely enough, this idea of lan-guage remains unexamined by him" (114). See also Miller, *Passion*, 211–212. Foucault's own statement may be found in his *Archaeology of Knowledge*, trans. A. M. Sheridan Smith (New York: Pantheon, 1972).

26. For useful overviews of works dealing with Foucault, with his method and substance, see Allan Megill's articles, "Recent Writing on Michel Foucault," *Journal of Modern His-tory* 56 (1984) : 499–511, and "The Reception of Foucault by Historians," *Journal of the History of Ideas* 48 (1987): 117–141. For a more extended review, see Megill's *Prophets of Extremity: Nietzsche, Heidegger. Foucault, Derrida* (Berkeley: University of California Press, 1985), especially chap. 5, "Foucault and Structuralism."
    For George Huppert's critique, see *"Divinatio et Eruditio*: Thoughts on Foucault," *Histo-ry and Theory* 13 (1974): 191–207, quotation on 204. The Vilar quotation appears in Megill, "Reception" (133). For the original, see Pierre Vilar, "Histoire marxiste, his-toire en construction," in Jacques LeGoff and Pierre Nora, eds., *Faire de l'histoire: Nouveaux problèmes* (Paris: Gallimard, 1974), 188. For another extremely negative judg-ment, see Mark Poster, *Foucault. Marxism and History: Mode of Production versus Mode of Information* (Cambridge: Polity Press, 1984), 72–74. Heinz Steinert has provided a well-documented, highly critical review of the German version of *Surveiller et punir*, see his "Ist es aber auch wahr, Herr F.? 'Überwachen und Strafen' unter der Fiktion gelesen, es handle sich dabei um eine sozialgeschichtliche Darstellung," *Kriminalsoziologische Bib-liographie* (Vienna) 19/20 (1978): 30–45. For a detailed and documented history cover-ing much of the same ground as Foucault, see Pieter Spierenburg, *The Spectacle of Suffering: Executions and the Evolution of Repression: From a Preindustrial Metropolis to the Eu-ropean Experience* (Cambridge: Cambridge University Press, 1984): "Foucault's picture of one system quickly replacing another is actually far from historical reality" (viii); for further comment on Foucault's method and substance, see 64, 108–109, 184, 206. An-other relevant critique is provided by Philip F. Riley, "Michel Foucault, Lust, Women, and Sin in Louis XIV's Paris," *Church History* 59 (1990): 35–50.

27. Megill, "Reception," 139–140. His listing is based on the work of Eugene Garfield, "Is Information Retrieval in the Arts and Humanities Inherently Different from That in Science? The Effect That ISI's Citation Index for the Arts and Humanities Is Expected to Have on Future Scholarship," *Library Quarterly* 50 (1980): 40–57. This report is based on 1977–1978 citations. The most-cited twentieth-century author, well ahead of

all others, is Vladimir Ilyich Lenin. He is followed by Sigmund Freud and, in third place, Roland Barthes.

I am assuming here that most citation is positive, that it in some way approves or commends the source in question. A flawed or fraudulent study, to be sure, might also gain considerable attention. Actual research on this question has found that the over-whelming majority of citations are approving. See the discussion in Eugene Garfield, *Citation Indexing—Its Theory and Application in Science, Technology, and Humanities* (New York: Wiley, 1979), 244–246.

Vyacheslav Karpov, an assistant of mine at OSU, reviewed a sample of twenty-five English-language articles that referred to *Discipline and Punish*. These were cited in the 1990 *Arts and Humanities Citation Index*. Eighteen of the references were positive, four neutral, and three negative. One of the negative comments was oblique, an opponent had relied on Foucault. A second was fugitive, a footnote reference. The third article centered on Foucault—it found Althusser's social theory better.

28. Following are the twenty-four English-language reviews or comments on Foucault's *Discipline and Punish*. Some are reviews of that book alone; some review several books. Some are commentaries, reflections after the first round of reviews. The list is incomplete. Sixty-six reviews are listed in Michael Clark, ed., *Michel Foucault, An Annotated Bibliography: Tool Kit for a New Age* (New York: Garland, 1983). This is not a random selection. I have chosen reviews appearing in leading "gate-keeping" journals for the educated public and leading scholarly journals in several key fields.

We have: Peter Barham, *Sociology* 13 (1979): 111–115; Robert Brown, *Times Literary Supplement* 16 June 1978, 658; Stanley Cohen, *Contemporary Sociology* 7 (1978): 566–568; Robert Coles, *New Yorker* 29 January 1979, 85–88; James Farganis, *Theory and Society* 10 (1981): 741–745; Jan Goldstein, *Journal of Modern History* 51 (1979): 116–118; Donald Goodman, *Cross Currents* 28 (1978): 378–382; David F. Greenberg, *Sociology and Social Research* 64 (1979): 140–143; Casey Groves, *Federal Probation* 43 (1979): 83; D. W. Harding, *Listener*, 15 December 1977, 802–803; Paddy Hillyard, *Community Development* 14 (1979): 163–165; Robert L. Hoffmann, *Historian* 41 (1979): 332–333; Athar Hussain, *Sociological Review* 26 (1978): 932–939; Roger Kaplan, *Commentary* 65 (May 1978): 83–86; David Thomas Konig, *History: Reviews of New Books* 6 (1978): 188; Richard Locke, *New York Times Book Review*, 26 March 1978, 3, 31; Frank McConnell, *New Republic*, 1 April 1978, 32–34; David J. Rothman, *New York Times Book Review*, 18 February 1978, 1, 26, 27; Louise I. Shelley, *American Journal of Sociology* 84 (1979): 1508–1510; Richard Singer, *Crime and Delinquency* 25 (1979): 376–379; Robert Sommer, *Civil Liberties Review* 5 (May–June 1978): 66–69; David W. Tarbet, *Eighteenth-Century Studies* 173 (1978): 509–514; Hayden White, *American Historical Review* 82 (1977): 505–506 (French edition); Gordon Wright, *Stanford French Review* 1 (1977): 71–78 (French edition).

A wider audience was introduced to the book by *Time* magazine, 6 February 1978, 92. George Russell criticized Foucault for "Delphic obscurity" but otherwise reported no faults in the book. Largely descriptive, the review itself ends on a Delphic note—the work is described as "haunting." Walter Clemons reviewed the book in *Newsweek*, 2 January 1978, 91. That review is also largely descriptive and it too reports no factual difficulties. His conclusion: *Discipline and Punish* "shakes our confidence that our own humane methods are improvements."

Gordon Wright has many skeptical comments in his later book. Following his initial exposition, he writes: "If one accepts [Foucault's] analysis of the eighteenth-century reform movement, it must be more on the basis of faith (and admiration for intellectual brilliance) than on the basis of compelling evidence" (*Between,* 22).

29. Patrick Colquhoun, *A Treatise on the Police of the Metropolis,* 5th ed. rev. and enlarged (London: H. Fry, 1797), 411–412.

30. Ibid., 415. Colquhoun was a "London police magistrate and a pioneer statistician and demographer." He was also a friend of Jeremy Bentham and a secret co-worker on several projects—including the panopticon. Through use of his connections, Colquhoun "was able to get Bentham at least a hearing for his views at the Home Office." See Hume, "Bentham's Panopticon," 714–715.

The information on the opposite tendencies in crime and punishment comes from easily accessible sources. The first figures and the Bentham quotation are from Edwin H. Sutherland and Donald R. Cressy, *Principles of Criminology,* 5th ed. (Philadelphia: Lippincott, 1955), 262, 284; chaps. 14 and 15 contain an extensive comparative review of punitive policies in the modern period. See also Ignatieff, *Just Measure,* 15–19. For a rich mine of information on "jury nullification," see Thomas Andrew Green, *Verdict According to Conscience: Perspectives on the English Criminal Trial Jury, 1200–1800* (Chicago: University of Chicago Press, 1985).

31. Richard Hofstadter, *The Paranoid Style in American Politics and Other Essays* (Chicago: University of Chicago Press, 1979 [original 1965]), 4, 6. The essay was published, in abridged form, in *Harper's* magazine, November 1964.

Two separate issues are present in such discussions: questions of evidence and questions of interpretative styles. One should, wherever possible, review evidence to determine whether planning, plot, or conspiracy was present in any given episode of policy making, and one should be ready to say yes, no, or not sure (insufficient evidence) with respect to those episodes. The argument of style involves a tendency, a regular inference, or imputation of plan, plot, or conspiracy without benefit of evidence or, as in the case of Foucault, regardless of evidence. While some people offer a priori arguments of plot, some others are casually dismissive, rejecting such options out of hand as conspiracy theories. For a useful discussion of an opposite and less discussed interpretative tendency, see William Domhoff's chapter "The Compulsive Style in American Social Science," in his *The Higher Circles: The Governing Class in America* (New York: Random House, 1970), 305–306.

32. One subsequent commentator has noted this feature of Foucault's work. William H. Sewell, Jr., writes: "The paranoic style should be recognizable to any reader of Foucault"; see his "History in the Paranoic Mode?" *International Labor and Working-Class History* 39 (spring 1991): 21–24. A double standard appears to be operating. Use of the concept of paranoia is approved and encouraged with respect to anti-Masons, Nativists, Poujadists, McCarthyites, anti-fluoridationists, and many others, but for one of "our own," for a fellow intellectual, the usage is taboo. Why, in this case, is sauce for the goose not sauce for the gander?

33. Foucault, *Discipline,* 128–129, 138, 214.

34. Ibid., 265, 271–272.

35. Ibid., 272, 285–286. This line of argument proved too much for two otherwise enthusiastic reviewers. Greenberg wrote: "That an international bourgeoisie conspired to di-

vide the working class by inventing the prison is unbelievable. Even if the prison has had this effect there is no evidence that it was intended" (*Sociology,* 141). Sommer wrote: "Nowhere does Foucault present any proof that representatives of the bourgeoisie planned the prison to succeed in producing delinquents, thereby diverting attention from their own illegalities" (*Civil Liberties,* 67).

36. For the references see note 28.
37. Stanislav Andreski, *Social Sciences as Sorcery* (New York: St. Martin's Press, 1972), 33.
38. Perry Anderson, *Considerations on Western Marxism* (London: New Left Books, 1976), 26 n2, 32, 49–53. Garfield's tabulation of most-cited authors from all centuries (in the *Arts and Humanities Citation Index,* 1977–1978) shows Karl Marx in second place (after Lenin, but ahead of Shakespeare, Aristotle, and Plato). "'Half of the citations to Marx," Garfield reports, "come from philosophy journals, with nearly two-thirds of these from one journal—*Deutsche Zeitschrift für Philosophie.*"
The arguments contained in the text, from the word *jeu* to this point, are not intended to be taken with full seriousness. As indicated, they make use of Foucault's method and as such do not pay strict attention to chronology, to the context of quotations, to the representativeness of persons, to impacts, or to causal connections. It is meant, in part, as a demonstration of what can be achieved through the use of these more relaxed epistemological standards. Not all of the statements contained there, incidentally, are mistaken or misleading.
39. Critics of science focus on established figures when pointing out examples of failed controls. They touch on Newton, Galileo, or Cyril Burt. Here it will be noted the failure of controls involves assessment of work by a leading figure among the "antiestablishment" critics.
A person whose name is often linked with Foucault is Jacques Derrida. For some insights into the processes of legitimation of his work in France and the United States, see Michéle Lamont, "How to Become a Dominant French Philosopher: The Case of Jacques Derrida," *American Journal of Sociology* 93 (1987): 584–622. Some comparisons are made there with Foucault and the reception of his work.
40. Megill, "Reception," 133–134.

Chapter Seven: Some Problems of Intellectual Life

1. See Karl R. Popper, *The Logic of Scientific Discovery* (London: Hutchinson, 1959), especially chap. 1. Strictly speaking, the scientific criterion, as Popper notes, is not verifiability, but falsifiability. It must be possible to refute or reject the claims on the basis of empirical tests (40–41). For a more recent review and discussion, see Stewart Richards, *Philosophy and Sociology of Science: An Introduction* (Oxford: Basil Blackwell, 1987), chap. 4.
2. The quotation is reported by Jack A. Goldstone in his "Capitalist Origins of the English Revolution: Chasing a Chimera," *Theory and Society* 12 (1983): 175.
3. See Thomas S. Kuhn, *The Structure of Scientific Revolutions,* 2d ed. (Chicago: University of Chicago Press, 1970). Sociologists routinely assert the implications of "their" basic assumption, that is, social influence as the key determinant of human behavior. The possibility of some genetic determination of behavior is either ignored, ridiculed, or, worse, condemned as morally suspect. Evidence on genetic impacts has appeared in leading sociological journals but this has had little evident impact. See Bruce K. Eck-

land, "Genetics and Sociology: A Reconsideration," *American Sociological Review* 32 (1967): 173–194, and Sandra Scarr and Richard A. Weinberg, "The Influence of 'Family Background' on Intellectual Attainment," *American Sociological Review* 43 (1978): 674–692. For a rare textbook account, see Gerhard Lenski, Jean Lenski, and Patrick Nolan, *Human Societies: An Introduction to Macrosociology*, 6th ed. (New York: McGraw-Hill, 1991), 11–13, 22–29.

4. The professors involved were, respectively, David Solomon and James D. Wright. As presented, the problem indicated is cathexis, a trained (or conditioned) psychological attachment to a given intellectual position. In concrete experience, the specific mechanism involved would not be immediately obvious and could not be determined without additional research. In the examples given here, the operative factor might have been cathexis (independent of any current influence), or it might have been actual or anticipated reactions of some "significant others" or of some reference groups. Another possibility is that both factors were operating. The seminal work on theory-saving behavior is that of Leon Festinger, Henry W. Riecken, and Stanley Schachter, *When Prophecy Fails* (Minneapolis: University of Minnesota Press, 1956).

5. For discussion and assessment of some of the theories discussed here, see Richard F. Hamilton, *Class and Politics in the United States* (New York: Wiley, 1972), chap. 2, and Hamilton, *Restraining Myths* (New York: Halsted-Wiley-Sage, 1975), chaps. 1 and 8.

6. That is the title given to the English translation of Julien Benda's *La trahison des clercs* (Paris: Editions Bernard Grasset, 1927). Many people, of course, are sensitive to the problem and have argued against it. See, for example, C. Vann Woodward's comment: "The historian must never concede that the past is alterable to conform with present convenience, with the party line, with mass prejudice, or with the ambitions of powerful popular leaders" (in Robin W. Winks, ed., *The Historian as Detective: Essays on Evidence* [New York: Harper and Row, 1969], 38). See also Seymour Martin Lipset, "The State of American Sociology," *Sociological Forum* 9 (1994): 199–220.
   The problem indicated in note 4 appears again here. Specification of the analytic possibility, of the hypothesis is easy, but determination of the actual processes involved is more difficult. Did the researcher distort the findings because of an inner compulsion, that is, out of a sense of loyalty to some movement? Or was it due to some actual (or anticipated) reactions of persons in that movement? Or were both factors operating?

7. C. Wright Mills, *The Sociological Imagination* (New York: Oxford University Press, 1959), 78. Mills was arguing for value-neutral research.

8. See Chapter 1, notes 8 and 11, for references.

9. For an overview, see Pamela J. Shoemaker, *Gatekeeping* (Newbury Park, Calif.: Sage, 1991).

10. This is based on the assumption that, in all settings, there are more conformists than nonconformists. If publication of a nonconforming finding required two or three unambiguously positive recommendations, and if journal referees "voted" their tendencies, the chances of "success" would routinely fall below 50 percent.
    There is a fair-sized literature on confirmatory bias. For an overview, see J. Scott Armstrong, "Research on Scientific Journals: Implications for Editors and Authors," *Journal of Forecasting* 1 (1982): 83–104, especially 88. An often-cited study is Michael J. Mahoney's "Publication Prejudices: An Experimental Study of Confirmatory Bias in the Peer

Review System," *Cognitive Therapy and Research* 1 (1977): 161–175. While certainly a suggestive and thought-provoking study, Mahoney's test does not appear to provide a pure experimental situation. The reversed results were not, at the outset, equally plausible choices.

11. See the works cited in Chapter 1, note 2.

12. Alan Hedley and Thomas C. Taveggia reviewed textbook treatments of a research finding from industrial sociology. The specific concern was the positive relationship between skill level and work satisfaction. Forty-one industrial sociology texts were examined "to determine if they discussed the skill-satisfaction relationship and cited specific empirical studies to document the discussion." Only fourteen, roughly one-third of the texts, provided that minimal information. The fourteen texts cited a total thirty-one studies in support of the conclusion. Hedley and Taveggia's examination of those studies found that "ten of the 31 studies (32%) originally cited in support of the skill-satisfaction relationship present no data on this relationship!" They also report that the demonstrated relationships are "much weaker than the textbook summarizations would lead one to believe." They point to the problem of reliance on secondary sources "rather than returning to the original sources for independent corroboration." In addition, textbook authors "typically do not note the limitations of the data they are describing." See Hedley and Taveggia, "Textbook Sociology: Some Cautionary Remarks," *American Sociologist* 12 (1977): 108–116. For another comment on textbook "constructions," see the letter by Steven Goldberg in *Contemporary Sociology* 8 (1979): 784.

13. Herbert Spencer lived from 1820 to 1903. Late in his life, he reported total sales of his books at 368,755 volumes. Elements of his work were picked up and transmitted in the writings of the American sociologist William Graham Sumner. For an overview of the Spencer and Sumner impacts, see Richard Hofstadter, *Social Darwinism in American Thought*, rev. ed. (Boston: Beacon, 1955), chaps. 2, 3. In the leading sociology texts of the first half of the century, those of Robert E. Park and Ernest W. Burgess and of Carl A. Dawson and Warner E. Gettys, Spencer's commanding presence may be appreciated with a quick review of the index listings. Few references to Marx and marxism appear in those texts and those few comments were, in a word, deprecating.

Crane Brinton put the question, in 1933, "Who now reads Spencer?" He added that "we have evolved beyond Spencer." Talcott Parsons began his influential book *The Structure of Social Action* with Brinton's question and conclusion, adding that "Spencer is dead." Parsons's book, which first appeared in 1937, was subtitled *A Study in Social Theory with Special Reference to a Group of Recent European Writers*. I am quoting from the 2d ed., (Glencoe, Ill.: Free Press, 1949). Spencer's decline is the only shift (of those discussed here) that in any way was significantly driven by new and compelling evidence, this being Franz Boas's critique of social evolution as a universal, unilineal history of inevitable progress. Jonathan Turner has reviewed the case and pointed up the injustice of the neglect of Spencer; see his *Herbert Spencer: A Renewed Appreciation* (Beverly Hills, Calif.: Sage, 1985). For a review of Spencer's "sociology of knowledge," see 22–29.

The divergent outlooks of French and German intellecturals are described by John Vinocur in "Europe's Intellectuals and American Power," *New York Times Magazine*, 29 April 1984, 60–78.

14. Professors with expert knowledge could easily provide a competent review of the Weber argument in the classroom. Some professors, however, those doubting the argument, might not do so routinely but would comment on request, that is, in response to a student's question. We do not, of course, know how sociology professors treat the thesis in their classes and therefore cannot be sure if appropriate comment, criticism, and referencing is provided there.

15. For many years the Parsons edition of *The Protestant Ethic* contained an obvious transcription error—the name of that exemplary bearer of the capitalist spirit, Benjamin Franklin, was initially given as Benjamin Ferdinand (50). It was not until the 1970s, forty years after original publication, that the correction was made. This error, unlike the others, is indeed trivial, one that would be recognized by any serious reader. The point here is the persistent indifference to obvious and easily corrected error. John Delane, the production manager of the Ohio State University Press, told me that such an error would have been "very easy to fix." It would have been "a three-minute job" in any subsequent printing.

16. This statement is intended as an indication of tendency as opposed to a categorical judgment. Max Weber clearly reached far beyond the boundaries of academic sociology. The statement applies particularly to subsequent readers and audiences. Foucault's reviewers vouched for his claims but, with rare exception, have not shown much knowledge of relevant historical literature.

17. Few sociologists, morever, would ever take a course in the sociology of religion or in economic history. Over the years, the increasing number of required methods courses in graduate programs have forced reduction in the number of content courses. The dropping of language requirements in the sixties and seventies meant a loss of intellectual breadth, or, put differently, greater intellectual provincialism.

18. The text is pointing to a fact, the differentiation of function. No evaluation of those functions is being suggested here. The distinction, moreover, is not categorical. Nonpublishing professors are found in "publishing" institutions and professors who publish are found in the "teaching" institutions. In addition, the plans or aims of an institution are not constant; they are, of course, subject to change. Although "publish or perish" is a standard, recurring theme, studies of the subject have regularly shown that most professors publish either nothing or very little. For most, publication is not a requirement and most do not "perish." A national study of social science professors undertaken in 1955 developed a productivity index with scores ranging from zero to five. The index was not particularly demanding. Publication of "at least one paper" meant a score of two (they were given a point for completion of a dissertation). Less than half of the professors, 46 percent ($N = 2,414$), exceeded that modest standard. See Paul F. Lazarsfeld and Wagner Thielens, Jr., *The Academic Mind* (Glencoe, Ill.: Free Press, 1958), 403.

A more comprehensive survey from 1969, sampling professors in all fields, found that 69 percent had never published a book; 53 percent had published no articles in the last two years; another quarter had published only one or two articles. Book publication is not usually expected in agriculture, business, engineering, or in the natural sciences.

Even in the social sciences and humanities, book publication was the exception rather than the rule. Three-fifths of the anthropologists had published one or more books; half of the economists had done so, those fields having the best showings. See Everett Carll Ladd, Jr., and Seymour Martin Lipset, *The Divided Academy: Professors and Politics* (New York: McGraw-Hill, 1975), 352–353, 264.

See also: Nicholas Babchuk and Alan P. Bates, "Professor or Producer: The Two Faces of Academic Man," *Social Forces* 40 (1962): 341–348; Norval D. Glenn and Wayne Villemez, "The Productivity of Sociologists at 45 American Universities," *American Sociologist* 5 (1970): 244–252; James L. McCartney, "Publish or Perish," *Sociological Quarterly* 14 (1973): 450, 600–601; William C. Yoels, "On 'Publishing or Perishing': Fact or Fable?" *American Sociologist* 8 (1973): 128–130; Robert Boice and Karin Johnson, "Perception and Practice of Writing for Publication by Faculty at a Doctoral-Granting University," *Research in Higher Education* 21 (1984): 33–43; and William J. Boyes, Stephen K. Happel, and Timothy D. Hogan, "Publish or Perish: Fact or Fiction?" *Journal of Economic Education* 15 (1984): 136–141.

19. For an overview of coverage in sociology texts, see Robert L. Herrick, "Nineteen Pictures of a Discipline: Review of Recent Introductory Sociology Textbooks," *Contemporary Sociology* 9 (1980): 617–626, and Theodore C. Wagenaar, ed., "Special Issue on Textbooks," *Teaching Sociology* 16, 4 (1988). For a more general treatment, see Harriet Tyson-Bernstein, "The Academy's Contribution to the Impoverishment of America's Textbooks," *Phi Delta Kappan* 70 (November 1988): 193–198.

20. See Jean D. Gibbons and Mary Fish, "Rankings of Economics Faculties and Representation on Editorial Boards of Top Journals," *Journal of Economic Education* 22 (1991): 361–372, and Lowell L. Hargens, "Impressions and Misimpressions about Sociology Journals," *Contemporary Sociology* 20 (1991): 343–349.

The phrase "on the cutting edge" is used to justify or legitimate a current focus. That might point to breakthrough thinking and research, or it might signal only a statistical frequency—it is what many people are doing. Put differently, it might simply be the trendy thing.

21. Paul Parsons, *Getting Published: The Acquisition Process at University Presses* (Knoxville: University of Tennessee Press, 1989); Walter W. Powell, *Getting into Print: The Decision-Making Process in Scholarly Publishing* (Chicago: University of Chicago Press, 1985). For an investigation of processes in several prestigious commercial presses, see Lewis A. Coser, Charles Kadushin, and Walter W. Powell, *Books: The Culture and Commerce of Publishing* (New York: Basic Books, 1982).

22. The best-selling introductory sociology text in the 1980s was the work of Ian Robertson, a writer, not a professional sociologist. In some respects, his work was better than many of the texts produced by sociologists. Neil J. Smelser, a sociologist of considerable eminence, is the author of a text now in its fifth edition. On the opening page, a question is raised about "the *scientific* study of society." By way of answer, Smelser tells about his student "Mark," who undertook a small research project, passing out survey forms "to students walking through Sproul Plaza" on the Berkeley campus. The author does not indicate that the student's nonrepresentative sampling procedure was inadequate, that it did not meet any reasonable scientific standard. See Smelser's *Sociology,* 5th ed. (Englewood Cliffs, N.J.: Prentice-Hall, 1995). The same example appears in the 3d and 4th editions.

An anonymous referee, commenting on Chapter 3 of this book, felt the review of text-book treatments of the Weber thesis to be superfluous and strongly recommended its removal. "Everyone knows," he wrote, that "textbook writers simply steal from each other and clone nonsense from nonsense."

For an overview of the problems facing one field, see Frederick L. Campbell, Hubert M. Blalock, Jr., and Reece McGee, eds., *Teaching Sociology: The Quest for Excellence* (Chicago: Nelson-Hall, 1985), especially chap. 9 by Reece McGee, "The Sociology of Sociology Textbooks."

23. See John H. Laub and Robert J. Sampson, "The Sutherland-Glueck Debate: On the Sociology of Criminological Knowledge," *American Journal of Sociology,* 96 (1991): 1402–1440.

24. The criminology text is Larry Siegel's *Criminology,* 3d ed. (Minneapolis: West, 1989), 126.

Friedrich Engels, another interested gatekeeper, wrote a series of reviews, several under pseudonyms, of Marx's *Das Kapital.* The Marx-Engels correspondence indicates prior discussion of placement and tactics. See the Marx-Engels *Werke,* (Berlin: Dietz Verlag, 1964), vol. 16, 207–309, or the Marx-Engels *Collected Works* (New York: International Publishers, 1985), vol. 20, 207–218, 224–259. Victor Hugo was another interested commentator. He, wrote reviews of his own works, which were then placed by his publisher. See James S. Allen, *Popular French Romanticism: Authors, Readers, and Books in the 19th Century* (Syracuse, N.Y.: Syracuse University Press, 1981), 94. In 1909, W. E. B. Du Bois published a biography, *John Brown.* A long, unsigned review in *The Nation* savaged the book; it was reprinted, later the same week, in the *New York Post.* The review was written by Oswald Garrison Villard, the owner of both publications and the author of a forthcoming biography of Brown. See David Levering Lewis, *W. E. B. Du Bois: Biography of a Race. 1868–1919* (New York: Holt, 1993), 360–361.

25. See Norval D. Glenn, "The Journal Article Review Process: Some Proposals for Change," *American Sociologist* 11 (1976): 179–185, and Von Bakanic, Clark McPhail, and Rita J. Simon, "The Manuscript Review and Decision-Making Process," *American Sociological Review* 52 (1987) 631–642. The latter article provides a detailed empirical study together with an extensive bibliography. See also Leonard D. Goodstein and Karen Lee Brazis, "Psychology of Scientist: XXX. Credibility of Psychologists: An Empirical Study," *Psychological Reports* 27 (1970): 835–838; Stephen I. Abramowitz, Beverly Gomes, and Christine V. Abramowitz, "Publish or Politic: Referee Bias in Manuscript Review," *Journal of Applied Social Psychology* 5 (1975): 187–200; Douglas P. Peters and Stephen J. Ceci, "Peer-Review Practices of Psychological Journals: The Fate of Published Articles, Submitted Again," *Behavioral and Brain Sciences* 5 (1982): 187–195. An extensive discussion of Peters and Ceci's important article appears in that issue.

26. Michael Smith wrote a critique of an established position in sociology and submitted it for publication to the leading journal in the field. A revised version was accepted for publication. See his "What Is New in 'New Structuralist' Analyses of Earnings?" *American Sociological Review* 55 (1990): 827–841. The editor, Gerald Marwell, gave Aage Sorensen, an advocate of new structuralism, the opportunity to respond, and his contribution was published in the same issue ("Throwing the Sociologists Out? A Reply to Smith," 842–845). Marwell subsequently apologized for the decision to invite this rebuttal.

Steven L. Rytina submitted an article critical of another established position. The article was accepted by William Parrish, the editor of *American Journal of Sociology,* who arranged for a symposium to involve leading proponents of that position. A subsequent editor, Marta Tienda, initially rejected Rytina's response to the proponents' criticisms. Then, with evident reluctance, Tienda allowed Rytina space for a severely limited response and allowed little time for its preparation. The proponents, in short, were given considerable advantage in this "exchange." See Rytina, "Scaling the Intergenerational Continuity of Occupation: Is Occupational Inheritance Ascriptive after All?" *American Journal of Sociology* 97 (1992): 1658–1688. The symposium then included two articles in the same issue commenting on Rytina's work, these by Robert M. Hauser and John Allen Logan (1689–1711) and David B. Grusky and Stephen E. Van Pompaey (1712–1728); for Rytina's response, see 1729–1748.

27. For a first look at some of the problems, see Harry L. Miller, "Hard Realities and Soft Social Science," *Public Interest* 59 (1980): 67–82. For a review of the treatment of several claims that were popular in the 1970s, see Richard F. Hamilton and James D. Wright, *The State of the Masses* (New York: Aldine, 1986), especially chaps. 1 and 2.

28. S. Robert Lichter, Stanley Rothman, and Linda S. Lichter, *The Media Elite* (Bethesda, Md.: Adler and Adler, 1986); Mark Snyderman and Stanley Rothman, *The IQ Controversy, the Media and Public Policy* (New Brunswick, N.J.: Transaction Books, 1988). For another something-out-of-nothing exercise, see Ben Bolch and Harold Lyons, "A Multibillion-Dollar Radon Scare," *Public Interest* 99 (spring 1990): 61–67.

29. Robert Rosenthal and Lenore Jacobson, *Pygmalion in the Classroom* (New York: Holt, Rinehart, and Winston, 1968). The quotation is from R. L. Thorndike's review of the work, in *American Educational Research Journal* 5 (1968): 708–711. When the initial replications failed to supply the needed confirmations, some researchers turned to uncontrolled classroom observation studies. These yielded "positive" results, and various publicists, neglecting the systematic evidence, passed on those results. For an early report on this experience, see Miller, "Hard Realities," 73–78. For a later and more comprehensive review, see Samuel S. Wineburg, "The Self-Fulfillment of the Self-Fulfilling Prophecy: A Critical Appraisal," *Educational Researcher* 16 (December 1987): 28–37; the same issue includes replies by Rosenthal (37–41) and by Ray C. Rist, the author of an observational study (41–42). Wineburg has a rejoinder, "Does Research Count in the Lives of Behavioral Scientists?" 42–44.

30. Wineburg, "Does Research Count," 43.

31. In 1985, Lenore Weitzman published a finding that "the economic status of women falls by an average of 73 percent after divorce." According to one account, this finding "undoubtedly ranks among the most cited demographic statistics of the 1980s." In this case, two researchers did review and challenge the claim. Their conclusion—"Weitzman's highly publicized findings are almost certainly in error." The critique is by Saul D. Hoffman and Greg J. Duncan, "What *Are* the Economic Consequences of Divorce?" *Demography* 25 (1988): 641–645. The 73 percent figure was still being presented as accurate and credible in journalistic accounts in 1992 (for example, in the *New York Times,* 3 May 1992). It also appeared in a half-dozen sociology texts published in the 1990s. For a subsequent review of this case, see Susan Faludi, *Backlash: The Undeclared War against American Women* (New York: Crown, 1991), 19–25. Weitzman's work is entitled *The Divorce Revolution* (New York: Free Press, 1985).

Chapter Eight: Social Misconstruction, Validity, and Verification

1. René Descartes, *Discourse on the Method of Rightly Conducting One's Reason and of Seeking Truth in the Sciences,* trans. Donald A. Cress (Indianapolis: Hackett, 1980), 6–12.

2. See T. C. Chamberlin, "The Method of Multiple Working Hypotheses," *Science* 148 (1965): 754–759. The article was originally published in *Science* in 1890 and it has been reprinted there on four subsequent occasions.

3. Horace Miner, *St. Denis: A French-Canadian Parish* (Chicago: University of Chicago Press, 1939).

4. Theda Skocpol, *States and Social Revolutions: A Comparative Analysis of France, Russia, and China* (Cambridge: Cambridge University Press, 1979), 140–144. One passing mention of religion appears, with respect to the revolutionary settlement (the king lost the right to intervene in religious affairs). No mention is made of religious issues as causes of the revolution or of religion as the driving force in the struggle.
   See too the work of Canadian social historian Bryan Palmer, *A Culture in Conflict: Skilled Workers and Industrial Capitalism in Hamilton, Ontario, 1860–1914* (Montreal: McGill-Queen's University Press, 1979). His account of urban working-class conditions in the nineteenth century neglected the communal factors so heavily stressed by Miner and placed all emphasis on the class factor. Only in the final pages of the book does religion surface; for his fugitive remarks on religion, see 238–239. Commenting on the likely results of possible subsequent research, Palmer writes: "More research may tell us much, but even the most diligent of historians will likely be forced to admit that this sphere of working-class life is shrouded in obscurity and ambivalence" (239). See also the examples reviewed in Chapter 4, note 46.

5. Alexis de Tocqueville, *Democracy in America* (New York: Knopf, 1963), vol. 2, 85–88, a chapter entitled "Some Characteristics of Historians in Democratic Times." For another discussion, one touching on some of the same themes, see Albert O. Hirschman, "The Search for Paradigms as Hindrance to Understanding," *World Politics* 22 (1970): 323–344.

6. On the replication question, see William Broad and Nicholas Wade, *Betrayers of the Truth* (New York: Simon and Schuster, 1982), chap. 4, and, James W. Neuliep, ed., *Replication Research in the Social Sciences* (Newbury Park, Calif.: Sage, 1991), especially the chapters by Rosenthal, Bornstein, and Neuliep and Crandall. See also the brief summary review in J. Scott Armstrong, "Research on Scientific Journals: Implications for Editors and Authors," *Journal of Forecasting* 1 (1982): 88–90. Replication studies, he argues, are very rare; two investigations showed the frequency to be less than 1 percent. One of those studies, signaling the need, found twelve of thirty replications "yielded results that conflicted with the original study." On the absence of replications, see Theodore D. Sterling, "Publication Decisions and Their Possible Effects on Inferences Drawn from Tests of Significance—or Vice Versa," *Journal of the American Statistical Association* 54 (1959): 30–34, and Jerold D. Bozarth and Ralph R. Roberts, Jr., "Signifying Significant Significance," *American Psychologist* 27 (1972): 774–775.

7. Robert A. Dahl, *Who Governs? Democracy and Power in an American City* (New Haven: Yale University Press, 1961); and G. William Domhoff, *Who Really Rules? New Haven and Community Power Reexamined* (Santa Monica, Calif.: Goodyear, 1978), especially 18–19, 33–36, 40–48, 109–110. For a discussion of the problems involved in field studies, see Richard F. Hamilton and James D. Wright, *State of the Masses* (New York: Aldine, 1986), 89–94.

8. Chester McA. Destler, "Wealth against Commonwealth, 1894 and 1944," *American Historical Review* 50 (1944): 49–72. The quotation is from 57.

9. Robert Bremner first brought this case to my attention. For further details I am indebted to Irwin Unger (letter of 24 June 1986) and Jerome L. Sternstein (letter of 24 August 1986). For an array of articles dealing with fraud in research, see *Society* 31, 3 (March–April 1994).

10. The concocted passages in this case were exposed by Henry A. Turner in *American Historical Review* 88 (1983): 1143. Two responses also appear there on 1143–1149. The systematic critique of the original work was undertaken by Ulrich Nocken, "Weimarer Geschichte(n): Zum neuen amerikanischen Buch 'Collapse of the Weimar Republic,' " *Vierteljahrschrift für Sozial- und Wirtschaftsgeschichte* 71 (1984): 505–527. For further discussion of the original work, see the debate in *Central European History* 17 (1984): 159–293. The critique of the revised edition is by Peter Hayes, "History in an Off Key: David Abraham's Second *Collapse*," *Business History Review* 61 (1987): 452–472.

The problem noted with respect to Foucault—inexpert reviewers—was very much in evidence in this case. As with Foucault's work, the enthusiasm of the reviewer increased with distance from the subject matter. Arthur Rosenberg's work on Weimar Germany, the volume given such warm praise by the sociologist reviewer, certainly deserves commendation. But it is a brief work, just over two hundred pages, lightly documented, and does not cover the crucial years—the final chapter is entitled "Das Ende 1928–1930."

11. See Stanislav Andreski, *Social Sciences as Sorcery* (New York: St. Martin's Press, 1972); Broad and Wade, *Betrayers;* Antony Flew, *Thinking about Social Thinking: The Philosophy of the Social Sciences* (Oxford: Blackwell, 1985); Stephen Jay Gould, *The Mismeasure of Man* (New York: Norton, 1981), chap. 6; and Alexander Kohn, *False Prophets* (Oxford: Blackwell, 1986).

12. Law reviews routinely check all citations for accuracy and substance, a practice called cite-checking. For various technical reasons, this is somewhat easier in law than in other fields. While that ideal is perhaps not possible for many scientific journals, the review of some sample of references, systematic or casual, could only have positive effects.

13. At one point, while refereeing articles for a leading sociology journal, I sensed that specialist historians were not regularly consulted for their comments. I asked both the editor and the appropriate deputy editor about their procedures. Both confirmed that my impression was correct. The conclusion about assessments of the Weber thesis is an inference based on material covered here in Chapter 3. For review and comment on the science critiques that bypassed competent reviewing, see Paul R. Gross and Norman Levitt, *Higher Superstition* (Baltimore: Johns Hopkins University Press, 1994).

14. Scott Armstrong took the conclusions from papers in four management journals and rewrote them so as to create two or three versions of varying levels of difficulty, this "without any apparent change in the content." A small sample of faculty members from leading management schools were sent the passages and asked to "rate the competence of the research" that was reported. In all instances, the "easy" passage was given the lowest competency rating. See Armstrong, "Unintelligible Management Research and Academic Prestige," *Interfaces* 10, 2 (April 1980): 80–86.

15. Larry Laudan, *Science and Relativism: Some Key Controversies in the Philosophy of Science* (Chicago: University of Chicago Press, 1990), xi.

Index